C

SSYRIAN EMPIRE
bout 720 B.C.)

Nineveh

BABYLONIAN EMPIRE
(about 570 B.C.)

Babylon

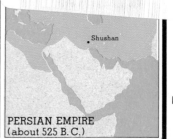

PERSIAN EMPIRE
(about 525 B.C.)

Shushan

1

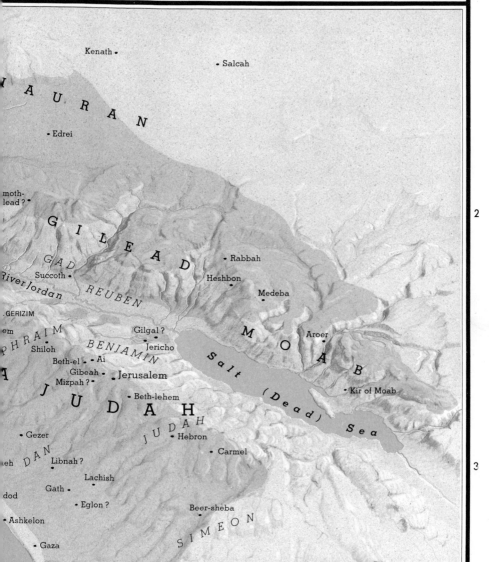

Kenath •

• Salcah

H A U R A N

• Edrei

2

moth-
lead ?

G I L E A D

GAD

Succoth •

River Jordan

REUBEN

• Rabbah

Heshbon

Medeba

M O A B

Aroer

. GERIZIM

em

EPHRAIM

Shiloh

Beth-el • Ai

Gibeah •

Mizpah ?

BENJAMIN

Gilgal ?

• Jericho

• Jerusalem

• Beth-lehem

J U D A H

Salt

(Dead)

Sea

• Kir of Moab

A

• Gezer

DAN

eh

Libnah ?

Gath •

dod

• Eglon ?

• Ashkelon

• Gaza

Gerar •

J U D A H

• Hebron

Lachish •

• Carmel

• Beer-sheba

S I M E O N

3

C

D

D0344993

The Dissected Plateau (Ch. XX).   An aerial view, taken in February 1967, looking southeast. In the left foreground the pre-Cambrian granite platform is exposed. In the center, running diagonally across the picture, is Wadi Ram, with the sandstone mountains of Jabal Ram on the nearer side (right center) and Jabal 'Ishrin beyond. The white on the top of these mountains is snow. In the top left hand corner are the sands of the Wadi Hasma.

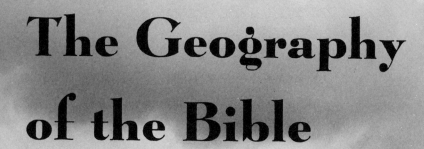

The Geography
of the Bible

NEW AND REVISED EDITION

Denis Baly

HARPER & ROW,
PUBLISHERS
NEW YORK
EVANSTON
SAN FRANCISCO
LONDON

To Richard and Rosemary Bird

THE GEOGRAPHY OF THE BIBLE is a complete revision of the 1957 edition
with the same title.

THE GEOGRAPHY OF THE BIBLE. Copyright © 1974 by A. Denis Baly. All rights reserved.
Printed in the United States of America. No part of this book may be used or reproduced
in any manner whatsoever without written permission except in the case of brief quotations
embodied in critical articles and reviews. For information address Harper & Row,
Publishers, Inc., 10 East 53rd Street, New York, N.Y. 10022. Published simultaneously in
Canada by Fitzhenry & Whiteside Limited, Toronto.

FIRST EDITION

Designed by Lydia Link

Library of Congress Cataloging in Publication Data

Baly, Denis.
  The geography of the Bible.
  Bibliography: p.
  1. Bible—Geography. I. Title.
BS630.B34 1974   220.9'1   73–6340
ISBN 0–06–060371–2

Contents

List of Abbreviations   vii

List of Illustrations   viii

Introduction   xi

Introduction to First Edition   xiii

Part One: General

1.   IN THE MIDST OF THE EARTH   3

2.   THE DEPTHS OF THE EARTH   15

3.   THE EARTH ON ITS FOUNDATIONS   28

4.   HAS THE RAIN A FATHER?   43

5.   THE RAIN OF THE MOUNTAINS   54

6.   NOT LIKE THE LAND OF EGYPT   69

7.   FOOD FROM THE EARTH   77

8.   STRAIGHT WAYS AND CITIES   91

9.   THE WILDERNESS AND THE WOODS   101

Part Two: Regional

10.   THE LAND BEFORE YOU   115

11.   THE COAST OF THE SEA   121

12.   THE LAND OF THE PHILISTINES   131

v

13.   THE RICH VALLEY   144

14.   GALILEE OF THE GENTILES   152

15.   BRANCHES OVER THE WALL   164

16.   THE HILL COUNTRY OF JUDAH   177

17.   THE ENTRANCE OF THE HAMATH AND THE ARABAH   191

18.   BEYOND THE JORDAN EASTWARD   210

19.   AMMON, MOAB, AND EDOM   226

20.   THE DESERT WASTES   241

Glossary of Geological Terms   253

Bibliography   257

Index of Biblical References   263

Index of Names and Subjects   271

List of Abbreviations

ANET   *Ancient Near Eastern Texts relating to the Old Testament* ed. James B. Pritchard. 2nd ed. Princeton University Press, 1955.

BA.   *The Biblical Archaeologist.*

BASOR   *Bulletin of the American Schools of Oriental Research.*

Geog. Journal   *Geographical Journal.*

Geol. Mag.   *Geological Magazine.*

IEJ   *Israel Exploration Journal.*

IJES   *Israel Journal of Earth Sciences.*

JB   *The Jerusalem Bible.*

JBL   *Journal of Biblical Literature.*

JNES   *Journal of Near Eastern Studies.*

JSS   *Journal of Semitic Studies.*

KJV   *King James Version of the Bible.*

NEB   *New English Bible.*

PEQ   *Palestine Exploration Quarterly.*

RB   *Revue Biblique.*

RCAJ   *Royal Central Asian Journal.*

RSV   *Revised Standard Version of the Bible.*

VT   *Vetus Testamentum.*

List of Illustrations

MAPS AND DIAGRAMS

1. *The Point of Balance*, showing how the major land and sea routes converge on Palestine. 5

2. *The Fertile Crescent.* 6

3. *The pattern of the Levant.* 7

4. *The realms of the Levant.* 9

5. *Rivers and wadis of Palestine.* 13

6. *Gondwanaland and Tethys.* 16

7. *The geological history of the Palestine area.* (After Picard.) 17

8. *Three theories of Rift Valley formation.* 23

9. *Quennell's theory of the formation of the Rift Valley.* (After Burdon, simplified.) 24

10. *Structural "network" in the Levant.* 29

11. *The Zone of Greater Complexity.* 30

12. *The structure of Northern Transjordan.* 32

13. *The structure of Southern Transjordan.* 33

14. *The structure of the Negeb.* 35

15. *The Judean Upwarp.* This is not an exact cut at any particular point, but is a "typical" block intended to illustrate the general features. 36

16. *The structure of Northern Cis-jordan.* 38

17. *The structure of Carmel and Samaria.* The dotted lines represent the original structure. The solid drawing below represents the present relief, showing how the basins are occupied by hills. 39

18. *North Cis-jordan and the Bay of Acre.* 40

19. *North–south section across Galilee.* 41

20. *Pressure conditions in summer.* (Information: *Atlas of Israel.*) 45

21. *Temperatures at Lod (Lydda).* Average temperatures during the day on the coast plain in both winter and summer, showing the cooling effect of the sea breeze during the middle of the day in summer. 46

22. *Relative humidity.* 47

23. *Mean and extreme maximums of daily temperature at Lod (Lydda).* 51

24. *Average annual rainfall.* 55

25. *Temperature and rainfall: Coast Plain.* The small, but very regular temperature range throughout the year should be noticed. 56

26. *Development of the rainy season.* 56

27. *Probability of rainfall in the Palestine area.* This diagram illustrates how great a chance one of the five places marked has of reaching a certain rainfall total. Thus, Haifa has a 95% chance of receiving 16 inches (400 mm.) of rain, an 80% chance of receiving 20 inches (500 mm.), a 5% chance of receiving 24 inches (600 mm.), etc. 57

28. *Temperatures in Haifa and Jerusalem.* 57

29. *Temperature and rainfall: Cis-jordan Hills.* Mount Kina 'anin in the north has a

greater total rainfall, but a smaller winter temperature range because of the influence of the sea. 58

30. *Temperature and rainfall: The Jordan Valley.* Notice the great summer temperature range in the dry south. 59

31. *Rainfall in Trans-jordan*, illustrating both how the rainfall decreases toward the south and the irregular pattern of the desert rainfall. 61

32. *Temperature and rainfall: The Southern Steppe*, showing the very regular temperature range of the coastal station and also the greater heat of inland Beersheba during the summer months. 62

33. *Temperature and rainfall: The Trans-jordan Plateau.* 62

34. *Maximum, minimum and mean temperatures at Amman during 1950.* This should be compared with Diagram 23. Unlike Lod, Amman, which is on the edge of the Trans-jordan desert, has its highest temperatures during the summer months and not during the siroccos of the transitional seasons. Nevertheless, the sudden rise of temperature caused by the siroccos of early April should be noticed, together with the drop in temperature when the siroccos end in May. The temperature range in winter is very small compared with that of summer, and in 1950 February was exceptionally cold. The drop in temperature in July is caused by the inflow of cooler air from the Mediterranean and is a surprisingly regular feature of the summer weather. 63

35. *Ten years of rainfall at Bayir in eastern Jordan*, showing the extreme irregularity of desert rainfall. 63

36. *The rainfall factor.* The "rainfall factor" is obtained by dividing the average annual rainfall in millimeters by average temperature in degrees centigrade for the rainy season, when almost all the growth takes place. Thus, a place on the highlands with an average annual rainfall of 650 mm. (26 inches) and an average temperature in the rainy season of 13° C. (55.4° F.) would have a rainfall factor of 50. (See A. Reifenberg, *The Soils of Palestine*, 1938, pp. 8–13.) 78

37. *Plant zones of Palestine.* (Based on the *Atlas of Israel*.) 79

38. *Trans-jordan settlements.* 92

39. *The land bridge of the Levant.* 95

40. *The routes of Palestine.* 95

41. *Regional names in the Old Testament.* Notice how the majority of these are outside, or on the edge of, the main area of Israelite settlement. 117

42. *The tribal territories.* 118

43. *The natural regions of Palestine.* 119

44. *The coasts of Asher* (northern and central sections). 122

45. *The coasts of Asher* (southern section). 125

46. *The Plain of Sharon.* 129

47. *The Valley of Craftsmen.* 132

48. *The Philistine Plain.* 136

49. *The Shephelah and the Judean Moat.* 140

50. *The Acco–Beth-shan route.* 146

51. *The passes across Carmel.* 149

52. *Megiddo*, showing the importance of the position at the junction of two great routes, both of which avoid the treacherous Kishon marshes. 150

53. *The four quarters of Galilee.* 153

54. *Upper Galilee.* 154

55. *Eastern Lower Galilee.* 158

56. *Western Lower Galilee.* 159

57. *Geology of the Tappuah district.* 165

58. *The Joseph tribes.* 165

59. *The highway from Bethel to Shechem.* 175

60. *The Saddle of Benjamin.* 178

61. *Judah.* 180

62. *The Huleh Basin.* 192

63. *The Jordan Valley.* 197

64. *The Dead Sea.* 203

65. *The Arabah and Edom.* (The Edomite region is discussed in Ch. XIX.) 207

66. *The Arnon Valley.* This diagram, showing the Arnon and all its tributary wadis, illustrates how a major scarp stream, cutting back along a line of weakness, has captured the drainage of the dip-slope. 212

67. *The plateau rim of Trans-jordan*, showing (a) the increasing height toward the south, and (b) how the major regions extend across the main canyons. The vertical height is, of course, greatly exaggerated for purposes of clarity. 213

68. *The land of Bashan.* 214
69. *Gilead and Ammon.* 220
70. *The plateau of Moab.* 230
71. *The heights of Edom.* 234

72. *The Plateau Desert and Wadi Sir-*
han. 242
73. *The Dissected Plateau.* 245
74. *The Wilderness of Zin.* 248

following page 26 Simplified geological map (in color)

PHOTOGRAPHS

I. The Navel of the Earth 4
II. Palmyra (the Tadmor of the Old Testament) 8
III. The Hamath Steppe 10
IV. The Mountains of Midian and the Wadi Ytem. 18
V. Jabal Ram 21
VI. Jabal adh-Dhakar 25
VII. "The bricks have fallen..." 25
VIII. Mar Saba in Jeshimon 37
IX. al-Buqei'a in Jeshimon 37
X. Mouth of the Zerqa Ma'in 42
XI. Storm over the Lake of Galilee 48
XII. Flooded Desert Wadi 49
XIII. Snow in Jerusalem 51
XIV. Morning Mist at as-Salt in Gilead 60
XV. Desert Plants in the Wadi Hasma after Rain 64
XVI. Tending Grapes in Transjordan 83
XVII. Living in Booths 83
XVIII. Date Palm near Aqabah 87
XIX. Olive Grove in Ephraim 88
XX. "A Lodging Place of Wayfaring Men" 92
XXI. Roman Milestones on the King's Highway 97
XXII. The Way to Edom 99
XXIII. The Highlands of Gilead 105
XXIV. "The lion shall eat straw like the ox" 107
XXV. The Coasts of Asher 126
XXVI. The Crusaders' Castle at Aphek 133
XXVII. The Standing Stones at Gezer 135
XXVIII. The Cliffs at Ashkelon 143

XXIX. The Rich Valley 145
XXX. Beth-shan 148
XXXI. Lower Galilee 161
XXXII. Wadi Beidan 166
XXXIII. Samaria 170
XXXIV. The Plain of Lebonah 176
XXXV. The Mount of Olives 182
XXXVI. "The Open Square before the House of God" 186
XXXVII. Gethsemane 188
XXXVIII. Bethlehem 189
XXXIX. The Landscape of Judah 189
XL. Caesarea Philippi 194
XLI. Waterfall near Banias 195
XLII. The Jordan near Adam 200
XLIII. The Monastery of the Temptation 201
XLIV. The Arnon Gorge 204
XLV. The Dead Sea 205
XLVI. Qa'a 208
XLVII. Canatha 217
XLVIII. Volcanoes at Shahba (Philippopolis) 218
XLIX. Herding Sheep near Salkhad (Salecah) 218
L. Gerasa: The Triumphal Arch 222
LI. Gerasa: A Colonnaded Street 222
LII. Eastern Gilead 223
LIII. The Mishor 229
LIV. Machaerus 231
LV. Kir-Hareseth 232
LVI. The Heights of Edom 238
LVII. Petra 238
LVIII. Petra: The "Urn Tomb" 239
LIX. The Plateau Desert 243
LX. The Dissected Desert 246
LXI. Subeita 249

Introduction

The kind reception given to the first edition of this book sixteen years ago has encouraged me to seek to bring it up to date. The first edition was written in the couple of years after I had left Jordan and come to live in this country, but nearly twenty years here of teaching both Old and New Testaments have revealed to me something of the problem that students of the Bible have when they try to visualize the biblical environment. I have tried to bear this problem in mind when writing the present edition.

It is a complete revision. Although the general form and thrust remain the same, every paragraph has been rewritten, most of them drastically, two entirely new chapters have been added, and on almost every page new information has been provided. The climatic diagrams have been brought up to date as far as possible, all the maps have been redrawn to provide fuller information, and the total number of maps has been more than doubled. The photographs have all been revised, and although some of the old ones have been kept because I did not think that I could improve on them, most are published here for the first time. I have paid a number of visits to Jordan, Israel, and the surrounding countries for further field research, the last trip being in March, 1972, when a phenomenally wet season clothed the entire landscape with color but prevented my getting quite a number of the pictures I had gone out specifically to obtain.

I have struggled to be conscious all the time of the needs of two groups of people. The scholar requires solid, detailed, and accurate information. Consequently, I have, as before, tried to make this book a serious geographical and biblical study. The beginning student and the more general reader, however, who have no geographical training, demand a simple and straightforward presentation. For their sake I have striven at every point for simplicity and clarity and tried to avoid, as it were the plague, unnecessary technical language. In all my research, alas, I have become unhappily aware of the impossibility of keeping fully up to date with three disciplines: geographical research, archaeological discovery, and biblical scholarship, especially when teaching full time and, this present year, once more taking over the chairmanship of a department. Let me assure the reviewers and critics that though they may find lacunae I have done my level best to keep myself informed.

I had hoped to have all this completed nearly a year ago, but an unfortunate spell in the hospital last summer interrupted my labors. The result was that the text was finished, but the maps and diagrams had to be drawn in the interstices of teaching and administration. I hope that this unavoidable delay has not unduly marred the final result and that whatever faults there may be, this new edition may at the very least prove useful.

As with any work of this kind my sincere thanks are due to far more people than I can enumerate. However, I should like to pay my respects to the memory of Père de Vaux, with whom so many of these ideas were discussed, to the École Biblique et Archéologique de St. Étienne and the Ecumenical Institute in Jerusalem for inviting me last March to give the lectures which provided the basis for Chapters VI and IX, to the Reverend and Mrs. John Wilkinson for all the help they gave on that visit, to Mrs. Crystal-M. Bennett of the British School of Archaeology in Jerusalem for information about Edom, and to Professor Basheer Nijim of the University of Northern Iowa for helping me to track down climatic data. I must extend my gratitude also to my wife for her endless patience and for performing the conjugal task of helping with the index, to the Elia Photo Service in the Old City of Jerusalem for the constant personal interest they have taken with my photographs, and to Mrs. Marcella Haldeman for typing the manuscript, and finally, though by no means least, to Kenyon College for making my last two visits to Jerusalem financially possible.

DENIS BALY

Kenyon College
April 1973

Introduction to First Edition

It is now more than sixty years since George Adam Smith first wrote his classic study *The Historical Geography of the Holy Land*, and since his day no one has attempted anything of quite the same nature in English. Even that other classic, *La Géographie de la Palestine* by Père F.-M. Abel, is twenty years old, and neither of these is now easily obtainable. There have, it is true, been certain smaller studies and also more than one "atlas" of the Bible, of varying geographical value, but nothing of the scale or nature of George Adam Smith's *Historical Geography*. Even the recent and beautiful *Atlas de la Bible* by Luc Grollenberg, which at the time of writing is being translated into English, is, strictly speaking, more historical than geographical.

However, the character of the country is changing rapidly on both sides of the armistice line, and it is unreasonable to wish that this should not be so, for it is neither desirable nor possible to keep Palestine in a glass case. Nevertheless, before the changes have proceeded too far there does seem to be a need for a study of the country, which may serve to assist the biblical scholar by giving him a picture of the stage whereon the history of our salvation had its place.

There are clearly two problems in any work of this kind. When the study is limited to the biblical period, it is difficult not to avoid the suggestion that the history of Palestine began with Abraham and came to an end in A.D. 70, an impression which is already too firmly implanted in the minds of many Western people. However, limits of some kind are necessary if the book is not to get completely out of hand; it cannot be denied that the events of the biblical period are those which most concern the ordinary American or British reader, and it seems, therefore, a useful place at which to begin, though obviously it is only a beginning.

The second problem is that expressed by a friend of mine, who read part of the manuscript and commented bluntly, "Theologians are not interested in geology, and geographers do not want theology in a geography book." There is much truth in what he said. Yet, on the one hand, it is impossible to understand what has been called the "personality" of a country without some knowledge of the structure and of the mechanism of the climate, and on the other hand, to attempt to study the Bible as if it were merely a work of secular history is to do violence to its nature. The moment one sets out to examine "the Land and the Book," it is necessary to take account of two facts: that the "Land," like any other land, is a complex and powerful thing, strongly influencing the lives and thinking of its people, and for this reason worthy of a thorough study in its own right; and that the "Book," from the beginning to the end of it, presupposes the existence of one God, who is both active and effective, and who, in Karl Barth's famous phrase, is always "the subject of the sentence." Therefore, a study of the "Land" which is merely superficial and rejects the discipline of examining how the whole environment is built, and a study of the "Book" which does not take seriously the nature of the biblical argument, are both of them studies without integrity. It is for the reader, and not for the author, to say whether this attempt to take account of both aspects of the subject has been successful. I can only say that, whatever blemishes the book may have, I have tried to write out of this conviction.

This book is the result of twenty years' work, fifteen of which were spent in the Palestine region, from 1937 to 1947 and from 1949 to 1954, when I was a member of the Jerusalem and the East Mission. During that time I visited every part of the country, and most of it very many times, by almost every means of transport known to the area, on foot, by bicycle, by horse, mule, and donkey, by car, by train, by boat and by plane (though I have to confess to my lasting regret that I never had occasion to ride on a camel). In the course of these journeys I met so many people to whom I owe a debt of gratitude that it is quite impossible to mention them all here. If this book should fall into the hands of any of them I hope they realize that it is only because they are so numerous that they are not thanked. However, three salutations must be given. The first is to the memory of Professor P. M. Roxby, under whom I studied at Liverpool and who first awakened in me an interest in the relations of history and geography. The second is to the members of the Civil Aviation Department in Palestine, many of whom later became members of the

Meteorological Department in Israel, who put themselves and all their records at my disposal during the whole of a long summer. The third is to the Arab Legion, to both the officers and men, who never failed to be both courteous and helpful at whatever time of the day or night I arrived on their doorstep. It is impossible to praise them too highly.

It cannot be pretended that life was always placid in Palestine, and as a result of the disturbances I twice lost a large part of my maps and notes. This has made it difficult always to trace the source of my information, and though I have done my best always to give credit where it is due, I may have slipped up somewhere. If I have, it is entirely unintentional and I apologize.

The photographs are all my own, and are chosen to illustrate those features of the country which are less commonly known. For this reason I have avoided the popular views of Jerusalem and the Lake of Galilee. Some readers may think that this is a pity, but such photographs can, after all, be seen in a great many books on Palestine. For the same cause I have thought it better to have more pictures of the country east of the Jordan, which is less well known.

A word of explanation is necessary about the spelling of place names. There is, of course, an official method of transliteration from Arabic, but I find that those people who do not know any Arabic find it irritating and confusing. Moreover, it is not used on most maps of the region. It has seemed better therefore, normally to use the spelling which appears on the maps, and where a name has become familiar to the public from their newspapers, to use that spelling, e.g., Amman and Aqabah instead of 'Amman and 'Aqabah. For Hebrew words I have tried to keep to the usage of the Revised Standard Version of the Bible. I know that this solution will not please the purist, but I hope that it may ease the path of the ordinary reader.

The Scripture quotations in this book, except where otherwise stated, are from the Holy Bible, Revised Standard Version, copyrighted 1946 and 1952 by the Division of Christian Education, National Council of the Churches of Christ in the United States of America, and are used by permission.

D.B.

Kenyon College
1957

PART ONE

General

CHAPTER 1

In the Midst of the Earth

*Go up to the top of Pisgah, and lift up your
eyes westward and northward and southward
and eastward, and behold it with your eyes.*
DEUTERONOMY 3:27

God, it has been said, worketh "salvation in the midst of the earth" (Ps. 74:12, and Bishop Arculf, who visited Jerusalem about A.D. 700, "observed a lofty column . . . in the middle of the city, which, at mid-day at the summer solstice, casts no shadow, which shows that this is the centre of the earth."[1] This belief was old even in Arculf's day, for in ancient times Jerusalem was held to be the *omphalos,* the navel, the place where order is established, where it is, as it were, funneled down, and from which it spreads out to "those who dwell at earth's farthest bounds" (Ps. 65:8). Other places in Palestine, it is true, had also been given this title: Tabor, the name of the impressive but lonely hill rising out of the Plain of Esdraelon, means "navel," and in Judges

1. Thomas Wright, ed., *Early Travels in Palestine* (London, 1848; reissued New York: Ktav Publishing House, 1968), p. 3.

9:37 Mount Gerizim is so described ("Look, men are coming down from the center of the land," i.e., the *tabur,* or navel, of the land). Yet in due time Jerusalem prevailed, and the word of the prophet was fulfilled,

It shall come to pass in the latter days
    that the mountain of the house of the
      Lord
shall be established as the highest of the
    mountains,
    and shall be raised above the hills;
and all the nations shall flow to it,
    and many peoples shall come and say:
"Come, let us go up to the mountain of
    the Lord,
    to the house of the God of Jacob;
that he may teach us his ways
    and that we may walk in his paths."
For out of Zion shall go forth the Law,
    and the word of the Lord from
      Jerusalem.
        [Isa. 2:2–3; Mic. 4:1–2]

This concept of the *omphalos* is very widespread indeed. Peking, the capital of the Middle Kingdom, is so called in Chinese tradition, Delphi in ancient Greek thought, Mecca by the Muslims, who in their worship all turn toward this center. Yet for those brought up in the biblical tradition, Jerusalem, despite its often violent history, has ever remained the point from which order proceeds, "the hope of all the ends of earth, and of the farthest seas" (Ps. 65:5).

I. *The Navel of the Earth.* The tower, dating from the Crusades, of the Church of the Holy Sepulcher, which was in medieval tradition the central point of the earth. The concept of Jerusalem as the center of the earth goes back to the Israelite monarchy.

Cartographers no longer use Jerusalem as their central point of reference, as did those who drew the map which now hangs in Hereford Cathedral, but the idea of Palestine is geographically, as well as theologically, central is not altogether unreasonable. It lies at that "point of balance" where the great land mass of the Old World is so constricted that a gigantic hand might get a grip upon it, inserting a thumb in the Mediterranean and the other fingers in the Black Sea, the Caspian, the Red Sea, and the Persian Gulf. All the great intercontinental routes must go this way, for in the isthmus of Sinai the continental mass is cut through almost entirely and Africa dangles by the merest thread. Here the routes which lead from Asia into Africa are pressed together into a narrow funnel, and the place of their assembly is Palestine. Here also the ships, nosing their way along the Red Sea, laden with the wealth of India and the East, and all the fragrant powders of the merchants, most nearly touch the busy maritime commerce of the Mediterranean, for there is less than 100 miles of land between them.

So lengthy are the roads and sea lanes which come together and so massive the history that boundaries must be set for our study, both in time and space. Of course, these will be somewhat arbitrary, as are all boundaries and frontiers, for neither in history nor in geography is it possible to set a limit and say, "This far shalt thou come and no farther." Yet some kind of restraint is essential if the undertaking is not to get completely out of hand. In time, therefore, we shall confine ourselves to the "biblical period," those 2,000 years from the days of Abraham to the destruction of Jerusalem by the Romans in A.D. 70, and in space to the Palestinian region, for convenience defined as the area covered by the two modern countries of Jordan and Israel. Within these limits the great majority of biblical events took place.

There still remains, however, the problem of names, for as anyone who has to deal with Middle Eastern geography knows to his cost, names tend constantly to take on political significance, and to be the cause of much recrimination. Therefore, it must be said clearly that *no name at all, whether "Israel" or "Palestine" or any other, will be used in its modern political sense, unless this is expressly stated.* The name "Palestine" will be used to mean "the country of the Bible," on both sides of the Jordan, in the sense in which it is used in many biblical commentaries. "Israel" will be kept for the ancient kingdom of Israel, lying to the north of the kingdom of Judah. In speaking of the two regions on either

side of the great Central Valley of the Jordan and the Arabah we shall speak of "Cis-jordan" and "Trans-jordan." The whole coastland, stretching from the borders of modern Turkey to Egypt, may be described as the "Levant Coast."

This coastland forms part of an area known to all students of the Bible and of ancient history as the Fertile Crescent, a huge sickle of inhabited and cultivable land lying between the sea, the desert, and the mountains: the realm of "order" confined and threatened by the realms of confusion and disorder. In the north are the vast elevated tablelands of Anatolia and Iran, some 3,000 feet in height, and divided from each other by the complicated Armenian mountain knot, the ancient kingdom of Urartu, dominated by the great peak of Ararat, nearly 17,000 feet above sea level. These plateaus are hemmed in on almost every side by great mountain

1   **THE POINT OF BALANCE**

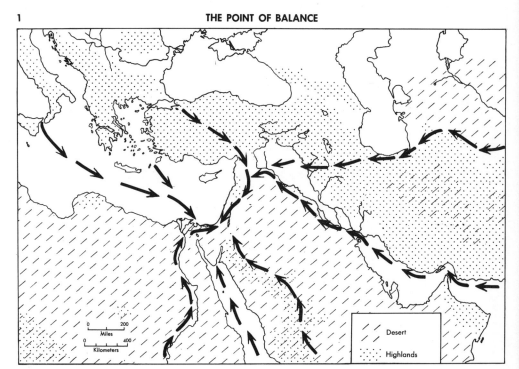

ranges, many of them well over 10,000 feet in height, the Taurus, the Pontic Mountains, the Elburz, the Zagros, the Makran and Suleiman ranges, the home of fierce tribes who again and again descended to raid and conquer the low-lying and ill-defended fields. To the west is the "tossing sea," trackless and frightening, "for it cannot rest, and its waters cast up mire and dirt" (Isa. 57:20). To the south and east are the grim, unwelcoming desert wastes, where men can find "no way to a city to dwell in" (Ps. 107:4).

The Fertile Crescent, which lies be-tween these three alarming obstacles to movement, is formed on the east by the broad land of Mesopotamia, watered by the Euphrates and Tigris, and by those other tributary rivers which flow down to join them from the Zagros. In the west is the Levant Coast, where the main lines of relief tend to run from north to south, that is, parallel to the

shore. Not only is movement here chan-neled in the same north-south direction, but moisture is ensured here where it might otherwise be deficient. The win-ter storms, moving in from the Medi-terranean, have to rise over two lines of highlands and thus must deposit their rain, especially on the western, or seaward, side. The leeward slopes to the east are very much drier.

The rainfall in the Levant decreases continually toward the south and in Cis-jordan finally peters out south of Gaza and Beersheba, where the culti-vated lands give way to wilderness. But not far away is that other great river valley, the Nile, which may be reached, though not easily, across the wasteland of Sinai. The Nile Valley and Mesopo-tamia, with their rich irrigated lands, support dense and prosperous agricul-tural communities, and between these two centers of power the Levant forms a bridge. All those who went down into

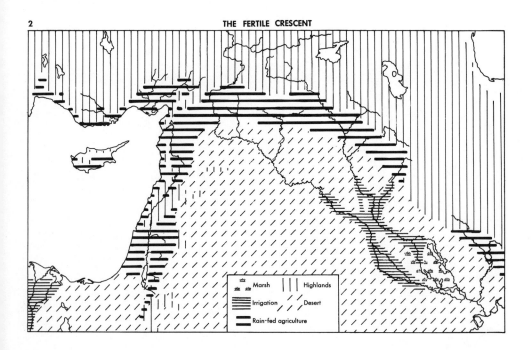

2   THE FERTILE CRESCENT

Marsh   Highlands

Irrigation   Desert

Rain-fed agriculture

Egypt, or journeyed from Egypt to Mesopotamia, had to travel the full length of it. No shortcut across the Arabian desert was normally possible, and the story of Palestine is very largely a history of the struggle between Mesopotamia and Egypt to control this Levantine bridge. Those of us who saw in World War II the British army moving northward from Egypt for the invasion of Syria, or returning for the defense of the Nile Valley, were watching nothing new, and those small Iraq forces which came later to contend with the troops of modern Israel were but ineffective descendants of the mighty hosts of Assyria which wiped out an earlier Israel like an "overflowing scourge" (Isa. 28:18).

Because the constriction between desert and sea is greatest in the south, in Palestine, the bridgelike character is here most pronounced, and the country has ever echoed to the tramp of the soldier or the more tranquil passage of the merchant. Only in the second century B.C. did the rise of imperial Rome cause it to take on a new character, that of a beachhead for the western powers, seeking to control the Land of the Five Seas. The double role of bridge and beachhead Palestine has maintained from that day to this, sometimes one and sometimes the other being dominant.

It is customary to divide the Levant into four north–south zones: the *Coast Plain*, the *Western Highlands*, the *Central Rift Valley*, and the *Eastern Plateau*. This is certainly correct, but it is only partly correct.

First, the main thrust of the structure is not from north to south, but from northeast to southwest, and the general tendency of the folded highlands is to run in this direction. This is most evident in the Lebanon and Anti-Lebanon mountains, but also in the uplands of

the Negeb south of Beersheba, and in the fact that the Dome of Gilead is structurally the continuation of the highlands of Judah. Many of the tremendous faults which cleave the Levant have also the same alignment, notably that marking the eastern edge of Mount Lebanon.

But imposed upon this northeast–southwest tendency is another, that of the north–south fault lines. Most striking are those which have carved out the great rift valley of the Jordan and Dead Sea, but another very evident fault scarp forms the eastern limit of the Nuseiriyeh Mountains in northern Syria. It is these north–south faults which have outlined the Western Highlands of

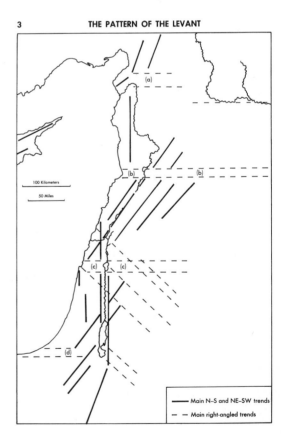

3   THE PATTERN OF THE LEVANT

100 Kilometers

50 Miles

(a)

(b)   (b)

(c)   (c)

(d)

—— Main N–S and NE–SW trends

– – – Main right-angled trends

Palestine, and present us, therefore, with the commonly accepted picture of a north–south pattern to the landscape.

Three important modifications of the north–south pattern must consequently be recognized:

1. The four zones do not continue directly all the way from north to south.

2. Almost always one of them may be said to dominate over the others.

3. Sometimes one of them almost completely disappears.

No less important, however, than the north–south zones is the fact that they are interrupted by a number of west–east depressions, or zones of structural weakness. These are quite definite, though occasionally they are obscured on the physical map. They are:

1. *The Aleppo-Euphrates Depression* in northern Syria. This includes Antioch, Aleppo, and the diversion of the Euphrates eastward in this area.

2. *The Homs-Palmyra Corridor.* This is the most remarkable of all because it can be traced right across to the Persian

11. *Palmyra (the Tadmor of the Old Testament).* Part of the great colonnaded street of the city of Palmyra, which attained its greatest splendor after the conquest of Petra in A.D. 106. It was an important oasis and caravan city in the long Homs-Palmyra depression which extended eastward from the Mediterranean to the Euphrates.

mountains. It starts in the west with the bay just north of Tripoli and the valley of the Nahr al-Kabir, dividing the Nuseiriyeh Mountains from the Lebanon, and includes, a little farther to the east, the Lake of Homs. In all this area volcanic basalt has poured into the depression and somewhat hidden it. The corridor continues eastward by way of Palmyra to Deir az-Zor on the Euphrates, not far from the ancient site of Mari. Here the Euphrates once more turns suddenly eastward as it enters the depression. Even farther east it may be that the valleys followed by the road from Kermanshah to Hamadan in Persia, possibly the biblical Ecbatana, are in some sense a continuation of this line of weakness.

3. *The Galilee-Bashan Depression.* This is by far the most complicated, because it is crossed by another depression running southeastward from Sidon toward the Wadi Sirhan. It is still further confused by great outflows of basalt which have blocked some of the valleys, damming the flow of the Jordan from the Huleh Basin to the Lake of Galilee, and the building the plateau of Moreh between the lake and the Valley of Jezreel. Despite these complexities, which render this area indeed confusing, the depression can be traced in the Bay of Acco, the valleys of Lower Galilee, the Lake of Galilee itself, and the line of the Wadi Yarmuq.

4. *The Beersheba-Zered Depression,* extending past Beersheba and the southern end of the Dead Sea to the Valley of the Zered, between Moab and Edom.

Although these west–east depressions are not always impressive on the physical map, their importance is beyond question, for they are all areas in which movement from west to east is easy. It is perfectly true that in the Levant the dominant line of movement is from north to south along the bridge between the desert and the sea, but these west–east depressions form zones of transverse movement interrupting the north–south passage. Moreover, they separate emphatically the way of life to the north from that to the south. There is no better example of this than the striking cultural boundary formed by the Homs-Palmyra Corridor in Syria. On the map, and sometimes indeed on the ground, this boundary is far from evident, and the casual traveler from Damascus to Homs by car is usually unaware that he has crossed it. However, south of this line there are no villages of the so-called beehive type; to the north they are so frequent as to be the rule, so persuasive is this physically unimpressive division between one culture and another.

Between these west–east lines lie four "realms," bounded by quite distinct clearly defined, limits, but each containing within itself a package of varied life styles, varied *modes de vie*. These four realms have each a dual quality, on either side of the great Central Rift. It is possible, therefore, to distinguish the following eight regions, and to give each of them a descriptive name to indicate something of its peculiar character:

1. *The Northern Realm,* where the eastern plateau, though not very high, is dominant. It may be divided into: (a) the Promontory of Ugarit and (b) the Pastures of Hamath.

2. *The Syro-Phoenician Realm,* the master realm of the four, and clearly dominated by the mountain element. We may therefore speak of: (a) the Mountains of Phoenicia and (b) the Gardens of Damascus.

3. *The Palestinian Realm,* where the Central Rift is at its most profound and separates decisively: (a) the hills and valleys of Cis-jordan and (b) the Table-land of Trans-jordan.

4. *The Realm of the Southland,* presided over by the towering plateau of Edom. This realm is divided into: (a) the Wilderness of the Negeb and (b) the Exaltation of Edom.

The northern realm is remote and enters only occasionally into the biblical record, but it is important because here come together all the routes from Assyria and Babylon, by way of the Euphrates, from Anatolia across the Cilician Plain, and by sea from Cyprus. The term "Promontory of Ugarit" for the western region serves to emphasize its extraordinary isolation, shut off as it was by the precipitous, and in ancient days forested, Nuseiriyeh mountains,

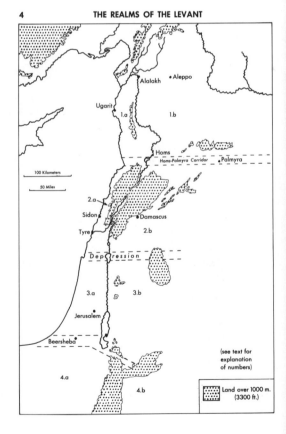

4   THE REALMS OF THE LEVANT

Aleppo
Alalakh
Ugarit
1.a   1.b
Homs
Homs-Palmyra Corridor   Palmyra
100 Kilometers
50 Miles
2.a
Sidon
Tyre   Damascus
2.b
Depression
3.a   3.b
Jerusalem
Beersheba
4.a
4.b

(see text for explanation of numbers)

Land over 1000 m. (3300 ft.)

and by the impenetrable marshes of the Ghab, where the Orontes meanders sluggishly in the choked Central Rift. Still today this isolation is demonstrated by the absence of mosques in the villages and the persistence of the sacred grove, used now mainly for burials. The important Bronze Age city of Ugarit in the extreme north existed for trade, and its existence was made possible by a narrow river valley connecting it with the interior.

To the east, on the here low-lying plateau, are the wealthy steppelands surrounding Hamath the Great (Amos 6:2). Rainfall in the far north is more plentiful, and here the farmer and the shepherd meet, for the land supports both good grassland and extensive wheat fields. It was always devoid of trees, and the beehive houses of the present villages reflect this lack of wood for roofing. Level and open, it offers no serious obstacle to the invader and seems to have had difficulty in maintaining its independence.

In the Syro-Phoenician Realm the lie of the land is SW–NE, opening out like a fan toward the north. The Mountain of Lebanon (*Jabal Libnan*), climbing straight out of the sea, dominates Phoenicia. It provided the timber, cypress, and cedar, and also, though grudgingly, the cultivated land, where the hard-won terraces rise one above the other to the uppermost line of abundant springs, 4,700 feet above sea level. Because the Mountain was thus agricul-

III. *The Hamath Steppe.* These unusual "beehive" type houses characterize the wide, open grassland where there was little or no wood for roofing. They represent a long-standing cultural tradition and are not found south of the Homs-Palmyra corridor or in the Euphrates valley.

tural, it gathered to itself the Central Valley, here itself so uplifted that the bottom of it near Baalbek is level with the highlands of Cis-jordan, and throughout history this has been attached persistently to the coast, despite the tremendous barrier between them. But because the Mountain offers so little land for agriculture, and because the coast plain here disappears, the inhabitants must seek their livelihood elsewhere, and Jabal Libnan has always "exported men," sending its sons far and wide, to settle across the sea and to trade with the motherland.

The Anti-Lebanon was less well watered and therefore much less attractive both to the woodman and the farmer. Once the trees had been cut down, the slopes reverted to barren scrub, the haunt of the wolf, the leopard, and the bear. The chief gift of the Anti-Lebanon is the spring line at its eastern foot, making possible a road between the mountains and the desert. Most glorious of all is the Ghouta, that vast oasis fed by Abana and Pharpar (2 Kings 5:12), in which Damascus is set like a jewel. All roads must pass through Damascus, for the Central Valley, which on the map looks so tempting, is far from easy. Especially in the south, where the mountain ranges come together and two fault systems cross, the way in and out is very difficult. Certainly this Central Valley did provide a route southward into Palestine, even as early as prepottery Neolithic in about 6500 B.C.,[2] but seldom for large armies and never for great commercial caravans. The wealth of the merchant flowed into Damascus.

The Syro-Phoenician Realm commanded the Levant both physically and

2. Diana Kirkbride, "Five Seasons at the Pre-Pottery Neolithic Village of Beidha in Jordan: A Summary," *PEQ*, XCVIII (1966), 59–60.

politically because there was no way of avoiding it and because no other Levantine power was able to conquer it and control it from a distance. Yet Damascus, so natural a center, never had a durable and extensive empire. It was strong only when both Egypt and Mesopotamia were weak, and it is, moreover, an oasis, an irrigation society, and expansion for such a society is strictly limited by the farthest point to which water can be brought. Beyond that absolute line is the wilderness, into which the oasis dweller feared to penetrate, and over which he had little control beyond, if he could, policing the trade routes. Even the greatest glory of Damascus, the 'Ummayad empire of the eighth century A.D., lasted no more than ninety years.

The Homs-Palmyra Corridor, which is the northern limit of the Syro-Phoenician Realm, was apparently the limit also of Israelite imperial ambitions (Num. 34:7–9; 2 Kings 14:25; Ezek. 47:15–17). But this was "vaulting ambition, which o'erleaps itself." Ancient Israel never made any attempt to subjugate Phoenicia, and indeed paid heavily for the Phoenician alliance which set her free to devote all her slender resources to the struggle with Damascus. But only temporarily could Damascus be reduced to a vassal position, a lowly status which she rejected at the earliest opportunity.

We now come to the Palestinian Realm, with which the greater part of biblical history is concerned. Its divisions are best understood if one bears in mind that the N–S Rift Valley conflicts with the main structural trend, which is NE–SW. If we imagine ourselves standing where Moses stood, on the Pisgah, the edge of the eastern plateau near the northern end of the Dead Sea, and of course facing westward toward Cis-jordan, we should have behind us and around us the Mishor, that remarkably level tableland which formed the territory of Moab. To the north on our right would be the swelling Dome of Gilead, a continuation structurally of the hill country of Judah. To the south, on the left hand, we should see the plateau rising again, steadily but gradually, toward the great heights of Edom.

The plateau edge presents a steep, precipitous wall to the west, cleft by four great canyons which are the most striking physical features of Transjordan: the Yarmuq, which is probably the "watercourse" of 1 Maccabees 5:40; the Jabbok, or modern Zerqa, which rises at Rabbah of the Ammonites, "the city of waters," where Uriah the Hittite was killed (2 Sam. 11:16–17; 12:27); the Arnon, or Mojjib, which was held to be the northern boundary of Moab (Judg. 11:18), and the Zered, which divided Moab from Edom. (Num. 21:12; Deut. 2:13).

In Cis-jordan the Coast Plain for the first time becomes an important feature. It is broken by the headland of Carmel near the modern town of Haifa and, though narrow to the north of this, widens out considerably to the south, first in the plain of Sharon and then in the Philistine territory between Joppa and Gaza.

The Western Highlands descend from the north in the two great steps of Upper and Lower Galilee to the low-lying plain of Esdraelon, which interrupts the Highlands just as Carmel interrupts the Coast Plain. There is therefore an important lowland corridor stretching southeastward from the sea to the Jordan Valley at Beth-shan. South of this plain the Western Highlands rise again to the ancient Israelite heartland, the tribal territories of Manasseh, Ephraim, and Judah. It must be remembered that the hill country of Judah in the south, which reaches more than 3,300

feet near Hebron, is continued structurally in the Dome of Gilead across the Jordan, and not in the highlands of Cis-jordan to the north of it, and this is the geographical basis of the historic difference between the southern kingdom of Judah and the northern kingdom of Israel. Judah is a part of a great upwarped region, which is cut by the deep rift of the Jordan Valley, and it is defended on all sides except the north by steep ascents; Manasseh, the center of the northern kingdom, is structurally a *basin,* despite the heights of Ebal and Gerizim, and it is readily open to invasion.

There remains the Realm of the Southland. Here the Western Highlands drop from the heights of Judah to the much lower uplands of the Negeb, where the land rises to no more than 2,000 feet, but to the east, across the Arabah Rift, the plateau of Edom towers 5,000 feet above the sea, and 6,000 feet above parts of the Rift. The winter storms, now rare and fitful in the south, sweep often unhindered across the lower-lying Negeb Uplands, but are forced to empty their moisture upon the majestic scarp of Edom. One must therefore distinguish in this realm between the wilderness of the Negeb and that narrow line of cultivable land, in ancient days even of woodland, which crowns the plateau edge in the east.

It is proper, therefore, to speak of the "Exaltation" of Edom, which so dominates the Southland that Seir as a regional name was pushed westward to include the Negeb. Much later the Nabateans from the same eastern plateau likewise extended their authority over the uplands west of the Rift. This domination of so large a realm from so tiny a base was possible because Edom had one thing in common with the much more luxuriant Phoenicia: she had so little agricultural land that she was forced to "export men." She became, therefore, the great land trader as Phoenicia was the trader by sea. Both of them had a reputation for wisdom and for pride. "You are indeed wiser than Daniel," said Ezekiel to the Prince of Tyre, "and no secret is hidden from you," but "your heart is proud, and you have said, 'I am a god' " (Ezek. 28: 3, 2). Similarly Jeremiah asked, "Has the wisdom of Teman vanished? . . . The terror you inspire has deceived you, and the pride of your heart, you who live in the clefts of the rock, and hold the height of the mountain" (Jer. 49:7, 16). Moab was also condemned for its pride (Isa. 16:6), but the proverbial wisdom of Edom and Tyre came to them by way of travel and commerce, from the fact that there was no room for them to stay at home.

Both the last two realms that we have been considering are cut in two by the Central Valley, the deep, divisive trough which extends from the borders of Syria to the Red Sea. When it first enters Palestine it stands some 500 feet (150 m.) above sea level, and the Lake of Huleh, which has now been drained, was 230 feet (70 m.) above the Mediterranean, but then the Jordan, cutting through the basalt dam, descends rapidly to the Lake of Galilee, 686 feet (209 m.) *below* sea level. This descent continues southward so that the surface of the Dead Sea is 1,284 feet (396 m.) below sea level, and the bottom of the sea very nearly another 1,300 feet (400 m.) below that. But in the realm of the Southland the great trough, here called the Arabah, rises gradually once more until at one point it is 660 feet (200 m.) *above* sea level. It then drops once more until it sinks beneath the Red Sea in the Gulf of Aqabah.

The Southland is without permanent streams, and even farther north in the Palestinian Realm the length of the summer drought and the porous nature of much of the rock have meant that such streams are few. There are, however, many deep wadis which were cut by the more vigorous drainage of the wetter "pluvial period," which prevailed in Palestine during the Ice Age of Europe. The Plain of Esdraelon is drained to the west by "the onrushing torrent, the torrent Kishon" (Judg. 5:21), though for most of the year this is no more than a sluggish brook. To the south of Carmel a few minor streams cross the Coast Plain to the sea, the most important being the Yarkon, which rises at Rosh ha-'Ayin (Ras al-'Ain, the ancient Aphek) and flows out not far north of the modern Tel Aviv.

5   **RIVERS AND WADIS OF PALESTINE**

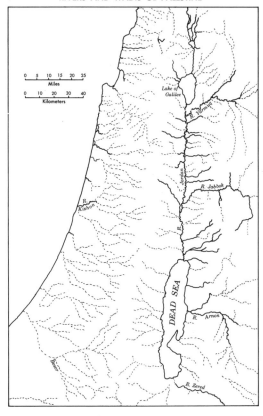

The Western Highlands form the water parting between these Mediterranean streamlets and the region of inland drainage which accounts for most of the Palestinian rivers and is centered on the Dead Sea. The largest river is the Jordan, which rises at the foot of Mount Hermon, and flows through the Lake of Galilee, to be joined between this and the Dead Sea by two important tributaries, the Yarmuq and the Jabbok, both from the Eastern Plateau, where the steep escarpment faces the rain-bearing winds. There are also some other, though smaller, scarp streams from the east, such as the Kufrinje, the Shu'eib and the Kufrein, but from the western bank it receives only the Harod (Jalud) and the Fari'a, neither of which is large. Similarly the Dead Sea receives from the east the Arnon and the Zered, as well as the smaller Zerqa Ma'in and Kerak wadis, but no permanent streams come down from Judah.

Likewise in the northern realms, though there is more rain there, the two major rivers are in the Central Rift. They rise near Baalbek, the Litani flowing to the south, and the greater Orontes to the north, and both of them break through to the sea. A large number of independent streams pour down the western slopes of the Lebanon and the Nuseiriyeh Mountains, but the eastward-flowing streams are fewer, the most important being the Barada (ancient Abana), which feeds Damascus.

Palestine, therefore, forms only a part of the Levant, and a minor part at that, for the geographical diversity of the Levant has hindered the development of any strong, unified country here. During the temporary periods of weakness both in Egypt and in Mesopotamia the tendency was for power to reside in Damascus, the most important single center in the area; only if Damascus was also weak could the kingdom of Israel rise to preeminence, and such preeminence was normally brief. It was certainly not because the ancient Israelites were more in number than any other people that the Lord set his love upon them (Deut. 7:7).[3]

---

3. In the first edition I concluded this first chapter by saying that in periods of great instability part of Cis-jordan might be governed from a capital east of the river, and that if history was anything to go by, the situation at that time, when most of the hills of Judah and Samaria were governed from Amman, was highly insecure and destined to be purely temporary. So it has proved. Nevertheless, I venture to suggest that the same history would indicate that the present expansion of the Cis-jordanian state is also destined not long to endure.

CHAPTER 2

The Depths of the Earth

My frame was not hidden from thee,
When I was being made in secret,
Intricately wrought in the depths of the earth.

PSALM 139:15

By far the greater part of man's activity is pursued upon the surface of the earth. Though men "search out to the farthest bound the ore in gloom and deep darkness [and] open shafts in a valley away from where men live" (Job 28:3–4), this is not their normal life. Therefore, any study of how man's thought and life is related to the land where he lives must concern itself almost entirely with the surface of that land. But this surface is not a matter of chance. The stage for man's activity, the hills and valleys, the fertile plains, the forbidding crags, and the dusty, sun-bitten deserts—these are brought into being by the slow, insistent processes of creation: the patient construction of the rocks, grain by grain upon the sea bottom; the titanic upheaval of the mountains, and the shearing effect of fault and rift; and by the constant onslaught of the climate, the fretting of

the rain, the shattering of the frost, and the hot, imperious sun. No land can be properly understood if these two processes are not studied, and it is with the first that we must begin. The connection of all this with the Bible is admittedly not immediately obvious, and some readers may perhaps be tempted to skip this chapter and the next. Yet, they should be patient, for these two chapters establish the basis for much that follows.[1]

The key to most of Palestine's geological history is that it has lain in a

---

1. The technical terms of geology may be strange to some readers, and so will be avoided as far as possible in these chapters. Where they must be used they will be explained. This may prove irritating to others to whom such terms are commonplace, but it seems unavoidable. A glossary of geological terms will be found at the end of the book.

zone of contact between a land mass and an ocean. The land mass, known to geologists as Gondwanaland, lay to the south and east, and the ocean, called Tethys, of which the present Mediterranean is but a remnant, lay to the west and north. It has therefore been a coastland, and the shoreline has never strayed far outside the region. Often it lay, very roughly, where the present Rift Valley now lies, but occasionally the land mass was thrust upward and the sea retreated westward, leaving the whole of our region as dry land. At other times the land mass was lowered and the sea flowed across into Transjordan and even, though rarely, beyond. The highest part was always the southeast, so that when the sea invaded the land it was the last to be covered and most quickly reappeared from the waves when the sea withdrew. In Cisjordan, therefore, which was the more

under the sea, the rocks result mainly from marine deposition, limestones, chalk, and the like. To the east, however, where the sea came more rarely, these marine deposits are thinner and the desert sandstones, formed upon the dry land, take their place, attaining, especially in southern Trans-jordan, tremendous thickness.

During the last 70 million years or so there were created those great mountain ranges which curve round the Fertile Crescent on the north and east, a process which seems to have been spread out over the whole of this period, and indeed cannot be said to be finished even yet. The effect of this on the Palestinian region was, however, limited by two factors:

1. The main mountain-building storm occurred in the region of Anatolia and Iran and was therefore separated from Palestine by the whole expanse of Syria.

6   **GONDWANALAND AND TETHYS**

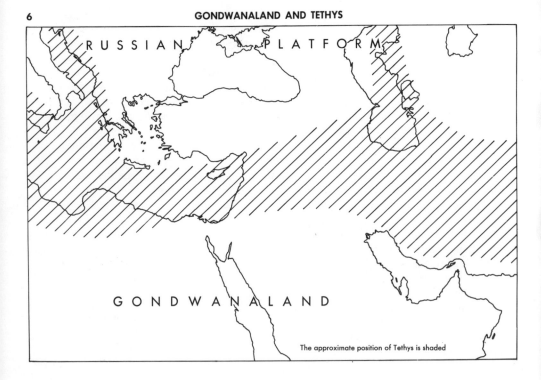

The approximate position of Tethys is shaded

Palestine was consequently affected, not by the full force of the storm, but by what Cole has well called the "ground swell,"[2] and the folding here is relatively simple.

2. The Palestinian rocks lie on the edge of the great solid block of Arabia. Unlike the more plastic sediments which underlay the ocean of Tethys, this vast crystalline mass resisted those pressures which folded and twisted the Anatolian mountains. It was to some extent warped by the pressure, but it could not be bent, and so folding of the sediments lying on top of it was severely limited. Nevertheless, the strain was so great that the block was broken, some parts being pushed up and others thrust down, while others again were rent ferociously apart. No part of the Palestinian realms was spared this slicing and shearing, but most awe-inspiring of all is the great Rift Valley, which has cleft the country from north to south and set asunder forever the East from the West.

The hugh stable block of Gondwana-land, of which the plateau of Arabia is a detached part, is very ancient indeed and came into existence long before the Cambrian period (see Fig. 5). It is exposed in the south of Trans-jordan, where in the mountains of Midian it stands 5,000 feet above the sea, and much less extensively in Cis-jordan near Elath. Evidence provided by these exposures indicates that in those long-distant days, more than 500 million years ago, some parts of Gondwana-land, then less resistant, had themselves been folded up into great ranges, the so-called Arabo-Nubid Mountains. These then suffered erosion, much of the debris being washed down into the

7   THE GEOLOGICAL HISTORY OF THE PALESTINE AREA

TIME (millions of years)	AGE	PERIOD	CIS-JORDAN	TRANS-JORDAN	ARABIA
6		Quaternary			
17	CAINOZOIC	Pliocene			
		Miocene			
43		Oligocene			
		Eocene			
55	MESOZOIC	Senonian / Turonian / Cenomanian (Cretaceous)			
40		Jurassic			
35		Triassic			
30		Permian			
70		Carboniferous			
40	PALAEOZOIC	Devonian			
30		Silurian			
70		Ordovician			
60		Cambrian			
c.2000	ARCHAIC	Pre-cambrian			

Palestine region, until at last only the roots of the mountains were left. All this happened while the continent still was dry land, so that what remained was a vast, relatively level platform on which sediments of the Cambrian Sea were laid down, as geologists would say, "unconformably."[3] The exposed portions of the platform consist mainly of pink and gray granite and deep red porphyry, penetrated by swarms of

2. Grenville A. J. Cole, *The Geological Growth of Europe* (London: Home University Library, 1914), p. 68.

3. Leo, Picard, *Structure and Evolution of Palestine* (Jerusalem: Geological Department of the Hebrew University, 1943), p. 29. Also *Atlas of Israel* (Jerusalem: Survey of Israel, Ministry of Labour, and Amsterdam: Elsevier Publishing Company, 1970). Notes to map III/1.

IV. *The Mountains of Midian and the Wadi Ytem.* The dark granite mountains in southern Trans-jordan where the underlying pre-Cambrian platform has been exposed. The wadi is floored with soft sand which reflects the rays of the sun almost as if there were water in it. It was an important routeway from the north to the Red Sea.

volcanic dikes, which themselves must be very ancient, since they have also been eroded and are not thrust up into the Cambrian sediments. The Cambrian Sea seems to have extended well to the east, since the dark Cambrian limestone is exposed both in the Zerqa Ma'in Valley and in the canyon of the Zered. Here it rests directly upon the ancient eroded platform.

We are still very much in the dark as to what happened in Palestine during the long Primary era. The coastline probably fluctuated, and from time to time the sea extended eastward, since marine strata occasionally appear between the layers of terrestrial rocks.[4] These, however, are thin, since

4. Efraim Orni and Elisha Efrat, *Geography of Israel* (3d rev. ed., New York: American Heritage Press, 1971), p. 9.

they were eroded when the land rose once more above the sea. The southeastern part remained fairly consistently as dry land, with normally, it would appear, a more or less desert type of climate. Here massive deposits of reddish sandstone, often thousands of feet thick, rest on the Cambrian limestone. This is the Nubian sandstone, which in southern Trans-jordan is carved and fretted into the fantastic cliffs of Wadi Ram and Jabal Tubaiq, and was laid down on and off throughout the entire period from the mid-Cambrian to the Cretaceous, and even a little later. It must not be forgotten, of course, that during this same time, while the wind was depositing the sand, it was also actively engaged in erosion. Recent research in some parts of Arabia and North Africa have shown that the grains of sand in these sandstone layers are aligned along well-defined axes, which may be the result of the prevailing winds. A careful study of these might, therefore, give us valuable information about the wind systems and the position of the equator and the north and south poles in early geological periods.[5]

During the Jurassic period the sea certainly spread eastward again, for Jurassic limestones are found both in the Wadi Zerqa (Jabbok) and in the Maktesh Ramon and Maktesh ha-Gadol (Wadi Raman and Wadi Hathira) in Cis-jordan. However, this was evidently intermittent, for the marine limestone strata are interrupted by layers of desert sandstone. Nor did it last very long in these areas. The southeast remained dry, but central and northern Cis-jordan remained longer under the sea, and limestone of the Albian series has been exposed by erosion in the center of the main arch both in Judah and in eastern Samaria.

During the Cretaceous period there developed a great transgression of the sea which laid down the larger part of those rocks which today comprise most of the settled areas of Palestine. At first the coastline lay only just to the east of the present Jordan, but little by little the waters spread east and south until by the end of the Cenomanian epoch they covered the whole region, except only that part of Transjordan which lies south of Ma'an. By Senonian times even the most southeasterly portion was under the sea. The Cenomanian limestones are therefore thickest in northern and central Cis-jordan, where they may be 2,000 to 2,500 feet thick, but only 1,000 to 1,500 in the south.[6] East of the Jordan they are also much thicker in the north, and the Gilead Dome resembles much of central Cis-jordan. They become thinner, however, toward the south and finally die away altogether. This great extension of the sea in the Cretaceous period covered up most of the earlier landscape, and the formation of the present landscape of much of Palestine may be said to have started at this time.[7] The first mild beginnings of the great mountain building seem indeed to belong to the Senonian, at the end of the Cretaceous period, and produced no more than a gentle folding in a southwest–northeast direction. One of the results of this is the raised middle section of the Wadi Arabah between the Dead Sea and the Red Sea, where in Jabal al-Khureij the valley bottom is humped up to about 650 feet above sea level.

After the Senonian, during the Eocene, the movements were of a somewhat different kind, and different parts of the coast were elevated and depressed alternately so that the sea extended inland first in one region and then in another.[8] It reached its greatest development in the middle of the period when it swept right across the present Saudi border into Arabia, but gradually the whole region was to be raised out of the sea. At first an island emerged in the form of an elongated dome, extending from Judah into Gilead, and by the end of the period the whole of Judah, Samaria, and eastern Galilee had probably become dry land.

5. W. B. Fisher, *The Middle East* (6th rev. ed., London: Methuen & Co., 1971), p. 21.

6. Geological Map of *Southern Palestine*, 1:250,000 (Jerusalem: Survey of Palestine, 1947). Also Picard, *Atlas of Israel*, III/1.

7. Yehuda Karmon, *Israel: A Regional Geography* (New York: John Wiley & Sons, 1971), p. 10.

8. Picard, *Structure and Evolution*, p. 36.

There was at this time also already a deep depression south of the Judah-Gilead dome, between Cis-jordan and Trans-jordan, which contained a large inland lake with its shore somewhere near Bethlehem. The Trans-jordan plateau stood at about 2,000 feet and the Cis-jordan hills at about 1,000, with most of the Judean wilderness roughly at the level of the inland sea.[9] To the east, where the land was higher, the Eocene Sea lasted only a short time, and Eocene deposits there are no more than 300 feet thick,[10] but in Cis-jordan they are as much as 650 to 1,000 feet.

During the Oligocene epoch the coastal plain of Cis-jordan remained under water, though it is difficult to determine the shoreline, since the rocks of this period may have been removed by erosion.[11] An arm of the sea still extended inland from Haifa to the Syrian desert, but all the rest of Palestine was dry land, and so it has remained. This is therefore a good moment at which to pause and examine the nature of the rocks which resulted from this long process of invasion and retreat of the sea, before we go on to study the effect of the mountain building, which did not take effect until later.

At the bottom, of course, is the granite platform of Arabia, which in southern Trans-jordan has been thrust up in a long narrow triangle to form the rugged and barren Mountains of Midian. Upon the eroded surface of this platform was laid down the dark Cambrian limestone which can be seen at one or two points in the deep valleys of Trans-jordan.

The massive thicknesses of Nubian sandstone, which is the major rock over so much of the south of Trans-jordan, are most frequently dark red in color, but some strata are white, yellow, purple, or a brilliant flamelike orange. Quennell[12] has distinguished four divisions of this sandstone, which was deposited, with a few brief interruptions by the sea, over a period of something like 350 million years:

1. The *Quweira Sandstone* of the Cambrian period. This is the most ancient and is normally a dark red in color. It rests unconformably on the granite platform, and it is out of this that the greater part of the rock-cut city of Petra is carved.

2. The *Ram Sandstone,* a coarse yellowish or white sandstone which in Jabal Ram overlies the red Quweira sandstones. The first tombs seen by the visitor to Petra at the entrance to the Siq are carved out of this rock. Both this and the Quweira Sandstone beneath it are crisscrossed by a system of joints which are eroded into deep narrow canyons, one of which is the Siq itself, the mysterious entrance to Petra, and another the smaller Siq at Beidha, a few miles to the north.

3. The *Umm Sahm Sandstone* of the Triassic and lower Jurassic periods, reddish or mauve in color, and darkening to purple on exposure. This is displayed over a wide area east of Wadi Ram, in which region is Jabal Umm Sahm, from which the name is taken.

9. G. S. Blake, "Geology, Soils and Minerals," in M. G. Ionides, *Report on the Water Resources of Transjordan and Their Development* (London: H.M.S.O., 1939), p. 52.

10. *Ibid.*, p. 93.

11. Orni and Efrat, *op. cit.*, p. 11.

12. David J. Burdon, *Handbook of the Geology of Jordan,* to accompany and explain the 1:250,000 *Geological Map of Jordan East of the Rift* by Albert M. Quennell (Amman: Government of the Hashemite Kingdom of the Jordan, 1959), pp. 26–37.

V. *Jabal Ram.* The great mass of red Nubian sandstone resting unconformably on the pre-Cambrian granite platform. Jabal Ram is the highest mountain in the Palestine area, reaching 5753 feet (1754 m.).

Unlike the two previous sandstones, it is not jointed.

4. The *Kurnub Sandstone* (late Jurassic and early Cretaceous). Described by Burdon as "multicolored,"[13] this may be pink, mauve, red, or white, and is often so loosely bound together as to be almost sand rather than sandstone. It is exposed in the Jabbok Valley, where it is very easily eroded and collapses, sometimes disastrously, in heavy rains, and also in Jabal Tubaiq, far to the southeast.

The kingdom of Edom, the "Red," derived its name from the predominant color of the Nubian sandstone, and the same rock carries the important deposits of copper, which were thought of as one of the great assets of the Promised Land, "whose stones are iron, and out of whose hills you can dig copper" (Deut. 8:9). The copper mines of Punon, the present Feinan, which may perhaps have been those worked in the time of Solomon, belong to the Quweira series.

The great Cretaceous transgression of the sea produced three major rocks: *Cenomanian-Turonian, Senonian,* and *Eocene.* The first of these consists usually of hard limestones, which are resistant to erosion and form excellent building stone. The Senonian is normally a soft chalk, while the Eocene may be either a hard limestone, as in central and eastern Galilee, where it is the source of some of the strongest springs,[14] and in the Abda plateau of the Negeb, or soft chalk not unlike that of the Senonian, as in the foothill regions of the Negeb and Judah and the western foothills farther north. This distinction between limestone and chalk is of vast importance. The hard limestones weather into a rich, deep-red soil, the typical Mediterranean *terra rossa;* being porous, they absorb the winter rain and pay it out regularly

13. *Ibid.,* p. 37.

14. Picard, *Atlas of Israel,* III/1.

during the long summer drought, justifying the description of the country as "a good land, a land of brooks of water, of fountains and springs, flowing forth in valleys and hills" (Deut. 8:7). To the Cenomanian belong the precipitous headland of Mount Carmel, the jagged palisades of the Maktesh ha-Gadol, and "Solomon's Quarries" in Jerusalem, from which the stone for the original Temple is reputed to have come. The Eocene has built the twin mountains of Ebal and Gerizim on either side of Shechem, from which in Deuteronomy the blessings and curses were ordered to be proclaimed (27: 11–13), and in Galilee the striking orange cliffs of Wadi Amad and the Valley of the Robbers.

The chalk is less fertile and useless for building, and Isaiah speaks of it contemptuously as "chalkstones crushed to pieces" (27:9). Nevertheless, it has two practical virtues, both the result of its softness: the soil is easily plowed despite its infertility, so that farmers often prefer it for cultivation, and the Senonian in particular is so little resistant that wherever it is exposed it is immediately worn away to form a valley. Although inclined to be slippery in wet weather, it normally dries rapidly and is worn by the passage of feet and vehicles into a hard, fairly smooth surface, unbroken by boulders. The valleys of Senonian chalk, therefore, have provided many of the roads of the country, especially west of the Jordan. The passes across the limestone hills of Carmel all follow narrow exposures of Senonian, and all the towns which served as capitals of the northern kingdom, Shechem, Tirzah, and Samaria, stand at junctions of similar valleys. The long, narrow moat which protected Judah on the west, dividing the Cenomanian hill country from the uplands of the Shephelah, is also

Senonian, and so is the valley of Aijalon, where the chalk has been preserved between two parallel faults and makes an easy approach to the mountains, pointing like a pistol at the heart of Judah. Here Joshua commanded the sun to stand still (Josh. 10:12). This is also the Ascent of Beth-horon, fortified by Solomon (1 Kings 9:17), the route followed by almost every army that invaded Judah, and the road down which Saul and Jonathan drove the Philistines after the victory at Michmash (1 Sam. 14:31). Had this thin layer of chalk not existed between the thicker limestone above and below it, the whole history of Palestine would have been different.

The tremendous earth movements which have given the country its present shape began in the Oligocene epoch, but had their greatest effect in the Miocene-Pliocene. Three different types of movement may be distinguished, though all took place concurrently throughout the period of mountain building:[15]

1. *Warping* of the underlying platform as a result of the strain imposed on it by the "Alpine storm" then taking place in what is now the mountain region to the north and east. This produced cigar-shaped arch structures which today form the major heights in Cis-jordan and Trans-jordan.

2. *Folding* of the softer sediments on top of this warped platform, producing an effect not unlike that of wavy hair on top of a person's head.

3. *Faulting* or shattering of the platform when the strain became greater than it could resist. This faulting is exceedingly complex and the causes of

15. Picard, *Structure and Evolution*, pp. 67–68; R. Freund, "A model of the structural development of Israel and the adjacent areas since Upper Cretaceous times," *Geol. Mag.,* 102 (1965), 189–205.

it still somewhat obscure. It forms part of a truly gigantic system of rifting stretching all the way from the borders of Turkey, though the Red Sea and the East African lakes, to Mozambique, a distance of no less than 60° of latitude. The basic cause of the rifting seems to have been a wrenching away of the peninsula of Arabia from the continent of Africa and, as part of this same movement, a separation of East Africa from the central part of the continent. In Palestine Cis-jordan was divided from Trans-jordan, but quite how this took place is a matter of much dispute. Some have argued that it is a true "rift valley," created by the tearing apart of the areas on each side and the consequent collapse of the central section, while others have supported an exactly opposite theory: that it is a "ramp valley," caused by the pressing together of the lateral areas so that they

8   THREE THEORIES OF RIFT VALLEY FORMATION

(a) Tension or Rift Theory. The two sides split apart and the central section drops down.

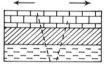 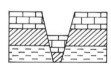

(b) Compression, or Ramp Theory. The two sides are squeezed up above the central section. The excess material (shown dotted) is removed by erosion.

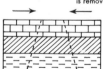 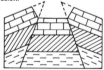

(c) Shear Theory. One block moves sideways away from the other.

have ridden up over the section in the center.[16] More recently Quennell has suggested that there was a shearing movement horizontally so that the Trans-jordan plateau moved some 67 miles northward in relation to Cis-jordan.[17] This, he argues, was the result of compression from the southeast. At first, while this was still slight, it caused only the minor folding, already mentioned, of the Senonian period. As the pressure intensified, the main thrust tended to move farther southward in a clockwise direction, and as the plateau broke under the tremendous pressure, the two parts of it tended to shift away from the main pressure in a counterclockwise direction; finally, as the compressive forces became even more intense and were by this time coming more or less from the south, the eastern block was pushed northward over a distance of 67 miles, the movement taking place in two steps, of 40 and 27 miles respectively. If the eastern block were once more shifted 67 miles southward, it is claimed, some important west–east faults in Cis-jordan would be continuous with similar faults in Transjordan, but there is on the other hand very little evidence of the compression in the Syrian region farther north which such a northward movement must have produced. Consequently, this theory has not so far won general acceptance.

In the early part of the main mountain-building period the sea still covered all the Coast Plain and extended inland

16. B. Willis, "Dead Sea Problem: Rift Valley or Ramp Valley," *Bulletin of the Geological Society of America*, Vol. 39, pp. 490–542.

17. Quennell's theory is summarized in Burdon, *op. cit.*, pp. 56–65, having been presented originally in papers read at the International Geological Congress in Mexico, Sept., 1956, and before the Geological Society, London, Dec. 12, 1956.

**9   QUENNELL'S THEORY OF THE FORMATION
OF THE RIFT VALLEY**

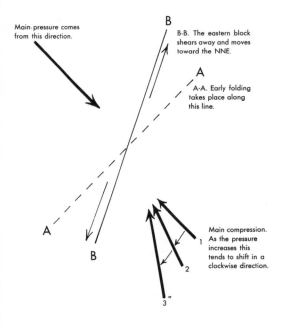

Main pressure comes from this direction.

B-B. The eastern block shears away and moves toward the NNE.

A-A. Early folding takes place along this line.

Main compression. As the pressure increases this tends to shift in a clockwise direction.

developed at this time. At the end of the Pliocene renewed faulting in the Rift Valley lowered the Jordan–Dead Sea Lake, and the streams on each side of the Rift were forced to erode their valleys once more to accommodate themselves to this new base level.

The faulting and fissuring of the Rift Valley also caused great eruptions of basalt which began in the middle Miocene and have continued down to historical times.[21] The earlier flows on the plateau of Bashan were quiet upwellings through cracks in the earth's surface, but the activity of the Pleistocene period was more violent and spewed out the mountains of Jabal Druze. The downfaulted basins of Lower Galilee, e.g., Sahl Battauf, belong also to the Pleistocene, and so does some of the faulting which carved the canyons of the Eastern Plateau. The basalt had already started to well out before this faulting, since in the north it has been pulled down into the Rift Valley, and basalt from Jabal Shihan is found on both sides of the Arnon canyon.

The cracking of the land is still not quite finished, for the fault shown on the geological map as running NNE from the center of the Gulf of Aqabah is very recent and has caused a 30-foot scarp in the gravel beds near 'Ain ad-Dafiyah.[22] Earthquakes still occur and are often mentioned in the Bible. In Numbers 16:30–31 it is considered as "something new" for the people coming from Egypt when "the earth opened its mouth and swallowed them up, with their households and all the men that belonged to Korah and all their goods." In the Psalms they are associated with the appearance of God

in the Haifa region and into the Beersheba Gap. In the Kurnub-Hosb region, southwest of the Dead Sea, there were probably sandy basins which received sediment from the surrounding hills.[18] During all this time the mountains were slowly rising, and by the Pliocene these basins lost their connection with the sea and became filled with sediment.[19] In Galilee the volcanic Hill of Moreh stood up as an island, but in time continued uplift raised the whole Gilboa-Moreh region out of the sea.[20] Carmel was also slowly beginning to appear above the Pliocene sea, and the faults which outline it

18. Picard, *Structure and Evolution*, p. 76.

19. Blake, *op. cit.*, p. 95.

20. Survey of Palestine, *Geological Map of Southern Palestine*.

21. Burdon, *op. cit.*, p. 47.

22. Survey of Palestine, *Geological Map of Southern Palestine*.

(18:7; 29:6), and again in 1 Kings 19:11, though on that occasion "the Lord was not in the earthquake." The great earthquake in the days of King Uzziah was long remembered (Amos 1:1; Zech. 14:5; possibly also Isa. 9:10), and the rending of the curtain in the Temple from top to bottom (Mark 15:38) is in Matthew attributed to an earthquake, for "the curtain of the Temple was torn in two, from top to bottom; and the earth shook and the rocks were split" (Matt. 27:51). Though Matthew's explanation may well be a later development, it is true that the Temple Area is on a line of structural weakness, and the Muslim shrines which stand there today have been damaged by earthquakes more than once in history, at least in 747, 1033, 1060, as we know from inscriptions recording the repairs,[23] and in recent years on July 11, 1927, and again in 1936. Slight tremors occur fairly frequently, and the latest one of any severity was on September 13, 1954.

The last volcanic eruption in Arabia is said to have been as late as A.D. 1256, but the most recent basalt outflow in Syria is dated about 4,000 years ago.[24] The Trans-jordan volcanoes probably ceased somewhat before this, though not so long before as to have faded from folk memory. Some scholars have seen in "the pillar of cloud by day and the pillar of fire by night" (Exod. 13:21–22) and in Mount Sinai "wrapped in smoke" so that "the smoke of it went up like the smoke of a kiln and the whole mountain quaked greatly" (Exod. 19:18) vivid memories of some volcanic eruption. So also in Psalms 104:32 and 144:5

and in the "continually smoking wasteland" of Wisdom of Solomon 10:7, though others would reject such interpretations completely. The destruction of Sodom and Gomorrah with "brimstone and fire from the Lord" and "the smoke of the land" which "went up like the smoke of a furnace (Gen. 19:24, 28) has also been seen as the memory of an eruption, but this seems

VI. *Jabal adh-Dhakar.* A mass of volcanic basalt which has forced its way to the surface through the Kurnub sandstone of the Wadi Hesa (The river Zered of the Old Testament).

VII. *"The Bricks have fallen . . ."* (Isaiah 9:10). Destruction wrought by an earthquake in the desert palace of Qasr at-Tuba, built by the 'Ummayads in the east of Transjordan in the 8th century A.D.

23. Alistair Duncan, *The Noble Sanctuary* (London: Longman, 1972), pp. 40, 44, 46.

24. Burdon, *op. cit.,* p. 4.

impossible, since the only example of basalt originating in the Rift Valley, rather than being pulled down into it, is the tiny exposure at Grain Sabt some 27 miles north of the Dead Sea and just to the east of the river.[25] Karmon has suggested instead that what is remembered is rather the uplifting of the salt mountain of Sdom, which caused the flooding of the shallow southern basin of the Dead Sea.[26]

Modern volcanic activity is confined mainly to the hot springs, such as those found by Anah, the Edomite, in the wilderness (Gen. 36:24). They are mostly east of the Jordan, e.g., al-Hammeh in the Yarmuq Valley and the strong springs at Zerqa Ma'in, but there are some also on the western shore of the Lake of Galilee. The remarkable preservation of such perishable materials as wood and meat in the Bronze Age tombs at Jericho has been attributed to the exhalation of volcanic gases through cracks along the edge of the Rift.[27]

The quieter activity of the Pleistocene was the deposition of sedimentary rocks in two separate areas: the Coast Plain and the Rift Valley.

1. *The Coast Plain.* Three different types of rock were formed here at about the same time. The first is the *kurkar,* a hard sandy limestone formed from solidified sand dunes. The lower *kurkar* beneath the surface seems to belong to the Pliocene. It forms a hard layer which seriously limits tree growth if it is less than 3 feet below the surface. The younger, Pleistocene *kurkar* has produced the narrow lines of low hills, rarely much more than 100 feet high, bordering the coast from Joppa northward. They may perhaps be "the heights of Dor" (Josh. 11:2—left untranslated in RSV as Naphath-Dor), since these hills are here well developed and played an important part in the defense of the town.

The second rock is the *Mousterian Red Sand* of the Plain of Sharon, a bright red or orange soil which is today the citrus soil *par excellence.* It occurs in patches divided by alluvium and is now believed to have been formed from stabilized dune sands which were sufficiently far from the sea for suitable vegetation to develop and produce the change. "Near the sea conditions are favourable for the formation of *kurkar,* at a distance of about half a kilometre conditions are more suitable for the formation of red sand."[28]

The third is *Loess,* formed of wind-borne material from the desert, and found in a great triangle west of Beersheba. Loess, it should be noticed, is also found on the Trans-jordan Plateau and has been deposited there during the last 2,000 years.[29]

2. *The Rift Valley.* At the beginning of the Pleistocene epoch there was a series of separated basins: the Aqabah Basin, the Jordan–Dead Sea Basin, the Tiberias–Beth-shan Basin, and the Huleh Basin. At first these last two were joined together, but the outflow of basalt in mid-Pleistocene times dammed the valley south of Lake Huleh. Below the dam the heavy rain of the mid-Pleistocene pluvial period brought into being a huge brackish lake, the Lisan Sea, which joined together the two middle basins, and in this were deposited the whitish-gray Lisan marls of the Jordan Valley and

25. *Ibid.,* p. 49.
26. Karmon, *op. cit.,* p. 14.
27. Kathleen M. Kenyon, "Excavations at Jericho 1954," *PEQ, LXXXVI,* (1954), p. 63.

28. Karmon, *op. cit.,* p. 16.
29. Burdon, *op. cit.,* p. 21.

Dead Sea region. At the same time tremendous masses of gravel were washed down by the rivers and choked the mouths of the wadis. In the Arabah they form vast alluvial fans which sometimes meet in the middle of the valley, but farther north the presence of the Lisan Sea meant a raising of the base level of the streams which entered it and the deposition of the gravel at the edge of the lake.[30]

Finally, about 9,000 years ago, the rains decreased and the Lisan Sea gave place to the present Lake of Galilee and the Dead Sea. This lowering of the base level once rejuvenated the rivers, now greatly reduced in size. The Jordan has carved a secondary valley, the *Zor,* well below the level of the Lisan marls, and the tributaries were forced to cut down again to the new level through the great piles of gravel which had accumulated in the pluvial period. At least one river, the Zerqa Ma'in, was unable to do this and carved a new valley for itself in the soft sandstone.

---

30. The strange absence of deposition from the rivers at the bottom of the main basin of the Dead Sea has been quoted by Burdon and Quennell in support of their thesis. They argue that "the present Dead Sea has opened since the erosion of the great wadis." *Op. cit.,* pp. 62–63.

CHAPTER 3

The Earth on Its Foundations

Thou didst set the earth on its foundations,
so that it should never be shaken.
Thou didst cover it with the deep as with a garment;
the waters stand above the mountains.
At thy rebuke they fled;
at the sound of thy thunder they took to flight.
The mountains rose, the valleys sank down
to the place which thou didst appoint for them.

PSALM 104:5–8

The most obvious structural division in the country is the great Rift Valley running from north to south and dividing the whole of Palestine into Cisjordan and Trans-jordan, but the pattern of faulting is far more complicated than this. We have already seen in Chapter I that the main structural trend of the Levant is from northeast to southwest, or more strictly NNE–SSW, and that the major upwards and folding lie in this direction. The tremendous fault which marks the eastern edge of the Lebanon mountains runs parallel to this, and in Palestine also we may trace some NNE–SSW faulting, such as that east of Gaza, Ashkelon, and Ashdod, marking the edge of the "Ashkelon Trough."[1] But imposed upon this NNE–SSW tendency is another, that of the north–south fault lines, of which the most obvious are those outlining the Rift Valley of the Jordan. It is these north–south faults which have helped to outline the Central Highlands of Palestine and present us with the commonly accepted picture of a north–south pattern to the landscape.

At right angles to these two major directions are other fault lines, from northwest to southeast and from west to east. NW–SE faults may be seen

1. This is shown in the *Atlas of Israel,* map III/3.

28

outlining Mount Carmel and the Valley of Jezreel, the valley of Fari'a east of Nablus, the Kerak Wadi and its continuation southeastward in the Fijj al-'Aseikir. West–east faults are common in northern Cis-jordan, such as the great scarp of ash-Shaghur, which divides Upper from Lower Galilee. We must therefore recognize a network of folding and faulting very much as shown in Figure 10.

With this in mind we may now turn to examine the structural pattern of the country as a whole. It may be divided into three broad zones running from west to east right across the Rift and dying away in the desert plateau east of the present Hejaz Railway. In the center is a *Zone of Relative Simplicity,* marked out on the north by a line drawn through Lod (Lydda), Ramallah, and Amman, the ancient Rabbah (Rabbath Ammon), and in the south by the Beersheba-Zered Depres-

10   STRUCTURAL "NETWORK" OF THE LEVANT

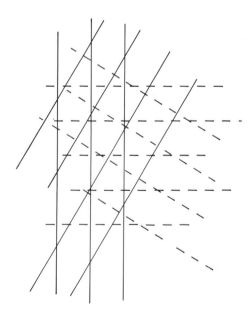

sion. To the north of this central zone lies a *Zone of Greater Complexity,* including Samaria, Galilee, and Gilead, and to the south the Realm of the Southland, which for our present purpose we may entitle the *Zone of Reversed Tendencies.*

1. *The Zone of Relative Simplicity.* Here the classic division of the country into Coast Plain, Western Highlands, Central Valley, and Eastern Plateau is most clearly seen. The undulating Coast Plain gives place to the single broad arch of the Highlands, moderately varied by the gentle folding of the overlying rocks. In Trans-jordan the broad and partly dissected plateau dips gradually eastward, and in the canyons of the Arnon and Zered can be seen the level, uncontorted strata lying one upon the other. On either side of the Dead Sea the fracturing has tended to pull the overlying strata sharply downward in plunging monoclines so that in places the layers of rock very nearly stand on end, as, for instance, the adh-Dhra' scarp west of Kerak, overlooking the Lisan Peninsula. "We have heard of the pride of Moab, how proud he was," said Isaiah (16:6), and in no small measure "his arrogance, his pride, and his insolence" were due to these cataracts of rock, behind whose defense he felt safe from invasion.

2. *The Zone of Greater Complexity.* Here the pattern is complicated by the fact that the strong NE–SW trend of the Lebanon–Anti-Lebanon and the N–S direction of the Jordan Rift are imposed upon each other (Fig. 11). The NE–SW direction is apparent in the line of the Judah–Gilead Dome and in the parallel line of Carmel–Upper Galilee–Mount Hermon. The long arm of Carmel, it should be noticed, extending northwestward from Samaria, runs *across* the main line of

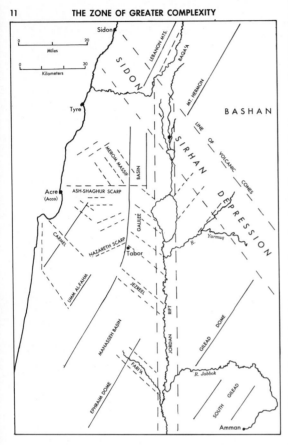

11   THE ZONE OF GREATER COMPLEXITY

Sidon, sharply cutting off the edge of Mount Hermon, and continues past Dera'a, to al-'Azraq and the Wadi Sirhan. It crosses the Jordan Rift in the Huleh Basin and divides Hermon from Upper Galilee.

From west to east we have the Galilee-Bashan Depression, separated from Upper Galilee to the north by the ash-Shaghur fault, the steep step which divides the Huleh Basin from Marj 'Ayoun to the north of it, and in the south the canyon of the Jabbok as it cleaves across the Gilead Dome. The Jabbok and the Fari'a enter the Jordan just south of the "Jordan Waist," where the Rift, cutting across the Judah-Gilead Dome, is no more than 2 to 3 miles wide.

3. *The Zone of Reversed Tendencies.* This is not entirely a happy term, but it indicates that here in the south we have to notice some important alterations in the normally accepted pattern. In Cis-jordan the upwarps lose their height and through much of the Negeb form uplands rather than highlands. In contrast the Rift Valley rises above sea level to 650 feet (200 m.) in Jabal al-Khureij. East of the Rift the plateau has been greatly disturbed by the complex faulting of southern Transjordan. The towering plateau edge, 5,000 feet above sea level, is formed not of a single plunging monocline but of a series of faulted steps which can be seen from the Arabah, with white sandstone resting on red, and the hard gray granite beneath that. South of Petra is a shattered area where the edge of the plateau cuts back southeastward along an extended series of minor faults,[2] and its place beside the Rift is taken by the Mountains of Midian, a gigantic wedge of granite pushed up between faults to over

the folding. The N–S direction is clearly apparent in the Jordan-Huleh Rift and may perhaps finally run out to the sea in the headland of Beirut. At right angles to these are the northwest–southeast faults and depressions and the west–east faults. Running from northwest to southeast we have (a) the long fault which divides Mount Carmel from the Plain of Esdraelon, and is continued in the little rift of the Wadi Fari'a and finally the northern edge of the Plains of Moab, (b) the narrow Valley of Jezreel, (c) the downfaulted plains west of the Lake of Galilee, and (d) that extensive zone of weakness which strikes southwestward from

2. Burdon, *op. cit.*, p. 54.

5,000 feet (1500 m.). Behind this is the fascinating wasteland of the Hasma and Jabal Tubaiq, where awe-inspiring mountains of rock rise from a bewildering sea of sand.

Trans-Jordan

East of the present Hejaz Railway the three zones are less apparent, and instead the broad plateau dips slowly northeastward toward the Wadi Sirhan, which extends from northwest to southeast and seems to be a filled-in rift.[3] A gentle undulation runs parallel to this across the plateau so that ridge of Jabal Mudeisisat and Jabal al-Jau-'aliyat, rising a little over 3,300 feet (1,000 m.), divides the basin of Wadi Hafira, 2,500 feet (750 m.), in the center of Trans-jordan. East of the Wadi Sirhan, and parallel to it, is the long barrier of basalt which so effectively blocked all transverse movement. This basalt has apparently poured out along "feeder dikes" which are part of the Wadi Sirhan system. The Wadi Sirhan today is not what the Westerner normally thinks of as a "wadi," but a prolonged broad depression, and the unsuspecting traveler across the often featureless, flint-strewn desert of eastern Jordan could easily cross the frontier and arrive in the wadi without being aware that he has done so. Its northwestern end, inside the present country of Jordan, is occupied by the salt marshes of al-'Azraq.

Between the railway and the plateau edge, with its long series of N–S faults, sometimes with a throw of 6,000 to 7,000 feet (1,800 to 2,100 m.), the division into three zones becomes apparent. The northern zone is dominated by the Gilead Dome, the only major fold east of the Jordan, with

3. *Ibid.*, p. 53.

parallel to it on the south another lesser fold extending northeastward from the Zerqa Ma'in, past Rabbah (Amman) to Qasr al-Hallabat. The Gilead Dome is cleft by the Jabbok, which rises at Rabbah, follows first a northeasterly direction, and then curves round to carve its way almost due westward to the Jordan. The northern section of the dome, formed of hard Cenomanian limestone, is rather higher and reaches over 3,600 feet (1,100 m.) in places. The Jabbok has cut through this limestone to the Kurnub sandstone beneath and in its lower reaches to the Jurassic limestone. South of the river the land rises again to the mountains around as-Salt and Sweileh, but these are cut by a line which starts at the fault marking the southeastern edge of the "plains of Moab by the Jordan" (Num. 22:1; 31:12; 33:48) and continues as a monoclinal fold which has produced the basin of al-Baqa'a near Sweileh.

To the north the Gilead Dome descends to the Plain of Bashan, which may be said to begin south of the Yarmuq in the region of Irbid and to extend far across the river to the foot of Mount Hermon. Although both sides of the canyon are essentially plateau country, there is a marked difference between them, since the river follows the edge of the basalt outflow. To the north, therefore, is the volcanic region, and to the south Senonian chalk.

The central, less disturbed, section of the country, "all the tableland of Medeba as far as Dibon" (Josh. 13:9) on the edge of the Arnon canyon, has remarkably level strata. To the south of the canyon the extinct volcano of Shihan raises its head above the level surface, which then continues unbroken to Kerak (Kir-hareseth), where the Crusaders' castle commands a mag-

12   **THE STRUCTURE OF NORTHERN TRANS-JORDAN**

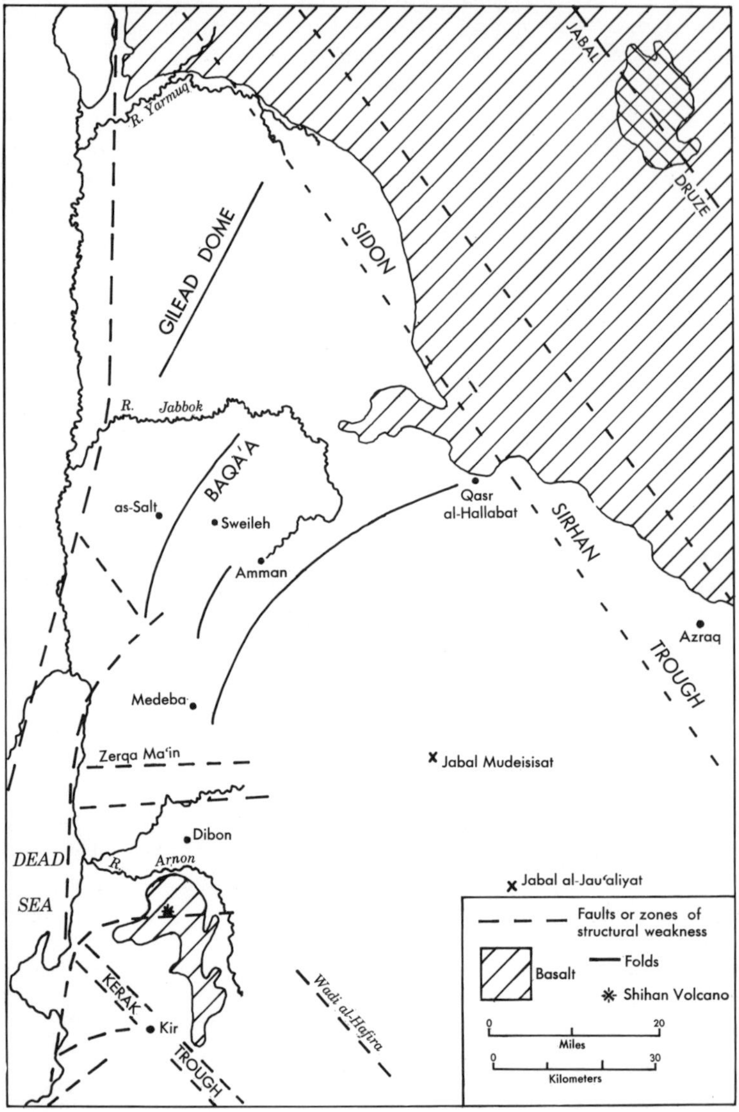

R. Yarmuq

JABAL

DRUZE

GILEAD DOME

SIDON

R. Jabbok

BAQA'A

as-Salt

Sweileh

Amman

Qasr al-Hallabat

SIRHAN

Azraq

TROUGH

Medeba

Zerqa Ma'in

✕ Jabal Mudeisisat

Dibon

DEAD SEA

R. Arnon

✕ Jabal al-Jau'aliyat

Faults or zones of structural weakness

Basalt

Folds

✳ Shihan Volcano

KERAK

Kir

TROUGH

Wadi al-Hafira

0   20
Miles
0   30
Kilometers

nificent view down the Kerak Rift northwestward to the waters of the Dead Sea. This rift valley is continued southeast of Kerak in the remarkably straight valley of Fijj al-'Aseikir, which though shallow is clearly defined and about one kilometer wide, and in the Wadi Gheish beyond it. South of

Kerak the ground rises steadily, though with little disturbance of the general plateau effect, until the gorge of the Zered. This canyon, like those of the Arnon and Zerqa Ma'in to the north of it, follows the line of a west–east fault.

South of the Zered the plateau

climbs more steeply until for a distance of 45 miles (72 km.) the edge is continuously over 5,000 feet (1,500 m.) and in places touches more than 5,600 (1,700 m.). One of the most marked differences in the structure here from that farther north is that the edge of the plateau is gashed in many places with faults, both parallel to the edge and cutting back into it to the east and southeast. Striking examples of west–east faults are those near Dana and Shaubak behind Feinan (Punon), and of NW–SE faults the Tafileh wadi and the faults which form Ras an-Naqb, the southern edge of the Edomite plateau.

South of Ras an-Naqb is the reticu-

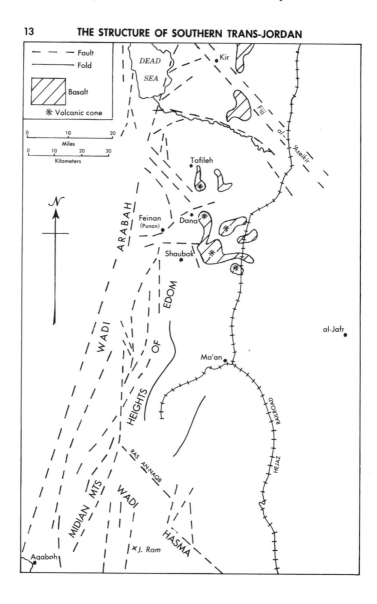

13   THE STRUCTURE OF SOUTHERN TRANS-JORDAN

lated landscape of the Hasma, created by rivers of the pluvial period cutting along the joints of the sandstone. On the western slope of the Edomite plateau the granite platform is exposed intermittently for almost its full length and then, south of Ras an-Naqb, continuously. Another pre-Cambrian feature is the long spine of dark red porphyry which in the Arabah crosses the mouth of the Wadi Dana.

Cis-jordan

West of the Rift Valley we find ourselves in a region with a more complicated structure and varied landscape. However, in one sense there is less diversity, since in most of the inhabited areas the rocks are largely Cretaceous and Eocene limestones and chalk. The basalt, so widely exposed farther east, is confined to a small area west and north of the Lake of Galilee, and the sandstones and granite are exposed only rarely in the Negeb. The main exceptions to the Cretaceous-Eocene domination are the more recent deposits of the Coast Plain and the Rift valley.

We have constantly to bear in mind Picard's three tectonic forms: warping, folding, and faulting. It was upwarping which produced the most important topographic feature—the great central backbone of highlands extending from north to south of the country —but the shape of these has been controlled by faulting. The upwarps, it will be remembered, run from SSE to NNW, that is, obliquely to the main N–S line of the highlands, and they are placed *en échelon*. The north–south alignment of the highlands is the result of the faults which have outlined them on either side, most noticeably in the east but also in the west.

The Negeb has three clear structural divisions:

1. *The Plateau of Paran,* divided by extended lines of west–east faulting from the beginning of the Sinai Mountains in the south and the Ramon Upwarp in the north. On the physical map it appears as a broad basin, modified by NE–SW folding, and drained to the northeast by the Paran and Zenifim wadis. Mainly formed of Senonian chalk, the center (about 1500 feet, 450 m.) is covered with gravel and alluvium brought down by the wadis, and around the edges the Eocene is preserved. The rim is somewhat higher than 2,000 feet (600 m.), but in the southeast, where the Cenomanian limestone is exposed, the land reaches over 3,000 feet (900 m.).

2. *The Central Upwarped Region.* There are two main upwarps, each of which has been broken open to form the remarkable *maksteshim,* or "erosion cirques," which are such a dramatic feature of this part of the country. Here the strain of the folding has caused a crack to develop along the top of the fold, and then the forces of erosion have opened up the crack to create a tremendous pit or "cauldron" (i.e., *maktesh*), enclosed within towering cliffs, broken only by the outlet in the northeast from which the *maktesh* is drained, and where the rare flash floods of winter break through to the Arabah.

The more southerly Ramon, or Khurashe, Upwarp is the higher, reaching 3,290 feet (1,003 m.) in the southwest in Har Ramon. Here is the largest of the cauldrons, the Maktesh Ramon (Wadi Raman), 22 miles long and 3 miles wide. The upwarp sinks toward the northeast, and the next, the Kurnub Upwarp, is considerably lower, for the land lies for the most part between 1,600 and 2,000 feet (500–600 m.), exceeding 2,000 in only relatively small areas. Three parallel folded ridges lie NE–SW along the upwarp: the Dimona ridge (Jabal Rakhma), the Hatira ridge (Jabal Hathira), the Hazera ridge (Jabal Hadhira). The last two have been broken open to form the Maktesh ha-Gadol (Wadi Hathira) and the Maktesh ha-Qatan (Wadi Hadhira). This last is the smallest of the *maksteshim* and is therefore probably the youngest, since erosion in it has not proceeded as far as in the other two.

On the southeastern side of the Hazera ridge the strata turn over and plunge headlong into the Arabah, and the traveler descends into a stark and jagged landscape, startling even in this country where extensive views are common. The present road from Beersheba to Sdom climbs down this precipitous slope by the Ma'ale Tamar, which confronts the canyon of the Zered on the far side of the Rift, here covered by the dazzling white marls of the Sebkha south of the Dead Sea. However, the first of the Israeli roads to be constructed from Beersheba to Elath crossed the Maktesh ha-Gadol and clambered down the Hazera scarp by the even more dramatic (and, it must be admitted, in those days frankly terrifying) road which has been identified with Ma'ale ha-Aqrabbim, the Ascent of the Scorpions, which formed the boundary of Judah (Num. 34:4; Josh. 15:3; Judg. 1:36) and was also the place where Judas Maccabeus defeated the Idumeans (1 Macc. 5:3). As describing the boundary, however, it is more probable that the term refers to the whole length of this impressive Niagara of rock.

The Kurnub Upwarp is divided from the Ramon Upwarp to the south of it by the broad sickle-shaped valley of Biq'at Zin (Wadi Murra), at the head

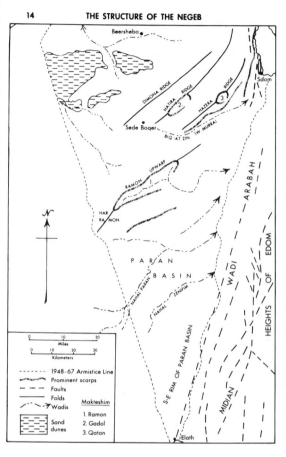

14   THE STRUCTURE OF THE NEGEB

of which stands today the kibbutz of Sede Boqer. Down this valley ran the Darb as-Sultan, by far the most important of the ancient roads from the Arabah to the sea, and one which never had to climb higher than 1,500 feet (450 m.). It led over into the third of the Negeb regions, the gentle seaward slopes southwest of Beersheba, largely covered by the only extensive inland sand dunes in the country.

North of the Beersheba Depression we enter the central *Zone of Relative Simplicity*. The Dimona ridge extends northeastward past the modern town

15   **THE JUDAEAN UPWARP**

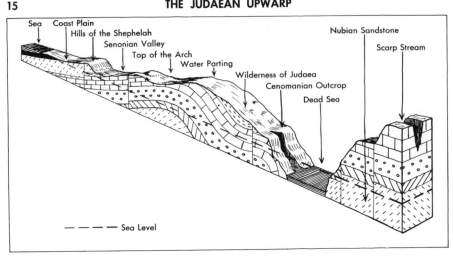

of Arad[4] to run out into the Dead Sea near Masada, but in general the topography is dominated by one broad arch, the Judean Upwarp, the secondary folds being here rather less obvious. The arch rises out of the Coast Plain to the west, reaches its greatest height north and east of Hebron, and then bends down abruptly toward the Dead Sea. If we were to cross over directly from Ashkelon on the coast through Hebron to Engedi on the Dead Sea we would pass through the following regions:

1. *The Philistine Plain,* a broad alluvial lowland with extensive sand dunes along the shore and a central *kurkar* ridge, never more than 330 feet (100 m.) in height, running parallel to the coast.

2. The wide outcrop of hard Eocene limestone, which forms the hills of the Shephelah, that bloody debating ground between the Philistines and the people of Judah.

4. The biblical Arad lay west of this in the broad valley which divides this ridge from the Judean Upwarp.

3. *The Judean Moat,* a thin valley of Senonian chalk effectively dividing the Shephelah from the mountains. This valley is so narrow that it is hardly apparent on the 1:250,000 map, but it was vitally important to the defenses of Judah.

4. *The Cenomanian Highlands,* or hill country of Judah. Erosion by the driving rain from the west has pushed the water-parting backward so that the highest land, on which Hebron, Bethlehem, and Jerusalem stand, lies east of the real top of the arch.

5. *Jeshimon,* where the dusty, infertile Senonian chalk produces the desolate Wilderness of Judah. The overlying Senonian has been eroded into smooth and gentle slopes, but where the wadis have cut through to the harder Cenomanian beneath, narrow rocky gorges take their place.

The northern limit of the Central Zone is the Saddle of Benjamin between Jerusalem and Ramallah, where faults curving inward from Aijalon on the west and Jericho on the east bring to an end the Senonian chalk on both

VIII. *Mar Saba in Jeshimon.*   The early Christian monastery of Mar Saba clinging to the side of the Wadi Nar east of Bethlehem where the fierce erosion of the Pluvial period has cut through the soft overlying Senonian chalk to form a gorge in the much harder Cenomanian limestone beneath.

IX. *al-Buqei'a in Jeshimon.*   This broad depression, believed by many to be the Valley of Achor of the Old Testament, represents an ancient lake bed which subsequently dried out.

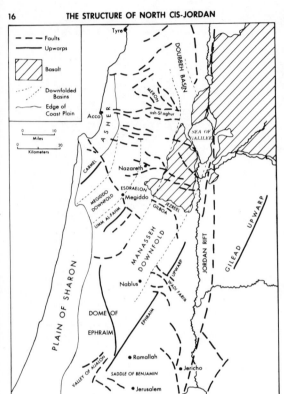

16   THE STRUCTURE OF NORTH CIS-JORDAN

through Jabal Kabir compresses the Jordan Rift from the west as does the Dome of Gilead from the east. The upwarp is here cut by a number of cross faults at right angles to the main NNE–SSW axis, the most important being the narrow rift valley of Wadi Fari'a which cleaves the mountains and gives easy access to the Jordan. It will be seen that here the main arch lies well to the east, and the central area around Nablus is, in fact, a basin. This is difficult to see on the physical map because the hard Eocene limestone which has been preserved in the center of the basin has been pushed up near Nablus until it forms the highest land in the region (Mount Ebal—3,083 feet, 940 m.). Nevertheless, the structure is important because the soft Senonian chalk is now enclosed within the rim of the basin instead of being outside the arch as in Judah, forming, therefore, communicating valleys inside Manasseh rather than valleys of defense outside it. One must therefore speak of the *gates* of Manasseh in place of the *walls* of Judah and Ephraim.

The northwestern edge of the basin is formed by the Umm al-Fahm Upwarp, beyond which to the northwest is the Megiddo Basin, and beyond that again the Carmel Upwarp. Once more this is not immediately obvious on the physical map, since the faults have cut directly across it and carved out a huge wedge of higher land pointing northwestward and reaching the sea at the Carmel headland. In this wedge the highest parts are the Cenomanian hills of the Umm al-Fahm and Carmel Upwarps, while the Megiddo Basin is somewhat lower, though still hilly because of the hard Eocene limestone preserved there. On either side of this central hilly portion is a narrow exposure of the Senonian chalk, immediately eroded to form the vital transverse

sides of the arch. The Ephraim Upwarp starts in the Central Zone, crosses the present Jerusalem–Nablus road north of Ramallah near Lubban, and continues into Jabal Kabir east of Nablus. In the territory of Ephraim immediately north of Ramallah, the Cenomanian limestone extends the full width of the highlands and is divided from the Coast Plain neither by the Senonian chalk nor by the Eocene limestone. There was therefore neither moat nor Shephelah west of Ephraim, but it was adequately defended by the cliffs and gorges eroded in the hard Cenomanian.

The continuation of the upwarp

17   THE STRUCTURE OF CARMEL AND SAMARIA

Carmel Upwarp   Megiddo Basin   Dothan Basin

Umm el-Fahm Upwarp

Jebel Kabir Upwarp

S

S

S

S

S = Senonian Chalk Valleys

valleys of Megiddo and Jokneam.

The territory of Manasseh also differed from that of Ephraim and Judah in the presence of a number of down-faulted basins floored with fertile alluvium washed down from the mountains, e.g., the plain of Dothan and Marj Sannur north of Nablus.

Farther north again lies the great corridor which stretches from the Bay of Acco (Haifa Bay) southeastward to Beth-shan, known in common parlance today quite simply as Ha-Emek, or "The Valley" *par excellence.* It is outlined by faults and divided into three very obvious sections (see Fig. 50, p. 146):

1. *The Jezreel Corridor* in the southeast, a narrow rift valley between the volcanic Hill of Moreh and the Eocene Mountains of Gilboa, Beth-shan at its eastern entrance stands on a high step

where the Jordan Rift cuts across the corridor.

2. *The Plain of Esdraelon* in the center. This is a rough triangle with a very straight base from Megiddo to Ibleam (near the modern Jenin) and its apex at the rounded hill of Tabor, around which the land has been collapsed by faulting. The isolation of Mount Tabor, which rises as steeply from the plain as Carmel rises from the coast, gave it an impressive majesty, and in ancient days both were accounted sacred. Hence Jeremiah says of Nebuchadnezzar, "Like Tabor among the mountains, and like Carmel by the sea, shall one come" (Jer. 46:18), and in Psalm 89:12 Tabor and Hermon joyously praise God's name.

3. *The Kishon Gate,* where the storied river squeezes through a very narrow passage between the Galilee

hills and the Carmel scarp to empty itself in the Bay of Acco.

The last of the mountain sections is best described by the name given it by Picard and Gilboa, the *Fault Block Complex of Galilee,*[5] since it is faulting, far more than folding, which has produced the present landscape. In principle the Basin of Manasseh is continued NNE toward the Lake of Galilee; the Umm al-Fahm Upwarp through the collapsed arch of Mount Tabor into the central hills of Lower Galilee; the Eocene of the Megiddo hills into the similar hills west of Nazareth; and finally the Carmel Upwarp into the elevated highlands of Upper Galilee. However, all this is almost completely obscured by faulting, here particularly intense because here the north–south rift system of the Jordan and the NNE–SSW Syro-Phoenician rifting meet and, as it were, engage each other. It is this engagement which has thrust down so deeply

the Esdraelon corridor, which apparently is still subsiding[6] and has so seamed the northern highlands with faults that the underlying structure is hardly visible.

The most evident division is the steep scarp of ash-Shaghur in the latitude of Acco, separating Upper from Lower Galilee. In Lower Galilee, to the south, the trough continuing the Manasseh Basin toward the NNE has been completely filled with basalt and stands today as the Plateau of Moreh, extending from the Valley of Jezreel to the Lake of Galilee. West of this the Cenomanian uplands, with a general level of 1,600 to 2,000 feet (500–600 m.), are so broken up by downfaulted basins, e.g., Biq'at Beth Netofa (Sahl al-Battauf, the Campus Asochis of the Romans), that passage across the hills is relatively easy.

Upper Galilee, north of the ash-Shaghur fault, is also much cut up by cross faulting in various directions, but

5. L. Picard, and Y. Gilboa, *Atlas of Israel*, III/3.

6. Karmon, *op. cit.*, p. 192.

18   NORTH CIS-JORDAN AND THE BAY OF ACRE

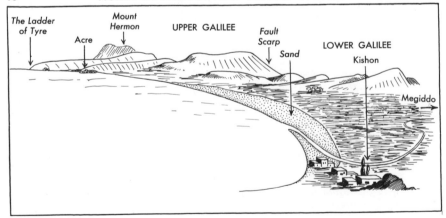

its general level is much higher. Most of it is over 2,600 feet and the central uplifted Meron block well above 3,000, Har Meron (Jabal Jarmaq), the highest point west of the Jordan, reaching 3,963 feet (1,208 m.). The land east of this, beyond the deeply incised gorge of Nahal 'Ammud (Wadi Leimun) is structurally the continuation northward of the downwarped trough which we first encountered in the Basin of Manasseh, but here it has been thrust up boldly into the elevated block of Mount Kina'an, again well over 3,000 feet (900 m.).

The Coast Plain is fairly quickly dealt with. Its features are:

1. The long straight coast, curving toward the southwest, and apparently the result of faulting.[7] From Caesarea to Jaffa wave erosion has carved out

7. Dov Nir, "Étude sur la Morphologie Littorale d'Israël," *Annales de Géographie,* LXVIII (1959), 425.

cliffs up to about 100 feet (30 m.) in height, but farther south extensive sand dunes have been deposited. A more limited area of sand dunes is found in the northern section, near the present Hadera, and cliffs in the south near Ashkelon.

2. The low narrow ridges of *kurkar* limestone which appear intermittently along the coast from Ras an-Naqura (Rosh ha-Niqra) to near Jaffa.

3. The Mousterian Red Sand of Sharon, i.e., south of Carmel to about 7 miles south of Lod. There are some isolated deposits south of this, but none to the north.

4. The large triangle of loess behind Gaza and Rafah, marking the junction of the Coast Plain with the Negeb wilderness.

The general outlines of the Rift Valley have already been dealt with. Here it is necessary to mention only

19   **NORTH-SOUTH SECTION ACROSS GALILEE**

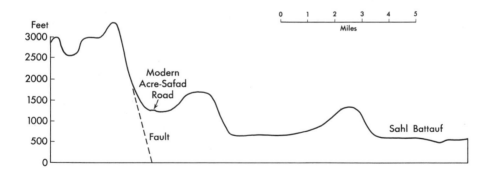

X. *Mouth of the Zerqa Ma'in.* The original exit of the Zerqa Ma'in into the Dead Sea was blocked by the mass of white gravel seen to the left of the picture and consequently, when the level of the Dead Sea was later lowered, the river was forced to carve out a new gorge on the right.

the important four basins: (Huleh, Galilee–Beth-shan, Dead Sea, and Southern Arabah) and to notice the sudden change in the north where the Syrian system of faults cuts across the N–S Jordan Rift, producing a very complex pattern. Here the valley floor is raised 1,000 feet (300 m.) above sea level, and one enters the structurally different, essentially upland, basin of Marj 'Ayoun.

CHAPTER 4

Has the Rain a Father?

Has the rain a father,
  or who has begotten the drops of dew?
From whose womb did the ice come forth,
  and who has given birth to the hoarfrost of heaven?

JOB 38:28–29

Four factors at least need to be taken into account in seeking to understand the climate of Palestine: (1) the movement of the major climate belts northward and southward in conjunction with the apparent movement of the sun from the northern tropic in summer to the southern tropic in winter; (2) the position of the country at the southeastern corner of the Mediterranean where the desert and the sea almost touch each other; (3) the proximity of the Sahara and the Arabian desert, with their extreme summer heat, and the Russo-Siberian plains, with their exceptional winter cold; (4) the fact that the main lines of relief run from north to south, parallel to the coast, that is to say athwart the movement of the cyclonic storms which bring the life-giving rain of winter.

The Palestinian year is divided into two major seasons: the dry summer

from mid-June to mid-September, and the rainy season in the cooler half of the year. This is a much more variable period, but may be said to extend roughly from mid-October to the middle of April. In between the summer and the rainy season are the very much briefer spring and autumn transitional seasons. The summer drought extends into these, and the greater part of the country has normally five continuous months without any rain at all, from the first week in May to the first week in October. It is better to avoid using the word "winter" for the rainy season, since to an English-speaking person this inevitably suggests a cold period, whereas in Palestine the cold weather is normally confined to the three months after Christmas, i.e., the second half of the rainy season. To a Palestinian the summer is so emphatically the prolonged drought (Ps. 32:4, "My strength was dried up as by the heat of summer") that winter means more than anything else that blessed season when the rain comes. In Arabic the word *shittah* is used impartially for both "winter" and "rain," and both end together in April when "lo, the winter is past, the rain is over and gone" (Song of Sol. 2:11).[1]

The Season of Summer

This is extraordinarily regular. It starts on about June 15 and finishes on about September 15, and during this period day after day is the same. In this season the dominant phenomenon is the monsoonal system of India, for the intense low pressure over the Indian subcontinent extends an arm round the foot of the Makran and Zagros mountains into the Persian Gulf and the Mesopotamian basin, while a secondary low pressure develops over the island of Cyprus. Although this is only a little island, the central plain of the Mesorea between two mountain ranges becomes exceedingly hot in summer, and the low pressure in this corner of the Mediterranean is therefore intensified. Far to the west, over the Azores, is a high pressure. Air tends to move parallel to the isobars, curving clockwise around a high pressure system and counterclockwise around a low. Consequently, the air movement over the eastern Mediterranean in summer is from north to south, but deflected around the pronounced Cyprus low so that it moves over Palestine from west to east. These northerly "Etesian" winds of summer may blow strongly and cause unpleasantly choppy seas, but they are steady and dependable, and for this reason summer was the period for shipping in the ancient world. The deflection of the wind around Cyprus makes it difficult for ships to beat westward against them (Acts 27:4), and those who delayed their journey into the more erratic transitional season would find their voyage "dangerous because the fast had already gone by" (Acts 27:9).[2]

The movement of the sun toward the northern tropic in summer results also in a northward movement of the warm upper air mass of the equatorial region, and the jet stream, which in the rainy season is over the Mediterrean, is also shifted northward. At the same time the lower air mass over the Mediterranean is relatively cool in relation to the upper air, and so there is little tendency for it to rise. All this means that summer air conditions in the eastern Mediterranean are remarkably stable, and though the air moving steadily in from the west toward Palestine is moist, it does not bring rain. What it does do—and both these effects are very important—is to moderate the heat and to bring dew all along the coast and on the western slopes of the mountains, though this does not occur in the Rift Valley south of Beth-shan during the summer months.[3] Dew is especially important in aiding agriculture in the Coast Plain south of Gaza, where there are as many as 250 nights of dew in the year as compared with 138 in Haifa. The reason

1. When I taught geography in Palestine I found that many students had great difficulty in visualizing a country like India with summer rain. Arabs in particular thought of "winter" and "rain" as synonymous, and so "summer rain" seemed to them a contradiction in terms.

2. "The fast" was Yom Kippur in late September.

3. D. Ashbel, *Bio-climatic Atlas of Israel* (Jerusalem: Meteorological Department of the Hebrew University, 1950), p. 51.

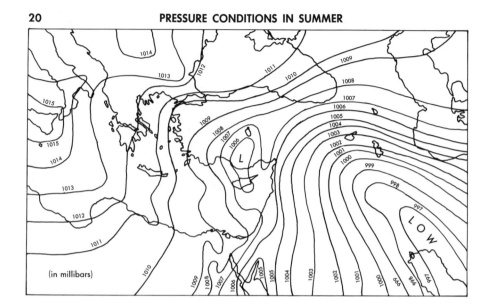

(in millibars)

for this great difference seems to be the rapid drop of temperature at night in the much drier regions of the south.

The value of the dew was well appreciated by the Israelites, for "Israel dwelt in safety . . . in a land of grain and wine; yea, his heavens drop down dew" (Deut. 33:28). The withholding of the dew is a curse and the granting of it a blessing, for it swells the grapes during the drought of summer. "As the Lord God of Israel lives, before whom I stand," said Elijah to Ahab, "there shall be neither dew nor rain these years, except by my word" (1 Kings 17:1). Haggai told the people that because of their follies "the heavens above you have withheld the dew, and the earth has withheld its produce" (Hag. 1:10; see also David's lament over Saul, 2 Sam. 1:21). But when Isaac blessed Jacob he said to him, "May God give you of the dew of heaven, and of the fatness of the earth, and plenty of grain and wine"

(Gen. 27:28), and Zechariah promised the people that in the days to come there would be a "sowing of peace; the vine shall yield its fruit, and the ground shall give its increase, and the heavens shall give their dew" (Zech. 8:12). Job also remembered how in the days of his prosperity, "My roots spread out to the waters, with dew all night on my branches" (Job 29:19). Dew can sometimes be so heavy that the flat roofs of the houses look as if it had rained, and Gideon wrung out "enough dew from the fleece to fill a bowl with water" (Judg. 6:38). In early morning the moisture often hangs like a thick mist in the valleys, even far from the sea on the Trans-jordanian plateau, "a cloud of dew in the heat of harvest" (Isa. 18:4; cf. Hos. 14:5; Mic. 5:7). Instantly the hot sun arises, however, it vanishes, and the mist was therefore a symbol of instability. "They shall be like the morning mist," said Hosea, "or like the dew that goes early away, like the chaff that swirls from the threshing floor or like smoke from a window" (Hos. 13:3; cf. 6:4).

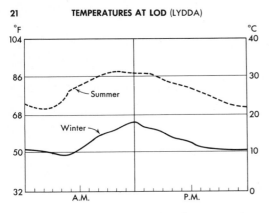

21   **TEMPERATURES AT LOD** (LYDDA)

The course of a normal summer day is fairly easy to foretell. On the Coast Plain during the early hours there is almost complete calm, so that smoke rises straight into the air and hangs lazily above its source. Sunrise produces an immediate rise in temperature, which remains within 5° F. of the day's maximum for as long as seven to nine hours. This early calm and the sudden rise of temperature make the early hours on the coast in many ways the most unpleasant of the day. The heating of the land, however, triggers the sea breeze, and regularly every day cool, damp air moves eastward across the coast to refresh the languid spirit and hold the temperature steady throughout the day.

The wind increases in strength and the maritime air piles up on the plain until shortly after noon it tops the mountains and pours like a torrent into the Rift. Its arrival east of the Jordan is somewhat longer delayed, but about three in the afternoon it overflows the plateau edge and swirls abruptly into the hot and dusty plateau villages, shaking every door on its hinges and the windows in their frames. It reaches these villages too late to restrain the sun, and the heat here on the high plateau is greater than on the very much lower Coast Plain. But it is both a refreshment and a profit, for by its steady draft the farmer may winnow his grain, tossing it up rhythmically in the long rays of the evening sun, so that the chaff is swept fluttering away and the grain drops back onto the ground in a glittering cascade. It is the wicked, said the Psalmist, who are "like the chaff which the wind drives away" (Ps. 1:4; cf. 35:5; Job 21:18; Hos. 13:3), and John the Baptist said of the one who was to come, "His winnowing fork is in his hand, and he will clear his threshing floor, and gather his wheat into the granary" (Matt. 3:12; Luke 3:17).

Soon after the sunset, calm again prevails on the coast, but about nine in the evening the land breeze starts. Because this is slowed down by its passage over rough ground and houses and because in any case it must strive against the general movement of the summer air from the west, it is much weaker and does not always establish itself, so that the night wind also sometimes comes from the sea.

The prolonged heat of a summer day is its most characteristic feature, but it must by no means be exaggerated; the summer climate, even on the Coast Plain, is a great deal more bearable than that of Washington D.C. or New York, or indeed of a large part of the United States at the same season. On the highlands the nights are cool, and even chilly, though the days may have been hot. The Rift is naturally hot, but at Tiberias and Beth-shan the arrival of the sea breeze brings relief, though farther south at Jericho it pours so tempestuously down the Judean hills, and is so warmed by its descent, that the effect is most uncomfortable.

22   RELATIVE HUMIDITY

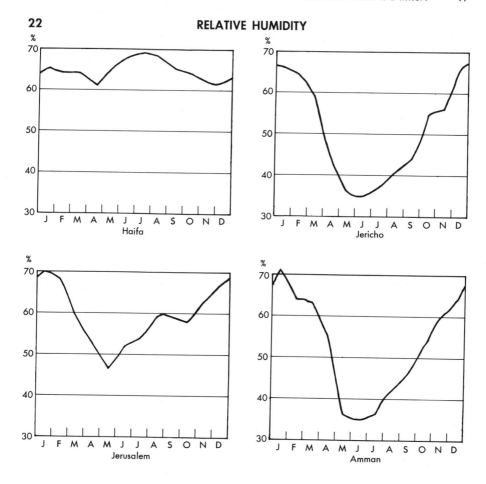

The Rainy Season

By contrast, this is completely un-predictable. No one ever knows when it will start and end, how much rain there will be, or how it will be dis-tributed throughout the season. At this period the air in the stratosphere is chilled, especially north of the moun-tain chain, because of the long polar night, but at the same time the waters of the Mediterranean, the Red Sea, and the Persian Gulf remain excep-tionally warm (56.3° F. in the eastern Mediterranean and 61.7° near the Palestinian coast). The jet stream is also shifted southward and sweeps powerfully from west to east, parallel to, but south of, the Alpine-Zagros-Himalayan mountain ranges. A strong high pressure system develops over the bitterly cold Russian-Siberian land mass and somewhat lesser ones over Arabia and the Sahara. Between the two lies a deep trough of low pressure along the Mediterranean and the Persian Gulf. All this makes for great instabil-ity in the atmosphere.

The vitally needed rain of winter re-sults from the passage of cyclonic storms along the Mediterranean trough, bringing damp maritime air from the Atlantic. Stimulated by their movement across the warm Mediterranean water, by the meeting of the warm continental air from Africa with the cooler continental air from Europe, and by the effect of the jet stream overhead, these cyclones are often rejuvenated en route, especially in the Po Valley, the Gulf of Sirte, and over Cyprus. They take four to six days to travel the full length of the sea and on their arrival in Palestine normally bring about three days of exceedingly heavy rain. On the first day and possibly the second also the rain is continuous and torrential and the whole world seems blotted out in a smashing tumult of water. Jesus quoted it as a well-known occurrence that a badly built house might collapse in the rainy season when the storms sweep in across the Palestinian hills and send their torrents

XI. *Storm over the Lake of Galilee.* The white paint of the boat stands out sharply against the dark thunder clouds which are building up to the north of Tiberias. Sudden and dangerous storms are characteristic of this lake and are mentioned in the Gospels. This photograph was taken in January, 1971.

flooding down the precipitous slopes into the Lake of Galilee and "the rain fell, and the floods came, and the winds blew and beat against that house" (Matt. 7:27). There is also a slightly comic picture in the Book of Ezra of the people sitting drenched "in the open square before the house of God, trembling because of this matter and because of the heavy rain" and protesting to Ezra that "we cannot stand in the open" (Ezra 10:9, 13). The later part of the cyclone is marked by slashing showers interrupted by fine periods. This extreme concentration of the rainfall is characteristic of most of the Middle East; Jerusalem receives all its rain in no more than about 50 days, but London, with about the same average total (22.4 inches, 560 mm.) has it spread over 168 days.

In a very good year the cyclones succeed each other with almost clockwork regularity once a week, but such a fortunate succession is exceedingly rare. Usually there are interruptions, sometimes lasting as long as a month, when dry air flows outward from the continental high pressure systems into the Mediterranean trough. Sometimes this is warm tropical air from the south or southeast, bringing days of sheer beauty, especially to the coast, where the winds are warmed still further by their descent over the mountains. Sometimes, however, it comes from the colder north, from two possible sources: from Europe into the rear of a Mediterranean cyclone, bringing cold air, occasional showers, and even snow to the Coast Plain; from the Asian high pressure to the northeast. This air is very dry and clear, and though warmed by its descent over the Zagros can cut across the Eastern Plateau with the sharpness of a whetted scythe. To explore the Trans-jordan desert in winter is to realize the truth of Gertrude Bell's remark, "The first rule when traveling in a hot country is to take one's thickest clothes." Nights are frosty and clear, and frost may persist also on the highlands during the day. This is the time when every cleft in the tableland of Moab is visible from Jerusalem 40 miles away, "and now men cannot look on the light when it is bright in the skies, when the wind has passed and cleared them" (Job 37:21).

The rainy season begins gradually during the second half of October, though sometimes the arrival of effective rain may be delayed until November or even till after Christmas. The air in these early days is still full of the summer dust, and with the building up of the first winter clouds in the west there are glorious sunsets, causing men to say, "It will be stormy today, for the sky is red and threatening" (Matt. 16:3). Sometimes these are merely deceptive, "clouds and wind without rain" and "waterless clouds, carried along by winds" (Prov. 25:14; Jude 12), and the farmers have to wait still longer before they can plow. Very often the first rains of the season come in sudden thunderstorms, for the damp air from the sea, moving in over the still-heated land, is thrust suddenly upward. " 'Prepare your chariot,' " said Elijah to Ahab on Mount Carmel, " 'and go down lest the rain stop you.' And in a little while the heavens grew black with clouds and wind, and there was a great rain" (1 Kings 18:44–45). Thunderstorms are normally very limited in extent, and there will be "rain upon one city and . . . no rain upon another city" (Amos 4:7), so that only in the fields upon which it has rained can the plowing begin.

The Palestinian longs for the rain with an intensity which cannot be put into words, and when "there is no rain on the land, the farmers are ashamed, they cover their heads" (Jer. 14:4). Even "the poor of the earth," who "lie all night naked, without clothing, and have no covering in the cold" (Job 24:4, 7), stand shivering in the pitiless downpour, repeating again and again, "Thank God for the rain! Thank God for the rain!" so thoroughly has it been drummed into their thinking that without the rain they die. Generally speaking, the more rain the better the harvest, but distribution is also important. In both 1937–38 and 1938–39 the totals were almost everywhere satisfactory on the Trans-jordan plateau (Kufrinje in Gilead had 30.6 and 32.2 inches, 765 and 805 mm.; Mazar in Moab 16.4 and 18.7, 401 and 470 mm.; Zerqa in the east of Ammon 8.2 and 6.2, 205 and 155 mm.; and H.3, far out into the desert, 5.7 and 6.2, 142 and 155 mm.), but in the first year the "former rains" were three months late in coming, and in the second they

XII. *Flooded Desert Wadi.* Water pouring down from the Negeb Uplands where there had been heavy rain and flooding across the road in the Arabah. Flash floods of this kind carry a great deal of sediment and can do a startling amount of erosion in a short time. The picture was taken in March, 1972.

began with torrents in the first week of October and continued evenly throughout the year. The first year's harvest was therefore only average, but the second a bumper crop. Flowers grew in rank profusion far into the desert, and the trains of the Hejaz Railway ran through them axle deep. Then indeed do "the pastures of the wilderness drip, the hills gird themselves with joy, the meadows clothe themselves with flocks, the valleys deck themselves with grain, they shout and sing together for joy" (Ps. 65:12–13).

The coldest weather normally come in January and February, and in this second half of the season the highlands receive most of their rain, though the Coast Plain has its maximum rain in the first half. This is because of the greater instability of the air in the earlier period, producing the coastal thunderstorms already mentioned; in the later period the land and sea temperatures are closer to each other and the air consequently more stable, so that the rain is delayed until triggered by the ascent of the air into the highlands.[4] Snow falls on the higher parts of the Western Highlands at least once almost every year and more frequently on the Eastern Plateau. The greatest snowfall recorded in Jerusalem was in February, 1920, when it lay at a depth of 3 feet (900 mm.), but the most widespread was the storm of February 5, 1950, when snow covered almost the entire country, even the oasis of Jericho. Jerusalem then had 27.5 inches (687 mm.), Acco on the coast 21.5 (537 mm.), and Tiberias in the Rift 6 inches (150 mm.). The Jabal Druze is snow-capped throughout the winter, and the snow-fed streams of the desert serve in Job as a symbol of deceitfulness:

My brethren are treacherous as a torrent-
bed,
    as freshets that pass away,
which are dark with ice,
    and where the snow hides itself.
In time of heat they disappear;
    when it is hot they vanish from their
    place.
The caravans turn aside from their course;
    they go up into the waste, and perish.
The caravans of Tema look,
    the travelers of Sheba hope.
They are disappointed because they were
    confident;
    they come thither and are confounded.
        [Job 6:15–20; cf. 24:19]

Snow is mentioned more than once in the Bible, but always as something unusual, as when Benaiah "went down and slew a lion in a pit on a day when snow had fallen" (2 Sam. 23:20; 1 Chron. 11:22), or when Trypho was prevented from coming to the help of his troops in Jerusalem because "that night a very heavy snow fell, and he did not go" (1 Macc. 13:22).

It is in midwinter also that hail is most common in the Coast Plain. "A storm of hail, a destroying tempest" (Isa. 28:2), can cause much damage, though rarely as much as the freak storm in the Valley of Aijalon when "the Lord threw down great stones from heaven upon them as far as Azekah, and they died; there were more who died because of the hailstones than the men of Israel killed with the sword" (Josh. 10:11). On May 23, 1957, hail "the size of small apples" fell again in the same region.[5]

In March the rainfall tends to taper off, and the final storm usually comes early in April, though there may be a slight sprinkle as late as early May. The "latter rains" are desperately needed to swell the grain and ensure a

4. Karmon, *op. cit.*, p. 27.

5. J. Katsnelson, "The Frequency of Hail in Israel," *IJES,* 16 (1967), 1–4.

23   MEAN AND EXTREME MAXIMUMS OF DAILY TEMPERATURE AT LOD (LYDDA)

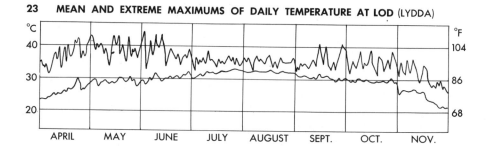

good harvest, and their failure is a sign of divine displeasure in Amos 4:7. In actual fact three-quarters of the rain tends to come in the three months of December–February, but so important is the beginning and the end that the former and latter rains are often spoken of as the most significant. "He will give you the rain for your land in its season, the early rain and the later rain, that you may gather in your grain and your wine and your oil" (Deut. 11:14; cf. Jer. 5:24; Hos. 6:3; Joel 2:23).

The Transitional Seasons

These last from early April to mid-June and from mid-September to the end of October. They overlap with the rainy season but are rather sharply divided from the true summer, and are characterized by two important phenomena: desert storms and the sirocco. In these seasons the high pressure over the plateau of Arabia is either not yet established or else beginning to break down. Thus, at the beginning and end of the rainy season the cyclones may penetrate farther inland, but because the land is hot at this time, convectional currents are strong and the rain is of the thunderstorm type, very limited in extent but also exceedingly heavy. The deserts and

XIII. *Snow in Jerusalem.* Snow on the Cisjordan highlands seems to have become more common during the last quarter of a century and may be expected in Jerusalem at least every five years. Snow falls on the higher and colder Eastern Plateau almost every year. This photograph was taken in the garden of Saint George's Hostel during the extraordinary cold spell of February, 1950, when snow fell even in Jericho, the only time that this has ever been recorded.

semideserts on their edges often receive most of their rain in these two
brief seasons, and a startling amount of
erosion in the desert wadis can be done
by the concentrated fury of these
storms.

The sirocco is "a hot wind from the
bare heights of the wilderness . . .
neither to fan nor to cleanse" (Jer.
4:11, KJV), useless, that is to say, for
winnowing, and bringing the parched
breath of the desert to scourge the
entire country. The word comes from
sharqiyyeh, meaning an east wind; in
Syria it is known as *shlouq* (a corruption of the same word), in Egypt as
khamsin, and in modern Israel as
sharav.[6] The sirocco proper seems confined to the transitional seasons, and
while it is blowing the temperature
rises steeply, 16 to 22° F. (9–12° C.)
above average, with only a slight cooling off at night. Relative humidity
drops by as much as 40 percent, and
every scrap of moisture seems to have
been extracted from the air. It is this
intense dryness and the fine dust in the
air which are so exhausting, for other
hot days, though troublesome, do not
have the same effect. People with a
heart condition, nervous complaints,
or sinus trouble are particularly affected, but even the mildest-tempered
person is apt to become irritable and
to snap at other people for no apparent
reason.[7] Tourists find the sirocco especially frustrating, for not only does
travel become fatiguing, but the fine
yellowish dust which fills the air drains
it of all color, blots out all but the immediate vicinity, and makes photogra-
phy a mockery. Even in the house one
is aware of it, for the dust penetrates
everywhere, and the soap dries on one's
face in the interval of putting down
the brush and picking up the razor.

The ferocity of a sirocco increases
as one goes toward the east, and to
leave the shelter of the house in Zerqa
or Mafraq is to step straight into an
oven. It is also oppressive in the Rift,
where it is further warmed by descent,
but on the coast the sea breeze may
give relief. Where the mountains come
close to the sea a strong sirocco pours
down the slopes like a flood, at 60
miles an hour or more, stirring the sea
into a fury. "By the east wind thou
didst destroy the ships of Tarshish"
(Ps. 48:7), and in Ezekiel's long con-
demnation of Tyre, "The east wind has
wrecked you in the heart of the seas"
(Ezek. 27:26). Since the sirocco is a
descending wind from the east, the
highlands have more days of sirocco
than the lowlands, but in all regions it

6. *Sharav* is used by Israeli meteorol-
ogists for any kind of exceptionally warm
air moving in from the east, and the *Atlas
of Israel* (map IV/3W) shows Jerusalem
as having annually no less than 100 days
of *sharav,* which is as many as all the days
of the two transitional seasons put together. Orni and Efrat (*op. cit.,* p. 141)
distinguish three situations likely to give
rise to *sharav* conditions: (a) *khamsin,*
in which air moving counterclockwise
around a low pressure over Libya approaches Palestine as a warm easterly
wind; (b) a low pressure reaching the
country from the Red Sea direction and
bringing with it unusually warm air, and
(c) *sharav,* "a barometric high develop-
ing over the country itself where the subsiding air is compressed and heated."
Though all this is true, it seems best to
separate sharply the conditions of the
transitional season because of their peculiar
physiological and psychological effects.
The term *khamsin* is in any case misleading because it is the normal Egyptian
word for the true sirocco, though coming
there from the Sahara.

7. W. B. Fisher suggests that the death
of the first-born in Egypt (Exod. 12:29–
30) may have been due to a *khamsin* and
says that the British term "round the bend"
was originally invented in World War II to
describe the effect of a sirocco (*op. cit.,*
pp. 57, 65).

brings the maximum temperatures of the year.

The end of a sirocco is marked by a sudden change of the wind to the west, a rise in humidity, a drop in temperature, and a wonderful sense of relief. The change in the wind is immediately obvious because the trees toss their branches, all the doors bang at once, and "there is the sound of the abundance of rain" (1 Kings 18:41).[8] Especially in autumn the new west wind brings heavy rain with it, for the sirocco results from the pulling down of desert air into an approaching low pressure. Palestinian farmers indeed say that "the east wind brings rain."

Biblical references to the sirocco are frequent. To Elihu it is inexplicable, "Do you know . . . the wondrous works of him who is perfect in knowledge, you whose garments are hot when the earth is still because of the south wind?" (Job 37:16–17), and to Hosea a symbol of uselessness, "Ephraim herds the wind, and pursues the east wind all the day long; they multiply falsehood and violence; they make a bargain with Assyria, and oil is carried to Egypt" (Hos. 12:1). It is everywhere an affliction, "his fierce blast in the day of the east wind" (Isa. 27:8). "When you see the south wind blowing, you say, 'There will be scorching heat'; and it happens" (Luke 12:55),

and when "God appointed a sultry east wind, and the sun beat upon the head of Jonah . . . he was faint; and he asked that he might die" (Jon. 4:8).

The spring siroccos destroy the winter grass and may damage the crops if they come too soon, and hence they appear constantly in the Bible as a symbol of the impermanence of riches or of human life, "for the wind passes over it, and it is gone, and its place knows it no more" (Ps. 103:16). "All flesh is grass and all its beauty like the flower of the field. The grass withers, the flower fades, when the breath of the Lord blows upon it . . . but the word of our God will stand for ever" (Isa. 40:6–8). Hosea said of the Northern Kingdom, "Though he may flourish as the reed plant, the east wind, the wind of the Lord, shall come, rising from the wilderness; and his fountain shall dry up, his spring shall be parched; it shall strip his treasury of every precious thing" (Hos. 13:15). Likewise Ezekiel asked of the rich vine of Judah, "Will it not utterly wither when the east wind strikes it—wither on the bed where it grew?" (Ezek. 17:10), and so also in the New Testament: "The sun rises with its scorching heat and withers the grass; its flower falls and its beauty perishes. So will the rich man fade away in the midst of his pursuits" (James 1:11).

---

8. The KJV is better here. The RSV translates המון הגשם as "rushing of rain," but this suggests the rain has already begun, whereas what is meant is this very characteristic preliminary noise.

CHAPTER 5

The Rain of the Mountains

They are wet with the rain of the mountains,
and cling to the rock for want of shelter.
JOB 24:8

The quick alternation of plain and mountain, plateau and rift, and the never-ending conflict between the desert and the sea bring great variety to the Palestinian climate and weather, and within a few miles one may pass from sharp cold to almost tropical heat, from drenching rain to the dusty wilderness. Even a modest variation in relief or aspect may give either the desert or the sea the advantage and bring places only a few miles apart under differing regimes. Jerusalem itself stands on such a divide. It has 22 inches (550 mm.) of rain a year, but 5 miles to the east begins the uncultivable Jeshimon, and while it is snowing in Jerusalem one may see offered for sale strawberries grown in the open air only 20 miles away at Jericho.

Six major rules determine the differences between the climatic regions:

1. Rainfall tends to *decrease* from north to south.

2. Rainfall tends to *decrease* from west to east, i.e., with distance from the sea.

3. Rainfall *increases,* however, on the seaward slopes of any hill or mountain.

4. Rainfall *decreases* again very sharply on the lee slopes toward the east.

5. Temperature tends to *decrease* with an increase in height.

6. The temperature *range,* however, tends to *increase* with distance from the sea and with any decrease in rainfall. Thus days on the inland plateau are often hotter than those on the Coast Plain 3,000 feet (900 m.) below.

The Coast Plain, including the central section of the Plain of Esdraelon. Here the influence of the sea is naturally greatest and the brutal sirocco strikes less often. Summers are hot, though the sea breezes exert a strong moderating influence, and throughout the year the relative humidity is high, averaging 65 to 70 percent, though decreasing inland by as much as 10 percent and even more in the Plain of Esdraelon. The daily range of temperature is small, only 13.2° F. (7.5° C.), and so there is little relief from the heat at night.

During the rainy season the same influence is felt. The daily range remains small, though not quite as small (16.2° F., 9° C., at Haifa) because of the more varied weather in this season. It is seldom very cold; snow is extremely rare, and frost has been recorded only four times in forty years at Tel Aviv. It is possible indeed to live not unhappily without heating in the house, though it is pleasant to have it in wet weather.

The rain usually starts earlier on the coast than it does inland and it lasts longer, though the total amounts decrease from north to south (Haifa, 25.3; Tel Aviv, 20; Gaza, 16; Rafah, 10—653, 500, 400, and 250 mm.). The totals also decrease as one moves away from the sea so that Ramleh, only 10 miles from Tel Aviv, has 17.6 inches (440 mm.), and Affuleh in the Plain of Esdraelon has 8 inches less (200 mm.) than Haifa 20 miles to the west.

As we have already seen, the maximum rainfall on the Coast Plain tends to come in the first half of the rainy season. Thus by the end of December Haifa has usually received 12 inches (300 mm.) and Jaffa 10 (250 mm.) but Jerusalem has had only 8 (200 mm.), though by the end of the year Jerusalem normally gets almost as much rain as Haifa and more than Jaffa.

The Hills of Cis-jordan. Here the range of temperature, both yearly and daily, is greater than on the coast. The climate is therefore more stimulating,

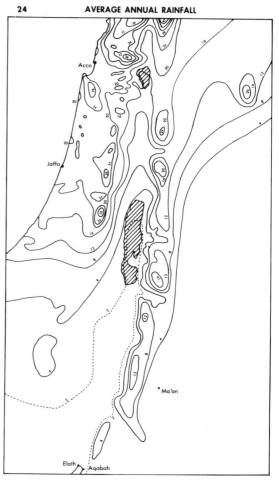

24   **AVERAGE ANNUAL RAINFALL**

for the hot summer days are relieved by cool, refreshing nights, and the rainy season is cold enough to merit the term "bracing." Because of the reduced humidity in the atmosphere this is true even at a moderate elevation, and at Nazareth, 1,300 feet in height and 19 miles from the sea, the summer heat is noticeably moderated when night falls. It will be seen from Figure 28 that the important difference be-

25   TEMPERATURE AND RAINFALL: COASTAL PLAIN

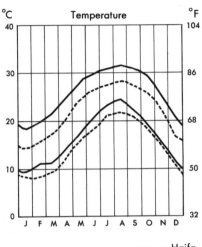

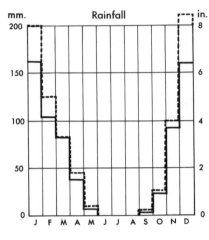

——— Haifa   - - - - Mt. Carmel

26   DEVELOPMENT OF THE RAINY SEASON

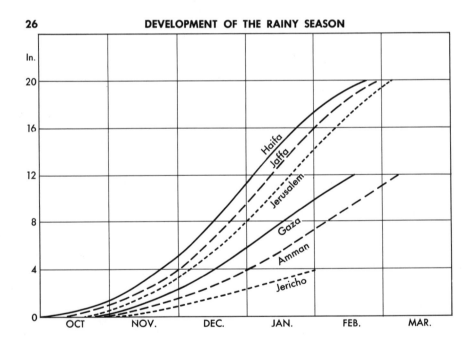

27   PROBABILITY OF RAINFALL IN THE PALESTINE AREA

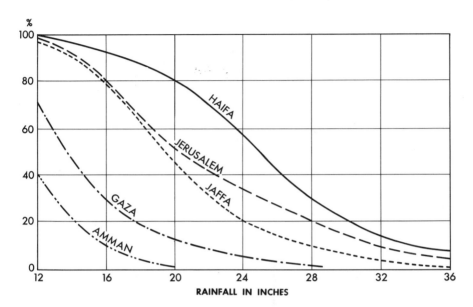

RAINFALL IN INCHES

tween the highlands and the coast is not in the matter of heat but in the intensity of the cold, both at night and in the rainy season. The daily range in January, it should be noticed, is actually less in Jerusalem than it is in Haifa.

The rain comes rather later in the highlands, but there is a greater possibility of years with heavy rainfall (see Fig. 27). As everywhere, rainfall totals decrease from north to south, though this may be modified by differences in altitude. Mount Kina'an in Upper Galilee (3,123 feet, 952 m.) has an average annual total of 29.5 inches (738 mm.); Nazareth in Lower Galilee (1,230 feet, 375 m.) has 25.6 inches (640 mm.); Sebastiyeh in the Central Highlands (1,510 feet, 461 m.), 22.2 inches (555 mm.); Jerusalem in Judah (2,600 feet, 793 m.), 22.4 inches (560 mm.); Hebron (3,183 feet, 970 m.), 19.44 inches (486 mm.); and Dhahariyeh, on the southern edge

28   TEMPERATURES AT HAIFA AND JERUSALEM

	HAIFA		JERUSALEM	
	°F.	°C.	°F.	°C.
Mean annual range	25.2	14.0	27.9	15.5
Mean daily range (January)	16.2	9.0	13.5	7.6
Mean daily range (August)	13.2	7.5	20.8	11.5
Mean daily range (year)	15.3	8.5	17.1	9.5
Average temperature in January	57.2	14.0	47.2	8.5
Average temperature in August	82.4	28.0	75.2	24.0
Average maximum in August	90.0	32.25	85.4	29.5
Average maximum in August	76.0	24.5	64.5	18.0

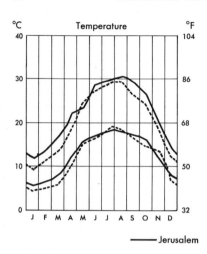

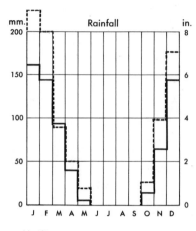

——— Jerusalem   ----- Mt. Kina'an

of the highlands (2,148 feet, 655 m.), 13.92 inches (348 mm.).

Included within this region is the promontory of Mount Carmel, despite its nearness to the sea. Its small temperature range indicates its proximity to the coast, but it belongs to the mountains by reason of the more moderate temperatures (regularly 5–7° F., 2–4° C. lower than those of Haifa) and its heavy rainfall of 28 inches. These figures may not sound impressive, but they mean the difference between the more enervating climate of the plain and the more stimulating climate of the hill country.

The Cis-jordan hills were the homeland of the ancient Israelites, and Chester McCown has said of their climate, "So far as health is concerned, the mountain-dwelling Hebrews were much more fortunately placed than either the Egyptians or the Babylonians; they were but little behind the Greeks and Romans."[1] This may well

1. Chester C. McCown, "Climate and Religion in Palestine," *Journal of Religion*, 7 (1927), p. 529.

be true, but we must not imagine that they necessarily thought so. The tempo of life was slower in those days, and the dry summer required little effort from the farmer beyond camping out in his vineyard to protect the vines. Therefore, though he was always glad that the heat should be subdued by "shade from a cloud" (Isa. 25:5), he did not find it too exhausting. Though he welcomed the rainy season with joy, he did not enjoy the cold. "Pray that your flight may not be in the winter," said Jesus, (Matt. 24:20), for January and February on the hills can be severe. Often it is cold enough to make a fire a real necessity, perhaps as late as early April (John 18:18), and even the wealthy were not really comfortable in these months, for they had little to warm them beyond an ineffective charcoal brazier (Jer. 36:22). Therefore ancient peoples often preferred the hotter places, and though Josephus found the summer air of Jericho unwholesome, he liked it so much in winter that he said it would be no exaggeration to call the place

TEMPERATURE AND RAINFALL: JORDAN VALLEY

30

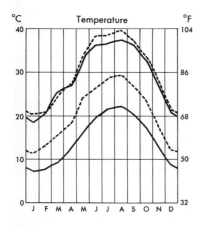

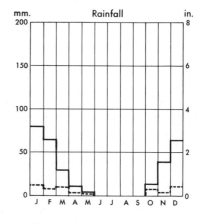

———Beth-shan   - - - - Sdom

"divine," a judgment with which hardly anyone would agree today.[2]

The Jordan Valley. This lies in a rain shadow where the moist air from the west is dried by its descent into the Rift, and rainfall totals are markedly lower than those on the highlands to the west. However, the normal decrease of rainfall from north to south still applies: Dan, at the foot of Mount Hermon, has 24 inches (600 mm.); Tiberias on the Lake of Galilee, 16 (400 mm.); Beth-shan, 12 (300 mm.); Jericho, 5; (125 mm.); Sdom at the southern end of the Dead Sea only 2 inches (50 mm.).

It would be wrong to think of the Jordan Valley as having a uniform climate, for there are very evident differences between the north and the south. South of the Jordan "waist" and especially around the Dead Sea desert conditions prevail, though decreasing northward. The Dead Sea itself creates local land and sea breezes northward and southward, drawing air inward at night and reversing this dur-

ing the day. The relative humidity is extremely low, but is somewhat modified by the intense evaporation. Temperatures are naturally high, the highest ever recorded at Sdom being 124° F. (51° C.).

North of the "waist," though summers are oppressively hot and uncomfortably prolonged (Beth-shan has six months with average maximum temperatures above 86° F., 30° C., as compared with three months at Haifa), the rainy season is cool and at Beth-shan cold enough to prevent today the growth of bananas. Around the Lake of Galilee temperatures tend to be higher in winter, both because of the effect of the lake itself and because the air descending the steep hillsides is warmed by compression. Here banana cultivation is again possible.[3]

The Huleh Basin has a large annual temperature range with a mean temperature in August of 81° F. (27.25° C.) and a January temperature of 52° (11.12° C.). This is because in summer the basin, enclosed is it is between

2. Josephus, *The Jewish War*, IV, 470.

3. Orni and Efrat, *op. cit.*, p. 156.

XIV. *Morning Mist at as-Salt in Gilead.* The westward facing valleys of the Trans-jordan scarp are often filled with thick mist in the early morning hours in summer, but this disappears rapidly as soon as the sun rises. This early mist is spoken of in Hosea 6:4 as a symbol of insincerity.

high walls, is prevented by the plateau of Upper Galilee from receiving the full effect of the sea breeze, but in winter cold air pours into it from the snows of Hermon.

The Plateau Edge of Trans-jordan. There are great similarities with the climate of the Cis-jordan hills, but since the edge of the Trans-jordan plateau is almost everywhere higher than the corresponding hill region to the west, rainfall totals tend to be greater, e.g., Jerusalem (2,600 feet, 793 m.), 22.4 inches (560 mm.); as-Salt (3,000 feet, 900 m.), 28 inches (700 mm.). Winter is colder because of this greater height, the distance from the sea, and exposure to the icy desert winds, snow being much more common here, and the roads more often blocked by it. Summer days tend to be hotter, for the sea breeze arrives too late to

moderate the temperature, though it is refreshing and stirs the villages to activity after the midday rest. At as-Salt, for instance, in the early part of the afternoon the air is still and the heat oppressive, but then at three in the afternoon, with almost clockwork regularity the fresh air from the distant sea overflows the plateau rim and pours down into the town, which suddenly is alive again. Children resume their endless games of tag on the flat housetops, and their fathers climb to the threshing floors to winnow the grain.

The summer nights are chilly, and the gray cool dawn is the time for movement from one village to another. Then it is that the mountain paths, so deserted at other hours, come to life, and men and women bring down to the market vegetables and baskets of grapes.

This region extends a long tongue

southward into Edom, where the great height somewhat counteracts the effect of the decreasing rainfall. That it does so decrease is shown by the following figures: as-Salt, 28 inches (700 mm.); Na'ur 21 (525 mm.); Mazar in Moab, 15 (375 mm.); Shaubak in Edom, 12 (300 mm.); and in the south the rain is sufficient to permit no more than a single line of villages along the rim.

The Steppeland. This is a marginal region, very often more pastoral than agricultural, with about 8 to 16 inches (200–400 mm.), of rain a year, lying north of the Negeb desert in Cis-jordan and east of the Trans-jordan plateau edge. Interrupted in the Rift where the rain shadow is so marked that the desert extends a long arm northward almost to the Jordan "waist," it is characterized by unexpectedly hot summers with prolonged drought, and during this time it displays features more typical of the desert than the cultivated zone.

The graphs for Gaza, Beersheba, and Amman well illustrate this. Gaza on the coast has, as might be expected, a very even and moderate temperature range, and Beersheba a greater one, but here it is caused not by increased cold but by the summer heat, and Beersheba has no less than six months with average daily maxima above 85° F. (30° C.). Amman on the plateau is, of course, much colder in the rainy season than either Gaza or Beersheba, but has much hotter summer days than Gaza despite its greater height. Amman, indeed, unlike the Cis-jordan hills, has its maximum temperatures in August rather than during the siroccos, hot though these may be.

Though the general pattern of the rainfall is similar to that of the other regions already considered, totals are lower than in any region except the drier parts of the Rift, and in any one year the rainfall distributed may depart

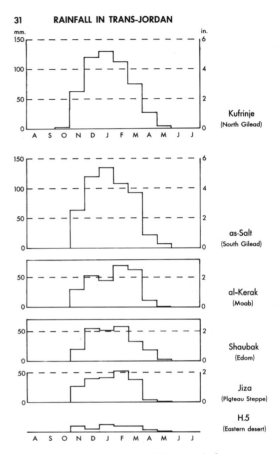

31   **RAINFALL IN TRANS-JORDAN**

Kufrinje
(North Gilead)

as-Salt
(South Gilead)

al-Kerak
(Moab)

Shaubak
(Edom)

Jiza
(Plateau Steppe)

H.5
(Eastern desert)

widely from the average. The graph for Amman shows that the eastern steppe receives its rain later and over a shorter period than the regions lying west of it.

The Desert Regions. These lie around the steppe to the south and east, including also the Arabah and, properly speaking, the Dead Sea region already considered. The change from one to the other comes very rapidly, even on the relatively level plateau. Thus, Jabal Amman (the part of the plateau in the center of the city) has an annual total of 15 inches (375 mm.); Amman airport, 3 miles northeast, 11 inches (275 mm.); and Zerqa, 7 miles farther, only 4.9 inches (123 mm.). The desert is not a place where rain never falls, nor

32   TEMPERATURE AND RAINFALL: SOUTHERN STEPPE

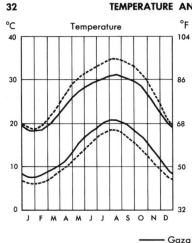

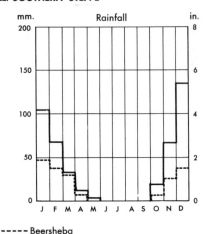

——— Gaza   ----- Beersheba

33   TEMPERATURE AND RAINFALL: TRANS-JORDAN

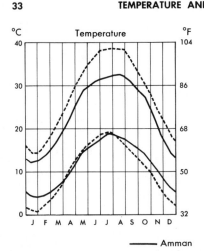

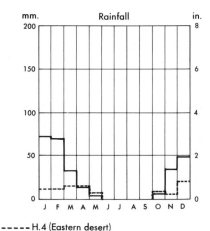

——— Amman   ----- H.4 (Eastern desert)

where rainfall is never sufficient for agriculture, but a place where the rain cannot be trusted. Rainfall totals vary from the norm in Haifa in 17 percent of the years; in Jerusalem, 21 percent; Beersheba, 26 percent; Bir Asluj in the Negeb, 43 percent; Auja al-Hafir on the Egyptian border (1967), 65 percent; and ath-Thamad in Sinai, 93 percent. More-over, in the desert the distribution is extremely erratic from year to year, and there is a strong tendency, noticeable in the Negeb, the Arabah, and the deserts of Trans-jordan, for much of it to come in heavy storms during the transitional seasons. Desert rainfall is limited in both extent and amount. In 1938–39 Ma'an had half its total rain-

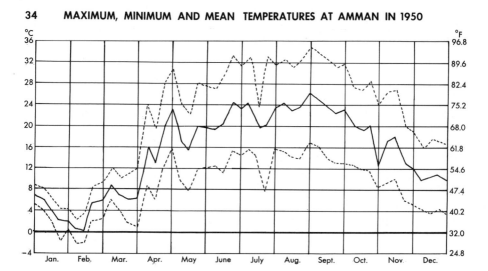

34   MAXIMUM, MINIMUM AND MEAN TEMPERATURES AT AMMAN IN 1950

fall for the year in a severe hailstorm one afternoon early in April, and in March, 1940, Wadi Ram had 1.6 inches (40 mm.) in one day, though only a few miles away there was no rain at all.

This may well be the explanation of the story told in 2 Kings 3:4–27 when Elisha promised the kings of Israel and Judah, encamped in the dry upper section of the Zered, "You shall not see wind or rain, but that stream-bed shall be filled with water, so that you shall drink, you, your cattle, and your beasts. . . . The next morning, about the time of offering the sacrifice, behold, the water came from the direction of Edom, till the country was filled with water" (vv. 17, 20). This unexpected supply came from a desert thunderstorm on the plateau to the east which filled the wadis and during the night poured down the Zered toward the Arabah.[4]

An interesting feature of desert rain-

4. I have myself seen a similar climatic phenomenon in the same region.

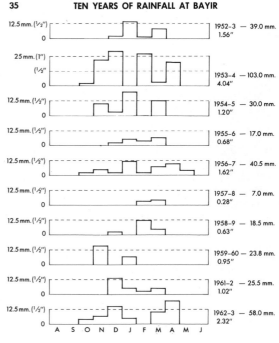

35   TEN YEARS OF RAINFALL AT BAYIR

12.5 mm. (½")	1952–3 — 39.0 mm.
0	1.56"
25 mm. (1")	
(½")	1953–4 — 103.0 mm.
0	4.04"
12.5 mm. (½")	1954–5 — 30.0 mm.
0	1.20"
12.5 mm. (½")	1955–6 — 17.0 mm.
0	0.68"
12.5 mm. (½")	1956–7 — 40.5 mm.
0	1.62"
12.5 mm. (½")	1957–8 — 7.0 mm.
0	0.28"
12.5 mm. (½")	1958–9 — 18.5 mm.
0	0.63"
12.5 mm. (½")	1959–60 — 23.8 mm.
0	0.95"
12.5 mm. (½")	1961–2 — 25.5 mm.
0	1.02"
12.5 mm. (½")	1962–3 — 58.0 mm.
0	2.32"
	A S O N D J F M A M J
12.5 mm. (½")	Average — 36.2 mm.
0	1.44"

fall is that it does not necessarily bear much relation to that of the better-watered lands, and extremely wet periods in Jerusalem may be dry in the Negeb and vice versa.[5] This, however, appears to be more in evidence between Judah and the Negeb than between the west and east of the Trans-jordan Plateau.

Desert temperatures are usually extreme with a large temperature range, both daily and annually. The desert is certainly not, as is popularly imagined, a place which is always hot. These rapid temperature changes result in powerful winds which occasionally create sand or dust storms. A true sandstorm approaches the observer like a gigantic wall; suddenly there is a howling wind and the air is filled with whirling sand which penetrates into the most tightly closed rooms. It is horrible while it

5. L. Shanan, M. Evenari, and N. H. Tadmor, "Rainfall Patterns in the Central Negev Desert," *IEJ*, 1967, pp. 174–75.

XV. *Desert Plants in the Wadi Hasma after Rain.* The winter of 1966-67 was a remarkably wet one and a considerable amount of rain fell even in the south of Trans-jordan. In this picture the dark leaves near the surface represent new growth springing up out of the sand after a thunderstorm.

lasts, but it ends as if cut off by a knife, and the air is immediately clear again. These sandstorms and the furious tempests of winter can rip the Bedouin encampments from their moorings and set "the tents of Cushan in affliction" (Hab. 3:7; see also Job 1:16, 19). A less ferocious result of the desert wind is "the whirling dust before the storm" (Isa. 17:13; see Ps. 83:13), those spinning "dust devils" which can be seen chasing each other across the plateau any day during the summer.

References to whirlwinds are common in the Old Testament, but it is not always clear what kind of wind is meant. When Elihu said that "from its chamber comes the whirlwind, and cold from the scattering winds," he surely meant the bitter southwest wind of a winter cyclone sweeping unrestrained across the plateau (Job 37:9; see also Prov. 1:27; 10:25; Jer. 23:19; 25:32; 30:23), but Isaiah 21:1, "As whirlwinds in the Negeb sweep on, it comes from the desert, from a terrible land," suggests the grim fury of a sandstorm. Isaiah 40:24 clearly defers to the parching effects of the sirocco, and Isaiah 41:16 to the strong afternoon breeze by which the farmers winnow their grain. The whirlwinds which carried Elijah up to heaven (2 Kings 2:1, 11), which Ezekiel saw (Ezek. 1:4), and out of which God spoke to Job (Job 38:1; 40:6) are surely meant to describe the devastating onslaught of a thunderstorm.[6]

Has the Climate Changed?

The answer to this very vexed question is both yes and no. That climate is

6. "Whirlwind" in the KJV, though not always in the RSV. The Hebrew word is either סופה or some form of the root סער.

not static but rather in a state of constant fluctuation is now beyond question, and it would be a great mistake to take any set of climatic figures as "normal." On the other hand there is equally little doubt that in the Palestinian area the general pattern of the climate has not seriously changed since 6000 or 7000 B.C.; the summers have been dry and the winters wet, and the same types of crops have been grown continuously in the region. The question, therefore, concerns the nature and magnitude of the variations of climate within this general pattern. Here, however, we run into difficulties. First, there is a tantalizing lack of evidence for the Levant region; records usually go back for only a relatively short (sometimes very short) period, documentary information for earlier periods is very rare, and studies of tree rings, lake levels, pollen deposits, etc., which have been so helpful elsewhere, have not yet provided in the Levant the kind of evidence we should like to have, though, of course, they have only just begun.[7] Second, there is still no general agreement about the causes of climatic change and as yet insufficient knowledge concerning all the factors involved. One thing, however, has become perfectly clear: climates throughout the world are not isolated from one another, but are integrally related. Therefore, any significant fluctuations in the distribution of high and low pressure systems are bound to have far more than merely local importance. That such fluctuations have taken place in the course

of the centuries is no longer a matter of doubt.

The most complete collection of evidence belongs to western Europe around about the latitude of 50°N, for here what may be called the "scientific" evidence of tree rings, glacial deposits, etc., is supplemented by a considerable body of documentary evidence about good and bad harvests, storms, exceptional cold and heat, and so on, for about 900 years and actual climatic records, going back to the eighteenth, and even seventeenth, centuries. On the basic of all this evidence it is now possible to recognize with some degree of certainty the following major climatic fluctuations:[8]

1. Disappearance of the glaciers from Britain somewhere about 8000–7000 B.C., though glaciers retreated only slowly in central Europe and the Brenner Pass in the Alps may not have become open until about 1800 B.C.

2. The "climatic optimum" - from about 4000 to 2000 B.C. with a milder and drier climate in western Europe than now. Around 5000 there had been a rather wetter period.

3. A relatively sudden change about 500 B.C., which has been described by more than one writer as "catastrophic."[9] This initiated a prolonged rainy, cool period during which the glaciers once more closed the Alpine passes for a

---

7. Quite a lot of work has been done in this area in Israel. A. Fahn, Naomi Wachs, and C. Ginzburg suggest, for instance, that the rainfall of the Negeb repeats a 100-year cycle, with the next minimum due between 1980 and 1990 "Dendrochronological Studies in the Negev," *IEJ,* 13 (1963), 291–99.

8. The most useful books or this subject for the general reader are C. E. P. Brooks, *Climate Through the Ages* (London: Benn, 1949), and H. H. Lamb, *The Changing Climate* (London: Methuen & Co., 1968).

9. "This change of climate was by far the greatest and most abrupt since the end of the Ice Age and its effect on the civilization of Europe was catastrophic," C. E. P. Brooks, "Geological and Historical Aspects of Climatic Change," in Thomas Malone, ed., *Compendium of Meteorology* (Boston: American Meteorological Society, 1951), p. 1008.

matter of some centuries. The maximum rainfall seems to have been about 400 B.C. and did not really begin to moderate until the beginning of the Christian era.

4. Secondary climatic optimum from A.D. 400 to 1200, reaching its peak about 800–1000. The west European "gulf of warmth" extended much farther north at this time, and the Arctic ice retreated.

5. 1200–1400 saw a renewed deterioration in the climate and exceptionally unstable weather, with a slight improvement after 1400.

6. The "Little Ice Age" of 1550 to 1800, with its peak during the first 150 years. This had disastrous effects in the Scandinavian countries and elsewhere in western Europe was marked by much colder, drier winters.

7. The recent milder period, which seems to have reached its peak in the first half of this century, with its wet, mild winters and warmer, drier summers. Since 1950 the evidence seems to be for a return of severer weather with colder winters and wetter, cool summers and for a cessation of the retreat of the glaciers. Snowfalls in Palestine have also become more frequent in these last twenty-five years. It is too early to say whether this is a purely temporary interruption, but, it should be noticed, many rainfall and temperature averages are based on figures for the first half of the century and may therefore be misleading.

There were, of course, fluctuations within these major periods, but the overall pattern seems established. It remains, therefore, to ask what relation these major fluctuations have to the climate of the Levant. It is exactly this question which is so difficult to answer. It has been claimed that there has been since 1750 "a close parallelism between rainfall fluctuations in Palestine and the middle latitudes of the Northern Hemisphere,"[10] but as we go further back the pattern is less clear. There is clear evidence that during the "Little Ice Age" the important Russian high pressure system in winter extended much farther westward than it does now,[11] but this could have had two quite contrary effects: the winter cyclones may have been deflected southward along the Mediterranean and thereby increased the rainfall in Palestine, or the European high may have joined up more frequently with the Saharan high pressure and blocked this passage. Another possibility is a combination of these two effects, resulting in an extension of the rainy season and possibly a somewhat more assured rainfall, but at the same time not producing any significant increase in the rainfall totals. There is, indeed, some evidence that this did happen in the period following the European "catastrophe" of 500 B.C. The weather diary kept by Claudius Ptolemaeus in the first century A.D. at Alexandria[12] indicates that

10. R. G. Veryard "A Review of Studies on Climatic Fluctuations during the Period of the Meteorological Record," in *Changes of Climate: Proceedings of the Rome Symposium Organized by Unesco and the World Meteorological Organization* (Paris: Unesco, 1953), p. 10.

11. See the maps in Lamb, *op. cit.*, p. 135.

12. Some authorities have suggested that the differences from the present Alexandrian weather indicate that the diary belongs to some city farther north, but this seems based on an assumption that climate cannot change. It is accepted as Alexandrian by both Brooks, *Climate Through the Ages*, p. 333, and Lamb, *op. cit.*, p. 7. C. Vita-Finzi has also argued from the geological evidence for a better distribution of rainfall in Palestine during the Roman period: "Observations on the Late Quaternary of Jordan," *PEQ, XCVI* (1964), 31.

the summer drought was shorter than at present with more thunder and weather changes in summer and more north winds in winter. On the other hand there are signs that the peak of the secondary climatic optimum (c. A.D. 800–1000) meant that with the northward extension of the Atlantic "Gulf of Warmth" the isobars across Europe ran north and southward, causing cold Siberian air to flow into the Mediterranean and producing the severe frosts of which we have record, with ice forming even on the Nile at Cairo on two occasions.

Another factor which may have been of great importance is the temperature of the oceans, though the effect of this might involve a long time lag. When the large masses of water were cold there would be little evaporation and therefore much less moisture in the air. When the oceans were warm there would be more moisture, with the probability of greater rainfall. It has been suggested that this may help to explain the rather sharp decline in Middle Eastern rainfall at the end of the Ice Age, when the melting ice kept the oceans cold.

A further possibility to take into account is that the eastern Mediterranean may have been a protected area, both by reason of the Alpine mountain chain and because the Mediterranean is a closed sea. Climatic fluctuations, therefore, may perhaps have been of much less magnitude than in northwestern Europe, where the penetration or retreat of the Gulf Stream plays such an enormous part in determining the weather.

All this means that any attempt to reconstruct theoretically the relationship between climatic fluctuations of western Europe and those of Palestine is fraught with danger. We must beware of assuming that because there was more rain in Europe there was necessarily more rain in Palestine, even though there is some evidence that in general this is true. We must also beware of taking for granted that changes in the settlement pattern of the steppelands indicate changes in climate. It is certainly possible that there is some connection, because the evidence for the effect of climatic fluctuation on populations movements elsewhere in the world is very strong, but most scholars would now argue that the alternation of settlement and nomadic pastoralism in the Palestinian area has rather a sociopolitical basis. This, of course, does not exclude the possibility of fluctuation in climate being a contributory cause, and in a recent important article Alan Crown has suggested the following tentative reconstruction.[13]

About 8000 B.C. temperatures began to recover from the cold of the last glacial period, but after 7000 B.C., though temperatures continued to climb, rainfall started to decrease. About 5700 B.C. there seems to have been a reversal: temperatures decreased somewhat and rainfall increased until about 5000 B.C. But then there was a sharp change, and from 4500 to 3500 B.C. hot, dry conditions prevailed and the desert spread outward. About 3500 cooler, damper conditions returned until about 2300 B.C., when once more there is evidence of renewed drought lasting until about 2000 B.C., with perhaps somewhat more assured rainfall than now just after 2000. He suggests that the increased rainfall after 3500 B.C. was responsible for the remarkable spread of Chalcolithic settlement into the Negeb and even into

13. Alan D. Crown, "Toward a Reconstruction of the Climate of Palestine, 8000 B.C.–0 B.C.," *JNES*, 31 (1972), 312–30.

Sinai. The next period of settlement in the Negeb in the Middle Bronze Age shortly after 2000 B.C., which most people, though not everyone (see below, p. 93 n. 1), would associate with the time of the Patriarchs, he sees as probably only partly related to the climate. The two later periods of settlement, during the Israelite monarchy and during the Nabatean-Roman period, he believes to be essentially the result of social, economic, and political conditions.

Unfortunately, after 2000 B.C. the evidences for climatic fluctuation are increasingly obscured by human activity in the country, but we must certainly beware, and beware emphatically, of assuming that the climate figures given in this book can be used unchanged for the patriarchal period, the time of the monarchy, the New Testament, or any subsequent era. That would mean that the Palestinian climate had remained static for 4,000 years, and this we can say with confidence to be impossible.

CHAPTER **6**

Not Like the Land of Egypt

*The land which you are entering to take pos-
session of it is not like the land of Egypt, from
which you have come, where you sowed your
seed, and watered it with your foot, like a
garden of vegetables; but the land which you
are going over to possess is a land of hills and
valleys, which drinks water by the rain from
heaven, a land which the Lord, your God, cares
for; for the eyes of the Lord, your God, are
always upon it, from the beginning of the year
to the end of the year.*

DEUTERONOMY 11:10–12

Despite the proximity of Egypt to Palestine, Israelite thought in general seems
to have been much less influenced by
Egyptian thinking than it was by that
of Mesopotamia. This is sometimes explained as a conscious rejection of the
Egyptian way of life, since Egypt was
the land from which the Israelites had
been delivered, and to which it would
be sinful to seek to return. The king, it
was said, "must not multiply horses for
himself, or cause the people to return
to Egypt in order to multiply horses,
since the Lord has said to you, 'You
shall never return that way again'"
(Deut. 17:16).

Certainly this conscious rejection may
have influenced the Yahwists,[1] but it
is unlikely to be the fundamental reason why Egyptian ideas made so little
headway among the general populace
—who, as the biblical record makes
clear, were not so dedicated—and why,
therefore, biblical writers make far
more use of Mesopotamian concepts
than they do of Egyptian. There is, it
is true, the similarity of Psalm 104 to
Ikhnaton's *Hymn to the Aton* and the
impact of Egyptian thought on the

1. I.e., worshipers of Yahweh, the
Israelite God (translated "the Lord" in
English versions).

teaching of the Wise, notably the close resemblence of Proverbs 22:17–24:22 to the Egyptian *Instruction of Amen-em-ope,* but nothing comparable to the influence of Mesopotamian mythology, or Mesopotamian systems of law, upon the Israelite way of life. These have their impact upon Israelite thought in general and are taken for granted, as it were, by the biblical writers, though they refine and transform them. The reason for this difference of attitude must be more basic than that of conscious rejection by the reformers; it lies rather in the very evident difference between the Egyptian and Palestinian cultural environment, a difference which is largely climatic. No society ever incorporates into its own way of thinking concepts for which it cannot already find parallels and affinities in its own culture. Completely foreign concepts, related to phenomena of which the people have no experience, are not for them meaningful. These they reject, while those which they do incorporate they rework and transform in the light of their own experience.

In Palestine, unlike Egypt as viewed through Israelite eyes, there is absolutely nothing that man can do to influence directly the source of his life. Egypt is wholly an irrigation culture, dependent upon an exotic river, whereas Palestinian agriculture is rain-fed, even the limited irrigation of the wadi bottoms and hillside terraces being clearly related to the winter rainfall. In Egypt the farmer watered the land with his foot,[2] whether this means his toiling to raise the water with a *shaduf,* or merely kicking a hole in the mud embankment around his field to allow the life-giving water to enter. In the land of Canaan, which "drinks water by the rain from heaven," man is absolutely helpless until that rain comes.

But this rain is quite unreliable even in the settled and agricultural area. "Can anyone understand the spreading of the clouds?" said Elihu to Job (Job 36:29), and his question is reinforced by the Lord himself, when he finally confronts Job in the storm, "Can you lift up your voice to the clouds, so that a flood of waters may cover you?" for who indeed "can tilt the waterskins of heaven, until the soil clogs together in a mass, and the clods cleave fast together?" (Job 38:34, 37-38) Even Phoenicia to the north, where the rainfall is more assured, can be the victim of both paralyzing drought and appalling floods, and in the time of Ethbaal, the father of Jezebel, there was a disastrously dry year, but "when he made supplication there came great thunders"[3]

No less dangerous is the possibility of severe and prolonged cold which, if it comes late in the season, may damage the fruit and at any time can wreak havoc among the flocks and herds. In the Middle East 1925 was a year to live long in people's memory, for even at Baghdad the thermometer went well below freezing. On January 28 of that year Gertrude Bell wrote of "an excruciating wind which cuts you like a knife. The sheep are dying like flies, the banyon trees and sweet limes are all killed . . . and all the young orange trees are dead. The people suffer horribly; the price of food has doubled and trebled. . . . In the north we hear that there is deep snow."[4] This was quite true. Writing

2. The RSV, for some odd reason, has "feet," which is quite incorrect.

3. Josephus, *Antiquities,* VIII, xiii, 2. This is often equated with the more prolonged drought in the time of Elijah (1 Kings 17:1).

4. *The Letters of Gertrude Bell,* ed. by Lady Bell (London: Ernest Benn, 1927), II, 721.

from Mosul at the end of winter, an American missionary said, "The snow fell as in Chicago . . . and remained for one month. . . . The food for the sheep was covered so that thousands of sheep died just before the spring lambing time. . . . The flocks with their shepherds wandered about, lost in the driving snow. Automobiles were sent out only to find a large portion of them frozen to death, their shepherds with them."[5]

These letters were written in Mesopotamia, but they admirably describe what can happen also on the Transjordan plateau. Lord Caradon has spoken of going out to visit a small Bedouin encampment in the Edomite territory after a heavy snowstorm and finding all the animals frozen to death in a grim circle around the tents, and all the people dead inside them.[6] Unfortunately it is precisely the interior steppelands, where flocks and herds supplement, or even replace, agriculture, that are more exposed not only to the possibility of drought but also to the danger of extreme winter cold. But these dangers are not confined to the steppeland, for "he gives snow like wool; he scatters hoarfrost like ashes. He casts forth his ice like morsels; who can stand before his cold?" (Ps. 147:16–17). Only the perfect housewife was "not afraid of snow for her household" (Prov. 31:21).

Frightening also was the "storm of hail, a destroying tempest" (Isa. 28:2), which might beat down the grain while it was yet awaiting the sickle, smash the tender flowers of the olives, and destroy the vines (Ps. 78:47; Hag. 2:17). "Therefore thus says the Lord God: I will make a stormy wind break

out in my wrath; and there shall be a deluge of rain in my anger, and great hailstones in wrath to destroy it. I will break down the wall that you have daubed with whitewash, and bring it down to the ground" (Ezek. 13:13–14).

In the Palestinian realm this insecurity is, as it were, compressed and intensified, because the rainfall decreases from north to south until finally, south of Beersheba, the grain fields fade away into the wilderness of the Negeb, "a land of trouble and anguish, whence come the lioness and the lion" (Isa. 30:6). This implacable reduction of the rain so desperately needed for agriculture brings the arid lands of the east closer and closer to the sea, and forces the farmer into an ever narrower strip, where the lands of chaos and disorder confront him directly.

But just how threatening and variable is the weather? Let us consider what happened in the space of only fourteen years, from 1955–56 to 1968–69.[7]

1955–56: A good year, with rainfall generally well distributed and extending from late October to early May. By the end of December the total rainfall had reached the annual average in some places, and by the end of the year the Judean hills and Trans-jordan plateau edge had had 150 to 170 percent of their usual totals. Deir 'Alla in the Jordan Rift had half the average annual total, i.e., 3.9 inches (137 mm.) in the month of November. However, severe damage and even loss of life were caused by hail and floods in December, and on November 8 as much as 10.8 inches (255 mm.) fell at Kafr Qasim on the edge of the coast plain, close to Rosh ha-'Alla (Ras al-'Ain).

5. Margaret Dean McDowell, *In the Land of Jonah and His Gourd*, ed. by Elizabeth Dean Fickett and Edmund W. McDowell (n.p., n.d.), pp. 31–32.

6. From a personal communication.

7. I am indebted for much of this information, though not all of it, to the valuable annual reports on the rainfall year by J. Katsnelson in the *Israel Exploration Journal*, Vols. 6–19, 1956–69.

1956–57: By contrast this season did not start until December, and the autumn was haunted by prolonged and serious siroccos, even as late as early December. But by a rapid change February was exceptionally cold, and Jerusalem had a snowfall of 16 inches (40 cm.), the greatest since 1950. The rain continued unusually late; there were damaging floods in the north on March 29, surprisingly heavy amounts of rain in May, and, even more startling, thunderstorms and heavy rain in the Negeb and Arabah in June. Jericho this year had 8.4 inches (211 mm.), which is 153 percent of the average total.

1957–58: The year started early, but the October rain was very localized, and this pattern continued throughout most of the year, with a very disturbing decrease in the second half. Ajlun, high up in Gilead, had no more than 2.2 inches (57 mm.) after the end of January, and Amman only half an inch (15 mm.). "I withheld the rain from you when there were yet three months to the harvest; I sent rain on one village and not upon another village, and the field upon which it did not rain withered" (Amos 4:7). It was generally a disastrous year for agriculture, and Beersheba had exactly half its normal total.

1958–59: This was another bad year. October rains were very variable, good in some places but absent in others, and then ensued a severe drought lasting until the beginning of January, but in the Negeb, on the Edom plateau, and in some other areas until February. By the end of the first half of the season Jerusalem had had only 17 percent, and Beersheba only 9 percent, of what they should have had by that time. February was the coldest month in sixty years, with heavy snow on the Judean hills and the Transjordan plateau, and snow even on the plains of the Negeb.

1959–60: Following an unusually cool summer, the winter rainfall was appallingly low, with only small amounts and in some places even drought until the end of December. However, the plateau edge of Edom, where the season usually starts late, had up to 2 inches (50 mm.) in November, an unusually high figure for that month. January rain was above average in the north and center of the Cis-jordan hills, but Judah and the Negeb had only 25 to 50 percent of the average. Totals, except in Upper Galilee, were extremely low, Jerusalem having only 8.4 inches (210 mm.) and Beersheba 3.5 inches (85 mm.). Both these figures were records, Beersheba surpassing its previous record in 1957–58. The Trans-jordan hills had half or less than half their normal totals, and Ma'an in the south of Jordan had no measurable rain at all throughout the entire season.

1960–61: This was an improvement, and the totals were almost everywhere close to the average, but the distribution was very uneven. The beginning and end of the year were marked by heavy floods in the marginal regions, in November in the Negeb and in April in the northern Rift, the first occasion on which cloudbursts have been recorded in the Rift Valley during this month. December and March were both unusually dry, but February was abnormal in that the rain in the center south and south of Cis-jordan was greater in the north. To a lesser extent this was true east of the Jordan as well, as-Salt having the quite unusual total of 9.3 inches (234 mm.) for the month.

1961–62: This year provided an excellent example of how untrustworthy the rain can be, for throughout the season it was very unevenly distributed from place to place. Thus, September had heavy rain on Carmel and in the Jezreel region, but not elsewhere; in

October there were floods in the Arabah, which is rare for this month; November had only 25 to 40 percent of the average for the month in most places, but there were floods in Lower Galilee. In December totals were generally rather above average, and very much above in Galilee, Gilead, and Moab, Madeba having half the average total for the year in one month. Thunder and hail were very widespread. January totals were about average in many places, but below normal in the south on the hill country of Judah (Hebron had only 1.6 inches, 40 mm.). February received the average amount in many parts of the hills and Trans-jordan, but was deficient in Galilee, and seriously so in the Negeb. In March most areas had only about 10 percent of the average, and the southern hills of Judah, the Negeb, and very many places on the Trans-jordan plateau had none at all. Such a dry February and March in the south is very serious. The rain in April came mainly on the 18th and 29th in heavy thunderstorms and hail, but these storms were often very localized. The Negeb had only 70 percent of the average for the year, but most places had about normal, and the Nablus-Jezreel region as much as 130 percent. However, this 130 percent was badly distributed, and Nablus had 24 inches (601 mm.), which is rather more than the average annual total, in the three months of December, January, and February and no more than 3.76 inches (91.4 mm.) in the rest of the season.

1962–63: This was an exceptionally bad year. Except only in Galilee the rainfall for the year was well below average and in the center, east, and south disastrously so. The season started well in October in many places, but November, which is a critical month for agriculture, was very dry and warm, Jerusalem having the warmest November for a century. In December and January rainfall, though good in the north, was deficient in Judah and on the Trans-jordan plateau. Jerusalem had only .68 inches (17 mm.) in January, the lowest figure recorded for this month in ninety years. February was also decidedly warmer than average, and February and March totals reached the average only in the north, where there were cloudbursts, hail, and floods as late as May 1 and even May 27 in the Upper Rift Valley. Except only in Galilee the total rainfall was very depressing. Jerusalem had only 47 percent and Beersheba a mere 1.7 inches (42 mm.), i.e., 21 percent of the average, the lowest figure ever recorded in some fifty years of observations, and less than half the previous record low in 1959–60.

1963–64: This was a complete contrast, for averages were almost everywhere exceeded, and Beersheba had 12.7 inches (318 mm.)—159 percent of the average and the second highest total ever recorded. October was generally wet, and December had some of the coldest temperatures for twenty years. January and February were unusually wet, and February very much so, for Jerusalem had 20 days of rain out of the 28 and the northern Huleh Basin no less than 23 such days.

1964–65: The rain did not start until the middle of November, but these initial rains were excessively heavy. Though the totals for the year were almost everywhere above average, the rain tended to be concentrated again in the three months of November, December, and January, and to die away after this.

1965–66: The "former rains" in October were excellent, but then followed a prolonged period of deficient rainfall from November through February. Such a situation can be extremely serious, since the grain starts to grow after the heavy October rains, but does not have enough depth of root to withstand a prolonged drought. On March 11 a storm developed at Elath and moved eastward, intensifying as it climbed the steep escarpment of Edom, and destroying much of the town of Ma'an and causing serious loss of life.

1966–67: Once again there were unusually good former rains in October, reaching as much as eight times the normal for the month in several places. Though November was somewhat dry, the rain was generally well distributed throughout the year, lasting even into May, with totals well above average. Snow blocked the approaches to Petra in both December and January, and at Beidha nearby in May "the campaign was halted slightly before the intended time not, as might be imagined, by imminence of war, but because a sudden freak storm completely flooded us out."[8]

1967–68: Yet again good former rains, though accompanied by an unusual amount of hail. The rainfall remained satisfactory until the beginning of February and then became seriously short. Further damage was done to crops in many places by heavy storms of hail on April 25 and May 13.

1968–69: For a fourth year running the October rains were very good in most places, and rainfall continued to be well distributed throughout the year, though it tended to be below average in February. The total was well above average in a large part of the country, about average in Jerusalem, but rather below in much of the Negeb.

The reader looking at this record as a whole must surely be struck by how many of the exceptional phenomena, many of which he knows from the Bible, are crowded into this very brief period. Amos 4 has already been mentioned in connection with 1957–58, but

8. Diana Kirkbride, "Beidha 1967: An Interim Report," *PEQ*, C (1968), 90.

"rain upon one village and not upon another village" would be just as true of 1961–62, when such erratic distribution persisted throughout much of the rainy season. The withholding of rain when there were yet three months to the harvest characterized not only 1957–58 but also 1962–63 and 1967–68.

Three successive years of drought occurred from 1957 to 1960, and in the last of these years farmers everywhere in Jordan, on both the east and the west bank, made the same lament, "We have had no rain for three years," exactly the phrase used of the great drought in the time of Elijah (1 Kings 18:1). By this they meant not that they had had literally no rain but that the rain had been quite insufficient to produce an adequate harvest. During this period Jerusalem had successsively 16, 17.4, and 9.2 inches (400, 436, and 230 mm.), i.e., 73 percent, 80 percent, and 42 percent of the average total for the year. For the three years together it received only 65 percent of what it normally receives in that time. The third year, which culminated this drought period, everywhere brought the lowest totals, but the other two were far more serious than the figures for the year might suggest, since in 1957–58 the second half of the season provided only about a quarter of the rain which normally falls in this period and in the following year the pattern was reversed: in the *first* half of the season the accumulated rainfall was only 17 percent of the amount which usually falls by the end of December.

The situation was far more disastrous in many of the marginal regions, of which Beersheba may be taken as an example. The average annual rainfall at Beersheba is 8 inches (205 mm.), but the figure was below this for six years running, coming close to it only in 1960–61, and the total was only 59 percent of the average total for a six-year period. Farmers without the help of irrigation, in an area where they are on the very margin of possible agriculture, cannot endure so prolonged a period of poor rainfall; under the conditions which prevailed in ancient Israel they would probably have had to move away, and much of the land would have passed, for either a shorter or a longer period, out of cultivation. The fluctuation of the margin of agriculture is, in fact, a very important feature of the countries bordering the south and east of the Mediterranean. It has been shown, for instance, that in Tunisia the 8-inch (200 mm.) isohyet[9] in 1944–47, a dry period, had retreated 125 miles northward from its position in 1931–34, which had been wetter, but that the 28-inch (700 mm.) isohyet had remained stationary.[10]

The year 1962–63 was a bad year everywhere, except only in the extreme north, but it was followed by two years generally above average. For such two years to occur in succession over the whole country is very rare and has been known only three times in the past eighty years, the other occasions being 1895–97 and 1904–6. Thus, in the very short space of eight years the country experienced both an unusually long drought and the uncommon phenomenon of two successive years of rainfall above the average.

These were not the only abnormal phenomena. There were, for instance, two exceptionally cold Februaries, in 1957 and 1959, the second being the coldest known for sixty years, with no fewer than seven days of snow in Jerusalem, and again extreme cold in December, 1963, when the temperature fell to 28° F. even in the Plain of Esdraelon,

and of course much lower on the highlands. In the spring of 1962 and again in 1968 there was hail in the time of the wheat harvest; when this happened at the beginning of the monarchy, it was regarded as a "great thing," so that "all the people greatly feared the Lord and Samuel" (1 Sam. 12:16–18). On February 20, 1964, there was prolonged and destructive hail in the Jerusalem area, and in February of the following year gales throughout the country on February 7, 8, and 9 caused widespread damage. In Galilee they reached record strengths exceeding 60 miles per hour (96 kph).

All this indicates yet again that "normal" figures in Palestine are very far from normal and the variations from them frequent and striking. Certain patterns, it is true, recur, but no one of them can be said to be especially characteristic, and there is no kind of rule about the order in which they come. Leo Krown has suggested there is evidence that a dry October is often followed by above-average rainfall, but that moderate rain in October is likely to be followed by below-normal precipitation, as indeed the Bedouin have noticed.[11] But this is not a rule, and it did not happen, for example, in 1938–39. It does indicate, however, that good "former rains" are not necessarily so desirable as is popularly believed, for a good October may be followed by a dry November which can do much harm to the young crops.

"Yahweh is a man of war; Yahweh is his name" (Exod. 15:3). So Miriam sang at the crossing of the Red Sea, and the early Israelites clearly thought of their God as coming to fight on their behalf in storm and tempest, before

9. I.e., a line joining places having the same amount of rainfall.

10. David Grigg, *The Harsh Lands* (London: Macmillan, 1970), pp. 166–67.

11. Leo Krown, "An Approach to Forecasting Seasonal Rainfall in Israel," *Journal of Applied Meteorology*, 5 (1966), 590–94.

which even the cedars of Lebanon cannot stand (Ps. 29:5). "Have you entered the storehouses of the snow?" the Lord demanded of Job. "Have you seen the storehouses of the hail, which I have reserved for the time of trouble, for the day of battle and war?" (Job 38:22–23; see Ps. 135:7). The stars in their courses fought against Sisera, and when God marched forth "from the region of Edom, the earth trembled, and the heavens dropped, yea, the clouds dropped water. The mountains quaked before the Lord" (Judg. 5:20, 4–5). In one of the very earliest psalms, quoted also in 2 Samuel 22, this theme is developed at length: "He bowed the heavens, and came down; thick darkness was under his feet. He rode upon a cherub, and flew; he came swiftly upon the wings of the wind. He made darkness his covering round about him, his canopy thick clouds dark with water. The Lord also thundered in the heavens, and the Most High uttered his voice, hailstones and coals of fire" (Ps. 18:9–13). Before him, indeed, "is a devouring fire, round about him a mighty tempest" (Ps. 50:3), and in the magnificent psalm added to the Book of Habakkuk we are told of how "God came from Teman, and the Holy One from Mount Paran . . . the mountains saw thee and writhed; the raging waters swept on; the deep gave forth its voice, it lifted its hands on high" (3:3, 10). Even long after the Exile the idea persisted as a poetic expression: "Thy glory passed through the four gates of fire and earthquake and wind and ice, to give the law to the descendants of Jacob, and thy commandment to the prosperity of Israel" (2 Esd. 3:19).

Sometimes, of course, the hoped-for deliverance did not come,

We have heard with our ears, O God,
 our fathers have told us,
what deeds thou didst perform in their
 days,
 in the days of the old:
thou with thine own hand didst drive out
 the nations. . . .
Yet thou hast cast us off and abased us,
 thou hast not gone out with our armies.
 [Ps. 44:1–2, 9]

This unpredictable weather left the Israelite farmer in perplexity, for he did not know in advance whether the vitally necessary rain would begin effectively in October or be delayed until January, and even after it began no one ever knew what would happen next. In times of drought men send "their servants for water; they come to the cisterns, they find no water, they return with their vessels empty" (Jer. 14:3), but when God says "to the rainstorms, 'Be fierce,'"

the floods of rain pour down unchecked.
He shuts every man fast indoors,
and all men whom he has made must stand
 idle;
the beasts withdraw into their lairs
and take refuge in their dens.
 [Job 37:6–8, NEB]

These torrential floods bring life to the land, but they also bring death, for they are often "a beating rain that leaves no food" (Prov. 28:3), sluicing the red earth of the fields into the wadis and staining the waters of the sea. Who knows, therefore, "whether for correction . . . or for love he causes it to happen?" (Job 37:13).

CHAPTER 7

Food from the Earth

*Thou dost cause the grass to grow for the cattle
and plants for man to cultivate,
that he may bring forth food from the earth.*
PSALM 104:14

The climate, the rock, and the plants which grow upon it are the soil-producing agents. In Palestine the prolonged summer heat and drought destroy much of the organic matter in the soil, leaving the surface parched and powdery. Intense evaporation sucks up the water in the soil by capillary action and deposits the natural salts in the upper layers, and then in the rainy season the same heavy storms which replenish the water supply wash away unprotected soil and leach out the salts from the surface. Considerable erosion also occurs everywhere in the dry summer, and in the steppelands and deserts throughout the year, by the powerful winds which sweep across the unprotected landscape. These forces of erosion are in fact so savage that once the natural vegetation cover has been removed, the soil is carried away more quickly than it is formed. It

has been well said that in Palestine there is no necessity actively to destroy the country; it is quite enough to do nothing. This dismal process has made such inroads throughout the centuries that over the whole cultivated region north of the Gaza-Beersheba-Jericho arc as much as six and a half feet of fertile earth have been removed since Roman times.[1]

The soils of Palestine fall into two major divisions: Mediterranean and Desertic, though it is necessary to distinguish also in both zones between the upland and mountain areas and those plain and lowland areas where the soils are formed mainly of material transported from other regions.

The soils of the Desertic Zone, with a

1. A. Reifenberg, *The Struggle Between the Desert and the Sown* (Jerusalem: The Jewish Agency, 1955), p. 46.

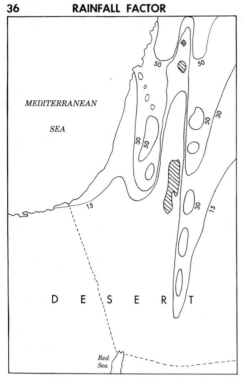

36   RAINFALL FACTOR

MEDITERRANEAN

SEA

D E S E R T

Red
Sea

The "rainfall factor" is obtained by dividing the average annual total rainfall in millimeters by the average temperature in degrees Centigrade for the rainy season, when almost all the growth takes place. Thus, a place on the highlands with an average annual rainfall of 650 mm. (26 inches) and an average temperature in the rainy season of 13° C. (55.4° F.) would have a rainfall factor of 50. See A. Reifenberg, *The Soils of Palestine*, 198, pp. 8–13.

rainfall factor of less than 15 (Fig. 36), are of only limited value for agriculture, except where alluvial soils have collected in the wadis. Much of the upland and mountain area is *hamada*, or stony desert, strewn with millions of small stones and boulders, though where *hamada* forms in the plains of the Negeb the soil is often thick enough to

permit cultivation if this pavement is cleared. Desert earth is typically red or yellow in color, yellow soils characterizing the Negeb and the east of Trans-jordan, where they are sometimes very deep, while red soils are to be found in the sandstone regions of the south of Trans-jordan. In the central Rift Valley are the grayish white Lisan marls, deposits of the Dead Sea in the course of its prolonged shrinking. Easily eroded into badlands, they are excessively salty and were not used for agriculture in ancient times. The dusty loess, brought by the desert winds and deposited in the wadis of the Beersheba region, sometimes many feet thick, is fertile and mercifully free from stones, but after the first rains a hard crust may form on the surface and prevent the penetration of water. Trees therefore do not grow in the loess, since the water cannot reach their roots, but cereals are possible, though these also are inhibited by the surface crust and the deficient rainfall.

Loess is a soil of the transition from the Desertic to the Mediterranean Zone. Where the rainfall factor is between 15 and 30 is the *moderately dry* area of the coastal lowlands south of Carmel, the Galilee–Beth-shan basin, and the Trans-jordan steppe. The last has brown soils, deepening in color as the rainfall increases, and forming excellent cereal country in the richer parts. The southern Coast Plain behind Gaza has brown steppe soils formed of loess mixed with alluvium, and this again is good for cereals. The Red Sands found in Sharon and in patches to the south break down into a bright red or orange soil with almost perfect moisture conditions. Today this provides the best citrus soil, but in ancient times it was forested and often isolated by marshes. On the landward side of the Coast Plain are the rich alluvial soils brought down from the mountains, but along the coast, especially south of Jaffa, are the barren sand dunes. In the Galilee–Beth-shan basin gray, permeable, *rendzina* soils formed on the Lisan marls. These are a clay loam type of soil which is valuable for agriculture, though sometimes too salty.

The *moderately wet* and *wet Mediterranean* regions (R.F. = 30–50 and over 50) are mainly uplands and mountains, though they include the plain of Esdraelon and the Huleh Basin. The lowland soils here are almost entirely dark brown alluvial soils, excellent for agriculture, though usually very ill-drained and subject to flooding. This is most serious in the Huleh Basin, and in biblical times the marshes here must have been formidable. Even in 1935 it was possible for a man to sink waist deep in mud in places.[2] In the papyrus marshes of the southern part of the basin dark-brown or black peat has formed to a depth of up to 25 feet.

Four types of soil may be distinguished on the mountains. The most valuable is the *terra rossa* of the Cenomanian limestone. It is suitable to the growth of all the typical Mediterranean crops, but may often be shallow, rather poor in humus, and easily washed off the hillsides. The Eocene limestone breaks down into the *brown forest* soils, similar to, but not so rich as, the *terra rossa*. The Senonian and Eocene chalk and chalky marl form a *rendzina* type of soil, which is rich in lime but poor in humus and somewhat infertile. It is whitish gray in color and easily distinguished from the two previous types. Finally there is the chocolate-colored

basaltic soil of the volcanic regions. This is similar to *terra rossa* and very fertile, but very often so choked with great boulders that the ancient farmer avoided it. Only on the interior of the plateau of Bashan, where it was less encumbered, could it be developed extensively. The lowland basins in the Western Highlands are floored with fertile alluvium, which is easily flooded but produces rich crops when it dries out after the rains.

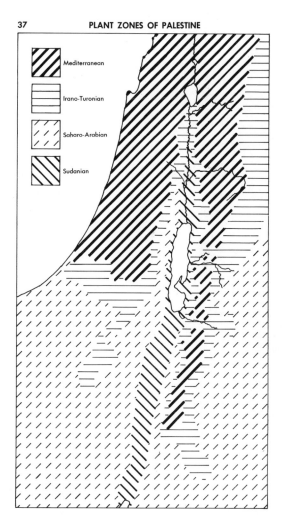

37   PLANT ZONES OF PALESTINE

- Mediterranean
- Irano-Turonian
- Saharo-Arabian
- Sudanian

2. Roger Washburn, "The Percy Sladen Expedition to Lake Huleh, 1935," *PEQ*, 68 (1936), pp. 204–10.

The plants which grow by nature on these soils are extremely varied, for Palestine stands at the junction of three of the world's major vegetation regions: *Mediterranean, Saharo-Sindian,* and *Irano-Turanian,* with a penetration by yet a fourth, the *Sudanian,* here isolated from its main homeland. As may be seen from the accompanying map (Fig. 37), the Mediterranean and Saharo-Sindian zones cover the greater part of the country, the first being found in Cisjordan north of the Gaza-Arad line and in Trans-jordan along the plateau edge, with an outlier in the Jabal Druze. Plants of this type must adapt themselves to the summer drought and often have long roots which burrow down in search of water. The trees and shrubs are frequently evergreen, but their leaves are small, often hairy, coated with wax, or thick and leathery to prevent evaporation. When "the winter is past, the rain is over and gone, the flowers appear on the earth" (Song of Sol. 2:11), or in actual fact soon after the rain begins, very many of them being bulbs which lay dormant during the summer, e.g., tulips, lilies, narcissus, anemones, and irises. The scorching siroccos of April, which destroy this multicolored carpet, are also probably the reason why there are relatively few different types of grasses. The typical trees are the Aleppo pine, the deciduous Tabor oak, evergreen Mediterranean oak, styrax, terebinth, carob, and pistachia. The dense thickets of the *maquis* include laurel, myrtle, broom, and rockrose.

The Saharo-Sindian plants are those suited to the great deserts of the Sahara, Arabia, and Sind, where there is very little rain, intense heat during the day, but sudden cold at night, often dropping below freezing in winter. At all times powerful winds, heavily charged near the ground with sharp particles of sand, may scourge the landscape. Plants, therefore, exist only with difficulty, and vegetation is scarce and stunted, but extremely sensitive to the presence of water. Where there is even the slightest increase in the supply, as in the most gentle depression, along the almost invisible drainage lines, and the edges of a blacktop road, the sparse plant cover immediately thickens. Desert plants must protect themselves against the persistent drought. Deciduous plants shed their leaves in the summer rather than in the winter cold, and evergreens have only the tiniest of leaves. Where there is some water *spina christi,* white broom, or tamarisk may grow. Elsewhere there is camel thorn or the aromatic sagebush and when there has been rain, but only then, a magnificent flowering of the dormant bulbs and seeds.

Between the Mediterranean and Saharo-Sindian zones is a narrow belt of Irano-Turanian Steppe vegetation, no more than a mile or two wide in Jeshimon, but broadening out in the Beersheba Depression and in the northeastern part of the Trans-jordan Plateau. In the Negeb it extends a narrow finger along the top of the uplands. In the true high steppelands of Asia, where this type of vegetation belongs, plant growth is twice interrupted, by the winter cold and by the summer drought, with the result that the growing season is very short. Here, however, it is rather the compression of the rainy season into three, or at the most four, months which effectively shortens plant growth, though on the eastern plateau the winter cold can also be a factor. In such conditions trees are absent and vegetation is stunted, consisting mainly of steppeland grasses and small shrubs, with a very brief but truly glorious flowering of annuals and bulbous plants in the spring. Often a vast expanse of dwarf

night-scented stock fills the air with per-
fume on the plateau east of Madeba,
and a little farther to the south the
"Moab lily" rears its head, a noble
purple iris so deep in color as to be almost black.

Finally, in the central and southern
Rift Valley and its tributaries the high
temperatures and especially the absence
of winter cold have made possible in the
oases "islands" of plants which belong
properly to the savanna region south
of the Sahara. Their presence is something of an enigma, but it may be that
they are relics of a great subtropical
forest which existed before the Sahara
came into existence.

Vegetation Regions

Coastal Sand Dunes. These have naturally a very sparse vegetation, but are
interesting for the intermingling here
of Mediterranean and Saharo-Sindian
plants. There is sufficient rainfall for
the first, but the water drains away so
rapidly through the loose sand that
desert types of plants can also grow.

Lowlands of Cis-jordan. Here there is
almost no natural vegetation left, and
instead there are orange groves, olives,
grain fields, market vegetables, and, in
many places in modern Israel, fish
ponds. In ancient times the alluvial soils
of Sharon and parts of Esdraelon were
probably marshy and the Mousterian
Red Sand was covered with forest, but
the better-drained alluvium had been
cleared for growing wheat. The Philistine section of the Coast Plain probably
always had few trees, except in the
valley bottoms, and barley rather than
wheat was grown. The Shephelah, composed of the somewhat less fertile
Eocene limestone, was noted for its
covering of fig sycamore (1 Kings

10:27), and though this was evidently
rather a despised tree (Isa. 9:10), the
stands were valuable enough to be made,
apparently, a royal preserve (1 Chron.
27:28).

*The Hill Country of Judah and
Samaria.* Today the usual vegetation
here is rough scrub, for the original oak
and pine forest has been completely
removed. Only on Carmel are there
still relics of the true, almost impenetrable *maquis.* Elsewhere this luxuriance
is not found and the vegetation is that
poorer type of *maquis* known as *garigue.*
Everywhere, however, the rule applies
that vegetation is always thicker on
the northern and western slopes, where
rainfall is greater and evaporation less,
than on the drier eastern and southern
slopes. This is an absolute rule throughout the whole of Palestine and applies
as much in the desert as in the forest,
and even on so small an elevation as
an archaeological tell. Modern reforesta-
tion has restored the thick pine forests
in many parts of the western slopes,
and experiments by the Jordan government on the edges of Jeshimon have
shown that once a cover of scrub woodland and shrubs probably extended a
few miles over the crest of the highlands.
It must always, however, have given
place rapidly to the poor steppe and
semidesert which confronts the visitor
today and carries a cover of short grass,
even on the northwestern slopes, only in
the wettest winters.

The Hills of Galilee. This region is
very similar to the preceding, but the
vegetation is much richer. On the
western slopes the *maquis* is even thicker
than on Carmel, and in many places the
hills are quite well-wooded, though the
trees are nowhere large. The forests of
Upper Galilee seem to have been cleared
by Roman times, and it is estimated
that in that period 97 percent of the

land was cultivated.[3] On these mountains may be found an admixture of plants of the Euro-Siberian type, characteristic of regions much farther to the north, e.g., the hawthorn, which is common around Safad, the plantain, and the wild pear.

The Trans-jordan Highlands. This consists of two "islands," the Gilead Dome as far south as a point almost level with the north end of the Dead Sea, and the plateau of Edom. Gilead in its natural state had a vegetation very similar to that of the hill country of Judah and Samaria, and still today carries in many places a fairly thick residual cover of forest and scattered woodland, mainly Aleppo pine, evergreen oak, and carob. On the old Amman-Jerash road, which crosses the Baqa'a, a sudden change may be observed from the oaks of the southward-facing slopes to the pines of the colder northern ones. On the bleak Edomite plateau the major tree was Aleppo pine, and the stands were still thick enough here in World War I for the Turks to find it profitable to build a special branch of the Hejaz Railway to obtain the lumber.

The Steppeland. Lying south and east of the Highlands, this has always been grassland. On the better steppeland immediately east of Gilead and along the plateau east of the Dead Sea, as well as in the southern part of the Judean hills, the vegetation is of the Mediterranean type, and there probably was at one time some scrub forest. To the east and south of this, and in Edom immediately east of the forest, is the poor steppeland with plants of the Irano-Turanian type. The plant cover is very thin indeed, and as far as the eye can

see the ground is bare in summer, though dotted with innumerable tiny bushes which turn green after the spring rains.

The Desert. This is seldom true desert, for though the hills are often quite barren, the wadis everywhere carry a thin line of saltbush and even tamarisk. On the high Ramon Upwarp are several hundred Atlantic terebinths, such as are found all the way from the Atlas to the Middle East, though with broad stretches of desert separating one patch of trees from the next.[4]

The Rift Valley. Here the warmth is like that of a forcing house, and where there is sufficient water, as in the Huleh Basin and along the Jordan, the vegetation forms impenetrable marsh or jungle. Examples of tropical plants are the papyrus of the Huleh Basin, which everywhere is not found north of about, 7°N, the *spina christi* trees so characteristic of the Arabah, and the doum palms close to Elath. In the Zor, the flood plain which the Jordan has carved in the Lisan marls, is a forbidding tamarisk jungle.

As little by little the land was cleared of its natural vegetation and prepared for agriculture, the Palestinian farmer began to grow what might roughly be described as the three cultivated equivalents of the natural cover he had removed. In place of the forest trees he grew olives; in place of scrub woodland, vines; and in place of the grasses, wheat and barley. These three provided "wine to gladden the heart of man, oil to make his face shine, and bread to strengthen man's heart" (Ps. 104: 15). When people in other countries said of the Israelites "Where is their God,"

---

3. B. Colomb and Y. Kedar, "Ancient Agriculture in the Galilee Mountains," *IEJ*, 21 (1971), 136.

4. Azaria Alon, *The Natural History of the Land of the Bible* (Jerusalem: Jerusalem Publishing House, 1969), p. 92.

XVI. *Tending Grapes in Trans-jordan.* This photograph was taken at the village of Faheis in the region known in the Old Testament as Jazer. Traditionally in Palestine vines have been grown with their branches spreading out close to the ground, where they can benefit from whatever moisture in summer that there is.

XVII. *Living in Booths.* From very early times farmers on the hills have camped out during the dry summer, either in tents or temporary huts, to protect the vineyards. This custom became the basis in the Israelite tradition for remembering the living in tents during the Exodus when they celebrated the "Feast of Booths" at the vintage season. This picture is taken in Trans-jordan in rough scrub country. In the background may be seen some of the vineyards.

Then the Lord became jealous for his land,
and had pity on his people.
The Lord answered and said to his people,
"Behold, I am sending to you
grain, wine, and oil,
and you will be satisfied.

[Joel 2:17–19]

The constant bracketing of these three
products together shows how they dominated the agriculture of the country
(Gen. 27:28, 37; Deut. 7:13; 11:14;
12:17; 14:23; 18:4; 28:51; 33:28; 2
Kings 18:32; 2 Chron. 31:5; 32:28;
Neh. 5:11; 10:39; 13:5, 12; Ps. 4:7;
Isa. 36:17; Lam. 2:12; Hos. 2:5, 8, 22;
Joel 1:10; Hag. 1:11), and to them we
should probably add the humble pulses
which Daniel and his companions ate
(Dan. 1:8) and by which Jacob bought
his birthright (Gen. 25:29–34). Deuteronomy 8:8 speaks of "a land of wheat
and barley, of vines and fig trees and
pomegranates, a land of olive trees and
honey," known in Jewish tradition as
the "seven species." Ecclesiasticus 39:26
has a slightly different list,

Basic to all the needs of man's life
are water and fire and iron and salt
and wheat flour and milk and honey,
the blood of the grape, and oil and
clothing.
All these are for good to the godly.

Milk and honey had long been associated with Palestine, for the promise
of the Exodus experience was that the
people would be brought into "a land
flowing with milk and honey" (Exod.
3:8; 13:5; 33:3; Lev. 20:24; Num.
14:8; Deut. 6:3; 11:9; 26:9; 27:3; Josh.
5:6; Jer. 11:5; 32:22; Ezek. 20:6, 15),
though at the time they often com-
plained that the reverse had happened
and that Moses had in fact brought them
out of a land flowing with milk and
honey to kill them in the wilderness
(Num. 16:13–14). Seen from the
wilderness, where the people had taken
refuge and where they were hungry and

thirsty, the hills of Palestine promised
excellent pasture for the animals and
wild honey dripping from the trees and
rocks (1 Sam. 14:25–27; Ps. 18:16;
Matt. 3:4; Mark 1:6).

When, however, they had become
settled in the land where "grain shall
make the young men flourish and new
wine the maidens" (Zech. 9:17) and
where rich olive oil replaced animal fat
for cooking, the once longed-for milk
and honey were despised and even became a symbol of poverty. Isaiah
warned Ahaz that as a result of his
misguided foreign policy the Assyrian
wars would have reduced the country
to such a state that yogurt and wild
honey would be the only food available,
for the farmers would have to take refuge with a couple of animals and
gather what food they could. "In that
day a man will keep alive a young cow
and two sheep; and because of the
abundance [the word is sarcastic] of
milk which they give, he will eat curds;
for every one that is left in the land will
eat curds and honey" (Isa. 7:21–22).[5]

"Three times in the year you shall
keep a feast to me. You shall keep the
feast of unleavened bread . . . for in it
you came out of Egypt. . . . You shall
keep the feast of harvest, of the first
fruits of your labor, of what you sow in
the field. You shall keep the feast of
ingathering at the end of the year, when
you gather in from the field the fruit of
your labor" (Exod. 23:14–16). The

5. Many commentators have suggested
that Isaiah 7:15 indicates the luxuriance
of the food that the child Immanuel would
eat, whether he is understood to be the
Messiah or Ahaz's son, or a child of
Isaiah's family. Some have even argued
that vv. 21–22 promise that a few would
continue to have plenty of food while the
majority went hungry. All such interpretations are extremely forced. The whole
tenor of the various oracles which make
up Isaiah 7–8 is the devastation of the
land by the Assyrian army.

list of feasts here quoted belongs to the "Covenant Code," and the parallel list in Exodus 34:18–24 to the "Ritual Decalogue," the two oldest collections of laws in the Old Testament, dating back almost certainly to the tenth century B.C. It is significant that all three feasts are agricultural, and there is no mention of the Passover, which does not seem to have been united with the Feast of Unleavened Bread until the final years of the monarchy, "for no such passover had been kept since the days of the judges who judged Israel, or during all the days of the kings of Israel, or the kings of Judah" (2 Kings 23:22). This innovation reflects the instructions given for the three feasts in Deuteronomy 16:1–17, part of "this book of the covenant" found at the time of Josiah's restoration of the Temple (2 Kings 22:8; 23:21).[6]

As the rainy season developed, the grain grew, "first the blade, then the ear, then the full grain in the ear" (Mark 4:28). By the beginning of April, "at the time appointed in the month Abib" (Exod. 34:18), though the exact date is not specified because the rainy season is so variable, came the barley harvest, "the time when you first put the sickle to the standing grain" (Deut. 16:9). This was the Feast of Unleavened Bread. Some seven weeks later, with the completion of the wheat harvest, came the "day of the first fruits, when you offer a cereal offering of new grain to the Lord at your feast of weeks" (Num. 28:26). Originally these feasts

must have varied not only from year to year but also from one part of the country to another, according to the time of the harvest, and probably the exact counting of days provided for in Deuteronomy 16:9 was designed to ensure a common celebration throughout the country. Somewhat later the idea of "first fruits" as distinct from the complete harvest became attached to the Feast of Unleavened Bread (Lev. 23:9), and hence the significance of Christ as the first fruits of those who are to rise from the dead in 1 Corinthians 15:20–23.

During the dry summer little could be done by the farmer because of the lack of water, but slowly there took place in this season the annual miracle of the vine, whose long root sucks up water from deep in the earth. In August and September the farmers went out to live in the fields in tents and little huts made of branches, in order to protect the grapes from the ravages of thirsty animals (Song of Sol. 2:15). This living in "booths" is an agricultural necessity, still practiced today on the hills of Trans-jordan, and apparently it was not until the compilation of the "Priestly Code" during the Exile that the tents were directly associated with those of the Exodus (Lev. 23:39–43).[7] Nevertheless, it is evident that from the beginning the religious teachers sought to extricate the feasts from their pagan interpretation and attach them securely to the Exodus experience (Exod. 23:15; 34:18). The vintage festival among the Gerasenes, previously accompanied by much vulgarity and drunkenness, was

---

6. Most scholars regard the elaborate description of Hezekiah's passover in 2 Chronicles 30 as unhistorical, since there is no hint of it in 2 Kings. The biblical evidence for the Israelite feasts is well presented in Roland de Vaux, *Ancient Israel* (New York: McGraw-Hill, 1961; paperback ed., 1965), pp. 484–517, though some scholars may dispute certain of his conclusions.

7. De Vaux (*ibid.*, p. 497), despite his encyclopedic knowledge of Palestine, has a curious misunderstanding here, for he distinguishes between the "huts" in the vineyards and the "tents" of the Exodus period. Actually, tents and huts were, and still are, used interchangeably at the vintage season.

similarly "baptized" when the region became Christian and was transformed into a ceremony commemorating the miracle at Cana of Galilee, annually performed in the cathedral courtyard at Jerash.

Whether the Feast of Booths was accompanied by a New Year festival (or was itself such a festival) celebrating the enthronement of Yahweh and his triumph over the forces of chaos is a matter of very much dispute. De Vaux rejects it, but others such as Johnson and Weiser argue strongly for it.[8] The weight of the evidence seems on the whole to favor a conscious recognition at the vintage season of the quite desperate need for water and the real danger of chaos and disorder if the rain did not come. When the Temple still existed water was drawn from the Pool of Siloam and poured upon the altar to symbolize this necessity, and "on the last day of the feast, the great day, Jesus stood up and proclaimed, 'If anyone thirst, let him come to me and drink'" (John 7:37). Therefore, there was probably a no less conscious recollection and celebration of the triumph of order over disorder both at the Creation and in the Exodus, and thereby the assurance that order would once more prevail in the year to come. The Creation and Exodus themes are tied together in a number of psalms, which were probably used at this festival (Pss. 74: 12–17; 89:1–18; 95, etc.).

The most important cereals were wheat and barley, the first being the more esteemed (Ps. 147:14). Barley is the product of the drier south and east and is probably "the standing grain of the Philistines" (Judg. 15:5). It will

8. *Ibid.*, pp. 502–6; Aubrey R. Johnson, *Sacral Kingship in Ancient Israel* (Cardiff: University of Wales Press, 1955); Artur Weiser, *The Psalms*, trans. by Herbert Hartwell (Philadelphia: Westminster Press, 1962), esp. pp. 35–52.

grow on poorer soils than wheat and does not need such a long ripening period, though it is easily spoiled by rain during the harvest. Olives, which ripen slowly and can be picked at any time in the early rainy season when the farmer has time to spare from his fields, are confined to those areas with a true Mediterranean climate. They can endure long periods of drought and will grow in very shallow soils where there is even less than 8 inches (200 mm.) of rain. They are, however, killed by prolonged frost, and the winter cold can be an important limiting factor. Except for Gilead, olives are more characteristic of Cis-jordan than of the eastern plateau, though recent experiments there have shown that they can be grown more to the south and east than was once believed, and indeed were so grown by the Romans. Vines are essentially a product of the hill slopes, and today the finest grapes come from Gilead, clusters of long, sweet, green fruit, which for table purposes are almost unparalleled. Grain was often grown between the olives and pulses between the vines, and together these four products constituted a system which both provided a well-balanced diet and could be operated by one man with the help of his family. The good wife is one who "works with willing hands" (Prov. 31:13), and "a son who gathers in summer is prudent, but a son who sleeps in harvest brings shame" (Prov. 10:5; see also Matt. 21:28–31).

So closely integrated were the grain and wine and oil that the Israelites, though they occasionally conquered other areas, never colonized any region where these three could not be grown together. According to the Syrians, the Israelite gods were "gods of the hills" (1 Kings 20:23), and for the Israelites themselves to leave the hills was to become strangers in a strange land, forced to "serve other gods" (1 Sam. 26:19), i.e., to live according to another system. They never, in fact, settled extensively either on the level plateau or the Coast Plain, and incorporated the Plain of Esdraelon only because it was enclosed by mountains and could be made part of their system, producing "the grain, the wine, and the oil" of Jezreel (Hos. 2:22). Even within their homeland the tribal territories often represent clearly defined agricultural regions, and some (e.g., Ephraim and Benjamin) have names which are clearly territorial rather than tribal.[9] On the well-watered dome of Ephraim the olive predominates over the other two, in the drier Judah, the vine, and in the downfaulted basins of Manasseh, wheat.[10]

It was the Israelite ideal that they should sit "every man under his vine and under his fig tree" (Mic. 4:4; Zech. 3:10), for then "you shall eat the fruit of the labor of your hands; you shall be happy, and it shall be well with you" (Ps. 128:2). Both vines and olives were symbols of richness and prosperity, Jeremiah speaking of a "a green olive tree, fair with goodly fruit" and also "a choice vine, wholly of pure seed" to describe Judah in the days of her greatness (Jer. 11:16; 2:21; cf. Ps. 128:3–4; Isa. 5:1–7; 27:2; Ezek. 19:10–14; Hos. 10:1; Matt. 21:33–41; John 15:1ff.). A good grain harvest also meant prosperity (Ps. 65:9–13; 72:16; cf. the New Testament use in Mark 4:2–20, 26–29; John 12:24; 1 Cor. 15:36–38).

Other summer fruits were the figs, whose early fruit was especially prized

XVIII. *Date Palm near Aqabah.* The date is near the limit of its cultivation in Palestine and belongs especially to the hot region of the lower Jordan valley and the Arabah, though some also grow on the Mediterranean coast. The date was especially valued for its high sugar content.

(Mic. 7:1; Hos. 9:10; Jer 24:2; Nah. 3:12), pomegranates (Deut. 8:8; 1 Sam. 14:2; Song of Sol. 4:3, 13; 6:7, 11; 8:2; Joel 1:12; Hag. 2:19), sycamore figs (Amos 7:14), pistachio nuts, and almonds (Gen. 43:11; Eccles. 12:5). The almond is the first fruit tree to blossom and is therefore in Hebrew *shaqed,* the "wakeful tree" (Jer. 1:11–12 has a play on words between *shaqed* and *shoqed,* "awake"). Besides these were the garden products, vegetables and spices, mentioned in Isaiah 1:8; 28:27, and Matthew 23:3.

Over against the agricultural economy, and to some extent intermingling with it, is pastoralism, which in Genesis is almost the only way of life mentioned. "The men are shepherds," said Joseph to Pharaoh (Gen. 46:32), and for them the keeping of flocks was more honorable than farming the land (Gen. 4:1–5). Their *miqneh,* their wealth, lay in their sheep, not "cattle" as English versions persistently but falsely translate it, and it was not until the Israelites took

9. Yohanan Aharoni, *The Land of the Bible,* trans. by A. F. Rainey (Philadelphia: Westminster Press, 1967), p. 193. Martin Noth, *The Old Testament World* (London: Adam & Charles Black, 1966), pp. 55–56.

10. This is discussed more fully in Denis Baly, *Geographical Companion to the Bible* (New York: McGraw-Hill, 1963), chap. 3.

over the Canaanite agricultural system that *miqneh* came to mean cows and oxen. Doubtless the people of the land were farmers, but the patriarchal stories have nothing to say about them.

The sheep were of the fat-tailed variety, providing milk, meat, and wool (Exod. 29:22), as well as the sheepskin coats so necessary to the shepherd for protection against the cold. Palestinian sheep are strong and can live outdoors throughout the year, but may die in large numbers if they are overdriven in the heat (Gen. 33:13), and this limits the mobility of the nomads that keep them. *Leben* (yogurt) made from the milk remains to this day an important part of the Bedouin diet, and the very poorest may have to make bread dipped in *leben* the whole of their meal. Naturally, the steppes are the sheep country *par excellence*, but sheep are kept also in almost every part of the hill country on both sides of the Jordan.

XIX. *Olive Grove in Ephraim.* The Cenomanian limestone of the Dome of Ephraim is particularly suited to the growing in olives and in Ephraim olives were the most important of the grain-wine-oil trinity.

Goats are often reared together with sheep, though they are able to range farther into the desert. A "flock of goats, moving down the slopes of Gilead" (Song of Sol. 6:5) is extremely destructive, and much of the tragic deforestation of the hillsides must be laid to their charge. They are kept for the same products as the sheep, but they have much less fat, and their hair is used for making those tents of Kedar, which are "dark but comely" (Song of Sol. 1:5).

The third of the animals of the pastoralist is the camel, which, though possibly domesticated early in the second millenium B.C., did not come into common use until the second half. These are really the only true desert animal which has been tamed, and are unable to live where something approaching desert conditions does not prevail. They quickly become ill in winter if the grass is too rich, and are therefore taken into the desert in this season, returning to the damper west only in the summer drought, being bred on the Trans-jordan plateau and brought into Cis-jordan for work in the summer harvest. By the time of the monarchy the camel had become the basic means of transport in the desert regions, though at an earlier date donkeys had been used wherever the wells had not been too far apart.

"The restive young camel interlacing her tracks" (Jer. 2:23) can cover as much as a hundred miles a day, and once she had been tamed sudden raids by the desert tribes upon the steppe became a real and constant danger (Job 1:13–17). The first of such attacks recorded in the Bible is that of the Midianites, who terrorized the Plain of Esdraelon when they came up "with their herds [*miqneh* here certainly means "camels" rather than than "cattle" as in RSV] and their tents, coming like locusts for multitude: both they and their camels could not be counted; so that they wasted the land as they came in" (Judg. 6:5).[11]

"Every shepherd is an abomination to the Egyptians" (Gen. 46:34), and all settled farmers, in fact, despise and distrust those who do not remain peaceably in one place, but are forever restlessly on the move. It was surely in a deprecatory sense that Amos described himself as "a herdsman and a dresser of sycamore trees" (Amos 7:14), for sycamore trees grow nowhere near his home at Tekoa on the borders of Jeshimon. Both phrases, therefore, meant that he was a wanderer. Though the kings of Egypt and Mesopotamia were described as the shepherds of their people, the biblical metaphor of the shepherd as a symbol of God's care for his people is a late one, and found only rarely before the time of Jeremiah (1 Kings 22:17; Pss. 23; 74:1; 79:13; 80:1; Isa. 40:11; Jer. 13:17; 23:1; 25:36; 31:10; 50:19; Ezek. 34:1–31; Hos. 13:5–8; Zech. 10:3; 13:7). It is, however, very common in the Gospels (Matt. 9:36; 10:6; 12:11; 15:24; 25:32; Mark 6:34; 14:27; Luke 12:32; 15:3–7; John 10:1–18; 1 Pet. 2:25).

Nevertheless, it was from the nomadic herdsmen that the Israelites learned to celebrate the Passover. When Moses told Pharaoh that they would go "with our flocks, and herds, for we must hold a feast to the Lord" (Exod. 10:9), the indication is that it was a feast already regularly celebrated by the shepherds, probably an animal sacrifice designed

to protect the flocks, and especially the newly born lambs, as the tribes began their arduous and sometimes dangerous trek to summer pastures.[12] It was taken over by the Hebrews in their desert wanderings and given a new interpretation in the light of the Exodus experience.

The animals of the settled people were the ass, the mule, the ox, and the horse. Horses were essentially animals of war, "more fierce than the evening wolves" (Hab. 1:8) in the eyes of the Israelites, whose hilly country was little suited to chariot fighting. Solomon seems to have traded in horses from Cilicia and Cappadocia and chariots from Egypt (1 Kings 10:28–29), though the text is unfortunately far from clear. The others were work animals, but the most prized of the three was the ox, which the farmer used for plowing the heavy soil, and which also fertilized the fields:

Where there are no oxen the barn is empty,
but the strength of a great ox ensures rich crops.

[Prov. 14:4, NEB]

The Palestinian farmer tended to see the ox as the symbol of meaningful existence, without which he feared that his life would collapse around him, for then he could not perform his essential function of bringing food out of the earth. For this reason, therefore, it became for him his "god," the mainstay of his world. It is true that the "golden calves" which Jeroboam I set up at Bethel and Dan (1 Kings 12:28–29) were intended not to represent God himself but to serve as his throne, but for all that Jeroboam came dangerously close to asserting the fundamental truth of the Canaanite agricultural system and rejecting the

---

11. It is perhaps worth noting that the camel is by far the largest animal in the country and very ungainly, so that it is quite absurd to explain away the picture of the camel trying to go through the eye of the needle (Mark 10:25), as many commentaries do. Jesus used exactly the same ridiculous contrast when he said the Pharisees were "straining out a gnat and swallowing a camel" (Matt. 23:24).

12. Martin Noth, *Exodus,* trans. by J. S. Bowden (Philadelphia: Westminster Press, 1962), pp. 88–92.

Exodus experience. With good reason the writer recorded that "this thing became a sin."

The life of the Palestinian farmer was not an easy one, and it is well described in Genesis 3:17–19:

Cursed is the ground because of you;
    in toil shall you eat of it all the days of
      your life;
thorns and thistles it shall bring forth to
      you;
    and you shall eat the plants of the field.
In the sweat of your face
    you shall eat bread.
till you return to the ground,
    for out of it you were taken:
you are dust
    and to dust you shall return.

The same book gives another picture of the hard life of the shepherd: "By day the heat consumed me, and the cold by night, and my sleep fled from my eyes" (Gen. 31:40). Both in the agricultural areas and in the steppe the poor were driven to desperate straits (Job 24:4–12). On the one hand there was the ever present threat of famine brought about by lack of rain or by a military invasion (2 Kings 6:24–29; Jer. 14:2–6), destruction by hail (Ps. 78:47), by locusts (Amos 7:1; Joel 1:2–2:10), or by blasting and mildew (Hag. 2:17). On the other there was the fear of desert raiding or destruction by storm (Job 1:13–19), when a man might cry out, "Suddenly my tents are destroyed, my curtains in a moment!" (Jer. 4:20). Against these things there was no protection, and over the head of the farmer hung the everlasting fear that he might build houses but not dwell in them, and plant vineyards but not drink the wine (Amos 5:11; Mic. 6:15; Hag. 1:6, 9).

CHAPTER 8

Straight Ways and Cities

He led them by a straight way,
till they reached a city to dwell in.
Let them thank the Lord for his steadfast love,
for his wonderful works to the sons of men.
PSALM 107:7–8

Palestinian farmers have always lived in villages rather than in isolated farms, because the houses must congregate where there is water, and for defense. East of the Jordan the possibility of settlement is determined also by the two areas of relatively level land, divided by the rugged westward-facing scarp. In the Ghor at the foot of the scarp, a chain of small settlements follows the spring line. These seem to have been more numerous in biblical times than now and perhaps even more numerous at an earlier date. The true area of settlement, however, is on the plateau. First come the fortresses along the plateau edge, positions of amazing strength, carved out by the deep wadis and left magnificently aloof; Bozrah and Tophel in Edom, Kir-hareseth in Moab, with its medieval castle, the Turkish capital of as-Salt, the Saracen castle at

Ajlun, all stand upon this line.

Behind these fortresses, and protected by them, are the scattered villages of the farmer, obtaining their water from springs or wells. More common in the wetter north, they thin out toward the south until finally beyond Kir-Hareseth they form but a single line with the castles. Beyond the present Hejaz Railway is the desert, but farther east still, at the foot of the basalt barrier, there are wells, and one important oasis, al-Azraq, at the head of the Wadi Sirhan.

In Cis-jordan such a schematic picture is not possible, but if a line is drawn from Beth-shan to a point a little east of Hebron and then in a curve through Beersheba to Gaza, the area of permanent settlement will be found to lie west and north of it. Since the Plain of Sharon was largely uninhabited and the plain south of that in the hands

91

38   **TRANS-JORDAN SETTLEMENTS**

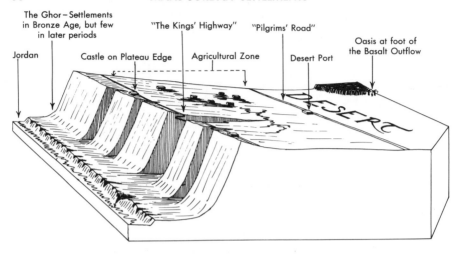

The Ghor – Settlements
in Bronze Age, but few
in later periods   "The Kings' Highway"   "Pilgrims' Road"

                                                                        Oasis at foot of
                                                                        the Basalt Outflow

Jordan   Castle on Plateau Edge   Agricultural Zone   Desert Port

DESERT

XX. "*A Lodging Place of Wayfaring Men.*"   The fortified "palace" or possibly caravanserai
of Qasr Kharaneh belongs to the 'Ummayad period of the 8th century A.D. and stands on the
desert track eastward from Rabbah (Amman) to al-Azraq. Strong rulers in the Palestine area
have always sought to control the surrounding desert and protect the merchant caravans.

of the Philistines, it will be seen that the area of effective Israelite occupation formed an inverted triangle with its base along the scarp dividing Upper from Lower Galilee and its apex at Beersheba. It extended, certainly, across the Jordan into Gilead, though the very limited mention in the Bible of places in Gilead suggests that this was a marginal area for Israelite settlement. That part of Palestine which the ancient Israelites could really call their own was extremely small.

Within this triangle there is today an interesting modification of the village distribution as one proceeds from south to north. In the south, where there is little water, Beersheba stands alone with almost no permanent settlements nearby. In the highland region around Hebron there are several large villages, but almost no small ones. Here there are more springs, but they are far apart, and cultivation is mixed with pastoral farming. Farmers, therefore, group themselves in large villages where there is water, and go out from this centralized settlement with their flocks. "Give me a present," said Achsah to Caleb; "since you have set me in the land of the Negeb, give me also springs of water" (Josh. 15:13–19; Judg. 1:11–15), for here near Debir water still is scarce.

Farther north between Jerusalem and Nablus rainfall becomes more assured and cultivation more general, and the pattern is reversed: there are many small villages scattered over the countryside, but few large ones. In the hills north of Nablus, however, the more plentiful rain permits both the scattering of small villages over the whole area and also the growth of several larger settlements.

Nevertheless, this recent distribution, though instructive, must be treated with the greatest possible caution when one looks back into the past, for it is evident that the pattern of settlement has varied throughout the centuries. This has been particularly true of the marginal areas, where the prolonged researches of Nelson Glueck have shown that both in the Negeb of Cis-jordan and in Moab and Edom on the eastern plateau the tide of settlement has ebbed and flowed across a very wide area. In four periods of ancient history the Negeb and parts of Sinai have been settled: Chalcolithic (3500–2900), Middle Bronze I, believed by most to have been the age of the Patriarchs (twenty-first–nineteenth centuries B.C.),[1] the Israelite monarchy, notably the tenth and ninth centuries B.C., and most important of all, the Nabatean-Roman-Byzantine period from the third century B.C. to the seventh century A.D.[2] The last three periods seem to be paralleled in Moab and Edom, though there we must certainly recognize a line of villages, lasting for at least 500 years, from 7000 to 6500 B.C.[3] Between these sedentary periods the land passed into the hands of the pastoral nomads. The extension of settlement into these marginal areas and its subsequent collapse some centuries later appear to be the result primarily of altered political and social conditions, but the possibility cannot be ruled out that fluctuations in the climate may perhaps have been a contributory cause.

Unquestionably in the better-watered regions the causes of change in the pattern of occupation are political and social, frequently occasioned by military conquest. Before the time of the Judges agriculture in Cis-jordan was limited by

1. This is, however, disputed by Yohanan Aharoni, "The Negeb," *Archaeology and Old Testament Study*, ed. D. Winton Thomas (Oxford: Clarendon Press, 1967), pp. 385–404.
2. Nelson Glueck, "The Negeb," *BA*, XXII (1959), 4, 82–97.
3. Diana Kirkbride, "Beidha 1965: An Interim Report," *PEQ*, XCIX (1967), 5–13.

the forests and the marshes, and confined, therefore, to the southern Coast Plain and the foothills, avoiding the forests and marshes of Sharon, the forests of Ephraim and Judah, and the swampy lowland of Esdraelon. The broken hill country all around Shechem and Lower Galilee had been brought under the plow and settlement extended also up over the Saddle of Benjamin between Judah and Ephraim, Jerusalem being apparently the chief town of this region.[4] For the eastern plateau we have much less evidence, but we should surely not be far wrong if we assume that the same conditions applied. Villages followed the spring line at the foot of the scarp and the grasslands of the plateau, but probably avoided the forests of Gilead. In Edom the main line of villages is just *below* the plateau edge, where the springs break out and where the forest was less thick. North of the Yarmuq, in southern Bashan, the city lists of Thutmose III and the Amarna correspondence, which must surely reflect the efforts of the pharaohs to maintain Egyptian control over the populated areas, indicate that settlement here extended an arm across the plateau to the foot of the Jabal Druze.[5]

The Israelite occupation led to the clearing of the forests and the establishment of agriculture on the hill country of Ephraim and Judah[6] and to a more moderate extent in Gilead. With the establishment of the Davidic monarchy this process was stimulated by the more effective political control and the coming into common use of iron tools. Extensive terracing developed in this period. Thereafter for many centuries the changes in the pattern were mainly the result of the grim desolation of war:

Your country lies desolate,
  your cities are burned with fire;
in your very presence aliens devour your
  land;
  it is desolate, as overthrown by aliens.
And the daughter of Zion is left
  like a booth in a vineyard,
like a lodge in a cucumber field,
  like a besieged city.

[Isaiah 1:7–8]

The conquest of the northern kingdom by the Assyrians in 722 B.C. and the ruthless exchange of populations left few there who "knew the *mishpat* of the god of the land," i.e., the accepted customs of the country, and the beasts of the forest moved in upon the once cultivated land (2 Kings 17:24–26). Similar devastation must have resulted from the Babylonian conquest of Judah. What happened after the Exile is far from clear, for we still know so little about the Persian period. The return of the exiles certainly must have increased the population in that small area of the hill country between Bethel and Hebron, and one would imagine that the Persian peace would bring wealth and a growth of population throughout the country. Nevertheless, Jerusalem remained much smaller than it had been in the latter days of the monarchy, and the Western Hill was not occupied again until the Hellenistic period, in the second century B.C. This new era begat a population explosion. We have already seen that settlement once more extended far into the Negeb, and great cities began for the first time to be built in Palestine.

4. Albrecht Alt, *Essays on Old Testament History and Religion*, trans. by R. A. Wilson (Oxford: Basil Blackwell, 1966), pp. 135–69. Manfred Weippert, *The Settlement of the Israelite Tribes in Palestine* (Naperville, Ill.: Alec R. Allenson., 1971).

5. Yohanan Aharoni and Michael Avi-Yonah, *The Macmillan Bible Atlas* (New York: Macmillan, 1968), maps 34 and 38.

6. B. S. J. Isserlin, "Israelite and Pre-Israelite Place-names in Palestine: A Historical and Geographical Sketch," *PEQ*, LXXIX (1957), 133–44.

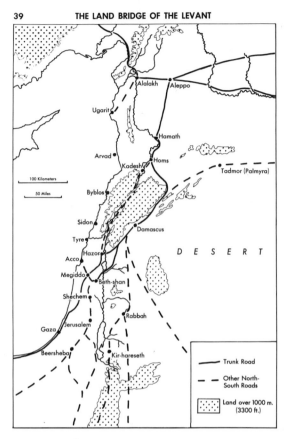

39   THE LAND BRIDGE OF THE LEVANT

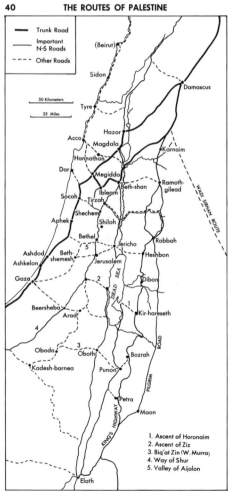

40   THE ROUTES OF PALESTINE

Interrelated with the settlements were the roads, which were no less conditioned by the availability of water and the nature of the landscape. Naturally, the primary purpose of any road is to enable people to move as directly as possible from one place to another, but travelers need water both for themselves and for their animals, and so the roads must go where the springs and wells are to be found. Secondly, all ancient roads were no more than what we today would call tracks, always rough, often rocky, and muddy or dusty according to the season. In an admittedly satirical letter, an Egyptian official about the end of the thirteenth century B.C. described the pass of Megiddo as "filled with boulders and pebbles, without a toe hold for passing by, overgrown with reeds, thorns, brambles, and 'wolf's-paw.' The ravine is on one side of thee, and the mountain rises on the other. . . . The horse is played out by the time thou findest a night-quarters. Thou seest the taste of pain!"[7] Where the more important roads descended to cross the wadis, which in a wet winter might make them impassable for weeks on end, some kind of causeway might very well be built to maintain the traffic, and the more powerful rulers would make use of forced labor to clear the major roads of boulders and make them serviceable for chariots and the swift movement of the royal couriers:

Pass through the gates.
Make a way for the people.
Bank up, bank up the highway,
    clear it of stones.
            [Isa. 62:10, JB][8]

Such a "highway" was called a *mesillah,* and was often marked out with waymarks and guideposts that men and women might consider well the highway, the road by which they went (Jer. 31:21). The clearing of the tracks and the maintenance of good communication were a necessity for efficient administration, the collection of taxes, continuance of trade, and the regular attendance at the national festivals, which was as essential to the coherence of society as it was a religious duty. Three times a year, when all was well, groups of pilgrims came from every village along "the highways of Zion" (Ps. 84:5), but when the destruction of the Temple made this no longer possible, it was said that "the roads to Zion mourn, for

none come to the appointed feasts" (Lam. 1:4). In times of national emergency and weakness, when "the envoys of peace weep bitterly, the highways lie waste, the wayfaring man ceases" (Isa. 33:7–8). The roads then became only too easily the haunt of brigands, and "travelers kept to the byways" (Judg. 5:6).

The major highways, or *mesilloth,* ran from north to south of the country, following the main lines of relief. Easily preeminent was the *Trunk Road,* connecting Egypt with the northern Levant, and from there with either Anatolia or Mesopotamia. Called by Isaiah "the way of the sea" (Isa. 9:1), and for this reason known by many scholars as Via Maris, it is the great artery, as it were, of the Levant. As we have seen (page 11), all the major roads of the northern steppeland were directed toward Damascus, and the Trunk Road came this way from Aleppo and Hamath the Great. There is some dispute as to which of two possible routes most of the traffic followed south of Damascus. One curved around the foot of Mount Hermon, crossing the Jordan just south of Lake Huleh and north of the basalt dam at the Bridge of Jacob's Daughters, and turning southward down the Rift at Hazor. It left the Lake of Galilee at Magdala (Migdal), climbed up on to the basalt plateau near the Horns of Hattin, and struck southwestward to Megiddo. This may well have been the more important road in at least certain periods of Old Testament history, for Hazor was a great city throughout the first three-quarters of the second millennium B.C.[9] "Formerly the head of all those kingdoms" (Josh. 11:10), its importance is attested by the Mari documents, and then after some three cen-

---

7. James Pritchard, *ANET,* pp. 477–78.
8. "Bank up" here means to build up banks alongside by clearing the road of stones, rather than to build up the road itself.

9. Y. Yadin, "Excavations at Hazor, 1958: Preliminary Communiqué," *IEJ,* 9 (1959), 74–78.

turies of eclipse it was refortified by Solomon and again by Ahab. The other road came south of the Lake of Galilee by way of the Yarmuq Valley to Beth-shan and then turned up the Valley of Jezreel to Megiddo. Some scholars to-day believe that this was actually the major route.

The road then crossed Carmel by the pass of Megiddo and pursued a narrow course between the foothills and the marshes of Sharon to Aphek. Once south of the Yarkon, it was free to swing closer to the coast, which it followed through Ashdod, Ashkelon, and Gaza, "the Way of the land of the Philistines" (Exod. 13:17), all the way to Egypt. "Gaza stands upon the verge of the Desert, and bears towards it the same kind of relation as a seaport bears to the sea. It is there that you *charter* your camels ('the ships of the Desert') and lay in stores for the voyage.[10] Here it was that men loaded "their riches on the backs of asses, and their treasures on the humps of camels" to take them to "a people that cannot profit them" (Isa. 30:6).

Second in importance was the *King's Highway,* which diverged from the Trunk Road at Damascus and continued due southward through Karnaim and along the edge of the Trans-jordan plateau, from one fortress to another, laboriously crossing the difficult canyons, past Petra and through the Wadi Ytem to the Red Sea. In the sandy waste of the Wadi Hasma the road to far distant Sheba diverged and led off into Arabia through Wadi Ram. These two roads were the most consistently important of the international routes passing through Palestine, but four other north–south roads were also much used:

1. *The Pilgrim Road*, so called be-

cause until the days of modern transport it was followed by the enormous cara-vans of Muslim pilgrims, traveling from Damascus to Mecca. It follows the level land southward from Damascus to Edrei just east of the great Trans-jordan wadis but west of the desert, passing through Ramoth-gilead, Rabboth Ammon, and Maon, and coalescing with the King's Highway just a little father south. It has the advantage of being generally very level, but in the south water becomes scarce and it is everywhere more open to Bedouin raids. When the government was strong enough to keep order in the steppeland, however, this road was

XXI. *Roman Milestones of the King's Highway.* These are in the Wadi Mojjib, the Arnon valley of the Old Testament.

10. A. W. Kinglake, *Eothen,* ed. by R. W. Jepson (London: Longmans, Green, 1935), p. 146.

likely to be greatly used by merchants.

2. *The Rift Valley Road*. Often a double road, using the springs on each side of the Rift, this is interrupted both by the cliffs of the Dead Sea and by the basalt dam north of the Lake of Galilee. Despite the arid nature of the country, the Arabah section was at times much in use for communication with the Red Sea, because water is available at reasonably frequent points, and also, of course, because of the copper mines (Deut. 8:9). On the west side it went through Oboth as far north as Engedi and on the east through Punon as far as the Wadi Kerak, "the descent of Horonaim" (Jer. 48:5; see Isa. 15:5). North of the Dead Sea both roads were resumed as far as the Lake of Galilee, but thereafter there was only one road, on the west, which led over the basalt dam through Hazor and along the foot of the Galilee Highlands but above the Huleh marshes to Abel-beth-maacah. Then it climbed up into the Plain of Ijon and passed through the Valley of Lebanon, swinging to the eastern side through Baalgad (Josh. 11:17; 12:7; 13:5), Baalbek, Lebo-hamath (i.e., probably "the entrance of Hamath" in RSV—Num. 34:8; Judg. 3:3; 1 Kings 8:65; 2 Kings 14:25), Riblah (Num. 34:11; 2 Kings 23:33; 25:6, 21; Jer. 39:5, 6; 52:9, 10, 26, 27), and Kadesh, scene of the famous victory of Rameses II in 1286 B.C. This was by no means an easy road in its southern section, because of the difficulty of the terrain, but it was used at times by the great invading armies, possibly because it provided a much better supply of food for men and animals than the Trunk Road to the east, and possibly also because it bypassed Damascus.

3. *The Water-parting Road* on the Western Highlands. Following the relatively level land between the steep valleys on either side, this went through,

or near, Hebron, Bethlehem, Jerusalem, Gibeah of Saul, Ramah, Mizpah, Shiloh, Lebonah, and Shechem, many of these standing slightly to one side, where the valleys had carved out better-defended sites. South of Hebron it continued through Beersheba and then southwestward to Egypt by "the Way to Shur" (Gen. 16:7). North of Shechem, which lies at the junction of two chalk valleys, the main road continued through Dothan and the Ascent of Gur (2 Kings 9:27) to enter the Plain of Esdraelon at Ibleam, but a more easterly branch ran through Tirzah toward Beth-shan.

4. *The Coast Road*. This was of only local importance north of Joppa, where the Trunk Road turned inland to Aphek, and in Sharon it could probably have been used only in summer, since the winter storms bring the sea right up to the cliffs.[11] Beneath the precipices of Carmel stood the little port of Dor, well defended (Judg. 1:27) but so isolated that it could not easily develop. It became Israelite under the United Monarchy (1 Kings 4:11). At Acco the Coast Road became again an important international route to Tyre, Sidon, Byblos, and the island of Arvad (Ezek. 27:8, 11). This was often a road of exceptional difficulty because of the high cliffs, and communication was really easier here by sea than by land. The satirical Egyptian official already mentioned was evidently well acquainted with it, for he says, "Let me tell thee of another strange city, named Byblos. . . . Once again—[thou] hast not trodden it. Pray instruct me about Beirut, about Sidon and Sarepta. Where is the stream of the Litani? What is Uzu like? They say another town is in the sea, named Tyre-the-Port. Water is taken [to] it

---

11. Yehuda Karmon, "Geographical Influences on the Historical Routes in the Sharon Plain," *PEQ*, XCIII (1961), 48.

by the boats, and it is richer in fish than the sands."[12]

Of the transverse roads from west to east three were of particular importance:

1. The lowland road following the foot of Carmel and Gilboa from Acco, past Harosheth of the Gentiles, Jokneam, Megiddo, Taanach, Ibleam, and Jezreel to Beth-shan and thence up toward Ramoth Gilead on the plateau.

2. From Aijalon up the Ascent of Beth-horon, over the Saddle of Benjamin, down to Jericho to cross the Jordan near Gilgal and climbing up on the plateau by way of Beth-jeshimoth to Heshbon.

12. Pritchard, *ANET*, p. 477.

3. From Gaza southeastward past Oboda (Avdat or Abda) down the Biq'at Zin (Wadi Murra) into the Arabah, across to Punon and up the Punon Embayment to Bozrah. Known to the Arabs as Darb as-Sultan (King's Highway), it has a "whole series of stone built villages or caravanserais along it,"[13] dating back to 3500 B.C. In the time of the Ottoman Empire a journey by camel from Gaza to Ma'an (ancient Maon) took five days.

Other transverse roads led from

13. Nelson Glueck, "The Negev," *BA*, XXII (1959), 86. Also "Archaeological Exploration of the Negev," *BASOR*, 159 (1960), 3–14.

XXII. *The Way to Edom.* The Wadi leading down to the Dead Sea from Kh. Ghazza in southeastern Judah. Despite the difficulty of the terrain this wadi carried an important road from Arad to the southern end of the Dead Sea. In the bottom of the wadi, slightly to the left of the center of the picture, may be seen the Roman fortress of Metzad Zohar.

Lachish to Hebron and down to Engedi by the Ascent of Ziz (2 Chron. 20:16), and from Beth-shemesh to Jerusalem, the road followed by the lowing cattle drawing the Ark (I Sam. 6:7–16) and perhaps by Amaziah when he went down to do battle with the king of Israel (2 Kings 14:11). From Hebron another road led southwestward by way of Arad to the southern end of the Dead Sea. There was also an easy route from near Socoh in Sharon to Shechem, by way of the Wadi Zeimar, passing by the foot of the hill on which Samaria stands. This is the modern road from Tulkarm to Nablus. In Galilee the most important west–east road, used also by international caravans, was the one known more recently as the Darb al-Hawarnah, from Acco by way of the downfaulted Sahl Battauf, Hannathon, and the valley of Jabneel to the southern end of the Lake of Galilee, where it joined the eastern branch of the Trunk Road.[14]

14. For those interested, the ancient road system is discussed in more detail in Yohanan Aharoni, *The Land of the Bible*, trans. by A. F. Rainey (Philadelphia: Westminster Press, 1967), pp. 39–57. Also Martin Noth, *The Old Testament World*, trans. by Victor L. Gruhn (London: Adam & Charles Black, 1966), pp. 84–93.

CHAPTER **9**

The Wilderness and the Woods

I will make with them a covenant of peace and banish wild beasts from the land, so that they may dwell securely in the wilderness and sleep in the woods.

EZEKIEL 34:25

"A king is an advantage to a land with cultivated fields," said Qoheleth (Eccles. 5:9),[1] but beyond the fields are other regions where the power of the strong ruler who protects the farmer is fiercely resented. Indeed, in the Atlas countries of North Africa its is customary to divide the land into *blad al-makhzan*,[2] the land of the storehouse or treasury, where people dutifully pay their taxes, and *blad as-Sibā'*, the land of the wild beasts and the wandering rebellious tribes—i.e., into the Land of Obedience and the Ferocious Land. This Ferocious Land would in Palestine comprise all the land that had not been settled and brought under the plow, especially the deserts and the forests, whether these

were on the mountains or in the Sharon plain.

To indicate "desert" one word prevails above all others in the Old Testament: *midbar,* which occurs 266 times. Others are *'arabah,* used 44 times in a regional sense for the southern Rift Valley, and more generally as "desert," 14 times; *horbah,* a dry, desolate, ruined place, 39 times; *tsiyyah,* land of drought, 18 times; *jeshimon,* desolation, 10 times; and *tohu,* the chaotic void, twice (Job 12:24; Ps. 107:40). These words are used almost exclusively as poetic parallels for *midbar,* and convey the impression that for the ancient Israelite the basic meaning of "desert" was "that which is beyond," "that which is dry," and "that which is desolate and deserted."

Who has cleft a channel for the waterflood,
　or a path for the thunderbolt;

---

1. If this is in fact the correct translation. The passage is much disputed.
2. It is from *makhzan* that we get our English word "magazine."

to cause it to rain on a land where no
   man is,
   on the *midbar,* wherein there is no man?
                               [Job 38:25–26]

Western scholars have often tended
to idealize the desert as a place of medi-
tation and a source of spiritual refreshment, and even to claim with Renan
that "le désert est monothéiste." This
belief has, it is true, some scriptural
foundation in the accounts of Jesus'
being "led by the Spirit into the wilderness to be tempted" (Matt. 4:1; Mark
1:12–13; Luke 4:1–13) and Paul's state-
ment that after his conversion he did not
go up to those who were apostles before
him, but went away into Arabia (Gal.
1:17). To idealize the desert, however,
is to misinterpret these passages, under
the influence, perhaps, of the puri-
tanical revulsion of the Desert Fathers
against the luxury and corruption of
city life. But this revulsion belongs to
the postbiblical period, and even the
Qumran community does not really fall
into this category. In more recent days
there has been a romantic identification
with desert as a place where a pure and
honest life is still possible, a nostalgia
characteristic of many of the great
Arabian explorers, but not, it must be
insisted, of the prophets.[3]

An affection for the desert is nowhere
to be found in the Bible. There the
midbar is always "the great and terrible
wilderness, with its fiery serpents and
scorpions and thirsty land where there
is no water" (Deut. 8:15; also 1:19),
and still in the New Testament it has
the same connotation, as when the
Epistle to the Hebrews speaks of the

faithful as men who "went about in
skins of sheep and goats, destitute, ill-
treated, afflicted—of whom the world
was not worthy—wandering over deserts
and mountains and in dens and caves
of the earth" (Heb. 11:37–38). It was
fitting that Jesus should meet Satan in
the wilderness, for it was the devils'
home,

            the haunt of jackals,
      an abode for ostriches,
[There] wild beasts shall meet with hyenas,
      the satyr shall cry to his fellow;
yea, there shall the night hag alight,
      and find for herself a resting place.
                               [Isa. 34:13–14]

We shall not understand the biblical
concept of the *midbar,* or the New
Testament *eremos* and *eremia,* unless we
grasp that it was thought of only with
fear, as a perfectly horrible place. "It
comes from the *midbar,*" said Isaiah,
"from a terrible land" (Isa. 21:1).

This *midbar* of which the Old Testament speaks is nowhere the great *erg,*
or sand desert, that we associate with
the Sahara or the interior of Arabia.
Erg was quite outside Israelite experience, for the Negeb and Sinai contain
only small patches of sand, and on the
eastern plateau patches hardly occur at
all. It is true that Dumah on the edge
of the great sand dunes of the Nafud,
and Tema, not far from its southwestern
corner, on the incense trade route, are
both mentioned in Isaiah 21:11–15 as
places to which men flee "from the
drawn sword, from the bent bow, and
from the grievousness of war,"[4] but to
the speaker himself, and certainly to all
his countrymen, these places would have
been known only by hearsay, from
travelers' tales and accounts of desert
fighting.

---

3. "I believed that . . . in those empty
wastes I could find the peace that comes
with solitude, and, among the Bedu, com-
radeship in a hostile world." Wilfred
Thesiger, *Arabian Sands* (New York:
Longmans, 1959), p. 5.

4. *Dumah* is read by some scholars as
Edom, parallel to Seir in the next line,
and this seems very possible.

The *midbar* is rather all that increasingly barren area which extends round Palestine on the south and east, and where there is, for all normal purposes, insufficient precipitation for rain-fed farming. Shemaryahu Talmon[5] has suggested the word "drift" as a suitable translation, in order to preserve a sense of the place where men drive out their sheep and goats to pasture if there has been enough rain ("the pastures of the *midbar*" in Joel 1:20; 2:22), but though the *midbar* certainly included this rough pastureland, it stretched well beyond it. "Wasteland" would be a better word, and better still the traditional translation of "wilderness," for "wilderness" carries with it two concepts which must always be borne in mind; that of *wildness* and that of the place where man is *bewildered*, confused, disoriented.

The *midbar* of Zin is in the Negeb, the *midbar* of Paran in northern Sinai, the *midbar* of Sin in southern Sinai, and the *midbar* of Shur close to where the Suez Canal is now (Exod. 15:22). In 1 Samuel 23:15, 24 the *midbar* of Ziph and Maon, on the parched slopes of the Rift Valley east of these villages, is clearly distinguished from the Jeshimon to the north of it. Here Jeshimon is a regional term, denoting the district east of Hebron, Bethlehem, and Jerusalem, between the cultivated land and the Dead Sea. But the Jeshimon is also *midbar* and is clearly described as such in 2 Samuel 15:23, where David is described as going eastward from Jerusalem into the *midbar*. In poetry the words are used as parallel to each other; "He found him in the land of the *midbar*, and in the howling waste of the *jeshimon*" (Deut.

5. Shemaryahu Talmon, "The 'Desert Motif' in the Bible and Qumran Literature," in *Biblical Motifs: Origins and Transformations*, ed. by Alexander Altmann (Cambridge, Mass.: Harvard University Press, 1966), pp. 31–63.

32:10); and "How often they rebelled against him in the *midbar*, and grieved in the *jeshimon*" (Ps. 78:40; cf. 106:14); and again, "I will make a road in the *midbar*, and rivers in the *jeshimon*" (Isa. 43:19, 20).

Also included in the *midbar* is all the poor steppeland, grading off into semi-desert, which on the eastern plateau presses in upon the cultivated land. The desolate area round the oasis of Damascus is called *midbar*, and in 1 Kings 19:15 Elijah is told to go to the *midbar* of Damascus, which apparently means that he is to keep clear of the highways and villages, where he might be subject to arrest. The river Arnon is described as "in the *midbar*" in Numbers 21:13, 18, and all the journey of the Israelites round the territory of Moab in the time of the Exodus was understood as part of their wanderings in the *midbar*. Consequently, very much of what was known as the *mishor*, or "tableland," east of the Jordan was in Israelite eyes *midbar*. Indeed, in Deuteronomy 4:43 Bezer, a city of refuge for the people of Reuben, is described as "in the *midbar*, on the *mishor*." Bezer is probably Umm al-'Amad, about halfway between Amman and Madeba, and still within the cultivable land, though near the edge of it. The other two cities of refuge east of the Jordan, Golan (Sahm al-Jaulan), just north of the Yarmuq gorge, and Ramoth Gilead (Tell Ramith), south of the Yarmuq, are similarly marginal towns, and both were probably thought of as being also on the edge of the *midbar*. The three cities west of the Jordan are different, for they are all famous ancient sanctuaries: Kedesh Naphtali (Tell Qades), Shechem, and Hebron. Thus, in the Land of Obedience a man who accidentally killed another was bidden to flee from "the avenger of blood," to some sacred place, where his person would be sacrosanct, but on the eastern plateau to take refuge on the borders of the Ferocious Land.

On the level Tableland the cultivated land ebbs and flows from year to year. In a good year the rain spreads far and wide, and there is standing water even beyond the great basalt barrier, but in a bad year, perhaps even the next year, the grain well to the west withers on the stem. People also move backward and forward. When there is good grass, and perhaps even more important, when there is a strong government, the villagers take their flocks far into the *midbar,* but when security is poor and drought presses, the nomads sweep in upon the farmers' fields. Thirty-five years ago houses in Madeba were still fortified against the Bedouin, and people vividly remembered their raids. There is therefore a wide zone of movement between the village territory to the west and the more brutal and desolate Ardh as-Suwan, the flint-covered plateau of what is now eastern Jordan. Across this zone runs the Pilgrim Road, a broad routeway of the wilderness spreading out over the level land, as much as 100 yards wide in places, one of those roads which Arab poets liken to "striped cloth." This is the zone of shepherds and merchants. In the south the plateau breaks away into the dramatic, colorful wasteland of Wadi Hasma and Wadi Ram, the majestic gateway for the incense route to southern Arabia. Here the watchmen of Edom, standing on the plateau edge at Ras an-Naqb, would have seen each year the caravan approaching,

> coming up from the *midbar,*
> like a column of smoke,
> perfumed with myrrh and frankincense,
> and all the fragrant powders of the
>   merchant.
>
> [Song of Sol. 3:6]

More rolling country is found in the *midbar* of Zin, where the wadis are shallow and cultivation in them often possible. As we have seen, it was inhabited by setled farmers at four times in its history, but during the long final period there were times of regression and return. Oboda and Nessana seem to have been built by the Nabateans in the third century B.C., but then to have collapsed before nomadic attacks about A.D. 126, and they were not rebuilt for at least a couple of centuries.[6] One undoubted reason for extending settlement into this part of the *midbar* was to bring under control the trade routes which have already been described. The rocky precipices on either side of the Rift are repellent indeed, though the exigencies of international trade demanded that they be climbed. They provide neither fields for the farmer nor pasture for the shepherd. Leopards are still known among the wild sandstone gorges of the eastern plateau, and even on the west bank of the Dead Sea one was killed only a few years ago. At the foot of these cliffs were the copper mines, extending much farther north on the eastern scarp, though we now know that those at Wadi Manei'yeh (Timna) on the western side are certainly late Bronze rather than early Iron Age, and so cannot be King Solomon's mines.[7]

East of the southern Arabah are the mountains of Midian, and in the south of Sinai the granite spreads out in a great tumbled sea of forbidding rock, rising to its greatest height in Jabal Katarina (8,651 feet, 2,637 m.). The southern route from Elath through these mountains past Jabal Katarina and the nearby Jabal Musa to Wadi Feiran has often

6. A Negev, "The Date of the Petra-Gaza Road," *PEQ,* XCVIII (1966), 89–98.

7. "Notes and Views" in *PEQ,* XCVIII (1966), 6–7; CI (1969), 57–59, contributed by Beno Rothenberg.

been identified with the route of Exodus, but recent researches have shown that although it was penetrated slowly, and considerably used, in the Chalcolithic period, it was apparently not used thereafter until the days of the Nabateans.[8] This seems to be a strong argument against the traditional identification of Jabal Musa with the "Mount Sinai" of the Bible, and we must therefore now look for this "Sinai" somewhere in the north of the peninsula or the Negeb, or possibly, as has sometimes been suggested, at Jabal Harab in the Madyan region of northwestern Arabia.

We now come to the question of what all this varied *midbar* meant to the people of ancient Israel. First, we should notice that the word is not used exclusively for the kind of drought-stricken and semidesert land that we have been examining so far. The "thorns and briars of the *midbar*" with which Gideon taught such a painful lesson to the men of Succoth (Judg. 8:7, 16) were evidently something far more serious than ordinary desert vegetation, and the story suggests that he drove them out into the cruel and tangled *maquis,* or the jungle of the Zor. Indeed, *midbar* could be extended in Israelite thinking into the *ya'ar,* which, though normally translated "forest," could also mean the thorny thickets and scrubland so characteristic of much of the Mediterranean coastlands.

Ya'ar is another word which poses the translator with a difficulty. There is no doubt that it is used for forests proper, such as the forests of the Lebanon (1 Kings 7:2; 10:17, 21; 2 Chron. 9:16, 20; Isa. 37:24; 44:14, 23; Zech. 11:2), but this is not necessarily the meaning everywhere. In one place

8. Beno Rothenberg, "An Archaeological Survey of South Sinai: First Season 1967/1968, Preliminary Report," *PEQ,* CII (1970), 18–19.

Ezekiel speaks of "the *ya'ar* of the Negeb" (Ezek. 20:46; Heb. 21:2), which cannot possibly mean "forest" in our sense of the word, though from the next verse he clearly envisages there being something in it to catch fire. The New English Bible translates *ya'ar* here as "the rough country of the Negeb," and this is probably correct, for the parallel word in Arabic, *wa'ar,* means rough and rugged ground, difficult of access, such as the basalt of Transjordan, but also the shrubland close to the seashore. Parallel to this seems to be the *ya'ar of* Isaiah 21:13, whether this is to be translated the rough country of Arabia or of the Arabah.

True forest was unquestionably far more extensive than now.[9] There is

9. B. S. J. Isserlin, "Ancient Forests in Palestine: Some Archaeological Indications," *PEQ,* LXXXVI (1955), 87–88.

XXIII. *The Highlands of Gilead.* Although much of the famous forests of Gilead have now disappeared, there is still a great deal of residual woodland, and this picture illustrates well the kind of landscape which ancient Israelites would have described as *ya'ar,* rough woodland which in those days would have harbored many wild animals.

mention of forest fires in Isaiah 10:17–18, Jeremiah 21:14, and Amos 7:4, and some of the place names suggest greater woodland than at present, e.g., Kiriath-jearim (correctly *kiriath-ya'arim,* the village of the woods, 1 Sam. 6:21, 1 Chron. 13:5, and probably also Ps. 132:6). The modern Arabic name for the now treeless eastern part of the Carmel range is Umm al-Fahm, or "mother of charcoal." Yet at their best such woodlands can never have compared with the majestic forests of Mount Lebanon, and when first-class timber was needed at any time for building or for ships it had to be brought from Phoenicia. The tall, straight trunks of cedar and cypress were floated down from Phoenicia, as when "they gave . . . carts to the Sidonians and Tyrians, to bring cedar logs from Lebanon and convey them in rafts to the harbor of Joppa, according to the decree which they had in writing from Cyrus king of the Persians" (1 Esd. 5:54–55; see also 1 Kings 5; 2 Chron. 2, as well as 2 Sam. 5:11; 1 Kings 9:27–28; 2 Chron. 8:17–18). "The House of the Forest of Lebanon" (1 Kings 7:2; 10:17, 21; 2 Chron. 9:16, 20; Isa. 22:8) seems to have been a large room in the palace built with great cedar beams and paneled with the same wood. The great height of the cedars fascinated the Israelites, who never saw anything comparable in their own country. They marveled that Solomon had made "cedar as plentiful as the sycamore of the Shephelah" (1 Kings 10:27; 2 Chron. 1:15), and Ezekiel likened Pharaoh of Egypt to a great cedar, with "its top among the clouds," which would nevertheless be destroyed (Ezek. 31:2 ff.).

Ya'ar is also used to mean the rough tangle of thickets and scrub which takes over when farming land is allowed to go out of cultivation, but where there is room for cattle and sheep to wander. "I will lay waste her vines and her fig trees . . . I will make them a *ya'ar,* and the beasts of the field shall devour them" (Hos. 2:12; Heb. 2:14). Isaiah speaks of "briars and thorns" in the same connection (Isa. 7:23–25), though he uses a different phrase from that of the Gideon story, and in 9:18 speaks again of "briars and thorns" as equivalent to *ya'ar.* In a somewhat similar manner *midbar* is used for the rough open pastureland in the neighborhood of Bethlehem, that same region in which in the Christmas story the shepherds kept watch over their flocks (Luke 2:8). When the young David came down from Bethlehem to join his brothers as they were fighting the Philistines, they said to him angrily, "Why have you come down? And with whom have you left those few sheep in the *midbar?*" (1 Sam. 17:28). In 2 Samuel 2:24 we learn of the *midbar* of Gibeon, which certainly includes the eastern slopes toward the Jordan, since that is the way by which Abner and his men fled (v. 29). But Gibeon is toward the west, and so here *midbar* must mean also the rough, uncultivated country between Jerusalem and Bethel.

Midbar, therefore, merges into *ya'ar,* and in Ezekiel 34:25, quoted at the head at the head of this chapter, they are equated: "they may dwell securely in the *midbar* and sleep in the *ya'ar.*" Also, very strikingly, in the otherwise strictly parallel metaphors in Isaiah 32:15 and 29:17, the word *midbar* in the one is replaced by the word "Lebanon," famous for its great forests, in the other. Together the *midbar* and the *ya'ar* were the Ferocious Land, dangerous and frightening and avoided by all sensible men. *Midbar* extends away from the cultivated land toward the barren deserts, and *ya'ar* toward the rich forests of the well-watered mountains, but they form together part of the same continuum, and the villager felt himself close to, and threatened by, both. The shepherd, it is true, took his flocks into their outskirts, but there was always the possibility of attack by lions, bears, and wolves.

Of all the features of Old Testament life probably one of the most difficult for modern man to think himself back into is the ever present menace of wild animals if one wandered too far from the vilage. They seem to have been a constant danger to both flocks and wayfarers, so that Jacob was able to say, "It is my son's robe: a wild beast has devoured him; Joseph is without torn to pieces" (Gen. 37:33). That the danger continued to be real is obvious from the frequency of the imagery in the prophets. "So I will be to them like a lion, like a leopard I will lurk by the way. I will fall upon them like a bear robbed of her cubs, I will tear open their breast, and there I will devour them like a lion, as a wild beast would rend them" (Hos. 13:7–8), and again, "as if a man fled from a lion and a bear met him; or went into the house and leaned his hand against the wall, and a serpent bit him" (Amos 5:19). Isaiah uses similar metaphors (31:4), and so does Zephaniah (3:3). There are stories of actual meetings between men and wild beasts, as when a young lion roared against Samson in the vineyards of Timnah (Judg. 14:5), and the young David

XXIV. *"The lion shall eat straw like the ox"* (Is. 11:7). This remarkably friendly and playful lion is to be found on the mosaic floor of a synagogue of the Roman period at Tiberias. During the Israelite monarchy, however, lions were a very present danger, as were many other wild beasts.

destroyed both a lion and a bear (1 Sam. 17:34). When the prophet who came from Judah destroyed the word of God, "a lion met him on the road and killed him" (1 Kings 13:24), and so the excuse of the sluggard, "There is a lion outside! I shall be slain in the streets!" (Prov. 22:13), for all that it was an excuse, was not as fantastic as it would be in our own day, or as it would have been in New Testament times. Lions were particularly associated with the tangled jungle of the Zor, along the banks of the Jordan (Jer. 49:19; 50:17; Zech. 11:3), and they impressed men both by their ferocity and by their majesty. "The lion, which is mightiest among beasts and does not turn back before any," was one of the four things which "are stately in their stride" (Prov. 30:29–30).

Desert animals were hunted on behalf of great kings like Solomon so that his table might be provided with "harts, gazelles, roebucks, and fatted fowl" (1 Kings 4:23), but for ordinary folk they were often as frightening as the savage *midbar* itself, which they thought of as full of poisonous snakes (Num. 21:6; Deut. 8:15; Isa. 30:6). Yet, despite their fear, they admired such animals, impressed particularly by their speed, their freedom, their strength, and their strangeness. God silenced Job by reminding him of the wild goats, the wild ass, "to whom I have given the steppe for his home, the salt land for his dwelling place" (Job 39:6), the wild ox, and the ostrich (39:9–18). The Psalmist in his distress cried out, "I am like a vulture of the wilderness, like an owl of the waste places; I lie awake, I am like a lonely bird on the housetop" (Ps. 102:6–7). Hosea compared Ephraim to "a wild ass wandering alone" (8:9), and in the Song of Solomon the gazelle is a constant image of speed (2:8–9, 17; 4:5; 7:3; 8:14).

Common to both *ya'ar* and *midbar* was the sense of disorientation and the ghastly fear of getting lost, for here there were no waymarks or guideposts for the stranger, nor easily recognizable tracks. The farther one penetrated into the *midbar,* the greater the danger of death from thirst, which in the most arid regions in summer can overtake a man in two days, or in the rocky regions of tumbling down some precipice, as the Sons of the Prophets feared had happened to Elijah (2 Kings 2:16). Psalm 23, usually interpreted in milder terms, must be understood instead against the background of the frightening *midbar,* where the shepherd leads his flock in search of fresh grass after the rain. The *shebet* and *misheneth* are the club he uses to drive off wild animals and the stout staff which helps him to make his way along the dark and rocky gorge, the *zalmaveth.*[10] Only by divine help is he guided along a "straight path."

Primarily, therefore, both *ya'ar* and *midbar* were realms of terror, the farther that one ventured into them. However, they were also both regions of refuge, places to which men fled when it became more frightening to remain at home, for there at least the enemies could not easily find them. How often in Palestinian history have the villagers become refugees, fleeing eastward into the *midbar,* "greatly distressed and hungry . . . enraged . . . cursing their God and their king," overcome by "distress and darkness, and the gloom of anguish" (Isa. 8:21–22; see also 21:13–15). But no less regular a pattern is the flight into

10. *Zalmaveth* occurs 18 times in the Old Testament, always in poetry. It seems to indicate a dark gorge in the wilderness where in the gathering gloom of evening wild beasts come out of their dens and robbers and evil spirits are abroad. Thomas D. Winton, "צלמות in the Old Testament," *JSS,* 7 (1962), 191–200.

the *midbar* of "everyone who was in distress, and everyone who was in debt, and everyone who was discontented" (1 Sam. 22:2), i.e., all those who felt themselves driven to break away from the established society because they found it oppressive and intolerable. Whether they were to be accounted wicked or righteous depended upon the point of view. They were certainly always malcontent, and certainly also some of them (but by no means all) took to guerrilla warfare and brigandage in their struggle against the authorities. The Elijah-Elisha stories reflect just such a period of incipient guerrilla fighting, the "troubling of Israel" for which Elijah and Ahab each accused the other (1 Kings 18:17–18). The miracle stories about Elisha, which have given the commentators so much trouble, fall more easily into place if one understands them as reminiscences of how people who had taken to the *midbar* and the *ya'ar* had managed to survive this grim period in their history. More peaceable, but no less dissatisfied, were those who at a much later date took refuge in the *midbar* among the community of Qumran.

It is thus that we must interpret the *midbar* of the Exodus experience. Various small groups, a "mixed multitude" (Exod. 12:38) of social misfits, both in the Egyptian Delta and also surely from Palestine itself, which was then under Egyptian control, fled from a life of bondage to that wasteland where the Egyptian writ did not run and where the Egyptian system, the Egyptian "gods," had no power. In this *midbar*, this land of meaninglessness and disorder, of death rather than life, there is neither food nor water, and—as is abundantly clear from their constant murmurings (Exod. 14:11–22; 16:3; Num. 14:2)—they fully expected to die of thirst and exhaustion. Yet it had been their experience that in the *midbar* they had found both food and water and had lived and not died; in the *midbar* they had entered into covenant; in the *midbar* they had been confronted by their God. This was in their eyes in no sense natural, for to the villager and town dweller, who flee to the *midbar* only when they have nowhere else to go, nature is no longer the source of meaning and order. Nature in the *midbar* is the enemy, and they had come to know there That which apparently had even the *midbar* under control and, as it were, forbade it to act according to its destructive nature. It was a fact that they had lived and not died. They had gone down "few in number," and they had "become a nation, great, mighty, and populous" (Deut. 26:5). This was not, however, a fact of nature; it was a fact of history: Once we were Pharaoh's slaves in Egypt; now we are free. Once we were no people; now we are a people.

It was therefore in the *midbar* that they had been forced to reject anything within nature as the means whereby the world could be interpreted and understood, as that fundamental Reality by which names can be given to everything and their significance be made known. It is on the basis of their experience in the *midbar* that their religion was of necessity aniconic, entirely without images, because nothing in the entire world of sense experience could be used to represent the Reality behind this experience, the Reality in terms of which everything in a world by nature meaningless had sudenly become endowed with meaning. "Thou shalt not make to thyself any graven image, or any likeness, of anything—of anything that is in the heaven above, or the earth beneath, or the water under the earth. Thou shalt not bow down to them or worship them" (Exod. 20:4–5; Deut. 5:8).

It is not the function of a geographer to preach a sermon, but one thing needs

to be emphasized: the enormous difference between what is loosely, but rather
inaccurately, called a "God of Nature"
and a "God of History," between the
world interpreted in terms of nature,
and therefore essentially upon its own
terms, and the world interpreted in terms
of historical events, in terms of what
happens to man. Nature makes no de-
mands upon man and cannot require that
he become other than what he is. History, however, insists upon a response.
Every historical event, coming upon him
as it were from outside, has the power
to say to man: What are you going to
do now? It is the historical event alone
which has the power to make all things
new.

This, then, is the basis of the centuries of struggle between Yahweh and
Baal, and it takes its start in the *midbar*.
It could not develop out of an agricultural situation. Consequently the attitude
of the true Israelite to the *midbar* was
ambivalent. It remained for him always
"the great and terrible wilderness" and
"a land of trouble and anguish" (Deut.
1:19; Isa. 30:6). Yet there he had been
found by Yahweh,

He found him in a desert land,
    and in the howling waste of the *midbar*.
        [Deut. 32:10]

I found Israel like grapes in the *midbar*.
        [Hos. 9:10]

There is among the prophets certainly
no nostalgia for the *midbar*, no sense of
it as an ideal place to which they long to
return, but they do insist upon the importance of the *midbar* and the significance of the Israelite experience there.
When Hosea realized that his world was
collapsing into disorder and meaninglessness, and that the people of Israel would
have to "dwell many days without king
or prince, without sacrifice or pillar,
without ephod or teraphim" (Hos. 3:4)

—i.e., without any of the symbols which
until then had given their world significance and stability—he insisted that
exactly in the midst of his terrifying
meaninglessness would they come to
know again the true source of meaning.

I will bring her into the *midbar*,
    and speak to her tenderly,
and there I will make . . .
    the valley of trouble a gateway of hope.
        [Hos. 2:14–15 (Heb. 16–17)]

The *midbar* is for Amos the realm of
Reality, the realm of truth and significance, against which present structures
and present activity must be tested.
"When you were in the *midbar* for forty
years, did you bring me sacrifices and
offerings, O house of Israel?" (Amos
5:25). Jeremiah indeed is able to speak
of this time as a honeymoon period:

I remember the devotion [the *hesed*]
    of your youth,
    and your love as a bride,
how you followed me in the *midbar*,
    in a land not sown
[i.e., not the world of agriculture].
        [Jer. 2:2]

In the New Testament the countryside
had become more civilized and ordered,
and references to wild animals are much
less common. The Gospels refer to foxes,
wolves, serpents, and scorpions (Matt.
3:7; 7:10; 8:20; 10:16; 23:33; Luke
3:7; 9:58; 10:19; 11:11–12; 13:32;
John 10:12). The devil is once likened
to a roaring lion (1 Pet. 5:8), but other
references to lions are drawn either from
the arena (2 Tim. 4:17) or from Old
Testament imagery (Heb. 11:33; Rev.
4:7; 5:5; 9:8, 17; 10:3; 13:2).[11]

11. Wild animals have continued to disappear from Palestine, the last crocodile
having been killed there in the nineteenth
century. In our own day, however, the rate
of extinction has been phenomenal, and
since World War I alone the country of
Jordan "has lost the wild ass, the fallow

Nevertheless, despite the Roman peace, there was still wilderness, and *eremos* in the New Testament has much of the same ambivalence as *midbar*. It is the wasteland, a desert or deserted place, the kind of place men arrive in if they wander too far from the village (Mark 6:35–36), including evidently rough pastureland (6:39). *Eremos,* no less than *midbar,* is a word of both terror and salvation. It is a place of hunger and thirst, where one is tried and tested to the uttermost, as in the temptations of Jesus (Mat. 4:1–11; Mark 1:12–13; Luke 4:1–13). It is essentially a place without food. "Where in the wilderness can we get enough bread to feed so great a multitude?" (Matt. 15:33), which is exactly the question asked by the multitude in the Exodus:

Can God spread a table in the *midbar?* . . .
Can he also give bread,
  can he provide meat for his people?
                [Ps. 78:19–20]

Yet it is, of course, exactly the place where men are fed with the bread of life (John 6:35). In Mark's thinking the Gentiles may be admitted to the community just because they also have wandered hungry and thirsty in the wilderness and found food there; they also have had an Exodus (Mark 8:1–10, and see below, p. 225). But the *eremos* is never a place to be desired. Mark thinks of Jesus as *"driven* into the wilderness" (1:12), and this kind of testing is something into which a man rightly prays not to be led (Matt. 6:13). Not until the postbiblical period does any sedentary person go into the desert to live because a desert life attracts him.

---

deer, the Syrian bear, the ostrich and the Arabian oryx. The cheetah and the Arabian and Dorcas gazelles and the once plentiful Houbara bustard now exist only in extremely small numbers." Guy Mountfort, "Birth of a Desert National Park," *GM,* XL (1967), 668.

CHAPTER 10

The Land Before You

Turn and take your journey, and go to the hill country of the Amorites, and to all their neighbors in the Arabah, in the hill country and in the Shephelah, and in the Negeb, and by the seacoast. . . . Behold, I have set the land before you.

DEUTERONOMY 1:7–8

Having so far considered the various factors which go to make up the land of Palestine, we must now turn to survey the land itself. We must not, however, for one moment imagine that what we see now as we travel to and fro is the landscape seen by the Israelites at any time in their long history, or even that familiar to Jesus and his disciples. From the time, some 9,000 years ago, that man first began to settle down and to cultivate the land, clearing the earth of stones to make his little fields, perhaps beginning tentatively to direct the waters of a stream onto the ground where he had planted his rough wheat and barley, from the time also that he began to keep animals and construct rude enclosures the better to protect and control them, the process of transformation had begun.

On the whole it was a process of amelioration, of softening the brutality of nature and coaxing it to bring forth food, pushing back little by little the borders of the *midbar* and the *ya'ar* and extending beneficent order into the domain of the wild beasts. Not all the processes were what we would call good. Overgrazing led at times to the destruction of the natural vegetation; the constant cutting of the forests for timber and for fuel laid bare the unshaded earth to the burning heat of the summer sun and permitted the slashing winter rains to beat furiously against the loosened soil, no longer restrained by the clutching tentacles of the roots, and sweep it irretrievably into the sea. Of course, the people at the time were unaware of the harm they were doing, for the supply of wood seemed to them inexhaustible. The savagery of war hastened the process, for "the trees which you know are not trees for food you may destroy and cut down that you may build siegeworks against the city that makes war with you, until it falls," though orchards and olive groves were in principle protected. "Are the trees of the field men that they should be besieged by you?" (Deut. 20:19–20). Nevertheless, not even these were always secure, for when the armies of Judah and Israel invaded Moab, "they felled all the good trees; till only its stones were left in Kir-hareseth," both cultivated and wild trees being destroyed together (2 Kings 3:25).

This process of spoliation is completely irreversible. When men flee from the drawn sword and the bent bow, the carefully cherished fields pass out of cultivation, so that "every place where there used to be a thousand vines, worth a thousand shekels of silver, will become briars and thorns" (Isa. 7:23), and it is necessary to hunt for food with bows and arrows. It is true that the fields may be patiently restored, but the land itself never reverts to the original forest. That has gone forever.

This process of change, of interaction between man and the landscape, has been going on for a very long time indeed. It began with the prepottery Neolithic. Excavations at Jericho have provided evidence of serious erosion from forest clearing during the Early Bronze Age (2600–2300 B.C.) when men first began to use metal tools for cutting trees,[1] and even earlier than this forests near Tell Beit Mirsim and Tell as-Duweir seem to have been cleared, possibly by burning.[2] Abraham, there-fore, did not enter a "natural" landscape in Palestine, and at least as early as his day the hillsides were in places terraced to hold the soil and provide better land for farming.[3] The establishment of the monarchy accelerated the processes of both salvation and destruction. On the one hand the increased population, now able to use iron tools, and needing more open land for settlement and more wood for fuel and building houses, made greater inroads on the forests, with consequent danger to the hillsides if ever they were neglected. On the other hand the greatest care seems to have been taken to ensure that the land so cleared was protected. On the highlands of Judah "preservation of cultivable land overrode in each case all other considerations in choosing the site of a settlement,"[4] and extensive terracing, both on the slopes and in the wadis, helped to prevent erosion. The invention of the plastered cistern some 200 years earlier had also promoted the extention of fortresses and villages into areas where there were few springs and wells.

The importance of this process of transformation cannot be overemphasized because it is so often forgotten. Nevertheless, the basic framework of the country has, of course, remained the same, and the striking difference between one region and another was not only recognized at a very early date but has stubbornly persisted despite every modification in the overlying vegetation cover. What we would call today the "natural regions" of the country were already known to the Israelite, though he did not think in our terms. Some of

1. Kathleen Kenyon, *Archaeology in the Holy Land* (New York: Frederick A. Praeger, 1960), pp. 133–134.

2. Isserlin, *op. cit.*

3. Nelson Glueck, *The River Jordan* (New York: McGraw-Hill, 1968), pp. 100–1.

4. R. Zon, "Agricultural Terraces in the Judean Mountains," *IEJ*, 16 (1966), 121.

the regional names which were in constant use we have already encountered, e.g., Shephelah, Sharon, Carmel, Negeb, Mishor, Jeshimon, Arabah, and Gilead. To these we must certainly add the *Galil*, from which probably developed the name "Galilee" (Josh, 20:7; 21:32; 1 Kings 9:11; 2 Kings 15:29; 1 Chron. 6:76; Isa. 9:1), the *Kikkar*, or plain of Lower Jordan and Dead Sea (Gen. 13:10–12; 19:25–29; Deut. 34:3; 1 Kings 7:46; 2 Chron. 4:17), the *Pisgah*, or edge of the Trans-jordan plateau (Num. 21:20; 23:14; Deut. 3:27; 4:49; 34:1), and the *Abarim*, the eroded slopes below the *Pisgah* (Num. 27:12; 33:47–48; Deut. 32:49; Jer. 22:20). *Bashan* (= smooth) and *Argob* (= clods of earth) for the level plateau of southern Syria, and *Edom* (= red) in the south of Trans-jordan, are also descriptive regional names.

All these are names for districts which, though clearly recognizable, lay beyond the borders of normal Israelite settlement. The *Galil* refers to that part of Galilee which had ceased to be Israelite (1 Kings 9:11), and in the time of Isaiah it was known as "the *Galil* of the foreigners" (Isa. 9:1). Gilead alone of these districts could be called Israelite territory, and even that, as we have seen, was marginal. Within ancient Israel the distinctive regions were no less apparent, and probably the tribal names were all in the first place regional names, taken over by the groups which settled in districts. The word "Ephraim" has the form of a regional name, and so also probably does Judah, which is used in a regional sense in 1 Samuel 23:3.[5]

The coastal region north of Carmel was apparently already known as "Asher" by the Egyptians of the thirteenth century B.C. before the time of the

5. See the discussion of this Noth, *Old Testament World*, pp. 63–75.

Exodus,[6] and in the biblical record itself we have more than mention of one tribe possessing land in the territory of another (e.g., Josh 16:9; 17:11), which suggests that the regional distinction was clearly recognized. None of this is the least surprising if we remember that the Israelites were primarily farmers, extremely conscious, therefore, of the various types of soil and climate conditions and strongly disinclined to move away into a region they regarded as "different" and consequently somewhat

6. Theophile James Meek, *Hebrew Origins* (New York: Harper & Brothers, 1936; Torchbook ed. 1960), p. 30.

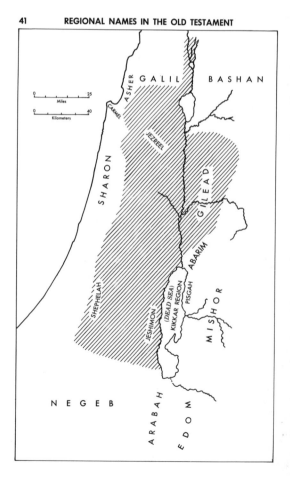

41   REGIONAL NAMES IN THE OLD TESTAMENT

suspect. This is a phenomenon well knows from farming communities in other parts of the world, and it is exceedingly unlikely that it did not prevail in ancient Palestine as well. We have already seen (p. 87) that there is an evident difference between the balance of crops in Judah, Ephraim, and Manasseh. Indeed, so strong are the resultant differences between one farming region and another that a marked separation develops between the communities, each having its own rhythm which does not easily mesh with that of the adjacent community. It is against this background that we must understand the persistent fighting and rivalry between the tribes even long after the establishment of the monarchy, the insistence of the Deuteronomic editors of the Book of Judges on the vital importance of a unity which transcended the agricultural differences, and the significance as a unifying factor of the three feasts, at which all male Israelites were required to come together.

With all this in mind, therefore, we may begin to "see what the land is, and whether the people who dwell in it are strong or weak, whether they are few or many, and whether the land that they dwell in is good or bad, and whether the cities that they dwell in are camps or strongholds, and whether the land is rich or poor, and whether there is wood in it or not" (Num. 13:19–20). For this purpose we may conveniently divide the land as follows:

A. The Plains of Cis-Jordan

1. *The Coasts of Asher*, i.e., the narrow coastal plain from the Lebanon border as far south as the Crocodile River.

2. *The Plain of Sharon*, from the Carmel range to the Yarkon River.

3. *The Valley of Craftsmen* between the Yarkon and the Sorek.

4. *The Philistine Plain*, south of the Sorek and north of Gaza.

5. *The Shephelah*, the hilly country between the Philistine Plain and the highlands of Judah.

6. *The Central Valley* of Esdraelon and Jezreel.

B. The Western Highlands

1. *Upper Galilee.*
2. *Lower Galilee.*
3. *The Basin of Samaria*, or Manasseh.
4. *The Carmel Range.*
5. *The Dome of Ephraim.*
6. *The Highlands of Judah.*

42   THE TRIBAL TERRITORIES

Miles
0   50
Kilometers
0   80

G A D. . Israelite Tribes
Syria . Foreign Nations
— — . Limit of Permanent Israelite Territory

43   **THE NATURAL REGIONS OF PALESTINE**

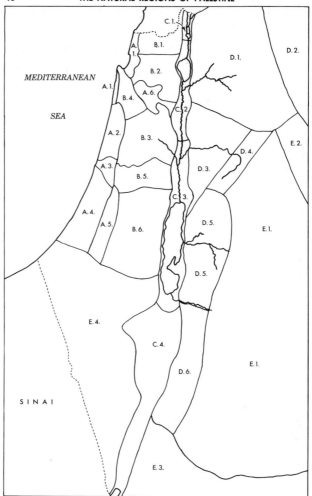

C. The Rift Valley

1. *The Huleh Basin.*
2. *The Galilee–Beth-shan Basin.*
3. *The Kikkar*, or the *Ghor*, south of the Jordan "waist."
4. *The Dead Sea.*
5. *The Arabah.*

D. The Plateau of Trans-Jordan

1. *The Plateau of Bashan.*
2. *The Mountain of Bashan.*
3. *The Dome of Gilead.*

4. *The Basin of Ammon.*
5. *The Tableland of Moab.*
6. *The Heights of Edom.*

E. The Deserts

1. *The Eastern Plateau Desert.*
2. *The Wadi Sirhan.*
3. *The Dissected Plateau of Trans-jordan.*
4. *The Wilderness of Zin*, i.e., the Negeb of Cis-jordan.

It will be seen that these regions could be arranged somewhat differently. The Arabah has been included here with the Rift Valley, to which it belongs structurally, but it might with equal justice be listed among the deserts. The Shephelah is not, strictly speaking, part of the Coast Plain and might well be treated separately. The ancient Israelites sometimes classed together the Sharon Plain with Mount Carmel (Isa. 35:2) because they were both thickly forested. Therefore, though the division offered here is both convenient and reasonable, it is by no means the only one.

CHAPTER **11**

The Coast of the Sea

Asher sat still at the coast of the sea,
settling down by his landings.

JUDGES 5:17

A.1. The Coasts of Asher

Although the impressive headland of Mount Carmel is the most obvious physical interruption of the Coast Plain, the true regional division, which has persisted through history, must be placed rather farther south at the marshes of the Crocodile River (Nahr az-Zerqa), which curves round the Carmel massif close to the modern town of Binyamina. Stretching away to the north of these marshes is a very narrow coastal zone, shut in by steep mountain slopes and usually less than 5 miles (8 km.) across. This is the region known to the ancient Israelites as "Asher." That the name is primarily geographical rather than tribal is quite evident from the manner in which it is used in the Old Testament. Dor, south of the Carmel headland, is said to be "in Asher" (Josh. 17:11), and the southern boundary of Asher was at Shihor-Libnath (Josh. 19:26), usually identified with

the Crocodile marshes. Toward the north, Asher is said to extend all the way "as far as Sidon the Great" (Josh. 19:28), which is a political impossibility, for Israelite territory never at any time came within sight of it, but it makes sense if the writer had the geographical region in mind.[1] The description of the territory of Asher in Joshua 19:24–31 is extremely difficult to follow, partly because only some of the sites can be identified, but largely because the places mentioned do not seem to be arranged in any very clear order. It would seem that the compiler had made use of more than one source of information and that he was also attempting to correlate the relatively small tribal territory of Asher with the much more extensive geographical region of

1. But it should be noticed that Joab's census is said to have included this region (2 Sam. 24:5–7).

121

44   **THE COASTS OF ASHER**
                                        (NORTHERN AND CENTRAL SECTIONS)

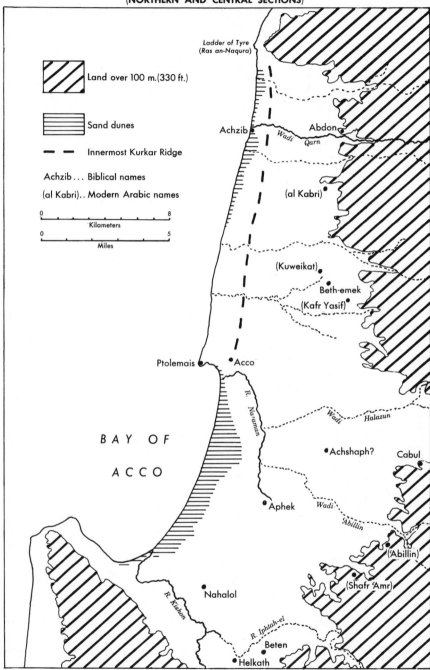

Land over 100 m.(330 ft.)

Sand dunes

Innermost Kurkar Ridge

Achzib ... Biblical names

(al Kabri) .. Modern Arabic names

0   8
Kilometers
0   5
Miles

Ladder of Tyre
(Ras an-Naqura)

Achzib

Abdon

Wadi Qarn

(al Kabri)

(Kuweikat)

Beth-emek

(Kafr Yasif)

Ptolemais

Acco

R. Na'aman

Wadi Halazun

Achshaph?

Cabul

BAY OF

ACCO

Aphek

Wadi 'Abillin

('Abillin)

(Shafr 'Amr)

R. Kishon

Nahalol

R. Iphtah-el

Beten

Helkath

the same name. At the very most the tribal lands on the coast must have been confined to that part lying between the two headlands of Carmel and Ras an-Naqura, the ancient "Ladder of Tyre."

Even so the region of Asher, however interpreted, played only a minimal part in Israelite history, and almost all the places listed as being in Asher occur only in these lists and do not figure as the scene of any historical event. Even Acco receives no further mention. In Joshua 11:1 and 12:20, it is true, it is said that the ruler of Achshaph was one of those defeated by Joshua, but this is a very shadowy claim, and even if true may perhaps refer to another place of the same name.[2] Harosheth, the headquarters of Sisera (Judg. 4:2, 13), is probably Tell al-'Amr on the edge of the Asher plain, but is is not mentioned in any tribal list, and significantly bears the name of Harosheth-ha-Goiim, Harosheth of the Foreigners. In 1 Kings 4:11, 16, Dor and Asher appear among the twelve administrative districts of Solomon, which suggests that for a brief period during the united monarchy there was some attempt to make this narrow coast plain part of the Israelite kingdom, but not, it would seem, for long, since later in Solomon's reign he was forced to cede twenty cities to Hiram of Tyre, one of which was Cabul (1 Kings 9:10–14).[3] We would probably not be far wrong if we thought of the tribe of Asher as belonging primarily to the western slopes of Galilee, though doubtless they tried to press down onto the coastal plain. According to Judges 1:31–32 the plain itself remained firmly in Canaanite hands in the early period, and the villages which

Hiram obtained from Solomon were possibly the territory of the tribe of Asher, which then ceased to be part of the Israelite state. Hiram would be anxious to get hold of these in order to protect the hinterland of his ports.

The tribe of Asher hardly enters into Israelite history, and the only time it is recorded as having played an active part was in support of Gideon against the Midianites (Judg. 6:35; 7:23). In the Song of Deborah the people of Asher are blamed because they "sat still at the coast of the sea" (Judg. 5:17), but probably they were in no position to rise against the forces of Sisera, who doubtless held all the towns of the region. After the cession of their territory to Tyre they cannot have been more than a rump tribe, and the Chronicler's account of Hezekiah's Passover (which, though historically dubious, may perhaps reflect the later attempts of Josiah to reunite the kingdom) recounts that "only a few men of Asher . . . came to Jerusalem" (2 Chron. 30:10).[4]

Although the tribe of Asher is little accounted of in the Israelite records, the region had the reputation of being prosperous:

Asher's food shall be rich,
   and he shall yield royal dainties.
[Gen. 49:20]

Blessed above sons be Asher;
   let him be the favorite of his brothers,
   and let him dip his foot in oil.
[Deut. 33:24]

This reputation was probably well deserved, for in this northern coastal region the rainfall is heavy and assured, with a yearly average in the north of more than 24 inches (600 mm.) and

2. Manfred Weippert, *op. cit.*, pp. 35–36n.

3. Cabul may be mentioned because it remained a border village. Aharoni, *Land of Israel*, p. 277.

4. If the reading "Asherites" for "Ashurites" in 2 Samuel 2:9 is correct, they were probably refugee groups who had fled to Gilead.

in the south coming close to that.

The plain of Asher south of the present Lebanese border may conveniently be divided into three parts. In the north is the narrow Galilee Coast, averaging about 3 miles wide. It is bounded by two promontories, the white chalk cliffs of Ras an-Naqura (the Ladder of Tyre) and the headland of Acco. In this section the *kurkar* ridges, which are an important feature of the Coast Plain in the center of the country, are much less prominent, and the two western ridges are in fact all but drowned by the sea. Only the eastern ridge is on dry land, and this forms a line of low hills (today marked by a line of Israeli settlements), some 100 to 120 feet (30–40 m.) high, parallel to the coast and half a mile inland. These are sufficiently broken to present little obstacle to the drainage from the Galilee highlands, and the six wadis from the east run more or less straight out to sea. The most important is the Wadi Qarn (Nahal Keziz), coming down from the lofty interior of Upper Galilee. Where it enters the plain stood Abdon on a rocky hill 479 feet (146 m.) in height, and at its mouth was the port of Achzib, protected by *kurkar* rocks. Farther up into the mountains the Crusaders built the castle of Montfort to control this constricted and difficult valley route.

The level plain between the hills and the *kurkar* ridge, being well drained and floored with fertile alluvium from the mountains, was too valuable to be taken up with villages, and in ancient times these followed the foothills and spring line, e.g., Abdon and Beth-emek. The later Arab villages also followed the same line, e.g., al-Kabri with its very important springs, Kuweikat, and Kafr Yasif, all of which have excellent olive groves.

The other important port was Acco, which during the Old Testament period stood at Tell al-Fukhkhar, 1¼ miles (2 km.) to the west of the modern Acre, probably at that time on the banks of the little river Naʻaman, which rises at Aphek to the south. The port of Ptolemais, the present Acre (Acco), was not built until the third century B.C. when a breakwater was constructed to protect the harbor from the southwesterly gales. Perhaps the old port of Acco may have become unusable at this time because of silting and the shifting of the course of the Naʻaman.

Acco stands at the western end of the tremendous fault of ash-Shaghur which divides Upper from Lower Galilee, presenting an almost unbroken face to the south. The central section of the plain of Asher, therefore, lying between Acco and the Carmel fault line, is an area of subsidence which has created the Bay of Acco (modern Bay of Haifa). No more than 20 feet above sea level in the center, it is divided into two parts by a slight swelling of the land where the Eocene limestone extends west of the village of Shafa ʻAmr. The coast, protected by Carmel from the scouring effects of the sea currents, is choked with sand dunes which block the mouths of the rivers and force them to turn northward, and as a result the plain, both north and south of the swelling, is ill-drained and marshy.

In the northern part the little Naʻaman, rising at Aphek, flows northward, collecting en route the waters of the ʻAbillin and Halazun from the Lower Galilee hills. These swamp the valley, and the marshes here are widespread, causing the routes from the downfaulted basins of Lower Galilee also to swerve northward and to foregather at Acco, which became the natural outlet for Galilee, and in Roman times for the rich granary of Bashan which lay beyond. One important route ran along the foot of the Shaghur fault to Ramah, one of the wall towns of Naphtali (Josh. 19: 36) and still today a very important olive-growing district. Another was the road through Hannathon at the western end of the Sahl Battauf (see p. 100).

South of the swelling the Iphtah-el (Wadi Malik), marking the border between Asher and Zebulun (Josh. 19:14, 27), is directed southwestward to join the Kishon, which enters the plain by an exceedingly narrow corridor near Harosheth of the Gentiles. This part of the plain is also choked and marshy, and it follows, therefore, that the ancient towns and villages avoided the rivers and kept either to the slightly higher land between them or to the Galilee foothills.

The name of Harosheth is preserved today in Jisr al-Harithiyeh, where the road from Haifa to Nazareth crosses the Kishon close to Tell al-'Amr. Here the mass of Carmel reaches its greatest height, towering nearly 1,600 feet (490 m.) in an almost sheer slope above the valley of the Kishon. When Barak was pursuing the defeated Sisera back to Harosheth (Judg. 4:16), the normally insignificant stream was a gorged and turbulent flood, for the battle seems to have been fought in a rainstorm (Judg. 5:20–21). It is no wonder that the Canaanite chariots were bogged down in the mud and at the mercy of the lighter-armed Israelites, so that "Sisera alighted from his chariot and fled away on foot." Through this same restricted defile ran also the important road from Megiddo to Acco which, once it had entered the Plain of Asher, hugged the Galilee foothills to steer clear of the marshes.

The third section of the Plain of Asher lies beyond the dramatic headland of Carmel and west of the Carmel massif. On the normal physical map this massif appears to be aligned toward

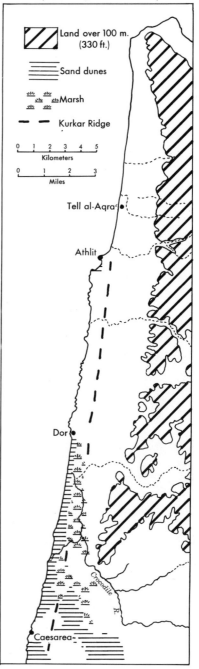

45 THE COASTS OF ASHER (SOUTHERN SECTION)

Land over 100 m. (330 ft.)

Sand dunes

Marsh

Kurkar Ridge

Kilometers
0 1 2 3 4 5

Miles
0 1 2 3

Tell al-Aqra'

Athlit

Dor

Crocodile R.

Caesarea

the northwest, and this indeed is the direction of the long arm which extends outward from the Western Highlands. But here in the seaward extremity this impression is somewhat misleading, for the western scarp of the massif runs almost due north and south so that the massif takes the shape of a vast prehistoric arrowhead pointing more or less northward. This can be seen quite clearly on any modern map by noticing the direction of the roads which follow the foot of the scarp on either side. The coasts of Dor, therefore, which form the southernmost section of the Plain of Asher, consist of a narrow coastal lowland some 20 miles (about 30 km.) long from north to south and only about 2½ miles (4 km.) wide.

It is physically much more akin to the Galilee coast than the Bay of Acco. North of Athlit (the Crusaders' Château Pélerin) the coast is sandy and straight, but to the south the *kurkar* ridges once more appear. The eastern ridge is almost continuous, and west of this, along the shoreline, is a second, more intermittent ridge. The eastern ridge in particular blocked the passage of the Carmel streams, and in fact, despite the strength of the streams coming down from the Carmel massif, there are no natural outlets through this ridge, those that exist being all artificial. In the Pluvial period the streams had drained to the sea, but with the decline in rainfall and at the same time a slight elevation of the land out of the sea,

XXV. *The Coasts of Asher.* A view, taken from Mount Carmel, looking across the narrow coast plain in the neighborhood of Dor, with the Mediterranean Sea in the distance. Today carefully cultivated, this plain was in ancient times thickly wooded.

they were no longer able to do so, and the ancient population had to cut channels in order to drain the marshes which were forming behind the ridge.[5]

Despite these efforts the narrow passage, about a mile and a half wide, between the ridge and the Carmel scarp seems to have remained somewhat marshy and forested, making movement by land very difficult. At the time of the Third Crusade the march southward along this corridor was impeded "by the thickets and the tall, luxuriant herbage, which struck them in the face, especially the foot soldiers."[6]

Though another, as yet unidentified, port seems to have existed in ancient times just north of Athlit, the only town in the whole of this district mentioned in the Old Testament is Dor, which in the fourteenth century B.C. was one of a series of small harbors that stretched along most of the Phoenician coast and were dominated at that time by Sidon. This was a period of great expansion in sea trade and consequently of increased wealth all along the coast. However, the upheavals of the thirteenth century and the invasions of the Sea Peoples in the latter part of it greatly altered the situation. Dor became the headquarters of a people called Thekel (or Tjeker), probably akin to the Sikel who gave their name to Sicily. Strongly defended on the landward side by the great forested block of Carmel, the marshes and woods at its foot, and the *kurkar* ridge immediately behind the city, Dor was almost impregnable, and the Israelites were

quite unable to take it until the time of the United Monarchy (Judg. 1:31). This isolation from the often turbulent land behind it gave the inhabitants of Dor a feeling of security from which they sucked out no small advantage. A good example of their freedom of action when no strong government mastered the landward approaches is shown by their treatment of Wen Amon, who came to them as an emissary from Pharaoh in about 1100 B.C., for not only did they maltreat him at Dor itself but they pursued him also to Byblos with eleven of their ships.[7]

After the division of the kingdom Dor was included theoretically within the territory of Israel, but since it is not mentioned at all in this period it is doubtful whether the Israelites were able to exercise much control over it. After 722 B.C. it passed into the hands of the Assyrians, who made it the headquarters of the province of Dor, extending southward to Joppa, an arrangement continued later by the Babylonians and Persians. In 219 B.C. it was besieged unsuccessfully by Antiochus III, and 1 Maccabees 15:10ff. records another prolonged siege by Antiochus VII (138–29 B.C.). After the building of Caesarea, Dor declined in importance, since its hinterland was so restricted. In New Testament times this part of the coast plain was included in the province of Syria to the north, indicating again its identification with the Phoenician coast.

A.2. *The Plain of Sharon*

South of the Crocodile marshes and the southwestern corner of the Carmel massif the Coast Plain suddenly widens and one enters the plain of Sharon, some 10 miles wide and 27 long (16 by 45 km.). There are only six references to

---

5. Dov Nir, "Artificial Outlets of the Mount Carmel Valleys through the Coastal 'Kurkar' Ridge," *IEJ*, 9 (1959), 46–54.

6. H. G. Bohn, *Itinerary of Richard I*, Bk. *IV*, pars. 12–14, quoted by G. Dahl in *The Materials for the History of Dor* (New Haven: Yale University Press, 1915), p. 116.

7. Pritchard, *ANET*, pp. 26, 28.

Sharon by name in the Bible: "They dwelt . . . in all the pasture lands of Sharon" (1 Chron 5:16); "Over the herds that pastured in Sharon was Shitrai the Sharonite" (1 Chron. 27:29); "I am a rose of Sharon, a lily of the valleys" (Song of Sol. 2:1); "The land mourns and languishes; Lebanon . . . withers away; Sharon is like a desert; and Bashan and Carmel shake off their leaves" (Isa. 33:9); "The glory of Lebanon shall be given to it, the majesty of Carmel and Sharon" (Isa. 35:2); and "Sharon shall become a pasture for flocks, and the Valley of Achor a place for herds to lie down" (Isa. 65:10). These passages by themselves, combined with our modern knowledge of the valuable citrus groves of the region, undoubtedly suggest to the ordinary reader something rich and desirable, but the ancient Israelites thought of Sharon as part of the terrifying *ya'ar*, and the Red Sand which today supports the golden orange groves was then covered with impenetrable oak forest. In Isaiah Sharon is classed with the thick forests of Lebanon and Carmel, and the "majesty" of Sharon is *hadar*, which has the sense of pride, of something swollen and ornate. It might almost be translated "extravagance," so that the desolate Arabah will receive "the extravagant riches of Carmel and Sharon . . . they shall see the prodigality of our God." In Isaiah 65:10 the *ya'ar* and the *midbar* are put side by side, and the forests and marshes of the one are to become a place where sheep may safely graze while the barren slopes above Jericho will carry enough grass for cattle. The most that could ever be hoped for from Sharon was grazing on the fringes of the forest, and it is significant that the headquarters of Benhesed was on the very edge of the region at Socoh (Khirbet Shuweikat ar-Ras), 400 feet above sea level (I Kings 4:10).

Sharon is bounded both in the north and in the south by rivers, the Crocodile River and the Yarkon, with its tributary the Wadi Qana (the Kanah which formed the boundary between Manasseh and Ephraim—Josh. 16:8; 17:9).[8] The drainage from the still well-watered hills to the east is plentiful, but there are only five exits to the sea, of which no less than three are confined to the most northerly 10 miles. The greater part of the center of the plain is occupied by a mass of Mousterian Red Sand anything from 150 to 300 feet (60–90 m.) in height, and the rivers are deflected round this, the Qana to join the Yarkon in the south, and the Iskanderun toward the north, collecting several wadis along its route, notably the Zeimar. A few miles farther north is the Wadi Mifjir (Nahal Hadera). West of the Red Sand are three *kurkar* ridges, all well developed. The first forms the coast itself and is under continual attack by the winter storms, which have cut a line of low cliffs rising to a height of some 200 feet (60 m.) near the modern town of Nathanya. These cliffs are slowly retreating under the onslaught of the sea. The central ridge is about half a mile inland and is the most continuous. The eastern ridge lies about 2 miles farther inland, and is the highest of the three, since it is covered by red sand. The troughs are today occupied by (a) the coast road, (b) the railroad,

8. See Yehuda Karmon, *Israel: A Regional Geography*, pp. 214–20, and "Geographical Influences on the Historical Routes in the Sharon Plain," pp. 43–60. A curious problem exists about the course of the river Qana, and Eva Danelius has suggested that it may have at one time reached the sea independently near the present Arsuf. This would then have been the boundary as described in the Book of Joshua. "The Boundary of Ephraim and Manasseh in the Western Plain," *PEQ*, XC (1958), 32–43.

46   THE PLAIN OF SHARON

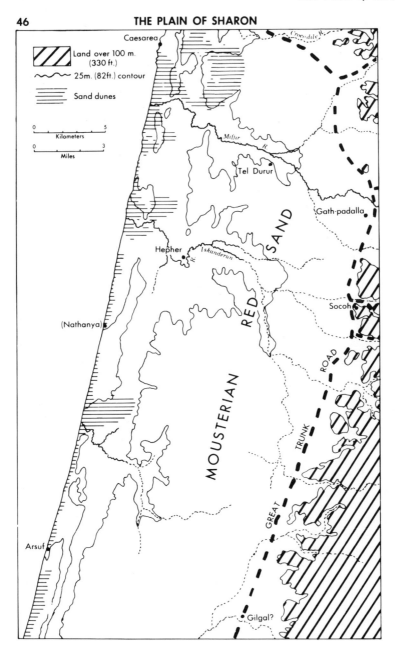

and (c) the road built in the period of the Mandate between the eastern ridge and the central mass of Red Sand, but in ancient times they were not in use because of the swamps at the river crossings.

Consequently, there are as it were two moats on either side of the central Red

Sand hills. In these the streams move but sluggishly, and tend to become choked with their own alluvium, and so they spread out into broad areas of swamp, which in places were permanent. These were particularly bad in the north, where there is a large area of dune sand, and even today flooding is common here in wet winters.

All this meant that Sharon was a place to be avoided, and historically its chief importance was that the vitally important Trunk Road skirted it on the east, hugging the drier foothills of the Highlands. After collecting the four routes across the Carmel passes this great highway ran through Socoh, guarding the route up the Wadi Zeimar to Shechem, southward to the source of the Yarkon at Aphek (Ras al-'Ain). Where it crosses the Qana is Jaljulya, which some have identified with the Gilgal of Joshua 12:23, though the RSV, NEB, and JB all agree in having "Galilee" here. A whole series of tells along this road gives evidence that during the Israelite monarchy there must have been a line of small settlements at the foot of the hills, but they find no mention in the Bible, and in any case most of them stand slightly above Sharon proper. No more than three show signs of having existed in the Bronze Age.[9]

The other place for little settlements was along the coast, where the coastwise shipping required frequent, usually nightly, stopping places. During the Early Bronze Age they were on the coast itself, for the boats were apparently beached every night, but the Iron Age harbors are farther inland, where the rivers cut through the innermost *kurkar* ridge.[10] Where the Iskanderun crosses this ridge is Tell al-Afshar, usually identified with Hepher,

mentioned in the list of Solomon's administrative divisions (1 Kings 4:10). Where the Yarkon cuts through the same ridge is Tel Qasile, an excavated site which has not yet been identified with any place mentioned in the Bible. On the coast not far from the Crusaders' town of Arsuf is Makmish, another excavated site, which existed in the first half of the monarchy and then again during the Persian period.[11] In the northern extremity of the interior, 2½ miles east of Hadera, is Tel Zeror (Tell Durur), which was first built about 2000 B.C. and then flourished intermittently, with from time to time long breaks in the occupation. The picture that we must have, then, is of a forbidding and unattractive jungle of oaks and marshes, occupied with any permanence only on its extreme eastern edge. Elsewhere, it would seem, settlements were started and later abandoned and then restarted again according to the fortunes of history.

The Romans extended their settlements into the interior, but for pasture rather than agriculture. Already the Greeks had built a harbor at Apollonia, later Arsuf, in the south of the region, and then Herod the Great built the imposing city of Caesarea, which at its zenith had 100,000 inhabitants. This was a triumph of engineering and construction, for an artificial harbor had to be built with breakwaters, water brought by aqueduct from Mount Carmel, and a network of roads laid out to connect the port with the interior of the country. Nevertheless, all this was done, and after the Romans took over the direct administration of Palestine they made the city their capital.

9. Karmon, *Israel,* p. 216.
10. *Ibid.,* p. 217.

11. N. Avigad, "Excavations at Makmish: 1958 Preliminary Report," *IEJ,* 10 (1960), 90–96; and "Excavations at Makmish 1960: Preliminary Report," *IEJ,* 11 (1961), 97–100.

CHAPTER 12

The Land of the Philistines

When Pharaoh let the people go, God did not lead them by way of the land of the Philistines, although that was near; for God said, "Lest the people repent when they see war."

EXODUS 13:17

On arriving at the Yarkon River in the journey southward we reach also, almost in one bound, the territory of biblical recorded history. It is indeed more than a little surprising that we have not reached it already, for though the largely uninhabited Sharon did not greatly concern the Israelites, the Trunk Road which skirted it on the east certainly did. Socoh, guarding the junction of this road with the route to Shechem, must surely have been important, and we know that the Northern Kingdom maintained an important garrison at Gibbethon, on the Philistine border (1 Kings 15:27; 16:15, 17), and must therefore have controlled the road which led to it. Probably it is because Sharon contained so few people that there was little of moment to record as the armies moved to and fro along the road; brigands there may have been, but no pitched battles.

South of the Yarkon may rather loosely be called "the land of the Philistines," not because the whole area belonged to them, but because in all this area they had to be reckoned with. Their true heartland lay in the southern Coast Plain, and from there they were always ready to expand outward into the surrounding territory.

A.3. *The Valley of Craftsmen*

This is an indeterminate title for an indeterminate region. The term occurs in Nehemiah 11:35, and may perhaps refer to the broad valley of the Wadi al-Kabir (Nahal Ayyalon), which runs northwestward across the center of the region. Some people have seen in the name a memory of the days when "there was no smith to be found throughout all the land of Israel; for the

47   **THE VALLEY OF THE CRAFTSMEN**

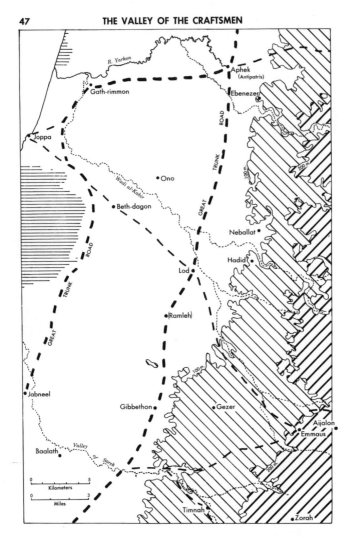

Philistines said, 'Lest the Hebrews make themselves swords or spears'; but every one of the Israelites went down to the Philistines to sharpen his plowshare, his mattock, his axe, or his sickle" (1 Sam. 13:19–20) in that far-off pre-Davidic period when the Philistines still guarded for themselves the secret of smelting iron.[1]

1. NEB leaves the term untranslated, and suggests also, as another possible translation, "Valley of Woods."

The northern border of the region is clearly the Yarkon River, but the southern limit is less easy to decide. Some authorities prefer to draw the line along the fault which runs southeastward past Ramleh, more or less along the line of the present Tel Aviv–Ramleh road,[2] but for our purposes it seems better to place it farther south, along the valley of Sorek (Wadi Surar or Sara), since

2. Karmon, *Israel*, p. 228.

the Philistine territory proper lay to the south of this.

Of the greatest importance was the town of Aphek, where the Trunk Road made its way between the powerful springs of the Yarkon and the foot of the scarp. There was no alternative to going through Aphek, for the Yarkon Valley, which until modern times was swampy and very easily flooded, constituted a major obstacle. Consequently, the site was fortified from very early days. It was well known to the Egyptians on their adventures northward, and is mentioned by Thutmose III and again in the Execration Texts. The ruler of "Aphek in Sharon"[3] is listed in Joshua 12:18 as among those defeated by Joshua, but almost certainly the city was never captured, for in the time of Saul it appears as a stronghold of the Philistines, where they gathered their forces together (1 Sam. 4:1; 29:1). Ebenezer, where the Israelites encamped on the earlier occasion, may be Majdal Yaba 2 miles to the southeast, guarding the route up into the mountains of Ephraim by way of the Wadi Sarida. In New Testament times an important road led up from the Yarkon springs toward Bethel, and it may have been by this that "the soldiers, according to their instructions, took Paul and brought him by night to Antipatris" (Acts 23:31), the Roman fortress on the same site. Today the springs form an important part of the modern Israeli water system; they are presided over by a ruined medieval Mamluke fortress and caravansary, and above it on the hill the remains of a Crusaders' castle.

From Aphek southward the roads splay out again, no longer restrained by the obstacles of Sharon. The western branch of the Trunk Road ran almost due westward along the higher land

3. This is almost certainly the correct reading, as in the Septuagint translation.

overlooking the swamps of the Yarkon, and from there one road went to Jaffa, while the main route turned southward and skirted the broad sand dunes which here begin to clothe the coast. Another eastern branch ran more directly south through Lod and Gibbethon to Ashdod, where the two roads joined. It was perhaps by this eastern route "that the commander in chief, who was sent by Sargon the king of Assyria, came to Ashdod, and fought against it and took

XXVI. *The Crusaders' Castle at Aphek.* The strong springs at Aphek, the modern Ras al-'Ain, or Rosh ha-'Ayin, meant that it was always an important staging post on the great Trunk Road south from Damascus to Egypt and a series of strong fortresses and caravanserais were built here. This picture shows part of the Crusaders' fortress on the hill above the springs.

it" in the year 711 B.C. (Isa. 20:1), though the direction as given in Assyrian records is not entirely clear.[4] Other roads from Aphek ran southeastward into the Shephelah.

The broad basin of the Wadi al-Kabir (Nahal Ayyalon) is covered with rich alluvium, and though it floods easily in wet weather it is excellent for grain when it dries out. The towns and villages characteristically stayed out of this low-lying land, both because of the danger of flooding and to avoid occupying good agricultural land. In the southeast it adjoins the Valley of Aijalon. This is the most important of all the routes leading up into Judah from the plain, and it differs from the other valleys in being a wide downfaulted basin instead of a river valley. Through it an easy road goes up past the two towns of Beth-horon, the lower and upper, and then on the highlands divides, giving access either to Bethel or by way of Gibeon to Jerusalem. It was in this valley that Joshua commanded the sun and moon to stand still (Josh. 10:10–15) and by this valley also that Saul and Jonathan drove back the Philistines after the victory at Michmash (1 Sam. 14:31). Lower Beth-horon was fortified by Solomon, and Aijalon by his successor Rehoboam, but in the days of the weak king Ahaz, Aijalon fell to the Philistines (1 Kings 9:17; 2 Chron. 11:10; 28:18). In about 166 B.C. Judas Maccabeus defeated Seron, the Syrian commander, here and in the following year won an important victory against Gorgias, who had encamped at "Emmaus in the plain" (Imwas—1 Macc. 3:13–24 and 3:28–4:25).[5] The strategic importance

4. Pritchard *ANET*, p. 126.
5. Whether this is also the Emmaus of the Resurrection story in Luke 24:13 is still a matter of considerable dispute. The phrase in 1 Maccabees 3:40, "Emmaus in the plain," suggests that there was another Emmaus elsewhere.

of this valley was demonstrated again in 1948 when the Arab Legion forces pressed down along it to cut the Israeli lifeline from Tel Aviv to Jerusalem, and until 1967 Jordan held here a salient which included both Yalu and Imwas. Controlling the northern slopes of the entrance to this valley were Shaalbim (Josh. 19:42; Judg. 1:35; 1 Kings 4:9) and Adithaim (Josh. 15:36).

The main road from Aijalon to Joppa went along the southern side of the Wadi al-Kabir through Lod and Beth-dagon (Josh. 15:41), where it crossed the two branches of the Trunk Road. Lod and Ono are always mentioned together. 1 Chronicles 8:12 says that they were built by the sons of Elpaal, which probably means that they were fortified towns of some importance. The mention of them in Ezra 2:33 and Nehemiah 7:37 suggests that they were among the places settled by the returning exiles and may perhaps have formed the extreme western boundary of settlement. Hence the plain of Ono would have been a suitable place for the untoward purposes of Sanballat and Geshem (Neh. 6:2). Joppa, the modern Jaffa, was the chief port used by Judah, though it was never part of their dominions, even in the days of the United Monarchy. It has the advantage of a small bay, perhaps connected with the fault line already mentioned, and partially protected by a *kurkar* cliff. The Wadi al-Kabir stream at one time flowed into this bay, possibly in biblical times, but at some period it seems to have changed its course toward the north, and now it joins the Yarkon.[6]

The land south of the Aijalon-Joppa road is rather higher and contains the last major area of Red Sand, also apparently forested in ancient times and avoided by the towns and villages. On either side of the broad alluvial valley

6. Karmon, *Israel*, p. 231.

east of it stood the powerful fortresses of Gibbethon and Gezer, commanding the frontier between the Philistine territory and the northern kingdom of Israel.[7] Gezer, on the edge of the Shephelah, had been an important stronghold of the Philistines before the time of David (2 Sam. 5:25; 1 Chron. 14:16; 20:4),[8] and was fortified by

7. H. Darrel Lance, "Gezer in the Land and in History," *BA*, XXX (1967), 34–47. The presence of some 15 to 20 *lmlk* (="for the king") jar handles here suggests that Hezekiah at one time controlled Gezer Aharoni, *Land of the Bible*, pp. 340–46.

8. William G. Dever, "Excavations at Gezer," *BA*, XXX (1967), 58–59.

Solomon (1 Kings 9:15), as the magnificent gateway of his period bears witness.

The Valley of Sorek, which brings this region to an end in the south, together with the Wadi al-Kabir, forms the area which in Joshua 19:40–48 is said to have been occupied by the tribe of Dan before they were forced to vacate it, presumably by the northward pressure of the Philistines along the trade routes. The whole region is transitional in more than one sense. It marks the change from the Red Sand and the marshes of Sharon to the drier south with its important exposure of Eocene and its sand dunes. It is the

XXVII. *The Standing Stones at Gezer.* Gezer was an important stronghold in the boundary zone between Israelite and Philistine territory. It is generally believed that these standing stones, belonging to the Bronze Age, represent the establishment of an important covenant between the neighboring peoples.

48   **THE PHILISTINE PLAIN**

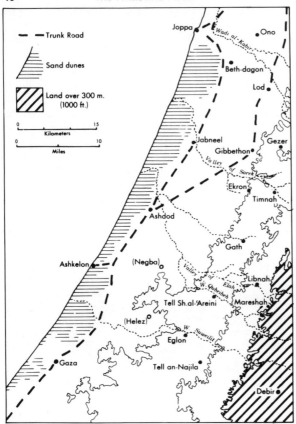

border zone between the Philistines, Israel, and Judah, each laying claim to part, and sometimes more than part, of it. It is also essentially a zone of trade routes, from north to south and from Jaffa to the hills, and all the settlements existed primarily to supply, control, and protect these routes.

A.4. *The Philistine Plain*

This is about 13 miles (21 km.) wide in the north but broadening in the south, where the coast curves away to the southwest. In sharp distinction from the coast of Sharon to the north there

are here broad sand dunes, extending as much as 3 miles (6 km.) inland, formed not of sand from the Nile, as was once believed, but of material brought down from the wadis, and especially the soft chalk and chalky limestone of the Shephelah.[9] The cliffs of the north appear here only very intermittently and are most important at the port of Ashkelon.

Once again we must distinguish a lower northern section and a higher southern section, the division between them being a line drawn from Ashkelon

9. Nir, "Étude sur la Morphologie Littorale d'Israel," pp. 424–36.

to Lachish. In the north a number of wadis from the Shephelah gather together behind Ashdod and enter the sea about 4 miles (6 km.) farther north; in the south the land, which was about 100 feet (30 m.) above sea level in the north, rises to as much as 650 feet (200 m.) behind Gaza in the gentle upfold known to Israeli geographers as the Helez-Negba anticline. Yet, although the land rises, the rainfall toward the south decreases and the influence of the desert makes itself more and more felt, and so, despite the formidable barrier of the sand dunes, sometimes 150 feet (45 m.) in height, there are no longer any marshes. Instead, the landscape is one of rolling downland, with wide valleys and distant views. The ancient forest gave way to open woodland, and in the south trees were confined to the valleys.

The role played by this region in history has, therefore, been very different from that of its counterpart to the north. Instead of the savage wastes heaped with greater riches of vegetation than they could easily bear, a hindrance to movement and settlement alike, this is increasingly open steppeland, full of good grainlands and famous towns, a land where movement is seldom impossible and often easy, but for that reason also a land often visited by war. The main branch of the Trunk Road ran behind the sand dunes, its course no longer determined by the necessity of avoiding swamps, but more and more by the need of finding water. In the northern section the villages still tend to keep to the higher part of the plain and the roads avoid the valleys, for the possibility of winter flooding is not yet exhausted, but in the south the villages creep down into the valleys, where water is easier to obtain, and roads cross hill and wadi indiscriminately.

Judges 15:5 speaks of grain and olive orchards, but the first is more characteristic of the region than the second, since here we are close to the edge of the true Mediterranean climate, the only climate in which the olive will consent to grow. Olive groves are found today on the coastal stretch near Ashkelon and Gaza, but on the rolling hills behind them wheat in the north, and barley and sheep in the south, take their place. The chief agricultural problem of this region is the increasing danger of drought, and so we must probably assume that when Elisha told the Shunammite woman to flee southward from Esdraelon to the land of the Philistines (2 Kings 8:1–6), the famine from which she fled was due, not to lack of rain but to the incessant war with Syria.

"Not only war swept the Maritime Plain. The Plague came up this way from Egypt." So quite rightly says George Adam Smith,[10] for the evil diseases of Egypt were proverbial (Deut. 7:15, 28:60; Amos 4:10), and the Philistines, who held the very gate Egypt, must have been particularly posed to them. It is hardly by accide that two of the best-known stories about this part of the country concern an outbreak of plague: the troubles of the Philistines while the Ark was in their territory (1 Sam. 5 and 6) and the destruction of Sennacherib's army, which at the time was warring against Libnah (2 Kings 19:8, 35–37).

The Philistines were moving into the southern Coast Plain at about the same time as the Israelites were occupying the hill country. In the thirteenth and twelfth centuries B.C. "the tempest of the Sea Peoples had lashed against the

10. George Adam Smith, *Historical Geography of the Holy Land* (New York: Harper & Row, Torchbook ed. 1966), pp. 118ff.

coast of Syria and Palestine, driving almost to the gates of Egypt . . . and the period of Egyptian domination over the land of Canaan came to an end."[11] The Philistines belonged to the second wave of these Indo-European people, against whom Rameses III fought in the great battle recorded on the walls of the temple at Medinet Habu, and it would seem that it was with Egyptian support that they were settled at the southern end of the Trunk Road. The biblical writers were well aware of the fact that these "uncircumcised" people had come from somewhere across the sea, and they described both the Philistines and their territory somewhat loosely as "Cretan" (either "from Caphtor" or "Cherethite"—Deut. 2:23; 1 Sam. 30:14; Jer. 47:4; Ezek. 25:16; Amos 9:7; Zeph. 2:5). Up to the time of the United Monarchy they became increasingly powerful and extended their authority northward along the Trunk Road as well as pressing upward into the hill country by way of the Saddle of Benjamin, from which they were ejected by Jonathan (1 Sam. 14). At the end of Saul's reign they had firm control of Beth-shan (1 Sam. 31) and even had penetrated down the Rift Valley as far as Deir 'Alla, and consequently this time had more or less surrounded the Israelites.[12] David smashed their power in a series of battles (2 Sam. 5:17–25; 8:1; 19:9; 1 Chron. 11:11–21), and though after the days of Solomon they continued to hold the southern end of the Trunk Road and to be a perpetual nuisance to Israel and Judah, they were never again a major threat.

Their five great cities were Gaza, Ashkelon, Ashdod, Ekron, and Gath

(1 Sam. 6:17). Gaza is one of the permanent sites in history, as necessary a place of habitation as Damascus, at the meeting point on the Trunk Road of the desert and the cultivated land. Ashkelon stands where a line of low *kurkar* cliffs marks a break in the sand dunes, its Philistine ruins surmounted by the remains of the greater Roman and medieval cities. Ashdod, farther north, like Gaza, is not on the coast but back behind the sand dunes, and in the later monarchy it had a stronghold on the shore at Ashdod-yam.[13] None of these towns controls a river crossing, for no longer do the streams provide any serious obstacle. Farther north along the road is Jabneel, overlooking the valley of the Sorek, and the most northerly extension of Philistine coastal territory was at Tel Qasile on the Yarkon. Tel Qasile seems to have been founded by the Philistines, but the others long predate them. Seagoing vessels had been developed at least as early as the third millennium B.C., and in the second millennium trade by sea took on considerable importance, reaching a peak in the fourteenth and thirteenth centuries, when this coast was in touch with Ugarit, Cyprus, Crete, Mycenae, and Egypt.[14]

The landward frontier of the Philistine territory was guarded by Ekron and Gath, about both of which there has been no little disagreement. Ekron is mentioned a number of times as a border city (Josh. 13:3; 15:11) or a

11. Aharoni, *op. cit.*, p. 246. See the whole section, pp. 245–53.

12. George Ernest Wright, "Fresh Evidence for the Philistine Story," *BA*, XXIX (1966), 70–86.

13. J. Kaplan, "The Stronghold of Yamani at Ashdod-Yam," *IEJ*, 19 (1969), 137–49.

14. See the account of the papers of Ruth Amiran, "Cultural Links between the Coast of Canaan and the Lands Overseas," and P. Delougaz, "Ships and Shipping in the Ancient Near East," in "Report on the Fifteenth Annual Convention of the Israel Exploration Society," *IEJ*, 10 (1960), 46–55.

city of the Philistines (1 Sam. 5:10; 7:14; 17:52; Jer. 25:20; Amos 1:8; Zeph. 2:4; Zech. 9:5) Apparently it was one of the centers of soothsayers, for whom the Philistines were noted (2 Kings 1:2; Isa. 2:6). It fell into the hands of Jonathan as a gift in 147 B.C. (1 Macc. 10:89) at the time of his successful campaign against the coastal cities. Most scholars agree today that it is to be identified with Kh. al-Muqanna', about 4 miles (6 km.) west of Timnah and overlooking a southern tributary wadi of the Sorek,[15] and if so it was, like Tel Qasile, founded by the Philistines.

The present most generally accepted site for Gath is Tell as-Safi, of which Aharoni says that it is "virtually the only fitting candidate in the region,"[16] though another recent claim has been put forward for Tell ash-Sharia' very much farther to the south.[17] Tell as-Safi, which guards the entrance to the important valley route of the Wadi as-Samt across the Shephelah, was previously identified with Libnah, which must now probably be placed at Tell Bornat on the Wadi Zeita farther south. Gath was the scene of constant fighting between the Philistines and the people of Judah, and as such it passed into the Hebrew language as a proverbial symbol of the hated Philistines themselves (2 Sam. 1:20; Mic. 1:10). The people of Gath seem to have been prepared to receive political refugees from Judah; David himself took refuge there (1 Sam. 27:2), and so did the slaves of Shimei, who was forbidden to leave Jerusalem (1 Kings 2:26–46). Possibly as a result of David's sojourn in Gath he was later able to have a

Philistine bodyguard commanded by Ittai from Gath (2 Sam. 15:18–22; 18:2, 5). It was captured by Uzziah (2 Chron. 26:6) and apparently largely destroyed. Amos seems to refer to it as recently laid waste (Amos 6:2), and it does not appear together with the other Philistine towns in the passages from the prophetic writings listed above for Ekron.

South of Gath a number of important tells, at present unidentified, mark the junction of the Shephelah with the Philistine Plain. Two of them have in the past been claimed as the site of Gath (Tell Sheikh al-'Areini and Tell an-Najila), but the archaeological evidence is against both these suggestions. Tell an-Najila has also been suggested as the site of Eglon, but it is more likely that this should be placed at Tell al-Hesi, about halfway between the two. Eglon was one of the cities, together with Lachish, Debir, Jarmuth in the north of the Shephelah, and Hebron, which responded to the appeal of the ruler of Jerusalem for help against Joshua and thereby provoked the great battle in the Valley of Aijalon (Josh. 10:3ff.). It was a city of considerable importance in the Bronze Age, but very much less so after its destruction in the thirteenth century B.C., an event which many would identify with the defeat by Joshua. An interesting reminder of the treacherous climatic conditions of this southern Philistine Plain is provided by the subterranean pits which in the Persian period were common in the Eglon region. They are believed to be storage pits for grain, in which a surplus could be kept against the danger of lean years.[18]

15. J. Naveh, "Khirbat al-Muqanna'-Ekron," *IEJ*, 8 (1958), 87–100, 165–170.

16. Y. Aharoni, "Rubute and Ginti-Karmil," *VT*, XIX (1969), 137–45.

17. Wright, *op. cit.* pp. 70–86.

18. Lawrence E. Stager, "Conditions and Grain Storage in the Persian Period at Tell el-Hesi," *BA*, XXXIV (1971), 86–88.

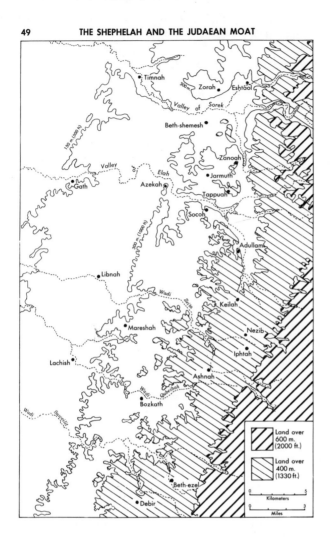

A.5. *The Shephelah*

It was George Adam Smith who first recognized that the word *shephelah,* or "lowland," is a definite regional term.[19] It occurs twenty times in the Old Testament (Deut. 1:7; Josh. 9:1; 10:40; 11:2, 16, twice; 12:8; 15:33; Judg. 1:9; 1 Kings 10:27; 1 Chron. 27:28; 2 Chron. 1:15; 9:27; 26:10; 28:18; Jer. 17:26; 32:44; 33:13; Obad. 19; Zech.

19. Smith, *op. cit.,* pp. 143–67.

7:7), and except for Joshua 11:2, 16, it always refers to this region between the Philistine Plain and the mountains. That it has this sense is clear from 2 Chronicles 26:10 and 28:18, for in the first passage the Shephelah is distinguished from the Plain, and in the second the Philistines, who lived in the Plain, are said to have made raids on the Shephelah. In Joshua 11, however, the word is twice used for some more northerly region. In verse 2 it is grouped with the northern hill country and the heights of Dor, while verse 16 speaks of "the Shephelah, and the Rift Valley, and the hill-country of Israel and its Shephelah." The first "Shephelah" in verse 16 is clearly the district between Philistia and Judah, but the "Israelite Shephelah" must be somewhere else. Very probably this northern Shephelah is the central section of the Carmel range between the Carmel massif and the hills of Umm al-Fahm, for it is composed of rock similar to that of the true Shephelah and is very like it in general appearance. There is reason to believe that the ancient Israelites would have been acutely aware of these similarities.

The Shephelah is a zone about 27 miles long (45 km.) by 10 miles wide (16 km.) and, like the Coast Plain, it is higher in the south than in the north. It is also divided down the middle into a lower western zone, which may be the result of erosion by the sea during the Miocene period,[20] and a higher eastern zone, reaching about 1,300 feet (400 m.) in the north and up to about 1,650 feet (500 m.) in the south. The whole region is one of rounded hills of chalk and chalky limestone, though protected from erosion by a hard limy covering called *nari*. Except in the broad transverse valleys and on the western slopes where the hills form only spurs with alluvial basins between them, it is not a fertile region, and very much of the hill surface was covered by rough scrub until quite recent times. In the Old Testament it was noted for the stands of fig sycamore, but as we have seen this was thought of in somewhat derogatory terms (1 Kings 10:27; 2 Chron. 1:15; 9:27; Amos 7:14).

Historically the Shephelah has always been a buffer zone. For the people of Judah, perched on their mountains, it

was the glacis which served as their first line of defense against the Philistines, but for the Philistines it was the first step toward the conquest of the hills. It belonged permanently neither to the one nor to the other, but was rather a debating ground whereon they waged their incessant bloody contests, so that at times the Philistines "devour Israel with open mouth," and at times Ephraim and Judah "swoop down upon the shoulder of the Philistines in the west" (Isa. 9:12; 11:14). The hills themselves are honeycombed with caves carved out in the soft chalk to provide lime for plaster,[21] and later used for refuge in the early Christian period.

All the valleys which cross the Shephelah have played their part in history. The Valley of Aijalon, which marks the northernmost limit, has already been described. The next valley, the Valley of Sorek, famous for the exploits of Samson, pierces the hill country like a trident, with all three prongs pointing at Jerusalem, though the steep, rocky ascents made these approaches less important than the Valley of Aijalon. On the northern side are Eshtaol and Zorah, with somewhere between them Mahaneh-dan (Judg. 13:25), and on the south is Timnah, where a young lion roared against Samson, and whence he took his first wife (Judg. 14:1, 5). Where it cuts through the Shephelah is the commanding side of Beth-shemesh, at which the Philistines handed back the Ark to the Israelites (1 Sam. 6:10–16) and where also Jehoash of Israel and Amaziah of Judah faced each other in battle (2 Kings 14:11; 2 Chron. 25:21), for it would appear that Jehoash, who was a strong ruler, was pressing the Philistines in this region, as did so many of the Israelite kings, when he was chal-

---

20. Karmon, *Israel*, p. 246.

21. *Ibid.*, p. 247. See also the description of them in Smith, *op. cit.*, pp. 167–71.

lenged by the foolhardy Amaziah. The result was that Jehoash was able to plunder Jerusalem (2 Kings 14:23–24), making his way thither by the same road as had been used earlier to bring the Ark to Kiriath-jearim (1 Sam. 7:2; 2 Sam. 6:2; 1 Chron. 13:6; Ps. 132:6).

Farther south is the Wadi as-Samt, the Valley of Elah in which Goliath was killed (1 Sam. 17:1–54), between Socoh and Azekah. Azekah is certainly Tell Zakaria, commanding the crossing of the valley by the road from Beth-shemesh to Mareshah, more or less along the junction between the western and eastern Shephelah (today the road southward to Beth Guvrin). Socoh, later to become one of the chief store cities in Hezekiah's reorganization of the Judean defenses,[22] is probably Kh. 'Abbad farther up the valley. At the point where the valley issued into the plain stood Gath.

The next valley southward is the Wadi Zeita. At its western end, in the Judean moat, stood Iphtah, probably the modern Tarqumiyeh (Josh. 15:42), and in the center it was controlled by Mareshah, the scene of a reputed battle of Asa (2 Chron. 14:9–10; see also Josh. 15:44; 2 Chron. 11:8; Mic. 1:15), on the impressive mound of Tell Sandahanna where the lower western Shephelah begins to break up into separate spurs running out into the plain. Consequently, Mareshah was a crossroads, where roads from Beth-shemesh, Libnah (Tel Bornat) farther down the Zeita Valley, and Lachish all meet. In the time of the Maccabees it was known as Marisa, and was an important stronghold of the Seleucid armies.

The last of the valleys is the Wadi Qubeibah, in which stand Lachish (Tell ad-Duweir) and, farther into the high

22. Aharoni, *Land of the Bible,* pp. 298, 340.

Shephelah, Bozkath (ad-Duwaiyima— Josh. 15:39; 2 Kings 22:1). Since Lachish and Mareshah command the routes up to Hebron, they were both cities of great importance. Lachish is mentioned five times in the Amarna letters and, as already mentioned, is said to have joined in the confederation against Joshua. It was also destroyed in the thirteenth century, but was strongly rebuilt during the United Monarchy and was apparently further fortified by Rehoboam (2 Chron. 11:9). In 2 Chronicles 25:27 we are told that the unfortunate King Amaziah fled there in vain for refuge. In the campaigns of both the Assyrians and the Babylonians it was besieged (2 Kings 18:14; Jer. 34:7), and from the later period, when "Lachish and Azekah . . . were the only fortified cities of Judah that remained," we have the famous "Lachish letters," which confirm this grim report.

On the eastern side of the Shephelah, dividing it from the highlands of Judah, is a long narrow valley running from north to south along an exposure of the soft Senonian chalk. Above it to the east stands the steeep scarp of the Cenomanian limestone. It may be traced from Aijalon through Eshtaol, close to the home of Samson (Judg. 13:25), and Zanoah to Tappuah, which is possibly the village of Beit Nattif (Josh. 15:34). South of this again is Adullam (Kh. Sheikh Madhkur), where David and his family took refuge from Saul (1 Sam. 22:1), and Keilah, where David delivered the inhabitants from the raids of the Philistines who were robbing the threshing floors (1 Sam. 23:1–5). Beyond this the valley is not so clear, but the steep westward-facing scarp continues past Nezib (Kh. Beit Nesib) to Iphtah, probably the present village of Tarqumiyeh (Josh. 15:43). Then there is a sharp bend of the scarp southwestward to Ashnah, the present Idna, and

XXVIII. *The Cliffs at Ashkelon.* Although much of the Cis-jordan coast is low lying and sandy, parts are marked by cliffs, especially where a *kurkar* ridge runs along the shore. These cliffs are often easily eroded and at Ashkelon even medieval buildings have collapsed into the sea. In the foreground parts of two Roman columns may be seen.

from there SSW along the course of the 1948 armistice line to Beth-ezel (Mic. 1:11), Debir (Josh. 10:38, 39; 11:21; 12:13; 15:15, 49; 21:15; Judg. 1:11; 1 Chron. 6:58), and finally to Ziklag (Tell al-Khuweilfeh), which was David's refuge in the latter part of his struggle against Saul and which at one point was sacked by the Amalekites from the Negeb (Josh. 15:31; 19:5; 1 Sam. 27:6; 30:1ff., 26; 2 Sam. 1:1).

This valley and the steep scarp beside it formed an important part of the defenses of Judah, for it meant that whereas the conquest of the Shephelah was a necessary preliminary to the conquest of the mountains, it was only a preliminary, and many famous armies have taken possession of the Shephelah and yet have failed to conquer Judah. The Philistines themselves, though they invaded the Shephelah again and again, never succeeded in gaining control of the mountains, and in the days of the Maccabean revolt the guerrilla forces of Judas were able to raid across the Shephelah and harry the Syrian army, even into the Coast Plain. The Syrians operated from the two strongholds of Gazara (Gezer) and Marisa (Mareshah), while at one point Judas encamped at Adullam (1 Macc. 4:15; 5:66; 2 Macc. 12:35, 38). In his turn Richard I of England, though he fortified and occupied the Shephelah, had to be content with but a distant view of the Holy City. Even in our own day the same strategic line has held, and at the end of the 1948 fighting Israel held the Shephelah and part of the moat, but the hill country was denied to them. They had held western Jerusalem because they were established there already, but only by the most determined efforts did they manage to keep control of the road which gave them access to the city.

CHAPTER 13

The Rich Valley

Woe to the proud crown of the drunkards of Ephraim,
and to the fading flower of its glorious beauty,
which is on the head of the rich valley of those
overcome with wine!

ISAIAH 28:1

A.6. *The Central Valley of Esdraelon and Jezreel*

Cleaving the Western Highlands, from Acco to Beth-shan, is the last of the lowlands west of the Jordan, the Bay of Acco, already considered as part of Asher, being itself the beginning. Then come in turn the Plain of Esdraelon and the Valley of Jezreel, the only areas of the western plains which lay entirely within the Israelite territory and a possession for which the people in the end paid dearly. It was the fact that this vital crossroads lay inside the borders of the northern kingdom that contributed in no small measure to its downfall a century and a quarter before the collapse of Judah, remote upon its windswept mountains to the south. Once Assyria had embarked upon her policy of expansion southward along the great Trunk Road there could already be

"heard a decree of destruction from the Lord God of Hosts upon the whole land" (Isa. 28:22).

Of the two plains that of Esdraelon is the larger, forming a triangle with its base along the foot of Carmel from Jokneam to En-gannim (the modern Jenin), a distance of some 20 miles (32 km.), and its apex at the modern settlement of Tel 'Adashim 18 miles (28 km.) due north of En-gannim. Through this plain the Kishon wanders in a long arc toward the northwest and enters the Bay of Acco by the narrow gap between Carmel and Galilee at Harosheth. Dry in its upper courses in summer, and only a trickle when it passes Harosheth, this famous stream is often a sad disappointment to visitors, but it is never fitting in Palestine to "despise the day of small things," and the importance of the Kishon was not exhausted by the part it played in the defeat of Sisera.

XXIX. *The Rich Valley.* This photograph is taken from the "Forty Oaks," and shows the narrow northwestern end of Esdraelon within the background the beginning of the "Galilean Shephelah." The straight line of eucalyptus trees marks the road from the Bay of Acco to Jokneam and Megiddo. In the foreground are the *maquis* and outcrops of Cenomanian limestone on the slopes of Carmel.

From about the middle of the straight eastern edge of Esdraelon the much narrower valley of Jezreel cuts southwestward to the Rift Valley between the limestone hills of Gilboa and the volcanic plateau of Moreh. In contrast to the almost level floor of Esdraelon, Jezreel descends gradually but steadily, passing below sea level in about 4½ miles (7 km.) close to the present 'Ain Harod and reaching −500 feet (−150 m.) at Beth-shan, some 7½ miles (12 km.) farther on. Here there is a sudden drop of another 250 feet (75 m.) down the steep step which forms the western limit of the Ghor.

Structurally the two plains form part of a complicated downfaulted region where the two different fault systems cross each other. The dominant line of faulting is from northwest to southeast, the direction of the base of the Esdraelon triangle and also the Valley of Jezreel. Other faults strike off at an angle to this, the most impressive being the NNE–SSW scarp just south of Nazareth which towers nearly 1,000 feet (300 m.) above the plain. Part of this scarp at Jabal Qafsa has been perhaps obviously, but certainly wrongly, called the Mount of Precipitation, the place where the Nazarenes attempted to lynch Jesus (Luke 4:29), but by hardly any stretch of the imagination could it be called "the brow of the hill on which their city was built." Another fault cuts back from this point toward Harosheth, and yet another is probably responsible for the almost straight eastern edge of the plain.

The whole expanse of Esdraelon is floored with alluvium, as much as 330 feet (100 m.) in depth, which has poured down into this rift valley. Although slightly higher in the southeast near En-gannim, the greater part of the plain is nearly level, about 150 feet (50 m.) above the sea and sloping very gently indeed to about 80 feet (25 m.), where the Kishon breaks through into the Bay of Acco. This slow descent is interrupted in the center by a narrow volcanic outcrop,[1] as it were a perpendicular dropped from the apex at Tel 'Adashim to the base at Megiddo, causing the land to rise very slightly, at the most no more than 100 feet (30 m.) above the surface. This is the merest swelling, and the slopes are so gradual that it is not clearly visible, even on the ground, although for the modern observer it is denoted by a line of white Israeli houses built along its crest.

The Kishon, small though it is, has to carry away the entire drainage from the surrounding hills, but it is twice hindered in this formidable task, once by the volcanic causeway and then again by the narrow defile through which it finds its way to the Bay of Acco. In consequence the two basins thus formed are only too easily flooded in winter, sometimes for prolonged periods, and W. M. Thomson, who knew the country well a century and a half ago, speaks of having "no little trouble with its bottomless mire and tangled grass."[2] In February, 1905, Gertrude Bell wrote even more feelingly of riding from Haifa to Jenin: "The road lay all across the Plain of Esdraelon . . . and the mud was incredible. We

1. Yehuda Karmon (*Israel*, p. 192) speaks of this as an anticlinal fold, but this seems to be incorrect.
2. W. M. Thomson, *The Land and the Book,* rev. by Julian Grande (London: Thomas Nelson and Sons, 1911), p. 429.

waded sometimes for an hour at a time knee deep in clinging mud, the mules fell down, the donkeys almost disappeared ('By God!' said one of the muleteers, 'you could see nothing but his ears!') and the horses grew wearier and wearier."[3] The northwestern basin is the more prone to swamps and marshes, but neither is free. The nineteenth-century traveler was warned to "beware lest he

3. *The Letters of Gertrude Bell*, I, 176.

50   THE ACCO—BETH-SHAN ROUTE

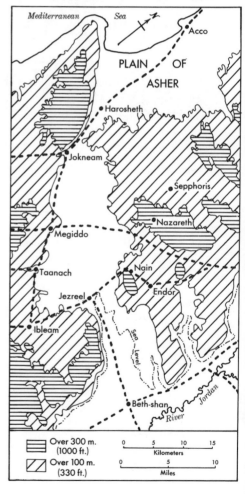

| | | Over 300 m. (1000 ft.) |
| | | Over 100 m. (330 ft.) |

Kilometers 0 5 10 15

Miles 0 5 10

camp within reach of the malaria engendered by the warm damp of the little rills,"[4] and the struggles of the early Jewish settlers in the first years of the twentieth century against this and other problems of the marshes which then existed are a famous part of the Zionist saga.

Yet it was always "the rich valley," for once dried out, the bottomless mud bears notable harvests. "Two things strike us forcibly in looking over the plain of Esdraelon," said Murray in 1868, "first, its wondrous richness . . . second, its desolation. If we except its eastern branches, there is not a single inhabited village on its whole surface, and not more than a tenth of its soil is cultivated. It is the home of the wandering Bedway . . . it has always been insecure."[5] Visitors in the nineteenth century differ greatly in their estimates of the area that was under the plow, ranging from 10 percent to 90 percent, but failure to cultivate seems always to have had some political cause. Insecure the valley certainly was in times of political weakness, and unless a strong government exercised its forceful control the danger of Bedouin raids was constant. Traveler after traveler bears witness to them, quoting almost without fail that weary time in the days of the Judges when "the Midianites and the Amalekites and the people of the East would . . . encamp against them and destroy the produce of the land" (Judg. 6:3–4). Yet the absence of villages in the plain, on which these writers so often comment, was not the result of desolation.

Even in times of prosperity the villages kept to the foothills, and houses were never built upon the cultivable land.

There are five gates to Esdraelon. The first is the constricted corridor which leads to the Bay of Acco, and opposite to it is the second, guarded by Jezreel (Zir'in) on the south and Shunem (Sulam) on the northern side. This is the Valley of Jezreel, never more than 2 miles (3 km.) wide, well supplied with water from the hillsides and a stranger to the cold of winter, but sometimes swampy and occasionally subject to dangerous flooding. The scarp of Gilboa dominates this passageway. It was from these slopes that Gideon saw the people of the East in the valley "like locusts for multitude, and their camels were without number" (Judg. 7:12), and here also that the army of Saul encamped before the disastrous battle in which both he and his son Jonathan lost their lives (1 Sam. 29:1).

At the southeastern end of the valley stands Beth-shan, the massive guardian of the Jordan gate, where every power that controlled the Trunk Road needed to have a strong garrison. In the days of the Egyptian empire this was an Egyptian city, and later the Philistines were established here, as evidenced by a typical anthropoid coffin of the Philistine type. It was never conquered by the Israelite tribes before the united monarchy, and when David overcame the Philistines he seems to have kept it as a royal city, without markedly changing the character of its inhabitants.[6] The fords across the Jordan opposite Bethshan are not difficult, and the ascent onto the plateau fairly easy, so that at times Beth-shan seemed to belong almost more to the eastern side than the west. Thus the Hellenistic and Roman Scythopolis, whose name may possibly

---

4. Canon Tristram, "Esdraelon and Nazareth," in *Picturesque Palestine, Sinai and Egypt*, ed. by Colonel Wilson (New York: D. Appleton, 1881), I, 262.

5. Quoted by Hanna Margalit, "Some Aspects of the Cultural Landscape of Palestine during the First Half of the Nineteenth Century," *IEJ*, 13 (1963), 214–15.

6. M. Avi-Yonah, "Scythopolis," *IEJ*, 12 (1962), 128.

XXX. *Beth-shan.*   In the background is the great mound of Tell al-Husn, the site of Old Testament Beth-shan, and in the foreground the ruins of the Roman theater of Scythopolis. This city controlled the gateway from the Jordan valley into the narrow Valley of Jezreel.

come from the settlement here of Scythian horsemen, was the only city of the Decapolis which stood on the western side of the Jordan, and very much earlier it was from Jabesh-gilead that "all the valiant men arose and went all night, and took the body of Saul, and the bodies of his sons from the wall of Beth-shan" (1 Sam. 31:12). It was from Gilead also that Jehu came by way of Beth-shan to slay "all that remained of the house of Ahab in Jezreel, all his great men, and his familiar friends, and his priests, until he left him none remaining," a policy of savagery which

prompted Hosea to use the name of Jezreel in execration (2 Kings 10:11; Hos. 1:5).

The third gateway is the moderately broad extension of the plain northeastward toward Mount Tabor, a rotund hump of a mountain, until quite recently forested, which stands majestically alone. This district could reasonably be considered either part of Esdraelon or the beginning of Lower Galilee, since here the plain is somewhat higher, about 350 feet (115 m.) above sea level, and forms a water-parting, the slopes of Tabor draining into the Jordan. Round the foot of the mountain came the Trunk Road from Hazor in the north to the pass of Megiddo and the Coast Plain. Tabor was from early times a sacred mountain, the "navel" of the land, and doubtless it was for this reason that Barak first gathered together here the warriors of Naphtali and of Zebulun (Judg. 4:6) before descending to rout the forces of Sisera.[7] The road to Jezreel and Samaria followed the edge of Mount Moreh through Endor, where Saul in his desperation consulted the witch, seeking the aid of those magic arts which earlier he had ruthlessly condemned (1 Sam. 28:3–25). About 2 miles farther along the road is Nain, where Jesus is reported to have raised the widow's son from the dead (Luke 7:11–17). The road then leaves the plain through the fourth gateway, the Ascent of Gur. This name is known only from 2 Kings 9:27 as the place where Jehu killed Ahaziah, king of Judah, as he was fleeing after the death of Ahab, but it is surely the narrow defile south of En-gannim (Beth-haggan in this story) leading to Ibleam and the tiny plain of Dothan. Here it was that Joseph came in search of his brothers (Gen. 37:17) and that later the king of Syria made a vain attempt to arrest Elisha (2 Kings 6:13). From this plain it is possible either to go up into the hills of Samaria or to turn southwestward into the Plain of Sharon.

The fifth gateway is threefold, where three fortresses guarded the passes across Carmel. These are Jokneam, Megiddo, and Taanach, spaced out about 5 miles (8 km.) from one another. Jokneam and Megiddo each stand at the entrance into the plain of those two chalk valleys which lie on either side of the "Israelite Shephelah," the low but rocky plateau in the central section of the Carmel

7. The course of the battle is somewhat obscure, and it may be that the stories of two encounters are here conflated.

range. Near Taanach a fault line striking southwestward across the hills has helped to create the Wadi 'Abdullah, a narrow defile up into the Cenomanian limestone. Beyond the present village of Ya'bud this road is joined by the road from Ibleam, and the two together make their way into Sharon by the Wadi Abu Nar.

Of these three routes, that past Megiddo was overwhelmingly the most important, as Thutmose III clearly recognized when he urged his army to seize it, "for the capturing of Megiddo is the capturing of a thousand towns! Capture ye firmly, firmly!"[8] This is

8. Pritchard, *ANET*, p. 237.

51   THE PASSES ACROSS CARMEL

PLAIN OF ASHER

Harosheth

Jokneam

ESDRAELON

Dor

Megiddo

Taanach

Caesarea

SHARON

Ibleam

Dothan

Kilometers

Miles

600 m. (2000 ft.)
300 m. (1000 ft.)
100 m. (330 ft.)

Socoh

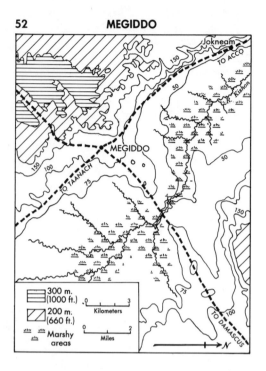

52   MEGIDDO

Jokneam
TO ACCO
Kishon
150
50
MEGIDDO
TO TAANACH
TO DAMASCUS

300 m.
(1000 ft.)
200 m.
(660 ft.)
Marshy
areas

Kilometers
Miles
N

would often be no other way across. The officers of Thutmose III, it is true, discussed the possibility of using other routes across the hills, but the goal was Megiddo, and the other passages were urged only as ways around to the same point. Megiddo did not only guard the pass. It stood at a crossroads, in fact at one of the great crossroads of the ancient world. It had been the seat of an Egyptian garrison in the time of their empire[10] and was an important Philistine city in the days of Saul. Solomon rebuilt it (1 Kings 9:15), and after its destruction by Shishak in 918 B.C. it was again strongly fortified, and the famous "stables" and underground water supply date from the time of Ahab.[11] Still later it saw the death of Ahaziah after he had been shot by Jehu at Ibleam (2 Kings 9:27) and the tragic defeat of King Josiah, who had gone north to check the advance of Pharaoh Necho against the Babylonians (2 Kings 23:29–30; 2 Chron. 35:20–25). In the days of the Romans there stood here the fortress of Legio Maximinopolis, whose name persists in the modern village of Lejjun.

The other towns held subordinate, yet strongly defended, positions. Jokneam stands at the northwestern end of the plain and therefore away from the main line of north–south trade. However, it is the only pass which has access to Dor, for the western approach is a double

because Megiddo controls not only a hill route but also the most natural route across the plain. The hill route is the Wadi 'Ara, well provided with springs and nowhere as high as 1,000 feet (300 m.) above sea level. The soft chalk wears away into a smooth, though admittedly bumpy, surface, and despite the narrowness of the pass there are few serious obstacles to the passage of chariots. The chief danger seems to have been of attacks by disorderly tribes from the *ya'ar* on either side as the army made its way in single file along the narrow road. The SW–NE line of this valley is then carried across the plain by the volcanic causeway to Tel 'Adashim, raised slightly but definitely above the clogging marshes on either side, and although in the dry summer after the harvest "the roads had no limit to their breadth,"[9] in the winter floods there

9. Smith *op. cit.*, p. 248.

10. Yohanan Aharoni, "Some Geographical Remarks Concerning the Campaigns of Amenhotep II," *VT*, XIX (1960), 177–83.
11. Yigael Yadin, "Megiddo of the Kings of Israel," *BA*, XXXIII (1970), 66–96. However, James Pritchard has questioned the usual interpretation of the "stables" in "The Megiddo Stables: A Reassessment," in *Near Eastern Archaeology in the Twentieth Century*, ed. by James A. Sanders (Garden City, N.Y.: Doubleday, pp. 268–76). We must probably think of them as storehouses or barracks.

one, and it has the further advantage of being the lowest of all the passes. Napoleon chose this route for his advance toward Acre, and in World War I General Allenby advanced against the Turks by both this road and the Megiddo Pass simultaneously.[12] In 1948 there was a decisive encounter at Mishmar ha-Emek, between Jokneam and Megiddo, which laid Galilee open to the Jewish forces.

The route by the Wadi 'Abdullah to Taanach is possibly the least attractive, since it is both narrow and steep and there is a climb up to more than 1,150 feet (350 m.). "Taanach by the waters of Megiddo," where the kings of Canaan fought against Barak (Judg. 5:19), seems to have flourished concurrently with Megiddo and not, as was once thought, in alternate periods,[13] but it was unquestionably the less important of the two, a residential rather than an administrative center. A Muslim fortress of the Abbasid period was later built on this site, and perhaps also a Crusaders' fort.

These routes into the region are the key to its history. We have seen that the "resting place was good, and that the land was pleasant" (Gen. 49:15), and Isaiah spoke of the "glorious beauty which is on the head of the rich valley" (Isa. 28:1), but fertile though the black earth is, the wealth which came by trade must always have been the greater. Of Zebulun and Issachar, who occupied these two plains, Zebulun to the west and Issachar in Jezreel, it was said that "they suck the affluence of the seas and the hidden treasures of the sand" (Deut. 33:19), and this in large measure was the cause of their downfall, for it was the weakness of this region that it was always too open to foreign influences.

Ill fares the land, to hast'ning ills a prey,
Where wealth accumulates, and men decay. . . .
[Goldsmith, "The Deserted Village"]

Trade brought wealth indeed to the Northern Kingdom, but the prosperity of the merchants caused an economic imbalance which earned the scathing denunciations of the prophet Amos, and trade brought also the perils of foreign worship and the strange influence of false gods. Moreover, the same roads which brought the merchants brought the soldier, "the trampling warrior in battle tumult" (Isa. 9:3), and under the heavy hand of the oppressor, Issachar "bowed his shoulder to bear, and became a slave at forced labor" (Gen. 49:15). It is by no accident that the very name of Megiddo has come to symbolize war in our own language, the Armageddon of Revelation 16:15, for this little corridor, the "Plain" *par excellence* of modern Israel, is the cockpit of Palestine. It could not but be that the great kings who strove to master the routes across it should sooner or later subdue the little kingdom which contained it.

---

12. The battle of Napoleon against the Turks in April, 1799, is vividly described by Tristram (*op. cit.*, p. 270) and that of Allenby in September, 1918, by Smith (*op. cit.*, pp. 266–68).

13. Paul W. Lapp, "Taanach by the Waters of Megiddo," *BA*, XXX (1967), 2–27.

CHAPTER 14

Galilee of the Gentiles

And he went about all Galilee, teaching in their synagogues and preaching the gospel of the kingdom and healing every disease and infirmity among the people.

MATTHEW 4:23

Immediately to the north of the Acco–Beth-shan corridor begins the region of Galilee, for Christians always to be associated with the Gospels and for Jewish people that region where their life took shape again after the appalling disaster of A.D. 70. Nevertheless, this region, so significant for the development of both Judaism and Christianity, entered very late into biblical history, and not until the days of the Maccabees do we learn of dramatic events taking place there, the first since Joshua is said to have driven his enemies back into the mountains after the conquest of Hazor (Josh. 11: 7–8). This is not to say that Lower Galilee at least was not the scene of such events, for an important international road ran across it through Hannathon to Acco (see above, p. 100), but they form no part of the biblical record. In times of strength the Israelites extended their control over it, but in the

days of weakness invaders from the north only too easily "brought into contempt the land of Zebulun and the land of Naphtali" (Isa. 9:1; see also 1 Kings 15:20; 2 Kings 15:29; 2 Chron. 16:4; 34:6).

Both the structure and the physical geography of Galilee are complicated, but it may be conveniently divided into four unequal quarters. The west–east dividing line, separating the north from the south, is the tremendous fault of ash-Shaghur cutting across the country from the direction of Acco to somewhat south of Safad and towering above the valleys beneath to a height of 2,000 feet (600 m.) or sometimes more. North of this is the high plateau of Upper Galilee, where the elevated sections are well over 3,000 feet (900 m.) and Jabal Jarmaq (Har Meron) reaches very nearly 4,000 (3,962 feet, 1,208 m.); to the south are the shattered hills

152

and downfaulted basins of Lower Galilee, which nowhere surpasses 2,000 feet (600 m.). The lower part of this fault scarp is followed today by a road running almost due east from Acco through the Shaghur Basin (Beth Kerem Basin) to near the present settlement of Parod. Close by here it meets another road running at right angles, which marks the division between western and eastern Galilee. This may be followed from Kfar Tavor in the south, at the eastern foot of Mount Tabor, northward through Eilabun to Parod, where it climbs up

into Upper Galilee, past Meron to join the present frontier road just west of Bar'am. No road continues at present, of course, across the frontier, but only a little to the north we may pick it up again at Yirun, just inside Lebanon, and follow it through Bint Jebail to Tibnine. In general, west of this line is an upwarped region and to the east is a downwarped basin, though this is not always immediately clear on the physical map because of the complications of faulting and volcanic activity.

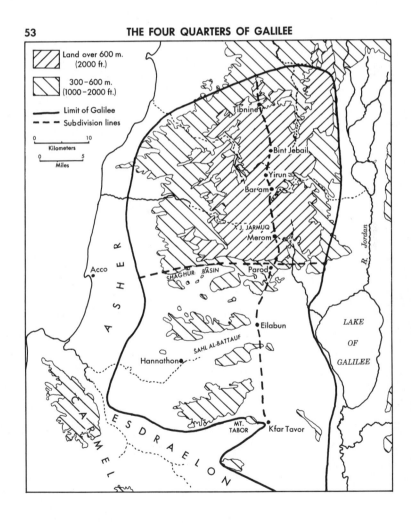

53   **THE FOUR QUARTERS OF GALILEE**

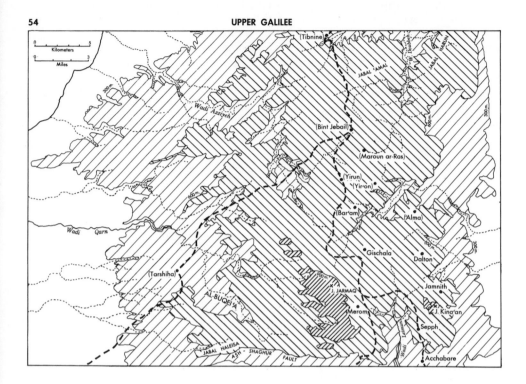

B.1. *Upper Galilee*

The geographical region of Upper Galilee is often described by Israeli geographers as being bounded in the north by the gorge of the river Litani,[1] but this is extending it too far. East of the city of Tyre there is a clearly marked west–east depression where the hills surpass 2,000 feet (600 m.) only in the extreme east close to the present Lebanon-Israel border. This transverse basin, no greater in height than Lower Galilee, cannot be considered part of the exalted plateau country, which must

1. "The natural boundary is formed by the gorge of the Litani River in the Lebanon" (Karmon, *Israel*, p. 178); "In the north it is delimited by the gorge of the Litani River" (Orni and Efrat, *Geography of Israel*, p. 73).

therefore be brought to an end just north of Tibnine. Actually the frontier itself forms a physical as well as a political division, for with one solitary exception (Maroun ar-Ras, southeast of Bint Jebail), all the land over 3,000 feet (900 m.) lies south of this line. Indeed, for the first 12½ miles (20 km.) of its course inland from Ras an-Naqura the frontier follows a great fault, which then curves northeastward toward Tibnine. In consequence, even within Upper Galilee itself we must notice a distinction between a northern and a southern section.

The western half of Upper Galilee is essentially a block of rough Cenomanian limestone, carved and fretted into the crags and precipices which are characteristic of this type of rock, and especially on its western slopes, clothed with dense and almost impenetrable *maquis*. Rainfall here normally exceeds 24 inches (600 mm.) everywhere, and 32 inches (800 mm.) in the higher regions. Dominating it all is the tilted central massif, thrust upward bodily by the faulting, and highest in the south and east, where it surpasses 3,000 feet (900 m.) over a wide area.[2] Immediately west of this massif is the lower-lying al-Buqei'a Basin (Emek Peq'in), and then west of this again a plateau of over 2,300 feet (700 m.), reaching its greatest height where the precipices of Jabal Haleisa (Har Shezor, 3,006 feet, 886 m.) overlook the Shaghur Basin of Lower Galilee beneath. The whole of this section of Upper Galilee is tilted downward toward the northwest so that the central massif and the Buqei'a Basin are drained by the two branches of the Wadi Qarn (Nahal Keziv), which unite just east of Tarshiha and flow in a deep gorge to the Coast Plain at Abdon. South of this the plateau is carved by a number of west–east faults into parallel spurs and short wadis. These, however, came to an end with the high scarp along which the frontier runs, and from Ras an-Naqura northward for some 10 miles (16 km.) the limestone block touches the sea and the coastal plain is abolished. In this section the fault lines run northeastward and the plateau is carved into a series of tilted blocks, rising in places to well over 2,500 feet (750 m.) and with their steeper slopes toward the southeast. The valleys between them are drained by parallel streams forming the headwaters of the Wadi 'Azziyeh, which has cut back southeastward to

2. Jabal Jarmaq, or Har Meron, is 3,962 feet (1,208 m.); Har Hillel, 3,513 feet (1,071 m.); Jabal Haidar, or Har Ha'ari, 3,437 feet (1,048 m.); Jabal 'Adathir, or Har Adir, 3,166 feet (1,008 m.).

capture them. The region comes to an end north of a line drawn from the village of 'Azziyeh northeastward to a point 2½ miles (4 km.) northwest of Tibnine.

The eastern half of Upper Galilee, which is much narrower than the western half, is also complicated. It is, as has been said, a long basin or trough, extending northward far into Lebanon. However, close to the frontier it is crossed by an upfold, which continues northward along the western edge of the Rift Valley. Where the narrow upfold crosses this eastern trough the land has been shattered and carved by faulting into small, almost rectangular blocks, crowned by three plateaus of basalt: Dalton (Dallita), 'Alma, and Yir'on (Saliha).

There are thus two troughs, separated from each other by this narrow ridge. The northern trough is very clear. It is a basin of Eocene chalk and limestone, about 2,000 to 2,500 feet in height (600–750 m.) drained by the Wadi Doubbeh, which cuts a remarkably straight course almost due northward to join the Litani River. To the west is the broken plateau of Jabal 'Amal southwest of Tibnine, and to the east the high ridge of Jabal Harun along which the present frontier runs.

The southern trough is less easy to see, for here the land has been thrust upward and the Eocene limestone forms the high mountain area of Safad and Jabal Kina'an (Har Kena'an, 3,122 feet, 955 m.), which is brought to a sudden end in the south where the Shaghur fault cuts across it at Akbara. These rocky heights are drained by the narrow gorge of the Wadi Leimun (Nahal 'Ammud), shut in between high cliffs, and flowing southward to enter the Lake of Galilee near Ginnosar. This remarkable valley is almost certainly the "waters of Merom" where the kings of Canaan encamped against Joshua (Josh. 11:5), probably where the Trunk Road crosses it beside the lake. Around the Safad block on the north and west is the somewhat more level Senonian plain, itself about 2,500 feet (750 m.) above sea level, and providing an important gap between Safad and the even higher central massif.

Upper Galilee gave to the north what every other important region in Palestine possessed, a region of escape. It is one of the *jibāl,* those uplifted islands of refuge away from the roads, which are such a powerful feature of the political geography of the Fertile Crescent. A *jabal* (pl. *jibāl*) is the normal Arabic word for an elevation of any kind, whether it be hill or mountain, just as a *wadi* is a valley of any kind, whether it has a permanent river in it or not. Thus one speaks of Jabal ash-Shaïkh for the undoubted mountain of Hermon, Jabal Quruntul for the impressive, but less majestic, Mount of the Temptation near Jericho, and Jabal Fureidis for what is no more than the hill of the Herodium near Bethlehem. *Jabal* alone, therefore, is an extremely general word. *al-Jabal,* however, used by itself in an absolute sense, is a regional term. If someone meets you on the road in the Hauran of southern Syria and says, "Are you going to the *Jabal?*" he has a definite mountainous region in mind, and it is not, as the unwary foreign visitor might suspect, the towering height of Mount Hermon, but Jabal ad-Druze, the inhabited mountain of Bashan. Elsewhere *al-jabal* can mean the precipitous slopes of the Lebanon, dotted with villages, the high plateau country of Jabal Nusairi, bordering the north Syrian coast, and the barren, unimpressive uplands of Jabal Sinjar, west of Mosul in northern Iraq. *al-Jabal,* therefore, always indicates a region apart, a recognizable cultural entity, the home of a people

who are observed to be different, and who preserve their identity by being different. Those who inhabit such a region are immediately distinguishable by their speech and their clothing, and by the sharp particularity of their religion, which usually preserves elements of much older cultures. These people resist emphatically, and often forcibly, integration into the dominant culture, and present, therefore, a quite intentional obstacle to cohesion.

Upper Galilee was such a region. It was difficult of access, for all the approaches were steep and the surface rocky, and movement from one part to another was hindered by the tangle of forest and scrub which covered every part not kept under cultivation. The variety of names born by the wadis as one passes from one section to another reflects the isolation of the villagers who in these fastnesses kept themselves to themselves. In the later Roman period a large part of Upper Galilee seems to have been brought under the plow, but even so much forest must still have remained, and when in the succeeding days agriculture declined, much of the land reverted again to *maquis* and scrub. W. M. Thomson, who often traveled across it 150 years ago, speaks of the difficulty of crossing the Doubbeh plateau because of the forest, and it is clear from his description that he means trees rather than *maquis*.[3] It is not surprising, therefore, that Upper Galilee stands so aloof from the biblical story.

Certainly there were roads, but they avoided both the high central massif and those regions where the complicated faulting had so broken the landscape that to travel from one place to another always meant going a long way around, as for instance in the Jabal 'Amal of southern Lebanon. Consequently, though

3. Thomson, *op. cit.,* p. 189.

Upper Galilee was crossed by travelers, large sections of it were left severely to one side. The most important road ran from Tyre to Tibnine, where later the Crusaders had a castle, and then southward along the division between western and eastern Galilee, following very much the route of the present roads. Bint Jebail stood at an intersection, for here a possible, but decidedly difficult, road led north of the Central Block southwestward past Tarshiha to Acco. The main road continued southward into the high plain between Jabal Jarmaq (Har Meron) and Safad, leaving on the left the little village of Jish, the home of Josephus' implacable enemy, John of Gischala. From this plain it was possible either to continue southward along the line of the modern road or to turn below the steep mountain of Safad to Akbara and follow the spur above Wadi Leimun, avoiding its narrow and precipitous gorge and arriving finally at the lake and the main Trunk Road. This road was much used in Hellenistic and Roman times. Aristobulus advanced up it to Gischala in 103 B.C. as part of his campaign to bring Galilee under Hasmonean control, by which was apparently meant only this region and Lower Galilee. This was also "Galilee" for Josephus, who was at one time commander here, for the campaigns of Vespasian that he describes are entirely confined to these two districts. Meeroth, Sepph, Acchabare, and Jamnith, which he says he fortified, are Meron, Safad, Akbara and Kh. Sheikh Banit, north of Safad.[4] Later on, in the time of the Crusaders, Safad was the seat of their chief castle in Galilee, and its ruins stood upon the hilltop of the city until the ghastly earthquake of January 1, 1837, so vividly described by Thomson.[5]

4. Josephus, *War*, II, 573.
5. Thomson, *op. cit.*, pp. 256–59.

After the destruction of Jerusalem in A.D. 70 and even more after the revolt of Bar Kochba (A.D. 131–35), when for a time the hopes of independence had flamed so strongly, Galilee offered a sanctuary to the Jewish people. After being established first at Jamnia, the Old Testament Jabneel, on the Coast Plain, the Sanhedrin moved to Lower Galilee, to Usha, Shefar'am, Beth She'arim, and finally to Tiberias. The great development in agriculture in Upper Galilee probably belongs also to this period,[6] and certainly also the superb synagogues, whose ruins stand still today at Meron, Bar'am, and elsewhere. These seem all to date from the fourth century A.D., since during the earlier years the people would still have been establishing themselves, and would not have had the wealth necessary for such buildings.[7]

B.2. *Lower Galilee*

This is structurally no less complicated, but it is rather easier to describe, for here we have no longer to recognize a northern and southern section, but are concerned only with the division between the west and the east along the line of the present Parod-Eilabun-Kfar Tavor road. One can trace across this region, running from south to north, the alternation of upwarp and trough which is so much more obvious beyond the Acco-Beth-shan corridor. The trough of Samaria continues northward through the length of eastern Galilee into the Wadi Doubbeh basin of Lebanon; the Umm al-Fahm upfold continues in the hills just west of the dividing road

6. Colomb and Kedar, *op. cit.*, p. 136.
7. Eric M. Meyers, A. Thomas Kraabel, and James F. Strange, "Archaeology and Rabbinic Tradition at Khirbet Shema': 1970 and 1971 Campaigns," *BA*, XXXV (1972), 2–31.

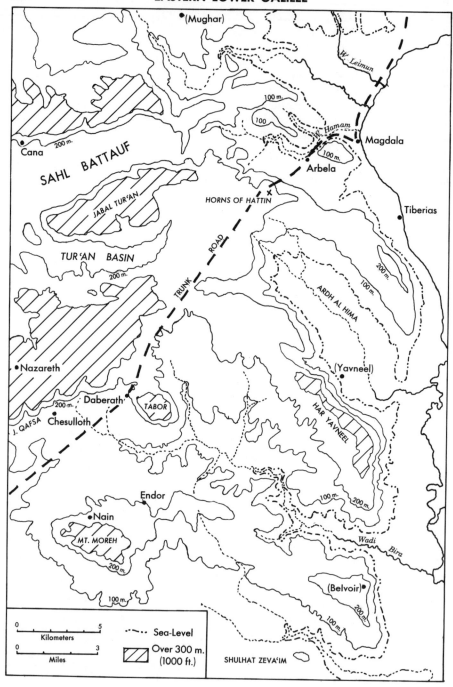

•(Mughar)

W. Leimun

100 m.

100

W. Hamam

Magdala

Cana
200 m.

SAHL BATTAUF

100 m.

Arbela

JABAL TUR'AN

HORNS OF HATTIN

Tiberias

TUR'AN BASIN

TRUNK

ROAD

200 m.

ARDH AL HIMA

200 m.

100 m.

•Nazareth

(Yavneel)

200 m.

Daberath

TABOR

HAR YAVNEEL

J. QAFSA   Chesulloth

Endor

100 m.   200 m.

•Nain

MT. MOREH

Wadi   Bira

200 m.

(Belvoir)•

200 m.

100 m.

100 m.

0					5

Kilometers

0			3

Miles

- - - Sea-Level

Over 300 m.
(1000 ft.)

SHULHAT ZEVA'IM

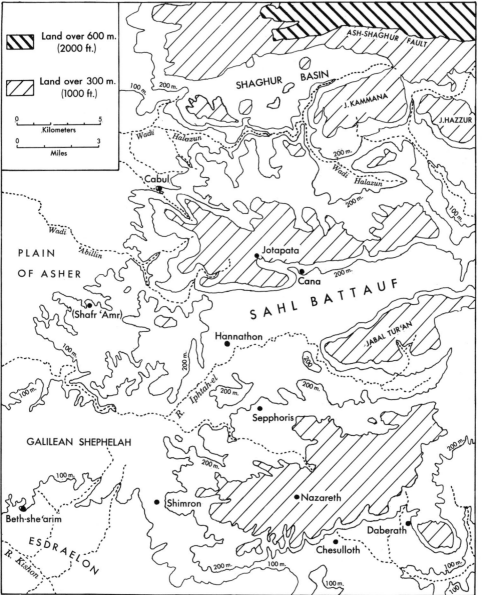

56   **WESTERN LOWER GALILEE**

Land over 600 m.
(2000 ft.)

Land over 300 m.
(1000 ft.)

0   5
Kilometers

0   3
Miles

ASH-SHAGHUR FAULT

SHAGHUR BASIN

J. KAMMANA

J. HAZZUR

100 m. 200 m.

Wadi Halazun

200 m.

Wadi Halazun

Cabul

200 m.

100 m.

Wadi *Abillin*

Jotapata

PLAIN

OF ASHER

Cana

200 m.

SAHL BATTAUF

(Shafr 'Amr)

Hannathon

JABAL TUR'AN

200

100 m.

R. *Iphtah-el*

200 m.

200 m.

200 m.

Sepphoris

200 m.

GALILEAN SHEPHELAH

100 m.

200 m.

Nazareth

200 m.

Shimron

Beth-she'arim

Daberath

ESDRAELON

Chesulloth

R. *Kishon*

200 m. 100 m.

100 m.

100

(Jabal Tur'an, Jabal Hazzur, and Jabal Kammana) and must have played its part in the uplift of the Jabal Jarmaq area; finally, the trough of the central Carmel range extends northward west of Nazareth. All this, however, as in Upper Galilee, has been very greatly disturbed by faulting and volcanic activity.

East of the dividing road the trough, here wider than in Upper Galilee, is filled with basalt, all the way from the edge of Jezreel to the borders of the Lake of Galilee. This is the Plateau of Moreh, where only in the bottom of the wadis have the winter streams cut down to the underlying limestone. The plateau is divided into a series of tilted blocks, with usually a steep scarp facing the northeast and a more gentle slope down to the southwest. The northern block is that through which the Wadi Leimun cleaves its turbulent way, but this has no northeasterly scarp, since it abuts onto Upper Galilee. The most northerly scarp, therefore, is that which overlooks Magdala and the Plain of Gennesaret (Ginnosar) and is followed today at its foot by the road from Mughar down to the lake at Majdal. Here, at Magdala (O. T. Migdal) there stood a fort to guard the Trunk Road as it left the lake shore and climbed up onto the basalt plateau through the narrow and dangerous valley known today as Wadi Hamam, but also by the more disquieting name of the "Valley of the Robbers." At the head of the valley was Arbela (1 Macc. 5:2) and the volcanic cone of the Horns of Hattin, where Saladin defeated the Crusaders in A.D. 1187. Beneath the basalt the caves which honeycomb the orange-colored Eocene limestone were only too often the haunt of brigands who plundered the caravans toiling slowly up the steep ascent. In 38 B.C., after a heavy snowstorm at Sepphoris, Herod the Great vigorously cleared out the rebels they harbored against him.[8]

The second scarp curves round southeastward from the Horns of Hattin themselves to press closely in upon the lake south of Tiberias, close to the hot springs and the tomb of Maimonides. The more gentle southwestern slope of this block dips down to Ardh al-Hima (valley of Yavneel), which is drained by the little Fajjas. The third scarp reaches the Rift Valley near the confluence of the Yarmuq with the Jordan and is known today as Har Yavneel, since the modern settlement of that name nestles at its foot. On the other side the block descends to the Wadi Bira (Nahal Tavor), a narrow and precipitous valley cutting down from the foot of Mount Tabor toward the Jordan. The fourth scarp is crowned at its southeastern end by the Crusaders' castle of Belvoir, 1,043 feet (312 m.) above sea level and more than 1,600 feet (500 m.) above the Rift Valley. Farther back, however, this scarp is less imposing, for the general tendency of this series of tilted blocks is to decrease in height toward the southwest. There is then one last low line of hills, on modern Israeli maps called Sheluhat Zeva'im, with a very much less definite scarp, overlooking the Valley of Jezreel.

Known to the Arabs as Bilad al-Hawa, the windy lands, this broken basalt plateau region was in ancient times never well populated, for the soil, though fertile, is rocky and difficult to cultivate, as well as deficient in water. It was apparently another region of refuge and is once so described in the Old Testament, for "Jotham ran away and fled, and went to Beer[9] and dwelt

8. Josephus, *Wars*, I, 304–13.
9. Probably al-Bira, 1¼ miles (2 km.) northwest of Belvoir.

there for fear of Abimelech his brother" (Judg. 9:21).

At the northwestern end of Sheluhat Zeva'im there rises the hill of Moreh (Jabal Dahi, or Giv'at Ha-More), 1,689 feet (515 m.) in height, which is not volcanic but a great block of Eocene rock thrust up by faulting. The basalt flowed round this hill, and only traces of what may be a thin original cover remain on the summit. The structure here is difficult to determine, but it seems that the Hill of Moreh and Mount Tabor may be part of the collapsed arch now forming the basin enclosed between these hills and the steep wall of Jabal Qafsa (Har Qedummim) near Nazareth.

In the larger western section we must notice, first north of Mount Tabor, a slight transverse trough extending east of Nazareth, and then a broad dome of Cenomanian limestone, increasing in height toward the north. It is, however, greatly dissected by fault basins running more or less from west to east. The first of these is the Tur'an Basin, used today by the road from Nazareth to Tiberias, with Jabal Tur'an (Har Tir'an, 1,797 feet, 548 m.) overlooking it on the north. Next comes the very much greater basin of Sahl Battauf (Biq'at Beth Netofa), the Campus Asochis of the Romans. To the north of this are the hills on which stood the formidable fortress of Jotapata, of which Josephus says that it was "almost entirely built on precipitous cliffs," and whose siege he describes at such length.[10] At their highest point these reach 1,844 feet (562 m.) Next comes the Halazun (Hillazon) Basin, drained by the Wadi Halazun to the west and dominated on the northern side by Jabal Kammana (Har Kammon) and Jabal Hazzur (Har Hazon), 1,961 and 1,916 feet in height

10. *War*, III, 158–339.

(598 and 584 m.). The last basin is that of ash-Shaghur (Biq'at Beth Kerem), bordered on its northern side by the tremendous wall of Upper Galilee.

These basins naturally provide a number of easy passages across Lower Galilee from Acco on the Coast Plain to the lake area, where they tend to converge on the little Plain of Gennesaret. Nevertheless, the roads are not always quite as easy as they appear on the map, for the exits at either end are sometimes closed, and the drainage finds its way to the sea by devious routes. Thus, the Tur'an Basin drains northward into the Sahl Battauf by a narrow cleft in the Cenomanian hills, and this in its turn drains southwestward by the narrow and zigzag valley of the Wadi Malik (Nahal Zippori), the Iphtah-el of the Old Testament. Similarly, the Basin of ash-Shaghur is drained southward into the Wadi Halazun, and the Halazun Basin northward into the same valley, which is a narrow, rocky gorge, unsuited to easy communication. In fact, anyone who has done much cross-

XXXI. *Lower Galilee.* This photograph shows the eastern end of the down-faulted basin of Sahl Battauf and in the far distance the great scarp of ash-Shaghur which marks the beginning of Upper Galilee to the north.

country walking in Galilee soon discovers that it is unwise to follow the wadis, however direct they may appear on the map, for as these leave the plateau, even from the low-lying basins across the western scarp to the plain, they become precipitous and sometimes quite impossible to negotiate.

This curiously indirect drainage has meant that some of the basins, and notably the Sahl Battauf, are waterlogged in the rainy season, though as a result they are floored with very fertile alluvium. Villages and roads, therefore, keep to the edges of the basins or climb halfway up the slopes of the confining hills. Here and on the alluvial fans the olives and vines are grown, while the rich black soil of the low-lying plains is reserved for fields of wheat.

South of the road which today connects Nazareth and Shafa ʿAmr (Shefarʿam) is the "Galilean Shephelah," a basin of Eocene chalk and limestone similar to the central basin of the Carmel range, and known in modern Israel as the Allonim hills. Although much of the region is chalky, it is covered with a hard crust of limy *nari*, which renders it exceedingly unattractive for agriculture, so that before 1948 there were almost no Arab villages here, and even today the kibbutzim and moshavoth are somewhat sparse. In ancient times it was clothed with oak forest and reinforced the division between the Israelite territory of Esdraelon and the Phoenician Coast Plain. It is therefore another of the Galilean regions of refuge, and after the Sanhedrin moved from Jamnia, three of the places where it met were on the edges of the Galilean Shephelah. At one of them, Beth Sheʿarim, close to the Kishon gap, a vast necropolis has been carved out in the caves of soft chalk beneath the hard *nari* capping. Simonias, fortified by Josephus, the Shimron of the Old Testament (Kh. Samuniyeh—Josh. 11:1; 12:20; 19:15), also stood on the southern edge of these hills. The scarp south of Nazareth formed the southern boundary of Zebulun, though they seem to have overflowed into the plain at the expense of the weaker tribe of Issachar, for Chesulloth (Chisloth-Tabor) is named in Joshua 19:18 as being part of Issachar, but in Joshua 19:12–13 it forms the boundary of Zebulun together with Daberath, which is also in the plain.

Today, of course, Nazareth is the chief town, but this is a Christian development, for in the time of the New Testament it was only a village. The most important center then was Sepphoris, the modern Saffuriyeh, about 4 miles to the northwest, on the main road from Ptolemais to Tiberias. This road ran almost in a straight line from Ptolemais around the western end of Sahl Battauf and then along the Turʿan Basin following the line of the present road. In the east it divided, one branch going to Tiberias and the other down the Ardh al-Hima to the Jordan Valley. It was a road of great importance for bringing grain from the eastern plateau to the Mediterranean.

When we are told that Jesus went about all Galilee, it is Lower Galilee and the shores of the lake that are meant, and it is therefore against this background that we must picture him. As he went from village to village across the cultivated hills, he would have skirted the fertile basins, rich with grain or in the winter deep in mud, taking perhaps a little over an hour to walk the full length of the largest of them. Even in the long summer, when the brilliant thistles took the place of flowers among the rocks and the stubble had gone from the fields, it would not have been a barren landscape, for there would still have been the verdant vineyards, and trees and shrubs must have been many. As he trudged the dusty foot-paths, he would have met the farmers with their laden donkeys, taking grapes and vegetables to sell in Sepphoris or the lakeside towns, profiting from the cool hours of the very early dawn to make their journey. Sometimes he would have used the great trade routes and encountered companies of soldiers and the lumbering caravans which carried the grain of Hauran or the rich fruits of Damascus. Never very far from the busy commerce and the restless coming and going of the Roman world, when-ever he was down by the lake he would have been in the thick of it. The "mer-chant in search of fine pearls" (Matt. 13:45), "a man going on a journey" (Matt. 25:14), the younger son who "gathered all that he had and took his journey into a far country" (Luke 15:13), as well as the farmers and the fishermen, would have been among the people he met as he visited the towns and villages round about.

Unfortunately, we know very little indeed about which towns and villages he did in fact visit, for away from the lakeside only three places in Galilee are mentioned in the Gospels: Nazareth, where he passed his boyhood, Nain, where he raised the widow's son (Luke 7:11), and Cana, where he turned the water into wine (John 2:1). Nain has already been mentioned on the slopes of Mount Moreh, and Cana is Kh. Qana, the ruined site on the northern side of the Sahl Battauf, even today called by the local Arabs "Cana of Galilee."[11] Apart from these brief ac-counts we are entirely in the dark.

---

11. Despite tradition, Cana was *not* at Kafr Kanna on the Nazareth-Tiberias road.

CHAPTER 15

Branches over the Wall

Joseph is a fruitful bough,
a fruitful bough by a spring;
his branches run over the wall.

GENESIS 49:22

The two Joseph tribes, Ephraim and Manasseh, occupied the central hill country south of the Acco–Beth-shan corridor, and from there they "sent their branches to the sea" (Ps. 80:11) and extended their control beyond the limit of the hills. The two tribal territories, however, represent different types of landscape, easily distinguishable from each other. In the Dome of Ephraim, situated due east of Joppa and Lod, the Cenomanian limestone extends from one side of the Highlands to the other. To the north of this it divides into two upwarps, of which the more obvious continues toward the NNE, gradually becoming lower, and finally disappearing beneath the lowlands of Beth-shan. The other extends along the edge of Sharon, though dipping in the center and rising again in the Umm al-Fahm upfold. Between these two arms is the Basin of Manasseh or Samaria, the beginning of that long trough which

stretches northward through Galilee into the present country of Lebanon. This basin structure is not immediately apparent on the physical map because the highest land is actually in the center of the basin, where the limestone enclosing the town of Nablus has been thrust up into the twin mountains of Ebal and Gerizim. There is thus in the Nablus region a reversal of the relief very similar to that which we have already noticed at Safad.

Surrounding the hard Eocene limestones in the center of the basin are the softer Eocene chalks and marls and the Senonian chalk, and these, it would seem, were thought of as typical of Manasseh, while the territory of Ephraim consisted of the rocky heights of the Cenomanian and Turonian. Unfortunately we do not have for Ephraim and Manasseh in the Book of Joshua a list of the towns and villages belonging to these two tribes, only the boundaries

being given (Josh. 16:4–17:13). In the
west the boundary between the two
consisted of the very clearly marked
ravine of the Wadi Qana, but farther
east it ran along the crest of the eastern
upfold through Arumah (Kh. al-'Urma,
crowning the mountain of the same
name) to Janoah (Kh. Yanun, though
probably the mountain immediately
north of it is intended as the actual
border), leaving the villages in the plain
to the northwest in Manasseh. However,
there is some confusion about how the
line ran from the Wadi Qana to Arumah.
Tappuah (Sh. Abu Zarad, close to the
village of Yasuf) is clearly said to be
on the boundary (Josh. 17:8), but the

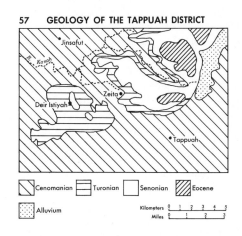

57   GEOLOGY OF THE TAPPUAH DISTRICT

Cenomanian   Turonian   Senonian   Eocene

Alluvium

Kilometers 0 1 2 3 4 5
Miles 0 1 2 3

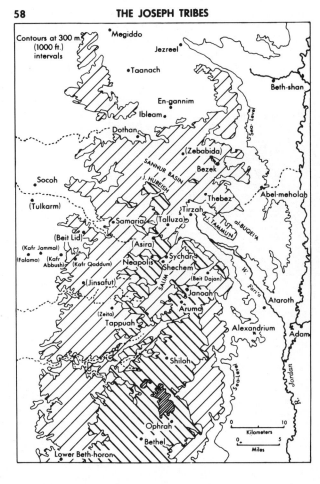

58   **THE JOSEPH TRIBES**

following verse says that the villages here, south of the river Qana, are "among the villages of Manasseh," but belong, nevertheless, to Ephraim. This is repeated in Joshua 16:9, where we are told that there were "towns which were set apart for the Ephraimites within the inheritance of the Manassites." It is interesting that the geological map shows that between the Qana and the highland of Tappuah there is a sickle of lower land, near the present villages of Deir Istiya and Zeita, where the softer Senonian chalks have been preserved. The conclusion that we must probably draw from this is that the Qana ravine formed the political division (streams are always suspect as natural boundaries), but that south of it there were villages whose fields were characteristically Manassite. Once again there is an attempt to correlate a regional term with an administrative one.

XXXII. *Wadi Beidan.* This leads from the ancient Shechem northwards towards Tirzah. The Senonian chalk valley followed by the road is rather hidden in this picture, but in the foreground is the rough karstic scenery characteristic of the hard Turonian and Cenomanian limestone and to the left and in the background the more rounded Eocene hill country which forms the center of the Basin of Manasseh.

B.3. *The Basin of Samaria*

There are, as has been seen, three subregions: the eastern upfold, the central heights within the basin, and the western modified upfold. It seems best to begin with the two upfolds and then move inward to the central basin, which is the heart of the region. If one draws a line along the eastern edge of the Valley of Aijalon, starting just north of Deiraban, about 2½ miles east of Bethshemesh, and continuing it due NNE in the direction of Beth-shan, it will be found that the soft Senonian chalk is interrupted by a fault scarp at Lower Beth-horon on the south side of Ephraim and then reappears on the north side at Tappuah, and after that it is unbroken until it is finally hidden beneath the alluvium of the entrance to the Jezreel Valley. This line of chalk is the continuation north of Ephraim of the Judean moat, but here it lies in the interior of Manasseh, and the main arch well to the west. In the SSW this arch is about 1,600 feet (800 m.) in height, but it dips gradually toward the NNE. Running more or less at right angles to the main axis are a number of faults which curve around southward toward the Rift Valley. At first these create narrow tilted steps, like the blocks of eastern Lower Galilee, with their steep scarp slopes toward the northwest. With the edge of Jabal al-Mahjara, however, this pattern changes, and now the scarp tends to be succeeded by a downfaulted basin before the hills are resumed.

The scarp of Jabal al-Mahjara curves around north of Janoah, and here the arch reaches its greatest height, 2,840 feet (866 m.) above sea level. This marks the limit of Ephraim, and below it on the north is the little plain of Salim, east of Shechem and extending as far as Beit Dajan. North of this again is Jabal al-Kabir (2,598 feet, 792 m.), whose sharp crags overlook the major break in the arch, the narrow rift valley of the Wadi Fari'a. Down this an important routeway ran southeastward from Tirzah in the chalk valley to the bridge of Jisr ad-Damiyeh across the river Jordan close to the site of the ancient Adam (Josh. 3:16). The headwaters of the river Fari'a, which flows down it, have cut back toward the Salim Basin to capture the wadis east of Shechem, and this section of Manasseh also, therefore, is drained into the Jordan.[1] North of this valley is Jabal Tammun, only 1,794 feet (547 m.) high, and then comes the basin of al-Buqei'a, at the northwestern end of which stands Tubas, the Thebez of the Old Testament. Finally, there are two further steps, drained toward the northeast by the Wadi al-Malih, so called from the hot springs of al-Malih at about the center of its course. Some authorities would place Abel-meholah, the home of Elisha (1 Kings 19:16), close to these springs, possibly at Tell al-Hila, but others would look for it east of the Jordan.

This long arch, so far to the east, is deficient in rainfall and, especially within the territory of Manasseh, is very largely *midbar,* only the westward-facing slopes being cultivated. In fact, if a line is drawn due south from a point about 2 miles (3 km.) east of Tubas, all the olive groves and villages will be found to lie west of this line. To the east is increasingly barren steppe.

Unlike the eastern upfold in which the hard Cenomanian-Turonian limestone is exposed for the full length of the arch, the western upfold is depressed in the center, and here, north of the Wadi Zeimar, the younger Senonian and Eocene are preserved until the struc-

ture rises again into the arch of Umm al-Fahm in the Carmel range. It is therefore a modified or interrupted arch rather than a continuous one as in the east.

Its structure is not simple. The Cenomanian-Turonian highlands extend as far north as the Zeimar Valley, the important passage which led into Manasseh from the Coast Plain. With the Qana Valley forming the southern boundary against Ephraim, the eastern limit of this subregion may be taken as the N–S line through the present villages of Beit Lid and Jinsafut. The rocky plateau west of this line descends southward from the Qana toward the Zeimar, from about 1,150 feet to about 650 (350–200 m.). The western edge is higher, reaching over 1,300 feet (400 m.) at a number of points all the way to the Zeimar. Although this plateau is of only moderate height as compared with the rest of the Western Highlands, it is composed of very hard rock carved up into steep crags and narrow, gorgelike valleys. The roads, therefore, everywhere follow the spurs between these valleys. Since it faces westward, it receives a considerable amount of rain, and the fertile *terra rossa* soil carries thick olive groves. In between these olive groves, however, the rocky ground is hostile to the farmer, and the surface of the plateau is consequently a patchwork of olives and rough scrub. As so often, villages tend to occur at the spring line where one type of rock gives way to another, and along a line drawn due west from Nablus there is today a series of villages (Kafr Qaddum, Kafr 'Abbush, Kafr Zibad, Kafr Jammal, and Falama) marking the junction of the Cenomanian and the Turonian. The Turonian to the north of this line forms a severer and more rugged landscape than the Cenomanian, and villages here are fewer.

1. Karmon, *Israel,* p. 321.

The Zeimar Valley follows a west–east fault line, and at its meeting of this route with the Trunk Road there stood, on the northern side of the valley, the city of Socoh (Shuweika). Today the road junction is at Tulkarm on the southern side. North of the valley the structure is complicated by faulting, and we encounter here the first beginnings of the more complex structure of Galilee. The southern part of this section is mainly Eocene and the northern Senonian. Where the two meet is the valley of the upper Mifjir, here known as the Wadi Abu Nar, containing the road which led from Dothan to the Coast Plain. The more easily worked chalk in this section north of the Wadi Zeimar lends itself to cultivation, and there are a number of large villages, contrasting with the smaller villages to the south. However, once again cultivation is confined to the better-watered western slopes, and therefore the whole of this modified upfold region is oriented toward the Coast Plain and the Trunk Road rather than to the interior of Manasseh at Shechem.

The heart of Manasseh is a trough extending to the northeast and enclosed between these two upwarped arms. Its basinlike structure is emphasized by the hills of Gilboa in the north, where the Cenomanian is once again briefly exposed on the edge of the Valley of Jezreel. In the center of this trough is an extended mass of Eocene which is surrounded by Senonian chalk valleys floored with alluvium brought down from the higher land on either side. The central core of this basin, formed of hard Eocene limestone, stands up as mountains (Ebal 3,083 feet, 940 m.; Gerizim 2,890 feet, 881 m.; Sheikh Salman in the southeast 2,667 feet, 810 m.; and Jabal Hureish at the northern edge of the central core, 2,496 feet, 764 m.). The northwestern slopes of this core of mountains are composed mainly of the Eocene chalk which is more easily worked, but nowhere is this core attractive to agriculture; farming is confined largely to the wetter west, and even here mainly to the lower slopes. Farther to the northeast it is broken up by downfaulted basins, continuing the line of the fault basins across the eastern arch. The Sanur Basin just north of Jabal Hureish continues the Wadi Fari'a, and the Zababida Basin a little to the northeast of this is an extension of the Buqei'a. Up against the Umm al-Fahm hills is the Basin of Dothan. In the very center of the core mountains are two very small basins, the result perhaps of solution of the limestone, which today contain the villages of Talluza and Asira ash-Shamaliyah with their olive groves.

Apart from these two small and isolated basins, the villages are found in the lower-lying land which surrounds this core, situated on the eastern side of these valleys at the foot of the better-watered westward-facing slopes, which carried the olives and vines, while the alluvial soil of the valleys themselves was planted with wheat. These interior valleys—rendered even more approachable, it should be noticed, by the two valleys across the enclosing upfolds, the Wadi Zeimar and the Wadi Fari'a—laid Manasseh open to invasion, and her history was largely determined by this fact.[2] Because of these open valleys

2. This was noticed and described, of course, by Smith (*op. cit.*, p. 219), but it is denied by Karmon (*Israel*, pp. 322–23). However, Karmon's argument cannot be said to carry conviction. The fact that "only a few roads cross Samaria" does not therefore mean that it was less open than Judea. The gates of Socoh, En-gannim, and the Wadi Fari'a are undeniable, to say nothing of the other route into Dothan from Gath-Padalla (i.e., Jatt by the Wadi Abu Nar; see Fig. 46. None of these could be easily defended.

with their easily worked soil this part of the hill country was developed considerably before the rest, and during the time of the Egyptian empire it receives frequent mention. With the decline of this empire in the reign of Ikhnaton, the city-state of Shechem was the center from which the notorious Laba'yu sought to expand into the surrounding territory of Esdraelon and the central plain. The Book of Joshua contains no account of the conquest of the Shechem area, and it is probable that there was a fairly peaceful mingling with the already plentiful population, a process in which the covenant recorded in Joshua 24 played its part.

It is a striking fact that although in the period of the Judges and up to the division of the kingdom the towns of Ephraim receive frequent mention in the Bible, and although the Ephraimites provided the leaders in the revolt which brought about that division,[3] yet, with the one exception of the sanctuary of Bethel on the southern frontier, no town in Ephraim occurs in the history of the northern kingdom. From the formation of the kingdom of Israel the dominant region was the territory of Manasseh. Manasseh's early history seems to have been a struggle to establish itself by securing the approaches, which could be done only by emulating Laba'yu and overflowing onto the plains. This meant that the Manassites took over territory traditionally belonging to other tribes (Josh. 17:11), which may be the reason why it was a man from Issachar, Baasha ben-Ahijah, who seized the throne from Jeroboam's son (1 Kings 15:27). It also meant that they brought within their borders not only the fertile lands of Esdraelon and Jezreel, but also a large section of the

Trunk Road and the vital crossroads of Megiddo, and extended their control across the Jordan into Gilead. Thereafter their supremacy was assured, but this did not mean that it was unchallenged. There was, it would appear, a strong tradition in the north that "covenant" meant agreement among the people, and this agreement had to be publicly given at Shechem if anyone was to be accepted in the north as king (1 Kings 12:1ff.). But the diversity of tribes within the Northern Kingdom, and their bitter resentment, led to constant revolts. Solomon's division of the kingdom into twelve administrative districts seems in part to have been an attempt to break up the swollen territory of Manasseh.[4]

The insecurity of the Northern Kingdom, once the power had passed to Manasseh, is reflected in two things: the strong garrisons required on the frontiers were often centers of military disaffection, and there was difficulty in finding a suitable site for a capital. No fewer than three military officers from frontier fortresses seized the throne of Israel: Baasha and Omri from Gibbethon (1 Kings 15:27; 16:17) and Jehu from Ramoth-gilead (2 Kings 9:1ff.), displaying the typical soldier's impatience with the ineffectiveness of the central government. As for the capital, the fact that the routes followed the Senonian chalk inside the rim of the basin meant that there was no natural focal point in the center, and such focal points as there were stood at junctions of low-lying valleys (Shechem and Tirzah) and were therefore useless for defense. It was not until Omri decided to build an entirely new city on top of a hill that a satisfactory stronghold was created.

3. Both Jeroboam and Ahijah the prophet were from Ephraim (1 Kings 11:26–40).

4. See Baly and Tushingham, *Atlas of the Biblical World,* p. 120.

All the towns mentioned in the Bible lie in the Senonian valleys with their easy communications. Four of them, including the first two capitals, are in the long narrow valley which divides the central core from the eastern arch, a valley known in its southern section today as Sahl Makhna. Here the road comes down from Bethel and Jerusalem. The first of these cities is Shechem. This is Tell Balatah near Jacob's well, famous from the story of the Samaritan woman in John 4, and the one real focal point in the territory of Manasseh. Sychar in John 4:5 is probably 'Askar, just to the north. The next town was Tirzah, the capital from the end of Jeroboam's reign until Omri built Samaria, 1 Kings 14:17; 15:33; 16:8–23), commanding the route which leads

XXXIII. *Samaria.* The Old Testament capital at Samaria was succeeded by the Persian, Greek and Roman cities. This picture shows the basilica of the Roman Samaria.

in from the Sanur Basin and down the Wadi Fari'a. The people of Tirzah seem to have resented the moving of the capital after it had been burned by Zimri (1 Kings 16:18), for a later usurper was from there (2 Kings 15:14). The third town was Thebez, where Abimelech was killed (Judg. 9:50–57) after he had attempted to make himself king at Shechem. This was another crossroads where a road from the Dothan Basin led through the Basin of Zababida to the Buqei'a. The last town is the least in importance, Bezek (Kh. Ibziq), where Saul gathered the tribes together before going to the help of Jabesh Gilead just across the Jordan to the east (1 Sam. 11:8). The other places mentioned are Samaria, Dothan, and Ibleam.

Samaria was an opulent but artificial city which flourished for some fifteen centuries, and then declined again into the obscurity from which it had sprung. Omri's buildings, and those of his son Ahab, are of excellent quality, and speak highly for the skill and craftsmanship of Phoenician workmen they employed. Superb fragments of ivory paneling have been found, evidently from the "ivory house" which Ahab built (1 Kings 22:39; Amos 3:15; also the reference to "ivory beds" in Amos 6:4). Though the city seems to have suffered under Jehu, it was again strengthened and adorned by Jeroboam II. Destroyed by the Assyrians in 722, it was again rebuilt and served as the provincial capital under the Assyrians, Babylonians and Persians. It was during this last administration that at one point Sanballat, the leader of the opposition to Nehemiah, was governor of the city. From the troubled years after Alexander date the magnificent fortifications of the Hellenistic period, but then it was largely rebuilt by Herod the Great, who renamed it Sebaste and crowned it with an enormous temple. It was this city which was the scene of Philip's preaching (Acts 8:4ff.). By the sixth century, however, Sebaste was declining, and when the Muslims conquered Palestine its glory was already over.

On the other hand, nothing could take away the significance of Shechem as a route center. Samaria had been built where the roads to Socoh and En-gannim divided and was therefore well placed to control the approaches from the Trunk Road, but Shechem was the "navel of the land" (Judg. 9:37), where the road from the north toward Bethel and Jerusalem met the road from the Coast Plain to the Jordan. Not just the city but the whole area seems to have been sacred from a very early date. All the elements of sanctity were there, the sacred well, attributed later to the patriarch Jacob (John 4:12), the sacred tree ("the oak of Moreh," of Gen. 12:6, the "oak which was near Shechem" of Gen. 35:4, and the "Diviner's Oak of Judg. 9:37), and the sacred stone (Josh. 24:26; note that it is set up "under the oak"). There is also the sacred mountain of Gerizim, though Ebal was apparently also accounted part of the sacred area. It is, however, perhaps significant that in Deuteronomy 27:11–13 Ebal is the mount of cursing and Gerizim the mount of blessing. Later, in the Persian period, a Samaritan temple was built on Gerizim, "this mountain" of John 4:20, and today the remnant of the Samaritans still sacrifice the Passover here, though the temple was destroyed by John Hyrcanus.[5] A temple

to Zeus Olympus, approached by a great flight of steps up the mountain, also stood upon Tell ar-Ras, the northernmost point of Mount Gerizim.[6]

Shechem was the *maqom,* traditionally the first place visited by Abraham upon his entry into the country (Gen. 12:6), and after the entry of the Israelites the bones of Joseph were interred here (Josh. 24:32). It was also the site of the great Bronze Age temple dedicated to Baal-Berith, the "Lord of the Covenant," mentioned in the story of Abimelech (Judg. 9:4, 46). It was built about 1650 and has been described as the "largest extant pre-Roman temple remains in Palestine,"[7] the fortifications of the same period being no less impressive.[8] It was destroyed about 100 years later by the Egyptian invasions and was then rebuilt in a somewhat modified form. It was this temple that was so brutally destroyed by Abimelech some time in the twelfth century B.C. (Josh. 9:46–49).[9] With the building of the new capital at Samaria, Shechem naturally had to take second place, but her position at the crossroads still gave her

---

5. For the religious importance of Shechem in antiquity see G. R. H. Wright, "The Mythology of Pre-Israelite Shechem," *VT,* XX (1970), 75–82; Bernhard H. Anderson, "The Place of Shechem in the Bible," *BA,* XX (1957), 2–10; Edward F. Campbell, Jr., and James F. Ross, "The Excavation of Shechem and the Biblical Tradition," *BA,* XXVI (1963), 2–27.

6. Robert J. Bull, "The Excavation of Tall ar-Ras on Mount Gerizim," *BA,* XXXI (1968), 58–72; also *BASOR,* 190 (1968), 2041.

7. Edward F. Campbell, "Excavation at Shechem, 1960," *BA,* XXIII (1960), 110.

8. George Ernest Wright, "The First Campaign at Tell Balatah (Shechem)," *BASOR,* 144 (1956), 9–20; "The Second Campaign at Tell Balatah (Shechem)," *BASOR,* 148 (1957), 11–28; Lawrence E. Toombs, "The Second Season of Excavation at Biblical Shechem: The Archaeological Results," *BA,* XX (1957), 92–105.

9. Robert J. Bull, "A Re-examination of the Shechem Temple," *BA,* XXIII (1960), 110–19; Lawrence E. Toombs and G. Ernest Wright, "The Third Season at Balatah (Shechem)," *BASOR,* 161 (1961), 11–55; "The Fourth Season at Balatah (Shechem)," *BASOR,* 169 (1963), 1–61.

a role to play, and she seems to have remained a center for the collection of taxes. In the days of Jeremiah men still came from Shechem to worship at the Temple in Jerusalem (Jer. 41:4). It was finally destroyed by John Hyrcanus in 128 B.C., and the Roman city that was built to take its place was Neapolis, 2 miles farther west, on the site of the present town of Nablus, which is a corruption of the Roman name.

In New Testament times Manasseh had become the country of the Samaritans, presided over by Herod the Great's magnificent city of Sebaste, and there must have been in those days a busy commerce along its roads. But the ancient enmity between the Joseph tribes and Judah had been still further embittered by the exchange of populations which the Assyrians had imposed on the city and region of Samaria (2 Kings 17:24–41) and by the differing histories of the two parts of the country in succeeding years. Many Jews thought it unsafe to travel through Samaria, although there is a strong tradition that Jesus himself had no hesitation in doing so (Luke 9:51–56; John 4:4). Later many Christians seem to have fled to Samaria as a place where they would be free from Jewish attack, and it became an important Christian center (Acts 8:1–25; 15:3). The separateness of Samaria is not yet at an end, and in recent years the people of the district of Nablus have shown themselves notably resistant to the government, whether it be that of the British Mandate, the Kingdom of Jordan at Amman, or the present Israeli authorities.

B.4. *The Carmel Range*

The routes across this region have already been considered in relation to the Plain of Esdraelon. It is, as has been said, clearly divided into three sections,

the Umm al-Fahm arch, the central basin, and the main Carmel Massif. At the junction of the first of these with the previous region of Manasseh there is a transitional zone. Physically it seems best to bring Manasseh to an end on the northern side of the Basin of Dothan and count the road from Taanach as one of the four routes across Carmel, for the land north of this basin rises to more than 1,300 feet (400 m.). Structurally, however, it should be noticed that the main exposure of Cenomanian limestone does not begin until beyond the Taanach road. The area southeast of this is a complicated fault zone in which the Senonian and Eocene have been preserved, and the older Cenomian is exposed only in a small triangle south of the present village of Ya'bad, with the highest point (1,253 feet, 382 m.) just beside Arraba, possibly the Old Testament Arubboth (1 Kings 4:10). The road from Taanach to Gath-Padalla, in fact, follows a fault line limiting the southeastern edge of the main exposure of Cenomanian limestone. Nevertheless, it is better to keep to the physical division, while recognizing the complication of the underlying structure, for historically the important fact was the channeling of movement by the scrub- and forest-covered uplands between Esdraelon and the Coast Plain.

No part of the Carmel Range is very high, for even two Cenomanian upfolds of Umm al-Fahm and the Carmel Massif nowhere reach as much as 2,000 feet (600 m.). Nevertheless, the whole region is exposed to the onslaught of the winter storms and is well watered, especially on the seaward side. Therefore it was in ancient times, and has remained until quite recently in history, difficult and frightening *ya'ar.* The rocky crags of the Cenomanian, with its fertile *terra rossa,* must have been thickly forested and even today carry a good covering of scrub woodland and maquis.

The Carmel Massif comes dramatically into biblical history with the contest between Elijah and the prophets of Baal (1 Kings 18:17–46). Whether the choice was Elijah's as the story would suggest, or whether there was already a move in the country toward Carmel to beseech Ba'al Hadad for rain, the site was well chosen. Remote and lonely, isolated by marshes, difficult to reach, clothed with impenetrable forest, Carmel had for the ancient mind a mysterious majesty which made men approach it with circumspection and awe, lest here they might encounter the gods. Its tangled thickets, the haunt of wild beasts[10] and the soaring eagle, were charged with that quality which has been called "numinous," terrifying and fascinating at the same time, because this was the domain of the "Absolutely Other." Even as late as thirty years ago people of the neighborhood spoke with caution of the "Forty Oaks," an ancient sacred grove still standing on the heights of Carmel, and held that an oath taken in this name was especially binding.[11] It was already known as sacred by the Egyptians[12] and to the Phoenicians, brought back by the southwest wind from their far-flung voyages, this striking promontory, the first that they would see after the flat land to the south, was the realm of Ba'al Hadad, the mighty god of the storm, who brought the slashing rain, surging in from the sea like a white wall of water, to the coasts

and slopes of Lebanon, and controlled the winds upon which their safety at sea depended. Père de Vaux has rightly said that we have here an "example of how Yahweh appropriated the mountains formerly consecrated to the old gods."[13]

Both Carmel and the Umm al-Fahm upfold have experienced small volcanic outflows, marking the highest parts of each of them, near al-Muhraqa (Karen Karmel), the traditional site of Elijah's contest, and the highland overlooking the pass of Megiddo. The central basin between them, the "Israelite Shephelah," has been much less disturbed. It consists of soft chalky limestone hills, normally less than 1,000 feet (300 m.) in height and just touching 1,300 feet (400 m.) close to Megiddo. It can never have carried the thick forest of the Carmel Massif, and it is therefore at first sight somewhat surprising that it should have proved such an obstacle. However, despite sufficient rainfall and singularly abundant springs, it shares the unattractiveness of its counterpart in Galilee. The present Arab villages are tiny and lacking olive groves, and there are remarkably few tells, indicating that in ancient times also it was little inhabited, for then it must have been rendered more difficult by a covering of oak and sycamore, which has now disappeared. Furthermore, it slopes up toward the northeast, and so the slopes facing Esdraelon are steep. It provides, therefore, an excellent example of how even a relatively slight obstacle can cause all movement to be diverted around it.

B.5. *The Dome of Ephraim*

It is possible to deal with this region somewhat more briefly than Manasseh

---

10. As late as the early nineteenth century leopards were fairly common on Mount Carmel.

11. But no longer today. When I last visited the Forty Oaks in January, 1970, it was a sorry mess.

12. Roland de Vaux, *Ancient Israel: Its Life and Institutions*, trans. by John McHugh (New York: McGraw-Hill; paperback ed., 1965), p. 260.

13. *Ibid.*, p. 281.

for two reasons: its structure is more simple, and it plays a much less continuous part in biblical history, with the unfortunate result that we know less about it. Structurally it is a well-defined dome or arch extending from the Coast Plain to the Rift Valley, and differing from the regions to the south and north of it in that here the soft Senonian chalk is hardly to be seen, for the important exposures of this rock to the south have been brought to an end by the faulting of the Valley of Aijalon and the scarp behind Jericho. Ephraim is therefore a great mass of hard Cenomanian limestone, with the older, but also hard, Albian limestone in the center. Throughout the whole region the rock is remarkably similar, though it is not, of course, uniform. There is, for instance, a distinct step-up of about 330 feet (100 m.) running northeastward through the present villages of Buruqin and Marda, marking the junction of two different layers of the Upper Cenomanian. This may be said to be the beginning of the true high plateau of Ephraim, for to the north is the rather lower western upfold of the Manasseh Basin. The Manasseh-Ephraim political boundary lay, as already noted, along the Wadi Qana, and the curious penetration of the Manassite valley landscape into the territory of Ephraim near Tappuah lay north of this step. The Roman boundary between Judea and Samaria in the New Testament period was a little to the south of the step, for it ran along the Wadi Sha'ir, one of the headwaters of the Sardia, which enters the plain near Majdal Yaba, "the Tower of Aphek." The southern boundary of Ephraim ran from the steep scarp behind Jericho through Ephron and Bethel on the water-parting and down to the plain by way of Beth-horon, theoretically as far as Gezer.

The plateau here is high, over 3,000 feet (900 m.) in much of the central section, and reaching 3,332 feet (1016 m.) in Tell 'Asur (the Baal-hazor of 2 Sam. 13:23), slightly to the east of a line drawn from Bethel to Shiloh; rainfall is plentiful, and the soil is everywhere the rich and fertile *terra rossa*. Until the Israelite occupation this region was but sparsely inhabited and densely forested, but with the gradual clearing of the forests olives took their place, "the finest produce of the ancient mountains, and the abundance of the everlasting hills" (Deut. 33:15). Today, over wide areas, the olive groves are almost continuous. Ephraim was also exceptionally well defended, for the wadis are rocky gorges and there are no easy routes leading up into the highlands. Once more the roads must follow the spurs between the wadis rather than the wadis themselves. In Roman times, although perhaps not earlier, a road ran westward from Gophna to Antipatris, and certainly in early days there was a road from Shiloh, following the southern rim of the Wadi Sarida through Zeredah, from which Jeroboam I came (1 Kings 11:26), and Ramathaim-zophim, the birthplace of Samuel (1 Sam. 1:1) and later the home of Joseph of Arimathea. The crags and forests of Ephraim made of this high plateau a stronghold in the perilous days of the Judges and indeed permitted the tribe of Ephraim to endow the whole of the northern kingdom with its name, but the same rocky and difficult terrain prevented easy communication within the region. Not only did the villages remain somewhat isolated from one another, self-sufficient and apart, but no major town developed within the region. It is no wonder that with the establishment of the monarchy power passed to the more open Manasseh and that the places which do occur in Ephraimite history lie close to the north-south road.

This road, "the highway that goes up from Bethel to Shechem" (Judg. 21:19), at first followed the water-parting and ran, therefore, along the heights east of the present road northward from Ramallah, avoiding the well-named "Valley of the Robbers" (Wadi Haramiyeh), which is the course of the road today. It skirted the edge of the little basin of Sahl Kafr Istuna, thus leaving the same sanctuary of Shiloh, on the northern rim of this basin, to the east,[14] and rejoined the present road at Lebonah, the modern Lubban. Ephron, marking a corner on the southern border of Ephraim (Josh. 18:15), "Ophrah" in v. 23), and possibly also the "Ephraim" of 2 Samuel 13:23 and John 11:54, is the present village of at-Taiyebeh, a couple of miles to the east of the road. This is one of a line of villages, running more or less NNE–SSW, which mark the eastern limit of cultivation. They lie beyond the water-parting at the beginning of the east-ward-facing slopes but above the steep scarps which initiate the barren steppe-lands. North of Lebonah the wadis from the west have pushed the water-parting far to the east, and so the road must now cross a series of valleys and ridges before entering Manasseh and the long chalk valley of Sahl Makhna.

Two sites alone in Ephraim have played an important role in history: Shiloh and Bethel, both of them sanctu-aries and both at one time places where the Ark was kept, apparently first at Bethel (Judg. 20:24–28) and then at Shiloh. Shiloh, the present Kh. Seilun, on the northern edge of the Sahl Kafr Istuna, is, it must be admitted, a most unimpressive site. The hills behind it rise fairly gently for some 350 feet, and at its foot the level ground opens out into the little plain. There is no clear reason why it should ever have

14. Noth, *Old Testament World*, p. 87.

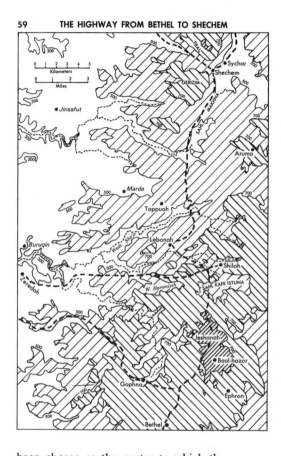

59   THE HIGHWAY FROM BETHEL TO SHECHEM

been chosen as the center to which the tribes should come up for the annual festival (1 Sam. 1:3), though in that forested era it may have been a place of security, or there may well have been here a sacred grove which has now disappeared. We can do no more than guess. There is no doubt, however, that the Ark was at Shiloh in the days of Samuel's youth, until its capture by the Philistines (1 Sam. 5:11). After this disaster the priests seem to have fled to Nob near Gibeah of Saul (1 Sam. 14:3; 22:11), but a sanctuary of some kind was still maintained, for the wife of Jeroboam I went there to consult the oracle (1 Kings 14:1ff.). It seems now probable that the destruction of Shiloh

XXXIV. *The Plain of Lebonah.* Lebonah, the modern Lubban, lay on the road northwards from Bethel to Shechem and in Turkish times the khan, or caravanserai, at the foot of the hill in the foreground of this picture marked the limit of "a day's journey from Jerusalem." Notice the ploughed alluvium of the valley bottom and the eroded hillsides of Cenomanian limestone. Also notice how the houses tend to keep to the foot of the hills away from the good farming land.

to which Jeremiah made reference (Jer. 7:12) was more recent than the Philistine capture of the Ark.

Bethel is likewise on no commanding site, but of its long importance as a religious center there can be no possible doubt. It stands on the northern side of the Saddle of Benjamin, and perhaps in the earliest days it was a Sanctuary where the road to the north entered the frightening *ya'ar*. During the time of the Judges and after the division of the kingdom it was certainly a border sanctuary, marking first the southern limit of Ephraim and later the frontier of the kingdom of Israel. First built about the year 2200 B.C.,[15] it is clearly already

15. James L. Kelso, "Excavations at Bethel," *BA*, XIX (1965), 36–43.

sacred in the patriarchal stories (Gen. 12:8; 13:3), and within this sacred area Jacob had his dream of the ladder reaching from earth to heaven (Gen. 28:10–17). It was later one of the three sanctuaries regularly visited by Samuel (1 Sam. 7:16). The greatest glory came, however, with its elevation by Jeroboam I into "the Temple of the Kingdom" (Amos 7:13), intended to rival the Temple at Jerusalem (1 Kings 12:26–33; 2 Chron. 13:8–9), dedicated to Yahweh, but clearly more than a little syncretistic. Bethel survived the Assyrian conquest of Israel and was still an important city in the New Testament, period, though it receives no mention there.

CHAPTER 16

The Hill Country of Judah

The scepter shall not depart from Judah,
nor the ruler's staff from between his feet,
until he comes to whom it belongs;
and to him shall be the obedience of the peoples.

GENESIS 49:10

B.6. *The Highlands of Judah*

To leave Bethel on the road southward and descend some 300 feet (about 100 m.) to the Saddle of Benjamin is to enter the Kingdom of Judah. "From Geba to Beersheba" (2 Kings 23:8) is 50 miles (80 km.) as the crow flies, but from the western edge of the mountains to the beginning of the eastern wilderness is only 15 miles (24 km.), with another 12 miles to the Dead Sea. It is therefore a small region, and half of it is desert.

Although in general the structure is that of a great arch between the Coast Plain on the west and the Dead Sea on the east, we begin to meet here for the first time the parallel NNE–SSW folding on top of the arch which is so much more apparent in the Negeb farther south. Thus, a line drawn from Ramah, just west of Geba, to Iphtah on the edge

of the Shephelah marks the division between the end of the Ephraim Upwarp to the northwest, extending here through the hills of Kiriath-jearim and dropping fairly quickly to the Judean moat at the Wadi Samt, and to the southeast the central upwarp of Judah. This stretches from just west of Adoraim (the present Dura) in the direction of Jerusalem, which may be said to mark the extreme end of it. South of Hebron the highlands are broadened by a further rippling of the surface, the first fold running through Juttah (Yatta) and the second through Maon (Kh. Ma'in).

In the north of the region is the Saddle of Benjamin, no more than 2,600 feet (800 m.) in the center, whereas the land to the north and south of it surpasses 3,000 feet (900 m.). In part the result of the dip between the Ephraim and the Judean upwarps, it is even more the product of the faults

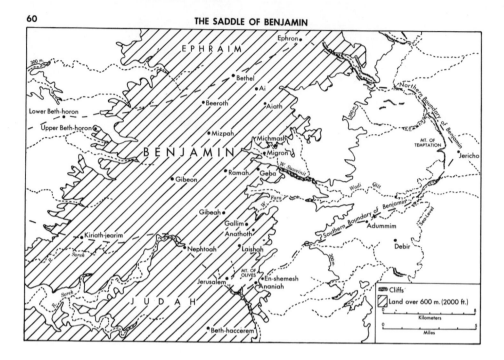

which have cut inward from either side of the arch and erosion from the wadis which here penetrate far into the highlands. Because of the lowering of the plateau and the relative ease with which it can be approached from both the west and the east, this was the first part of the true highlands to be penetrated, and already before the days of the Israelites much forest cover had been cleared and numerous settlements established. It is a crossroads and a zone of movement, no more than 10 miles broad (16 km.) in the center, but the scene of a quite startling amount of biblical history.

The extent of the saddle is defined fairly exactly by the boundaries of the tribe of Benjamin, who took possession of it in the Israelite period. These start in the east at Jericho and open out westward, the southern boundary going

up beside the Wadi Qilt and then past Adummim and the "Inn of the Good Samaritan" along the line of the present Jericho road round the Mount of Olives and Jerusalem on the south, and thence westward to Nephtoah (Lifta) and along the rim of the northern branch of the Sorek to Kiriath-jearim. The northern boundary follows by the fault scarp of the Mount of Temptation, "the shoulder north of Jericho" (Josh. 18:12), to Ephron (Taiyebeh), along the line of the present road to Taiyebeh, overlooking a deep rocky gorge to the north. From Ephron it turns south to Bethel and then westward to the edge of the hills just south of Lower Beth-horon. These boundaries are, in fact, for a large part routes still in use today.

In the center the limits were Bethel in the north and Jerusalem in the south, and on the level plateau between them are many towns well known from Scripture. Only 2½ miles (4 km.) north of the Old City of Jerusalem, perched on a small hill, is the small fortress of Gibeah of Saul, where he administered rough justice seated under a tree (1 Sam. 15:34; 22:6), and another couple of miles farther north is Ramah, the home of Samuel, who anointed him to be king (1 Sam. 10:1ff.). Just east of Gibeah is Anathoth, the birthplace of Jeremiah, with below it the rocky gorge of the Fara, the "Euphrates" where he hid the waistcloth (Jer. 13:1–11), and a little to the northeast of Ramah is Michmash, where Jonathan routed the Philistines (1 Sam. 14:1ff.). The crags of Bozez and Seneh (v. 4) enclose the Wadi Suweinit, which joins with the Fara to form the Wadi Qilt, flowing out at Jericho. West of the Jerusalem-Bethel road is Gibeon, where twenty-four young stalwarts from the forces of Abner and Joab engaged in single combat and where Joab later killed Abner (2 Sam. 2:12–17; 3:26–27).

The northern boundary of Benjamin was the frontier between the kingdoms of Judah and Israel, Bethel marking the southern edge of Israel, and Geba the northern limit of Judah. Between the two towns was a kind of no man's land which from time to time each country tried to take for itself. Not long after the revolt of Jeroboam, Abijah of Judah pushed northward beyond Bethel as far as Jeshanah, halfway to Shiloh (2 Chron. 13:19), but he did not hold the territory for long, since in the next reign "Baasha king of Israel went up against Judah, and fortified Ramah, that he might permit no one to go out or to come in to Asa king of Judah" (1 Kings 15:17). Ramah is but 5 miles from Jerusalem, and in desperation Asa "took all the silver and gold that were left in the treasures of the house of the Lord and the treasures of the king's house

. . . and sent them to Benhadad . . . king of Syria, who dwelt in Damascus," begging him to attack from the north. This he did, thrusting far into Galilee, and forcing Baasha to withdraw from Ramah. "Then King Asa made proclamation to all Judah, none was exempt, and they carried away the stones of Ramah and its timber, with which Baasha had been building; and with them King Asa fortified Geba of Benjamin and Mizpah" (1 Kings 15:16–22; Mizpah is Tell an-Nasbeh, another frontier town just south of the present Ramallah).

All this coming and going across Benjamin served not only to foster war but to endow the land with sanctity. Centers of pilgrimage are often those places where roads meet and where men must come together for trade (Mecca, Chartres, and Kiev come rapidly to mind) or that central point on a promontory where the merchants gather after the winds and tide have driven them to almost any inlet of the surrounding coast (Santiago di Compostella in Spain, Canterbury in England, and St. David's in southwest Wales are all such places, and so at one time was the megalithic fane of Carnac in Brittany). Moreover, those places which are swept by the blast of the ruthless and the angry storms of war must have some place of refuge and sanctuary where the traveler may have assurance of safety. So it was in Benjamin, and many of the towns already mentioned for other reasons were sanctuaries of repute. Of course, in the unregenerate days before the Deuteronomic reform every little hamlet had its altar, and as many as the villages were the gods (Jer. 11:13). But Bethel, Mizpah, Ramah, and Gibeon were more than this; they were places of assembly to which people came from far and near. As we have already seen, upon this road one might meet "men

61   **JUDAH**

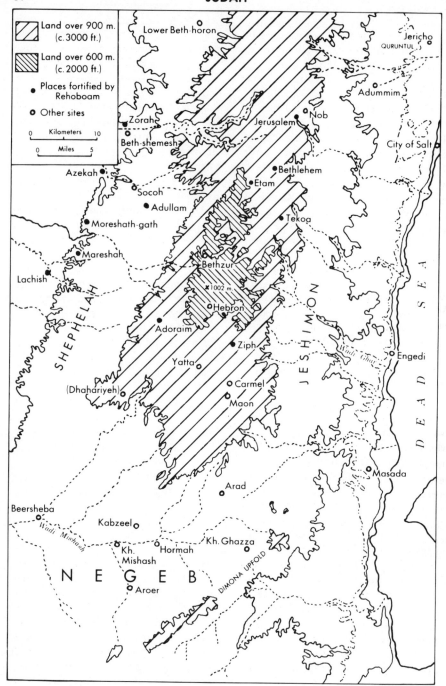

Land over 900 m. (c. 3000 ft.)

Land over 600 m. (c. 2000 ft.)

• Places fortified by Rehoboam

○ Other sites

Kilometers   0 — 10

Miles   0 — 5

Lower Beth-horon

Jericho

QURUNTUL

Adummim

Zorah

Jerusalem

Nob

City of Salt

Beth-shemesh

Azekah

Bethlehem

Etam

Socoh

Adullam

Moreshath-gath

Tekoa

Mareshah

Lachish

Bethzur

× 1002 m.

S H E P H E L A H

Hebron

J E S H I M O N

Adoraim

Ziph

Engedi

Wadi Ghar

Yatta

D E A D   S E A

(Dhahariyeh)

Carmel

Maon

Masada

Arad

Beersheba

Kabzeel

N   E   G   E   B

Kh. Mishash

Hormah

Kh. Ghazza

DIMONA UPFOLD

Wadi Mishash

Aroer

going up to God at Bethel," carrying with them their kids, their wine, and their bread as an offering (1 Sam. 10:3). It was near Ramah that Deborah gave counsel (Judg. 4:5), and there Samuel administered justice and offered sacrifice on the high place (1 Sam. 7:17; 9:12). At Mizpah the tribes "assembled as one man" to consult the oracle and to dedicate themselves before some common enterprise (Judg. 20:1ff.; 1 Sam. 7:5ff.; 10:17), and in those last sad days after the Temple in Jerusalem had been destroyed it became for a time the center of government (Jer. 40:7–12). It was because Gibeon was a place of sanctuary that Joab and Abner met there (1 Sam. 2:12), and before the building of the Temple it was "the great high place," where Solomon offered sacrifice (1 Kings 3:4); the Tent of Meeting was there (1 Chron. 21:29), and even after David had brought the Ark to Jerusalem he saw to it that the sacrifices at Gibeon were maintained (1 Chron. 16:37–42).

South of Benjamin is the territory of Judah itself, draped over the back of the Judean arch and dragging its skirts in the desert dust. It has four clearly defined regions: the Mountain, the Wilderness, the Lowland, and the South (Josh. 15:21, 33, 48, 61). The list in Joshua of the cities of Judah seems to belong to the later monarchy, perhaps the days of Hezekiah or Josiah, for the royal seal impressions stamped on storage jars, belonging to the late eighth and seventh centuries B.C., carry the names of four cities of Judah, apparently administrative centers, which reflect this fourfold division. Socoh was the center for the Shephelah, Hebron for the mountain, Ziph for the Negeb and perhaps the southern mountain, and the still mysterious *mmst* may have been the government storehouses at Jerusalem for the produce of Benjamin and the

few villages of Jeshimon, which were all in the north.[1]

Of these divisions, the Shephelah, or "Lowland," has already been considered with the Coast Plain as a region in the early days disputed with the Philistines; the district of the Judean Negeb in the south was identical with the territory of Simeon (compare Josh. 15:21–32 with 19:1–9) which Judah later absorbed; and the wilderness of Jeshimon was largely uninhabited. The essential Judah was therefore the Mountain, the "hill country" of the Bible. This is indeed a *jabal* in the absolute sense, an inhabited highland and the home of a fiercely independent people, set apart upon a rocky plateau, only half of it cultivable and the other half desolate wilderness, but well guarded by nature. On the west the plunging monocline of the Judean arch, and the narrow Senonian moat, discouraged the invader, and on the east the rocky gorges of the barren Jeshimon and the stern cliffs of the Dead Sea provided double protection. On the south the arch dips toward the Beersheba Basin and the Senonian chalk curves around the highland and spreads up into the depression between the Yatta and the central upfolds. Here the defenses are less impressive, for the slopes are more gentle, although the southern end of the hard Cenomanian limestone is marked by a sudden descent of some 650 feet (200 m.) about halfway between Hebron and Beersheba, just south of the present adh-Dhah-

1. Aharoni, *Land of the Bible*, pp. 340–46. Yigael Yadin has argued that the cities were store cities for time of siege, with Ziph for Jeshimon and *Mmst* (founded after the last editing of Josh. 15) somewhere in the Negeb. But this seems to leave *Mmst* even more speculative, unless it is Kurnub, as some have proposed, and to allot to Ziph a region with only a handful of villages, which was hardly even besieged. Yadin, "The Fourfold Division of Judah," *BASOR*, 163 (1961), 6–12.

XXXV. *The Mount of Olives.* A dramatic view of the Mount of Olives from the south. It is not really a mountain, but a rather higher part of the plateau. The tower belongs to a Russian Orthodox convent.

ariyah. This marks the real edge of the mountain and the border with Simeon, later to be incorporated as the Negeb district. Before 1967 the armistice line ran quite remarkably close to this division. Only on the north, where the plateau of Benjamin could be so easily approached from Aijalon, did Judah lie open to the invader.

It is instructive to pause for a moment here and examine the places which, Rehoboam fortified to secure the heart of Judah after the division of the kingdom, (2 Chron. 11:5–12). Jerusalem, Bethlehem, Etam, Beth-zur, and Hebron all lay along the spine of Judah and the important north–south road, and in the west he maintained control of the heights of the Shephelah and the Judean moat by strengthening Zorah, Azekah, Adullam, Moreshath-gath (rather than Gath, the Philistine city, as in the Hebrew text), Mareshah, and Lachish. Tekoa, on the edge of Jeshimon, gave added protection to Bethlehem, and Ziph and Adoraim in the south guarded the approaches to

Hebron. These last two represent the greatest withdrawal to an interior line of defense, for south of them there is another step down, all the land over 2,600 feet (800 m.), except the hill of Juttah, being to the north. The edge of the mountain at adh-Dhahariyah and the southern district beyond, not yet as fully incorporated as it was to be in the days of Uzziah, served as a defensive glacis from which it would be possible, in times of stress, to withdraw. The approaches to Benjamin from the west were guarded by his fortification of Aijalon (lower Beth-horon had been fortified by his father, Solomon, 1 Kings 9:17). He did not, however, fortify the northern border of Benjamin, for it was still hoped at this time that the kingdom could be reunited by more tolerant methods (1 Kings 12:21–34).

Etam, Adoraim, and Ziph stand at the edges of the high interior plateau, which is everywhere above 3,000 feet (900 m.), the highest point being Kh. Khallat Batrakh at 3,345 feet (1020 m.) just north of Hebron. The 3,000-foot contour, in fact, coincides closely with the limits of the plateau. This is quite remarkably narrow, no more than 6½ miles wide (10 km.) in the Hebron region and shrinking in the center to less than 2 miles where the Wadi Ghar, the Engedi Valley, cuts back into the eastward slopes. The limestone surface has been dissolved in many places into hollows in which the soil has collected, and these are cultivated for wheat. On the terraced slopes are grown the vines, the chief crop of Judah, for here the increasing cold of winter and the decreasing rainfall discourage the production of olives, though the Judean heartland is not, as sometimes imagined, beyond the limit of olive cultivation. Today the Muslim prohibition of wine and the existence of imported cane sugar have restricted the growing of grapes to production for the table, but in the past wine was consumed in large quantities, and from the grapes rich treacle was prepared to supply the need for sugar. Then the greater part of the population must have encamped around the watchtowers in summer to protect the vineyards, for the parable of the man who "had a vineyard on a very fertile hill" and who "digged it and cleared it of stones and planted it with choice vines; he built a watchtower in the midst of it, and hewed out a wine vat in it; and he looked for it to yield grapes," belonged to the life of every Judean farmer (Isa. 5:1–7). Below the 3,000-foot contour, however, cultivation is abruptly interrupted and villages are very few, on the west because of the rocky slopes and gorges overlooking the moat and on the east because once the ridge is passed drought immediately prevails. Only where the land drops more gradually in the south does cultivation continue in the broad valleys. North of Etam, where the beginning of the Ephraim upfold widens the highlands, the plateau

is between 2,600 and 3,000 feet (800–900 m.), and here in the neighborhood of Bethlehem is the richest part of Judah. Olives, grain, and vines are all grown profusely, the hillsides and wadi bottoms are carefully terraced, and good husbandry is bountifully rewarded. Only a couple of miles beyond Bethlehem to the east, however, begins the implacable Jeshimon.

Along the water-parting, between the valleys and crags on either side, ran the highway, though not, it should be noticed, *through* the towns and villages. These all stood to one side, where the steep valley slopes, which the road avoided, gave them protection.

The district of the Negeb, to the south, once the land of Simeon, is the broad Beersheba depression, drained to the west by the Wadi Shenek (Nahal Besor). Since permanent cultivation comes to an end at the Wadi Mishash, one of the headwaters of the Shenek, flowing through Beersheba, this must be taken as the geographical division. Beersheba was as much the southern limit of the country as was Dan in the north, and was no less a border sanctuary, having been sacred from very early times. Samuel's sons were judges at Beersheba (1 Sam. 8:2), and Amos spoke scornfully of the pilgrimages thither (Amos 5:5). This wadi was one of the lines of defense for Judah, as exemplified by the powerful tells along its course.[2] Tell al-Milh may possibly be Hormah, long remembered as the place where the Amalekites blocked the approach of the Israelites (Num. 14:45; Deut. 1:44), and Kh. Gharra, the largest of the Iron Age tells in this region, may be Kabzeel, the home of Benaiah, "a doer of great deeds" (2 Sam. 23:20; 1 Chron. 11:22). At the

2. See the valuable discussion of this region by Y. Aharoni in "The Negeb of Judah," *IEJ*, 8 (1958), 26–38.

farthest end of this line is the strong fortress of Kh. Ghazza, one of the "uttermost cities of the tribe of the children of Judah toward the border of Edom southward" (Josh. 15:21, KJV).

North of this line of fortresses is the undulating territory which marks the end of the Judean folds to the north and the beginning of the Negeb folds to the south. Kh. Gharra stands at the end of the Maon upfold and Kh. Ghazza toward the northern end of the Dimona upfold. Between these upfolds are broad basins of fairly level land in which marginal cultivation and grazing are possible. The widest of these is the eastern basin between the Maon and Dimona upfolds. This was country of the Kenites (Judg. 1:16), in which stands the high tell of Arad, occupied in the Early Bronze Age (about 2900–2700 B.C.) and then not again until the time of the monarchy, when it became an important fortress with a sanctuary that shows remarkable parallels to the Temple in Jerusalem.[3] The only undoubted Yahwist place of worship so far excavated, this was certainly a border sanctuary, sanctifying both the military control and also the limit of the band of order and obedience against the ferocious land of the *midbar*.

The last of the districts of Judah is Jeshimon, so admirably described by Kinglake in *Eothen*: "Before me, and all around, as far as the eye could follow, blank hills piled high over hills, pale, yellow, and naked, walled up in her tomb for ever the dead and damned Gomorrah." It descends in a series of

fault steps, ever more jagged and precipitous, with gently rolling chalk hills on top, but breaking into wild and sinister gorges where the narrow wadis eat their way down to the sea. Though there is some pasture for the goats, which seem at times to browse on the stones of the field, it is only in the richest spring that there is more than a faint haze of grass, and such scrub as there is grows on the northern slopes where there is shelter from the blistering heat of the sun.

Save only for the few forts in the north, this region has never held cities of habitation, though the Bedouin encamp on its waste in the springtime, and from time to time in history it has given refuge to those who shunned the towns. Far back in the Chacolithic period (second half of the fourth millennium B.C.) almost every cave in the wadis near the Dead Sea was occupied, though why, and from whom, the people fled we do not know.[4] The monasteries of Mar Saba and Mar Jirius, clinging to the sides of the narrow gorges, each of them with only a dozen monks today, are the last relics of much greater communities, 4,000 souls or more, in the heyday of the Desert Fathers.

David fled here to escape from Saul, roaming with his followers around the southeast between Carmel, Ziph, Maon, and Engedi until the king of Israel came out to seek his life "like one who hunts a partridge in the mountains" (1 Sam. 26:20). Traditionally, also, it was to the north of Jeshimon that Jesus came after his baptism, and the Monastery of the Temptation, clutching the precipice of Jabal Quruntul, preserves this tradition. There is no need to try to pin

3. Y. Aharoni, and Ruth Amiran, "Excavations at Tel Arad: Preliminary Report on the First Season, 1963," *IEJ*, 4 (1964), 131–47; Y. Aharoni, "Excavations at Tel Arad: Preliminary Report on the Second Season," *IEJ*, 7 (1967), 233–49, and "Arad: Its Inscriptions and Temple," *BA*, XXXI (1968), 2–32.

4. N. Avigad, Y. Aharoni, and P. Bar-Adon, "The Expedition to the Judaean Desert, 1961," *IEJ*, 12, *Nos.* 2–3, 1962. It is possible, of course, that it was better watered at that date.

down any one place as the site of his experience, but upon the higher hills of Jeshimon it was in his day in a sense possible to see "all the kingdoms of the world in a moment of time" (Luke 4:5). There one might stand, looking out across the Ritt, and discover the whole plateau edge of Trans-jordan in one amazing panorama. In the far south were the lands of the Nabateans, shimmering in the haze which hovers over the Dead Sea, and Petra, hidden in their cliffs, rich with all the fabled wealth of the East. Immediately opposite lay Perea and the castle where Herod imprisoned John, once the lands of Moab and Ammon. Farther to the north were the cities of the Decapolis, heirs to rich heritage of Alexander and of Greece, and all around was then the power of Rome. "All this authority and their glory" was there gathered together in one single landscape as they would have been displayed in hardly another place in the world.

Of the six "cities" of Judah in Jeshimon (Josh. 16:61), only Engedi about halfway along the shore of the Dead Sea could be said to be worthy of that name. The City of Salt is now usually identified with Kh. Qumran, also just beside the Dead Sea, and the others were no more than forts, either on the border at Debir and Adummim, where the "Inn of the Good Samaritan" now stands, or guarding the road through the level basin of al-Buqei‘a above the cliffs of Qumran. This has been identified with the Valley of Achor, where Achan and his family were put to death (Josh. 7:26), but the identification can be no more than tentative, for the indications in the Bible are far from exact.[5] In New Testament days Herod's fortress of Hyrcania stood above this

basin on the western side,[6] and today the charming Muslim sanctuary of Nabi Musa is at its northeastern end.

During two periods of history military necessity demanded the building of roads across Jeshimon: the Israelite monarchy because of the wars with Moab and Edom, and the Roman period in the days of Masada and Bar Kochba. There had always been a route from Hebron to Engedi, perhaps the Ascent of Ziz (2 Chron. 20:16), but the old tracks were cleared and improved by the kings of Judah. The Roman engineers were more thorough in their methods, cutting passages through the rocks and paving where necessary. In the days of the monarchy the main military road went from Arad past Kh. Ghazza and down the Wadi Muawwat (Nahal Zohar), at the bottom of which there is today the ruin of a Roman fortress. It is the only route without sheer cliffs, but it is very lacking in water.[7]

When David first began to reign, his capital was at Hebron, suitably and centrally placed as long as he controlled only Judah, but when the northern tribes joined him in the eighth year of his reign he sought a site more central to the whole country and not identified with any of the major tribes. For this reason he captured Jerusalem and built his capital there. This is "the city where David encamped" (Isa. 29:1), built where the road up the rim of the Sorek and that from Jericho cross the water-parting road. This last is the "Ascent of Blood" (Adummim), by which name it is still known in Arabic today from the patches of red ocher to be seen near

5. F. M. Cross and J. T. Milik, "Explorations in the Judaean Buq‘ah," *BASOR*, 142 (1956), 5–17.

6. G. R. H. Wright, "The Archaeological Remains at el-Mird in the Wilderness of Judaea," *Biblica*, XLII (1961), 1–21.

7. These roads are discussed in more detail in M. Harel, "Israelite and Roman Roads in the Judaean Desert," *IEJ*, 17 (1967), 18–42.

the "Inn of the Good Samaritan." It is the road followed by the unhappy King Zedekiah when Jerusalem was besieged by the Babylonians and "a breach was made in the city; the king with all the men of war fled by night by way of the gate between the two walls, by the king's garden, though the Chaldeans were around the city. And they went in the direction of the Arabah. But the army of the Chaldeans pursued the king, and overtook him in the plains of Jericho" (2 Kings 25:4–5). It was followed very much later by Jesus when "he went ahead, going up to Jerusalem" (Luke 19:28). The journey from Jericho to Jerusalem normally took two days, and halfway along the road was a caravansary and a fort near Adummim. Here travelers could rest for the night and the authorities could exercise control

of the often brigand-infested road. It was a dangerous journey in the time of Jesus, and traditionally the caravansary at Adummim was the one he had in mind when he told the story of the Good Samaritan (Luke 10:29–37). This may be so, of course, but there is nothing in the story to say that the inn was not in Jericho. As late as the Arab rebellion against the British in 1936–39 the dangers of this road in a time of civil strife became again very apparent.

The city of Jerusalem itself stands where three steep-sided little wadis gather together to form one wadi, the course of the "River of Life" in the vision recounted in Ezekiel 47:1–12. The three wadis are the Kidron, the Tyropoeon, and the valley of Hinnom. Between the first two a long narrow spur extends southward, and it was on this

XXXVI. *"The Open Square before the House of God"* (Ezra 10:9). The great sanctuary at Jerusalem was essentially a large open space in which stood the temple building, the "house" for God, entered only by the priests. It has retained to this day the character of a vast enclosed open space, though it is now a profoundly sacred Muslim shrine called "the Noble Sanctuary." The stone pavement in this picture was first constructed by Herod the Great. The buildings and arches are Muslim.

spur that the first town was built.[8] This was the town taken by David and was strongly defended by steep descents on every side except the north. This was therefore the area for expansion; here he built his palace, and here his son, Solomon, built the Temple on the threshing floor of Araunah the Jebusite (2 Sam. 24:18), the flat land on the plateau such as is found outside every Palestinian hill village, where farmers thresh and winnow the grain. Though at first confined to this spur, there is now evidence that by the eighth century it had expanded across onto the western hill, the valley between being probably the *Maktesh*, the "Mortar" of Zephaniah 1:11. After the return from the Exile the city was once more confined to the eastern spur and was not extended westward again until the great building schemes of Herod the Great spread out the city to both the west and the north.

The Temple stood where the glorious Haram ash-Sharif, the "Noble Sanctuary" of the Muslims, now stands, and in New Testament days two bridges led across the Tyropoeon Valley to the western hill. There were then two fortresses, one on the western hill where the present citadel now stands and the other, called the Antonia, on the eastern hill overlooking the Temple from the north. It was certainly to the Antonia that Paul was carried through the excited crowd after he had been arrested in the Temple courts (Acts 21:27–36), and traditionally this is also the scene of Jesus' trial. Indeed the ancient pavement, often identified with the *Gabbatha* where Pilate sat to pronounce the sentence of execution (John 19:13), now under the convent of the Soeurs de Zion, is one of the most impressive sights for the visitor to Jerusalem. However, it is now clear that this pavement is of the same date as the triumphal arch, part of which is still to be seen extending across the street outside, and which was certainly built by the Emperor Hadrian as the eastern gateway to his new city of Aelia Capitolina after A.D. 135.[9] Jesus, therefore, must probably have been tried in the Citadel on the western hill and have been taken from there to Golgotha. This means, of course, that the traditional Via Dolorosa, hallowed by the prayers and pilgrimages of the devout, is not the actual route.

On the other hand, we may now speak with more confidence than formerly of the site of the Church of the Holy Sepulcher, which has in the past been much questioned, rather particularly by Protestant scholars. The chief difficulty for accepting this site as the true position of Jesus' crucifixion and resurrection has always been that it is at present well within the walls, and was believed by many authorities to have been within them in the first century A.D. Unfortunately, Josephus' description of this wall, the so-called "second wall," is so vague as to be of no help at all.[10] However,

8. The growth of the city is described in detail, with a series of seven maps, by A. D. Tushingham in Baly and Tushingham, *Atlas of the Biblical World*. Further excavations, of course, have been going on since these maps were drawn. For the evidence of the extension of the city to the western hill in the late eighth century see Ruth Amiran and A. Eitan, "Excavations in the Courtyard of the Citadel, Jerusalem, 1968–1969 (Preliminary Report)," *IEJ*, 20 (1970), 9–17; N. Avigad, "Excavations in the Jewish Quarter of the Old City of Jerusalem, 1969/70 (Preliminary Report)," *IEJ*, 20 (1970), 1–8; Second Preliminary Report, pp. 129–40; M. Avi-Yonah, "The Newly-found Wall of Jerusalem and Its Topographical Significance," *IEJ*, 21 (1971), 168–69.

9. P. Benoit, "L'Antonia d'Herode le Grand et le Forum Oriental d'Aelia Capitolina," *Harvard Theological Review*, 64 (1971), 135–67.

10. *War*, V, 146.

XXXVII. *Gethesemane.* One of the most attractive features of present-day Jerusalem is the great variety of architectural styles which is the result of people from all over the world wishing to build a shrine here. This picture shows the Russian church in the Garden of Gethsemane.

the recent excavations by Kathleen Kenyon have shown that where the Holy Sepulcher stands today was apparently outside the city walls until Hadrian had this area filled in for his new buildings in Aelia Capitolina.[11] This does not prove, of course, that the present church does in fact stand on the site of the Crucifixion, but we no longer have

11. Kathleen Kenyon, *Jerusalem: Excavating 3000 years of History* (London: Thames and Hudson, 1967), pp. 146–54.

serious reason to reject it.[12]

During the whole of the monarchy, following the division of the kingdom at Solomon's death, Jerusalem, the capital of Judah, stood very dangerously close to the frontier, a mere 5 miles from the border towns. In Isaiah 10:23–34 the prophet envisages the Assyrian advance in staccato phrases suggestive of speed: "He has reached Aiath; he has by-passed Migron, left his baggage train at Michmash, and gone over the pass. He has encamped at Geba; Ramah is terrified, and Gibeah of Saul has fled. Cry for help, people of Gallim; listen, Laishah, and answer them, Anathoth. Madmennah is in flight; the people of Gebim are running away. This very day he will halt at Nob and shake his fist at the mount of the daughter of Zion, the hill of Jerusalem."[13] These places are not strung out many days' journey from each other as are Calno, Carchemish, Hamath, Arpad, Damascus, and Samaria, which the king of Assyria himself had quoted (Isa. 10:9–10; 37:12–13), but are all close to Jerusalem. Aiath, the first of them, is no more than 10 miles (16 km.) distant, and Nob, where the dread conqueror will stand "this very day," is probably at-Tur on the Mount

12. G. M. Fitzgerald rightly says, "One ought to bear in mind a fact, often ignored, that Eusebius, with earlier authorities available to him, claims for Jerusalem and Aelia a church and a succession of bishops beginning with James the Less, one of the family of Jesus Christ, and only broken in the sense that before the Second Revolt they are said to be 'of Circumcision,' that is of the Judaeo-Christian element, whereas Bishop Mark and his successors at Aelia were not so. But there is no reason to support that a short interval of time need break a tradition which one would naturally expect to be faithfully handed down." "Palestine in the Roman Period, 63 B.C.–A.D. 324," *PEQ*, LXXXVIII (1956), 48.

13. Author's translation.

XXXVIII. *Bethlehem.* Some of the great columns in of Justinian's basilica which now line the nave of the Church of the Nativity, standing over the cave which Christian tradition has long associated with the birth of Jesus. Beneath the floor are remains of the mosaic floor of the earlier church from the time of the Emperor Constantine.

XXXIX. *The Landscape of Judah.* A characteristic view of the Judaean landscape showing the denuded slopes of Cenomanian limestone where the natural terracing of the rock has been developed by the farmer into terraces for agriculture. The bottom of the wadi has also been terraced by building walls from one side to the other. Terracing in Judah seems to have begun early in the Israelite monarchy.

of Olives, where Jesus stood and wept over the city (Luke 19:41).

George Adam Smith says of Judah that one cannot live in it "without being daily aware of the presence of the awful deep which bounds it on the east,"[14] and that may well be so for the foreigner, for whom the Jordan Rift is a peculiar phenomenon. But those who have grown up beside it all their lives know that on this side at least they are well protected. On the other hand they cannot but be aware of the danger of "evil from the north and a great destruction" (Jer. 4:6) and of the ease with which the invader could make his way up the Valley of Aijalon. It was perfectly possible then to leave Jerusalem at midday and walk as far as the edge of the hills on the west, there to look right across the Coast Plain and see, perhaps, the smoke rising from the plundered villages, and then return on foot to the city before the gates were closed at sunset. So close stood Jerusalem to the invader, and it cannot have been only once in the history of the kings of Judah that "his heart and the heart of his people shook as the trees of the forest shake before the wind" (Isa. 7:2).

Judah's strong natural defenses on all sides but the north, and her position aside from the great Trunk Road, gave her a breathing space in times when the imperial rulers went forth to war, but only a breathing space, and Jerusalem was ever haunted by the fear of war. It is therefore by no accident that a prophet is so often called a watchman (Isa. 21:6; Ezek. 3:17; 33:7; Hab. 2:1). Of the rulers it might be said, "They prepare the table, they spread the rugs, they eat, they drink" (Isa. 21:5), thinking, as they so frequently did, that by some skillful piece of diplomacy they had contrived to postpone the danger, saying, "We have made a covenant with death, and with Sheol we have an agreement; when the overflowing scourge passes through it will not come to us" (Isa. 28:15). But the prophet knew that when he saw "riders, horsemen in pairs, riders on asses, riders on camels," then he must hearken very diligently (Isa. 21:7). The people might try to shut their eyes to the danger and say to the prophets, "See not . . . prophesy not to us what is right . . . let us hear no more of the Holy One of Israel" (Isa. 30:10–11), and their more superficial counselors might tell them, "You shall not see the sword, nor shall you have famine, but I will give you assured peace in this place" (Jer. 14:13), but never was it to be so.

---

14. Smith, *op. cit.*, p. 178.

CHAPTER 17

The Entrance of the Hamath and the Arabah

Jeroboam restored the border of Israel from the entrance of Hamath as far as the Sea of the Arabah, according to the word of the Lord, the God of Israel, which he spoke by his servant Jonah, the son of Amittai, the prophet, who was from Gath-hepher.

2 KINGS 14:25

C.1. *The Huleh Basin*

It is now possible to drive all the way down the Rift Valley from Dan in the extreme north to Elath in the south, a little more than 300 miles by road (about 500 km.). This can be done in haste in well under a day, but it should not be, for it is a remarkable journey, perhaps one of the most remarkable in the world, from the plentiful springs of the Jordan to the desert of the Arabah, from the snows of Hermon to the desolation of the Red Sea. The Palestinian Rift, as we have already seen (p. 29), is structurally not continuous with the Valley of Lebanon. Their direction is not the same, and they stand at markedly different levels, the northern

Rift being everywhere an upland valley, rising to over 3,000 feet (900 m.) at Baalbek, while the Palestinian valley is everywhere lowland, indeed for the most part below sea level, and reaching as much as 650 feet (200 m.) only at one place in the Arabah.

The rift valleys meet on the present frontier between Israel and Lebanon, where there is a steep and sudden step of some 400 feet (125 m.) followed by a less abrupt, but still rapid, descent of another 4 miles (6 km.), separating the fertile basin of Marj 'Ayoun to the north (1,650 feet; 500 m. above sea level) from the Huleh Basin, which is everywhere below 350 feet (110 m.).

Near the town of Marj 'Ayoun (or Jdeideh) in Lebanon is Tell Dibbine,

191

62   THE HULEH BASIN

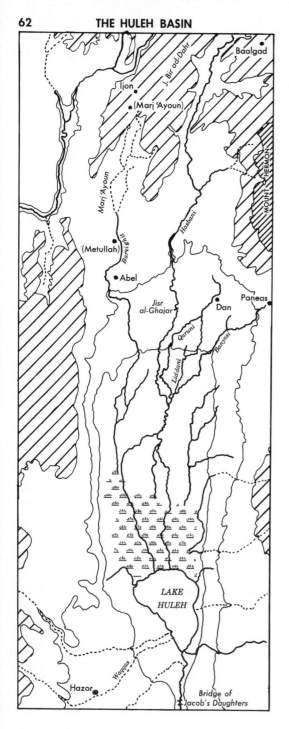

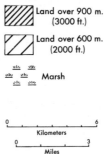

the site of Ijon, once an Israelite out-post which was captured by both Ben-hadad of Damascus and Tiglath-pileser of Assyria (1 Kings 15:20; 2 Kings 15:29), and immediately north of it the complex structure of southern Lebanon confines the road to a very narrow passage. This is the limit of the reputed conquests of Joshua, Baalgad (Josh. 11:17) being probably the present town of Hasbaya on the lower slopes of Mount Hermon. The constricted Lebanese Rift is here divided lengthwise by the fault block of Jabal Bir ad-Dahr, and on either side of it run two of the four headwaters of the Jordan. The basin of Marj 'Ayoun to the west is drained by the smaller Bareighit, which leaps over the threshold in a series of charming waterfalls near Metullah and postpones its junction with the Jordan until just before the Huleh marshes. On the east of the ridge is the Hasbani, the longest of the Jordan streams, rising near Hasbaya and then flowing southward in a narrow valley through wild and deserted limestone country until it crosses the present frontier at Jisr al-Ghajar about 400 feet above sea level.

Towering above Marj 'Ayoun on the east stands Hermon, the long and lovely mountain which brings the Anti-Lebanon to an end, climbing up from the plain to a height of 9,230 feet (2814 m.). Heavy with snow in winter and retaining a few patches even during the hot summer months, it is variously named in the Bible, for "the Sidonians call Hermon Sirion, while the Amorites call it Senir" (Deut. 3:9; 4:48; Song of Sol. 4:8). Some have identified Hermon with the "mighty, many-peaked mountain" of Psalm 68:15, but this is more properly to be equated with the Jabal Druze. From the foot of Hermon burst forth the swelling fountains of the Liddani and Banyasi, springing fully grown from the mountain not far from each other at Tell al-Qadi and Banias, altogether glorious, for their rushing torrents foster lush green vegetation even in the height of summer.

This is a curious corner of Palestinian history, for though it is far from the great centers of Israelite life, it keeps recurring in the records. The sudden change from the Palestinian to the Lebanese Rift and the majestic barrier of Hermon have made of it a frontier throughout history, and here Syria, Israel, and Phoenicia met. Abraham is said, in a story whose historical authority is difficult to determine (Gen. 14:14), to have pursued his enemies as far as Dan and beyond, and in his day Dan was already a strongly fortified city.[1] It was probably some time during the eleventh century B.C. that the people of Dan, themselves driven out and searching for somewhere to settle, smote the inhabitants of Laish "with the edge of the sword, and burned the city with fire" (Judg. 18:27). Before this savage attack the people "dwelt in security, after the manner of the Sidonians, quiet and unsuspecting, lacking nothing that is in the earth, and possessing wealth. . . . They were far from the Sidonians and had no dealings with any one" (Judg.

1. A. Biran, "Tel Dan," *IEJ*, 19 (1969), 121–23.

18:7), but afterward the name of Laish was changed to Dan and it became the most northerly town in the country. Lurking in their thick woodlands, the people of Dan were "a lion's whelp, that leaps forth from Bashan" (Deut. 33:22), and they harried the travelers on the roads from the north "as a viper by the path, that bites the horse's heels so that his rider falls backward" (Gen. 49:17), but when a mighty army came from the north, Dan was the first to suffer, for no invader dared leave this nest of vipers to threaten his lines of communication (1 Kings 15:20; 2 Kings 15:29). So distant a tribe could often pursue a role somewhat independent of the central government, and it was at Abel-beth-maacah (Tell Abil just across the valley) that the rebel Sheba sought refuge (2 Sam. 20:14), but in his day the authority of the king in Jerusalem was strong and widespread, and so his flight was in vain.

Bound up with the frontier role of these remote towns was their religious significance, for they were all border sanctuaries, and at two of them the rocks pour forth the water of life in profusion. This is a numinous region indeed, where the rich forests close in upon the fields and the snow-clad mountain looms mysteriously above. Nowhere was the proclamation of order in face of the enveloping wildness of nature more necessary, for in no other Israelite settlements were the young lions, roaring after their prey, quite so close. It is a mysterious world of superabundant life, and all of the three towns on this northern border were places to which men came for counsel and ghostly strength. "They were wont to say in old time, 'Let them but ask counsel at Abel,' and so they settled a matter" (2 Sam. 20:18), and at Banias, the Paneas of old, one may see carved in the rock face the niches for Pan which recall

XL. *Caesarea Philippi.* At Banias (ancient Paneas) one of the sources of the Jordan pours out in a swift torrent from the foot of Mount Hermon. Here one may still see the niches dedicated to the god Pan. In the Gospel story this is the place where Peter confessed that Jesus was the Christ.

his ancient worship. From the beginning the Danites at Laish set up a graven image (Judg. 18:30); later Jeroboam I made it one of his royal sanctuaries (1 Kings 12:29; 2 Kings 10:29), and Amos derided those who say, "As thy god lives, O Dan!" (Amos 8:14). The great high place, with its monumental flight of steps which may be from the time of Ahab, has recently been excavated.[2]

At Paneas Herod built a temple dedicated to the Emperor Augustus, and when Philip became tetrach of this

2. A. Biran, "Tel Dan," *IEQ*, 20 (1970), 118–19.

region, the name was changed to Caesarea, called Caesarea Philippi to distinguish it from the important seaport on the coast. It was here at Caesarea Philippi, in the haunt of pagan worship, where stood the shrines of the state and the mysterious forest deities, that Jesus chose to ask his disciples the critical question, "Who do you say that I am?" (Mark 8:29), and Peter answered him, "You are the Christ," you are the person we have all been waiting for. This was the death sentence upon the gods by whom they were surrounded and in a sense also the death sentence of the Christ himself, for "immediately he began to teach them that the Son of Man must suffer many things, and be rejected by the elders and the chief priests and the scribes and be killed and"—herein lay the difference—"after three days rise again" (Mark 8:31).

Many would identify Mount Hermon, whose slopes rise steeply above Caesarea Philippi, with the Mount of the Transfiguration, though more traditionally it is associated with Mount Tabor. We can no longer be certain. If it was either of them, it is strange that the name is not given, for the names of both were as much a part of common speech as that of the Mount of Olives. At this late date, alas, we must be content to celebrate the event and no longer know the place.

The Huleh Basin which lies to the south of these towns is very small, only some 14 miles long by 5 miles wide at the most (22 by 8 km.). Until it was recently drained there was at the southern end the small lake of the same name, certainly much larger in biblical days than recently, for over the centuries it steadily filled with sediment. Behind it the streams lost themselves in watery marshes, and tangled thickets of papyrus, here growing in strange isolation from its normal home in the Sudan. On either side steep slopes hemmed the basin in, and the road from the north clung to the edges of Galilee until it reached the basalt dam behind which this desolate swamp had formed.

The Trunk Road vaulted the Jordan just below Lake Huleh by the Bridge of Jacob's Daughter,[3] the only possible crossing point, since to the south the river enters the confines of the basalt gorge, whose walls stand as much as

3. The name has nothing to do with the Patriarch Jacob, but comes from the Daughters of St. James who had a convent here in the days of the Crusades (Karmon, *Israel*, p. 166).

XLI. *Waterfall near Banias.* The abundance of water springing out of the rock, the dense forests of oak, and the towering mountain of Hermon above all made of the extreme north of the Jordan valley a region of mysterious sanctity from the very earliest times that we know.

1,000 feet (300 m.) above the stream. About 7½ miles in length (12 km.), this dam is a rough, but fairly level plateau. Just north of it a number of streams flowing down toward the lake area from the Galilean hills have built up a wide alluvial fan encroaching on the lake from the southwest. Where the road from the north crossed one of these, the Waqqas (Nahal Hazor), stood the important stronghold of Hazor, close to where this road was joined by the Trunk Road from across the bridge.

Excavations in recent years have demonstrated that indeed "Hazor formerly was the head of all those kingdoms"

(Josh. 11:10), for in the so-called Hyksos period the city covered some 180 acres, which is an enormous area for an ancient tell.[4] It is the only city in Palestine to be mentioned in the Mari letters and apparently had commercial relations with both Mari and Babylon.[5] Evidence of this close relation with Mesopotamia is to be found in the excellent system of irrigation and drainage canals, which were begun in the eighteenth century B.C.[6] The city was completely destroyed in the late thirteenth century, presumably by Joshua, and after this it carried intermittently for a time only a small settlement. It was fortified again by Solomon (1 Kings 9:15), although only on part of the tell, and then more strongly in the time of Ahab. It is to this period that the city owes its quite remarkable underground water system, more than twice the size of that at Megiddo, with provision for donkeys to go up and down at the same time to the hidden well. The development at this time of such highly sophisticated methods of supplying the great fortresses with water in time of siege, which involved sound geological knowledge of where the water was to be found, reflect the necessity of resisting the formidable invasions of first the Syrians and then the Assyrians.[7]

In contrast to the basalt region farther south, the basalt plateau between Huleh and the Lake of Galilee carries many evidences of early settlement. To the Roman period belong the somber ruins of Chorazin, built out of the black and difficult rock and in New Testament times an unresponding witness of the mighty works of Jesus (Matt. 11:21).

C.2. *The Galilee–Beth-shan Basin*

At the north end of the lake the river Jordan, now slightly more than 600 feet (200 m.) below sea level, breaks free from the confinement of the valley and crosses a small alluvial plain to enter the lake. This little heart-shaped body of water, only 12 miles long by about 7 miles as its widest point (18 by 12 km.), is shut in by hills on nearly every side. The broadest plain is the tiny triangle of Gennesaret in the northwest, and in the northeast also, near the Jordan mouth, the hills withdraw a little from the shore in the region known as al-Buteiha. Nowhere are the shores impassable, and there is space for a track all the way around the lake. Rainfall is here still sufficient for farming without irrigation, though both Gennesaret and al-Buteiha are also watered by permanent streams which can be used for his purpose. The warm winters and very long, hot summers encourage growth wherever there is water, and almost every kind of Palestinian crop is to be found. In spring the gaily colored slopes glow with a brilliance which may perhaps be equaled in some other fortunate places in the country but is certainly never surpassed.

Today this lake has a placid beauty, with distant Hermon presiding over the green, enfolding hills, and is a wonderful retreat for those who wish to meditate upon the gospel story. But they should not imagine it was so quiet in the time of Jesus. It was not then a scene of rustic beauty, but bustling with life. A dozen sizable towns stood close to its shores; fishing was an im-

4. Yigael Yadin, "The Fourth Season of Excavation at Hazor," *BA*, XXII (1959), 19–20.

5. A. Malamat in "Report on Fourteenth Annual Conference of the Israel Exploration Society on *Safad and Upper Galilee*," *IEJ*, 8 (1958), 277–83.

6. Yigael Yadin, "Excavations at Hazor, 1968–1969," *IEJ*, 19 (1969), 8.

7. *Ibid.*, pp. 12–17.

Contour interval: 300 m.
(c. 1000 ft.)

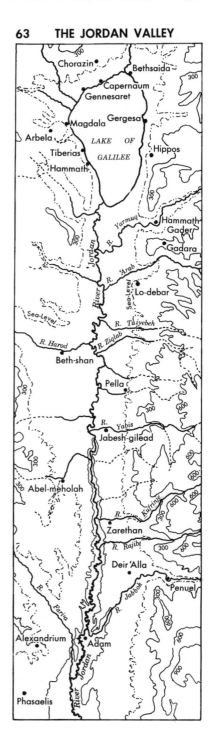

63   THE JORDAN VALLEY

portant industry, the fish being pickled for export at Magdala, conveniently close to the Trunk Road, and boats brought from Bashan the grain that was to be sent to Rome. It was not therefore among simple village folk that his mighty works were done, but among the city dwellers of Chorazin, Bethsaida, and Capernaum, and it was they who were condemned because they did not respond to the itinerant preacher whom many of them doubtless feared as politically subversive.

Capernaum, the center of his activity, is at Tell Hum in the northwest, and Bethsaida, the birthplace of Philip, Andrew, and Peter (John 1:44), at al-'Araj in the northeast. The dignified synagogue at Capernaum cannot be the one mentioned in the Gospels (Luke 7:5), for it belongs to the third or even fourth century, though of course it may stand on the same site. However, there has recently been discovered in the fishermen's quarter of first-century Capernaum what may be the earliest evidence of Christian worship that we have, a private dwelling in which the chief room has apparently been modified to permit the gathering together of early Christians to "proclaim the Lord's death until he comes" (1 Cor. 11:26).[8] Tiberias was then an entirely Gentile city, and there is no record that Jesus ever entered it, though there seems little doubt that he was not averse to going to Gentile territory. It was famous then

8. Père V. C. Corbo, "Capernaum," *IEJ*, 18 (1958), 197–98.

as now for the hot springs near Tiberias, the Hammath in Naphtali of Joshua 19:35, and known in Roman times as Amathus. The Roman Tiberias, which was well fortified, lay south of the present town, between the steep hillside and the lake. There are other hot springs a little way up the Yarmuq Valley at al-Hammeh, and here also the Romans had their baths. Still other hot springs, rising beneath the lake, provide amusement for the swimmer.

The eastern side of the lake was Gentile, the region of the Decapolis (Matt. 4:25; Mark 5:20; 7:31), and it is clear from the Gospels, especially Mark, that in those days when people looked across at the lights on the other side of the lake they were aware that over there were men and women who did not keep the feast; it was the haunt of a legion of unclean spirits, whose stammering inhabitants could proclaim the gospel only after they had been given the power to do so (Mark 5:1–20; 7:31–37).[9] Where on the eastern shore the incident of the Gadarene swine took place is obscure, since the name is rendered variously as Gergasene, Gerasene, and Gadarene. Gergesa is probably al-Kursi, opposite Magadala, but the other two were more distant, and both important Decapolis cities, Gadara at Umm Qeis on the southern edge of the Yarmuq canyon and Gerasa at Jerash, far away in the hills of Gilead. The city of the Decapolis which was closest to the lake was Hippos, crowning a conical hill isolated by deep wadis just behind the present kibbutz of En Gev.

South of the lake the Rift, from here to the Dead Sea known as the Ghor, continues agreeably for about another 25 miles (40 km.) until the narrowing at the Jordan "waist" is reached. There is still sufficient rain for cultivation, even without irrigation. The river, though meandering continually, is not yet too far beneath the general level of the plain to be easily fordable, and it may be crossed at many points. From the eastern side comes the Yarmuq, bringing to the confluence as much water as the Jordan itself, and then a series of swift scarp rivers, the 'Arab, the Taiyebeh, the Ziqlab, and the Yabis, as well as smaller, less permanent streams. The Yabis is believed to be the "brook Cherith, which is east of the Jordan" (1 Kings 17:3), where Elijah took refuge in the famine. Along the eastern edge of the plain, where water is plentiful, there was a line of towns and villages, either at the piedmont springs or just a little way up the valleys. Umm ad-Dabar, a couple of miles south of the 'Arab, may perhaps be Lo-debar (= Debir on the border of Gad, Josh. 13:26; 2 Sam. 9:4), of whose recapture Amos spoke so scathingly (Amos 6:13). Rather farther south, in the little Wadi Malawi, is Pella (Kh. Fahil), already known in the Amarna letters and in the time of the New Testament one of the cities of the Decapolis. After the destruction of Jerusalem in A.D. 70 a number of Christian refugees came here to live. At the entrance to the Wadi Yabis stood Jabesh-gilead, which sent men secretly at night to rescue the body of Saul in remembrance of the time when he had saved them from the Ammonites (1 Sam. 11:1–11; 31:8–13; see also the story in Judg. 21:8ff.).[10]

---

9. That Mark told the story of Legion and the Gadarene swine in the light of Psalm 65:5–8 has often been pointed out. Beyond the lake were the "farthest bounds" of the land (i.e., *eretz*, land or earth).

10. Some authorities would place Jabesh-gilead at Tell Maqlub, much farther up the Yabis valley, and this is quite possibly right.

C.3. *The Kikkar, or the Ghor*

South of the Jordan "waist," a few miles south of the Yabis, the mountains close in upon the Rift from either side. Today the road runs at the foot of the eastern upfold of Manasseh to the west of the Jordan, but the ancient towns were at the spring line to the east. The modern tourist may here look across the Jordan trough 1,000 feet (300 m.) below sea level to Tell as-Sa'eidiyeh, the ancient Zarethan, where the bronze vessels for the Temple are said to have been made (1 Kings 7:45–46), and beyond to the great wall of Gilead rising 4,000 feet (1200 m.) above the river. Zarethan stands close to the important river Kufrinje, which comes down from near Ajlun, and here also there was a well-protected approach to the water supply, with provision for the animals to come up and down at the same time.[11] The next permanent stream is the Rajeb, and then the canyon of the Jabbok. About a mile north of the Jabbok, at the foot of the scarp, is Tell Deir 'Alla, once believed to be the site of Succoth. We now know that this cannot be so, though the region round about was certainly a metalworking one, using for fuel either wood from the hills or else the thickets of the Jordan. First occupied in the sixteenth century B.C., it was an open sanctuary of considerable significance and a center of pilgrimage. The Bronze Age sanctuary was destroyed by an earthquake followed by a fire, and in the early Israelite period the site was not permanently occupied, but visited seasonally in winter both to work the iron and for religious festivals. It has been suggested that here was the border sanctuary, containing "an altar of great size," which led to a dispute between the people west and east of the Jordan (Judg. 22:10–34). Intriguing, but still obscure, inscribed clay tablets and inscribed plaster fragments have been found here, and it is quite evident that it was at one time a very important center.[12]

As the Ghor opens out it is joined by the Jabbok and the Fari'a, both of which are deflected southward before the confluence. Here is the last of the fords before Jericho and the site of Adam (Josh. 3:16), where more than once in history when swollen with melting snow and heavy rains "the Jordan overflows its banks throughout the time of harvest," the strong spring floods have undermined the soft marl cliffs and dammed for a time the course of the river. Guarding the entrance to the Fari'a Valley stood the Herodian fortress of Alexandrium.

Now the climate is much drier and the valley wider, as much as 10 miles (16 km.) in places, and now also appears fully developed the threefold division of the Rift. First, sloping steadily from the hills on either side, is the true *Ghor,* where are the pasturelands and, if water is available, the cultivated fields. But then, nearer the river, the ground breaks away into the desolate badlands of the *Qattara,* which exhibit in miniature all the features of a dissected desert landscape, containing in manageable size the plateaus, buttes, and mesas which elsewhere are seen on a much grander scale. Uncultivated and uncultivable, it is exhausting to explore, for the ash-gray marl is horribly slippery

---

11. James B. Pritchard, "The First Excavations at Tell es-Sa'idiyeh," *BA*, XXVIII (1965), 10–17.

12. H. J. Franken, "The Excavations at Deir 'Alla in Jordan," *VT*, X (1960), 386–93; XI (1961), 361–72; XII (1962), 378–82; XIV (1964), 377–79, 417–22. Also "Notes and News," *PEQ*, CI (1969), 2.

after rain and when dry crumbles under-
foot.

In these badlands the Jordan has
carved a trench, the *Zor,* in which it
twists and writhes through an impenetrable tangle of tamarisk and other
shrubs. This is the *gaon ha-yarden* of the
Old Testament, the "Pride of Jordan,"
then the home of lions and wild boars
(Jer. 12:5; 49:19; 50:44; Zech. 11:3),
and it was this, together with the *Qattara,* which made such a strong division
between the peoples on either side. The
Jordan itself is, it must be confessed, a
narrow, muddy, and almost despicable
stream, which is nowhere difficult to
cross, though the swift current may
sweep away the unwary. Naaman not

unreasonably thought it less atractive
than the clear streams which fed the
gardens of Damascus (2 Kings 5:12).
However, so difficult to penetrate are
the two regions which enclose it that
rivalry and bitterness plagued the relationship of the people to the east and
west (Josh. 22; Judg. 8:4–17; 12:1–6,
21:8–12).

Though the Lower Ghor is increasingly desert, this does not mean that it
was altogether uncultivated. Far back
in the time of Abraham there were many
little settlements along the edges of the
eastern hills, and the Roman genius
brought water in lengthy aqueducts to
feed the palm groves of the western
plain. Phasaelis (Kh. Fasayil), Archelais

XLII. *The Jordan near Adam.* A photograph taken looking northeastward, showing the
uplifted Dome of Gilead in the background with, to the left, the valley of the Jabbok coming
down to meet the Jordan. In the foreground the sinuous Jordan river winds through the
flood plain of the Zor (here cleared of its tangle of thick vegetation) and enclosed by the
badlands of the Qattara. It is the undercutting of these marl cliffs which has occasionally
dammed the Jordan at this point.

XLIII. *The Monastery of the Temptation.* Clinging to the steep cliffsides of Jabal Quruntul is the monastery built on the traditional site of the Temptation of Jesus. At the foot of the cliffs may be seen the beginning of the oasis of Jericho.

(Auja at-Tahta), and all the district of Jericho were intensely cultivated, and above Jericho, on the scarp known today as the Mount of Temptation, stood the Herodian fortress of Docus to guard the various roads up into the hills. The towns in the plain were never easily defendable, and Jericho seems to have been content to belong to whoever was strongest, for though theoretically it was in Benjamin, Ephraim also laid claim to it (Josh. 16:7; 18:21). The stories in 1 Kings 16:34 and 2 Kings 2:4–6 suggest that it was then in Israel rather than in Judah. George Adam Smith says of it caustically, "She has been called 'the key' and 'the guardhouse' of Judaea; she was only the pantry. She never stood a siege, and her inhabitants were always running away."[13] In view of the remarkable defenses of the prepottery Neolithic city discovered by Kathleen

13. Smith, *op. cit.*, p. 183.

Kenyon, this stricture is no longer as apt as it was, but in biblical times it certainly seems to have served primarily for provisions rather than for military purposes.

On the other side of the Jordan at the north end of the Dead Sea, where a fault scarp has cut back into the plateau, are the well-watered "plains of Moab" (Num. 22:1). Here also agriculture started in very early days. The waters of Nimrin (Isa. 15:6) are the present Wadi Shu'eib, leading up to the town of Salt, and the little village of Shunat Nimrin on the edge of the plain still carries the name. Abel-shittim (or Shittim, Num. 33:49; Josh. 2:1, 3:1; Mic. 6:5) is Tell al-Hammam, where the Wadi Kufrein enters the plain, and Beth-peor (or Baal-peor; Deut. 3:29; 4:3; Josh. 13:20; Hos. 9:10) is at the very corner of the plain where the Wadi Hisban comes down.   ·

Certain sites, however, still elude us. There is no general agreement about Gilgal, important though it was, though it seems to be somewhere between Jericho and the river, nor can we identify "Bethany beyond Jordan" (John 1:28).[14]

C.4. *The Dead Sea*

South of Jericho the width of the valley shrinks again to about 6½ miles (10–11 km.), the steep scarps approach each other, and the entire plain disappears beneath the surface of the Dead Sea. This unique body of water, 50 miles long by 10 miles wide at the most (80 by 16 km.), lies 1,274 feet (396 m.) below the level of the Mediterranean and about as much as that again at its

deepest point, in the northern basin; it occupies almost exactly the center of the Palestinian Rift, with its two ends about 110 miles (185 km.) from Dan to the north and from Elath to the south. It is not only the lowest place on the earth's surface, but also the most salty body of water in the world, a little more than a quarter of the total volume being composed of such minerals as magnesium chloride, sodium chloride, calcium chloride, and potassium chloride. This excessive density is the result entirely of evaporation, for the tributary streams around the shores contain no more solid matter than is normal, though there are, it is true, a number of hot saline springs round its shores. One of these, on the eastern side, is Zara, the ancient Callirhoe to which Herod the Great was brought for treatment, and farther up the same wadi the steaming waterfall of Zerqa Ma'in. On the west there are hot springs near Engedi and farther south at En Bokek. A heavy bluish haze hangs more or less constantly during the day over the water, which is poisonous to fish and quite remarkably unpleasant to taste. Swimming in it is amusing, for one bobs about like a cork, but the swimmer comes out covered with salt which is very painful if it gets into the eyes or any sore. Moreover, people have been drowned by getting their heads under water and then not being able to use their arms and legs to right themselves. The surface is usually calm and, because of the great density, not easily ruffled by a light breeze. But the powerful winds which rush down the western slopes in the late summer afternoons can stir up the whitecaps, and in the rainy season dangerous storms may develop. Rain is rare, the average for the year being only about 2 inches (50 mm.), and if it does fall, it is likely to come as a heavy thunderstorm.

14. Kh. al-Mafjir, Kh. al-Athelah, and Suwanet ath-Thaniyeh have all been suggested for Gilgal. The "Gilgal" of 1 Samuel 11:12–15 may perhaps be Tell Deir 'Alla.

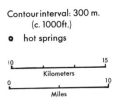

Contour interval: 300 m.
(c. 1000 ft.)

o   hot springs

Kilometers

Miles

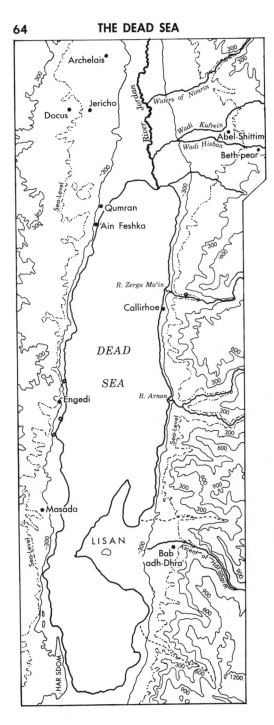

64   **THE DEAD SEA**

The two sides of the Dead Sea are not the same. On the west the Cenomanian limestone cliffs leave a very narrow coast, along which today an excellent road has been built, but on the east the Nubian sandstone cliffs, rising straight out of the water, forbid any passage at all. The western shore is in a rain shadow, and no rivers flow into the Dead Sea from this side, but there are at a number of points springs at the foot of the cliffs and here intermittently through the centuries there have been small settlements. The chief of these and the most permanent has always been Engedi, fed by a strong spring, and close to Qumran is the spring of 'Ain Feshka which supplied the farm for the community. Recently it has become apparent that for a time in the later monarchy a number of points between these two springs were briefly occupied, a discovery which raises questions about the identification of the "cities" in the Judean district of Jeshimon.[15] Some of them may have been here. Above the Engedi spring has also been discovered a sanctuary of the second half of the fourth millennium B.C., which seems to have been in that time a place of pilgrimage. It is very possible that the hoard found in the "Cave of the Treasure" is the cultic material from this sanctuary which had to be hidden when

15. "Notes and News," *PEQ*, XCIX (1961), 61.

the priests were forced to leave.[16]

Ten miles south of Engedi is the massive, isolated table mountain of Masada, 160 feet (49 m.) above sea level and therefore 1,307 feet (445 m.) above the Dead Sea. Here, as is well known, Herod the Great strengthened the Maccabean fortress and carved out a palace from the perpendicular northern face,

16. P. Bar-Adon, "Expedition C—The Cave of the Treasure," in *IEJ*, Vol. XII, 1962, parts 3–4, "The Expedition to the Judean Desert." Also David Ussishkin, "The 'Ghassulian' Temple in Ein Gedi and the Origin of the Hoard from Nahal Mishmar," *BA*, XXXIV (1971), 23–39.

XLIV. *The Arnon Gorge.* This shows the narrow Arnon gorge close to its mouth. The figures wading in the river are dwarfed by the gigantic sandstone cliffs. It is possible to penetrate only for a short distance because soon the way is blocked by precipices and waterfalls.

and here took place the grim end to the Jewish revolt against the Romans. This palace and fortress guarded a ford across the Dead Sea to the Lisan Peninsula, only 2½ miles (4 km.) from the eastern shore, a ford which existed in Roman times, but which has not always been possible.[17] Both the Lisan Peninsula and the plain at the foot of Masada are composed of the same unattractive material as the *Qattara* and form dissected badland plateaus about 350 feet (110 m.) above the Dead Sea. Finally, at the south end of the western shore is the extraordinary salt mountain of Har Sdom (Jabal Usdum), about 7 miles long (11 km.) and 742 feet (240 m.) above the Dead Sea. It is a long thin plateau, fretted and dissolved into peculiar pinnacles and tunnels. It was formed very late in geological history, and it is possible that its creation may have some relation to the story of Sodom and Gomorrah (Gen. 19:29; see above, p. 26).

Just where Sodom and Gomorrah were is still a mystery, though the most reasonable suggestion seems to be that they were somewhere in the very shallow basin of the Dead Sea south of the Lisan Peninsula, which is nowhere more than 25 feet (8 m.) deep. The convulsion which thrust up the salt plug of Har Sdom may also have lowered this section of the Rift and allowed the waters of the Dead Sea to flood over toward the south, destroying the five small settlements on the extended oasis of the Zered. Unfortunately no research, aerial or other, has yet revealed any traces of such settlements beneath the water.

Along the southern part of the eastern shore and behind the Lisan Peninsula, wadis from the plateau have dropped

17. The last time it is recorded was in 1846. See T. J. Salmon, and G. T. McCaw, "The Level and Cartography of the Dead Sea," *PEQ*, 1936, pp. 103–11.

their sediment and provide water even in summer. Here is a charming and prolonged oasis, where a multitude of products can be grown, as at Jericho and Engedi. It suffers, of course, from the same enervating heat and also from its remoteness from markets. However, it was certainly cultivated, and the Ascent of Horonaim led up beside the Wadi Kerak to Kir-hareseth. It has been suggested that the large Early Bronze Age cemetery discovered at Bab adh-Dhra' near the entrance to this ascent may perhaps have served as a burial area for Sodom and Gomorrah and the other Cities of the Plain before their destruction.[18]

North of the peninsula, almost all

18. Paul W. Lapp, "Bab edh-Dhra' Tomb A 76 and Early Bronze I in Palestine," *BASOR*, 189 (1968), 12–41.

the way to the north end of the Dead Sea, the rugged, perpendicular cliffs of sandstone block every attempt at passage around their foot. This forbidding coast is broken only twice by narrow gorges where the plateau streams finally debouch into the Dead Sea, piling up little deltas of tangled vegetation and heaps of dead wood swept down by the winter floods. The lesser of these gorges is the Zerqa Ma'in, with Callirhoe at its mouth, and the greater is the Arnon, a constricted passage indeed between towering sandstone cliffs. It can be penetrated for some hundreds of yards, but then the way is blocked by waterfalls and further advance is checked.

The Dead Sea is today important for its potash, but in ancient times it was valued for its salt and for the bitumen which sometimes floats to its surface.

XLV. *The Dead Sea.* This picture is taken on the eastern side near Bab adh-Dhra'. Beyond the narrow bay may be seen the shining white marl of the Lisan peninsula and beyond that again the steep eastern slopes of the plateau of Judah. Masada is to the extreme left of this picture.

The Romans knew it as Lacus Asphaltitis. In New Testament times it seems to have been controlled by the Nabateans, who exported the bitumen to Egypt for use in embalming, and Cleopatra's desire to control the Dead Sea and Jericho may reflect a desire to control the supply of bitumen and balsam.[19] It was also important for transport, and the Madeba Map shows ships plying upon it. How much it was so used in Old Testament times we do not know, but it seems probable that it was, not only for trade but also by raiding parties. Much doubt has been cast upon the authenticity of 2 Chronicles 20:1–30, where it is said that "some men came and told Jehoshaphat, 'A great multitude is coming against you from Edom, from beyond the sea; and behold they are at Hazazon-tamar' (that is Engedi)," but it probably indicates a remembrance of the kind of thing which happened from time to time.

C.5. *The Arabah*

This may conveniently be divided into two sections by the sill of higher land, Jabal al-Khureij or Gav ha-Arava, somewhat to the south of its center. Everywhere it is desert, with an average rainfall of no more than one inch (25 mm.) a year, though in the better-watered wadi bottoms there are scattered *spina christi* trees, characteristically umbrella-shaped by the strong desert winds, and a line of camel thorn or sagebush. A rare thunderstorm, it is true, may cover

19. Philip C. Hammond, "The Nabatean Bitumen Industry at the Dead Sea," *BA*, XXII (1959), 40–48. Emmanuel Anati has also suggested that the development of prepottery Neolithic Jericho as a fortified city is related to its trade in salt, bitumen, and sulfur, which is found in the Lisan marls. "Prehistoric Trade and the Puzzle of Jericho," *BASOR*, 167 (1962), 25–31.

the ground with fresh grass and revive the dormant flowers, but they cannot long endure, for the sun is without mercy. Only under extreme economic pressure, as when the Nabateans maintained the affluent trade routes, has it proved feasible to conduct any agriculture here. For the whole length of the Arabah the eastern side is much higher than the western and receives also the greater rain, and so the wadis from the east have the greater power of erosion and have built up their alluvial fans sometimes well across the center of the Rift.

As we proceed south from the Dead Sea it is first necessary to skirt the transitional zone of the Sebkha, a broad and desolate salt flat which during the latter years of the last century, when the sea was higher than it is now, was under water. It is surrounded by a line of low cliffs marking the limit of Lisan badlands, similar to those of the peninsula. At the foot of these cliffs there is a line of little springs, such as 'Ain Khanazir, 15 miles (24 km.) south of the Dead Sea, and fairly profuse desert vegetation.

The badlands continue for another 10 miles (16 km.), but by now the valley is widening out to its greatest extent. First on the west the Negeb Uplands swing back into the low Wadi Murra (Biq'at Zin), the most important and persistent route over to the Mediterranean. On the north the entrance to the wadi is overlooked by the steep Ascent of the Scorpions, and on the south the low hills of Har Mazeva (Jabal al-'Ashu'shir), the last remnant of the Ramon anticline, intervene between the middle section of this valley and the Arabah. On the Arabah side of these hills are two important springs, 'Ain Hosb (Hatzeva) to the north and 'Ain Weiba (Yahav) to the south. 'Ain Weiba has been identified with Oboth (Num. 33:43) and 'Ain Hosb with

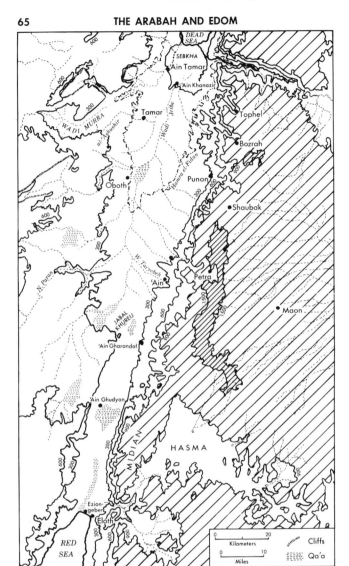

Tamar, which was fortified by Solomon (1 Kings 9:18), but neither of these identifications is certain, and others would place Tamar farther north at 'Ain al-'Arus, at present called 'Ain Tamar.

Then on the other side of the Rift the rocky wall of Edom also withdraws into the Punon Embayment. Across the mouth of this embayment is the porphyry dike of Hamra al-Fidan, and within it were the copper mines of Punon, the modern Feinan, at Kh. an-Nahas and Kh. al-Maqteh. Upon the spine of al-Fidan there stood an Iron Age fortress to protect the mines, which, though exhausted today, were once of great importance. Although there are a number of mines at the foot of the long exposure of Nubian sandstone, towering 5,000 feet (1,500 m.) above the valley floor, the group around Punon were of special value. Here there was a plentiful supply of water, which would have permitted the working of the mines even during the summer, and this is almost certainly the place where Moses raised the brazen serpent in the wilderness (Num. 21:4–10; 33:42–43).

The whole eastern wall is intensely dramatic, since the Trans-jordan tableland is here at its highest, and the rough red sandstone ascends in jagged cliffs and precipices. It is well nigh impassable, for the winter storms have carved the rock into deep, unfinished gorges, and only rarely does one of the gorges provide a possible route onto the plateau. The most important of these is the Wadi Musa, by which the caravans from the Arabah clambered up to

XLVI. Qa'a. The water which after rain pours down the otherwise dry wadis into the southern Arabah creates broad areas of mud flats, which then dry out into the cracked surfaces seen here. Dry and dusty at most times, but dangerously slippery after rain, qa'a is a common feature of true desert.

Petra, but even this is notoriously difficult. Here in the Arabah are Bir Madhkur and 'Ain at-Taiyebah, 7 miles (11 km.) apart, and at both these places the Nabateans established forts to guard the route.

In contrast to this jagged, unscalable wall the western side of the Rift is less impressive and at times loses the effect of a scarp altogether. It is only a third the height and is made up of tumbled chalk and limestone hills, drained northeastward by the long Wadi Jirafi (Nahal Paran), which comes from far to the south. The wadis from both east and west gather in Wadi Jeibe, which carries the flash flood water northward toward the Dead Sea.

The southern section of the Rift beyond the dividing sill is markedly different. Quite suddenly it narrows to no more than 6 miles (10 km.), and now there are steep cliffs on both sides. On the east the granite Mountains of Midian run for the full length, and to the west the Nubian sandstone appears at last in the south, typically sheer and difficult. Finally the granite is exposed here also. Where the Midian granite on the east is separated from the Edomite plateau to the north of it there is a shattered zone, clearly visible from across the Arabah as a jumble of sand and sandstone, where multiple faulting has permitted passage into the broad interior of the Hasma.

Another new feature of this southern section is the broad, flat areas of *qa'a*, formed where sediment has been washed down into the valley bottom, but where, because of the small rainfall, there is insufficient drainage to carry the sediment all the way to the Red Sea. These are dried-out mud flats and are excessively slippery after rain. Here also the alluvial fans on the east are no longer greater than those on the west, for the granite is more resistant to erosion.

The important springs are three: 'Ain Gharandal, on the eastern side at the entrance to the Hasma, across the shatter zone; 'Ain Ghudyan (Yotvata), in the center on the western side; and Aqabah, in the far south, again on the east, with its rich supply of water and its green, luxuriant palm groves. This was the biblical Eloth (Num. 33:35) and a bone of contention between the people of Judah and the Edomites.

The temptation which caused the kings of Judah to covet control of the long passage of the Arabah was both its rich supplies of copper and the trade to which the Arabah was the gate. It is now clear that the mines at Jabal Manei'yeh on the western side, the so-called King Solomon's Mines, were not worked in Solomon's time at all, but earlier, first by the Egyptians, as shown by the impressive Egyptian temple discovered here, and later by the Kenites and Edomites. They ceased to be used by the tenth century B.C.[20] Tell al-Kheleifeh, at the head of the Bay of Aqabah, was apparently not so important for copper smelting as was once thought, though it certainly was used for metalworking. It is probably the Ezion-geber of the Old Testament and seems to have been an industrial and mercantile caravansary. A striking feature of its construction is the alternation of bricks and wooden beams, known elsewhere in the Rift Valley and used also in building the Temple (1 Kings 6:36).[21] This was designed to prevent collapse during an earthquake and is a method of building still used in the mountains of southern Turkey today.

20. Beno Rothenberg, "Ancient Copper Industries in the Western Arabah: An Archaeological Survey of the Arabah, Part I," *PEQ*, XCIV (1962), 5–71. Also additional notes in *PEQ*, XCVIII (1966), 6–7; CI (1969), 57–59.
21. Nelson Glueck, "Ezion-Geber," *BA*, XXVIII (1965), 70–87.

From Ezion-geber went out the "ships of Tarshish," which returned the following year bringing with them "gold, silver, ivory, apes and peacocks [possibly baboons]" (1 Kings 10:22), as well as incense, spices, and ebony (perhaps the "almug" of 1 Kings 10:11). When Solomon's ships penetrated to the southern end of the Red Sea, the Queen of the South, alarmed by this threat to her monopoly, came herself "with a great retinue" to look into the matter. It cannot, however, have been easy for the Judean kings to maintain control of this long route, a journey of several days from Beersheba for the slow-moving caravans. Moreover, once in the Arabah, they had to run the gauntlet of the proud Edomites, anxious themselves to control the trade, and occasionally endure the risk of sudden flash floods which, when they occur, "are mighty and rage horribly" (Ps. 93:3–4, BCP). Even at Ezion-geber they had to beware lest the Edomites pour down from the heights and attack them. Only when their strength was at its greatest could the kings of Judah stretch out and grasp this precious harbor.

Solomon was the first to build a fortress at Ezion-geber (1 Kings 9:26), but the Edomites regained it after his death. Once again in the days of Ahab and Jehoshaphat the Edomites became the vassal of Judah, for "there was no king in Edom; a deputy was king" (1 Kings 22: 47). Jesoshaphat, therefore, fitted out a fleet at Ezion-geber, but it was destroyed before it could put to sea, probably because the Edomites revolted (1 Kings 22:48). The third and final time that Judah gained control was in her last period of greatness, when Uzziah "built Elath and restored it to Judah" (2 Kings 14:22), but in the days of the ineffective King Ahaz it passed out of Judean hands for good (2 Kings 16:6).

CHAPTER 18

Beyond the Jordan Eastward

Gad and Reuben and half the tribe of Manasseh have received their inheritance beyond the Jordan eastward, which Moses the servant of the Lord gave them.

JOSHUA 18:7

Anyone who stands upon the eastern edge of the Judean hills sees the ground drop away in front of him in a succession of tumbled yellow slopes and the clouds dissolve into nothing above his head, as the air starts its tumultuous descent into the rift. Twenty-five miles or so to the east is an almost unbroken wall of rock, dwarfed by the distance, but still tremendous, and poised above it are the clouds, forming again where the air is cooled by its steep ascent from the Jordan. This wall is the edge of the great Arabian tableland and stretches, very nearly in a straight line, the extreme length of the country, from the foot of Hermon to the Red Sea.

It one goes there, snaking down between the barren hills of Jeshimon and across the muddy Jordan, he goes to another type of country. This is immediately apparent on leaving the hot and dusty lowlands of the Ghor to climb up beside the waters of Nimrin. The frowning honey-colored cliffs, the rushing stream, and the glorious pink oleanders in the valley bottom all proclaim a different landscape. This impression of "otherness" is heightened when at last the road toils up onto the plateau and the vast, unlimited steppes open out toward the east. The classic trinity of grain and wine and oil is no longer so apparent, for though Jordanian experiments have shown that olives will grow farther east, where once the Romans grew them, they do not easily flourish on a plateau so scoured by icy desert winds in winter. Moreover, the vine also decreases as the hill slopes give place to level tableland. Excellent wheat and barley, however, continue until at last decreasing rainfall makes all cultivation impossible and the animals alone survive, sheep and goats and camels and the magnificent Trans-jordan horses. Only Gilead, where wheat and olives and grapes could be grown together, was ever colonized effectively by the Israelites. Everywhere else remained foreign territory.

We are concerned in the first place with the settled, western section of the plateau and must leave the more barren lands east of the Hejaz Railway until later.[1] Here two methods of dividing the country into its natural regions, the physical and the cultural, to some extent conflict with each other. The physical divisions are the more obvious and are the result of the natural drainage pattern. The heavy rains of winter are concentrated upon the towering plateau edge and the land immediately behind it and then rapidly die away toward the desolation of the eastern desert. This rain runs off in two directions: either straight down the steep scarp into the Rift, or else eastward along the more gentle dip-slope. The scarp streams are naturally the stronger and erode more quickly because they flow very much faster. The eastward-flowing streams flow less swiftly and move, moreover, toward a region of decreasing rainfall. Occasionally the scarp streams, already more powerful, have been assisted still further by lines of structural weakness, and have cut back far into the plateau to capture the waters of the weaker dip-slope streams. The result is a system of small plateau wadis, directed toward the east, and then gathering themselves together to form the main wadi, which carries a permanent stream.[2] At first

1. See Chapter XX.
2. The reader is reminded that in Arabic *wadi* means any kind of valley, whether it has a stream in it or not. The word has come to have a technical sense in geography of a desert-type valley with water only after rain. However, it is better to avoid this technical use when dealing with a country where Arabic is the spoken language, and all valleys are called *wadis*.

this may flow along the desert rim, but then it turns westward and cuts its way down through a magnificent canyon to the Jordan or the Dead Sea. Four of these canyons are of particular importance: the Yarmuq in the north, the Jabbok, the Arnon, with its tributary the Wala, and the Zered in the south, though other scarp streams, e.g., the Zerqa Ma'in, are in the process of cutting back into the plateau.

These four great clefts provide evident possible frontiers and today the boundaries of administrative districts. They were certainly regarded as frontiers by some Old Testament writers, for the Arnon is described as "the boundary of Moab, between Moab and the Amorites" (Num. 21:13), and the Jabbok as "the boundary of the Ammonites" (Deut. 3:16). In this passage from Deuteronomy, Reuben and Gad are said to have been allotted the land between the Jabbok and the Arnon, and in Judges 11:12–28 Jephthah argues that the Ammonites can have no complaint against the Israelites, because Israel has not extended beyond the boundaries formed by these rivers.

Nevertheless, it is clear from the Jephthah story that the Ammonites did not agree that their territory was confined to the wilderness beyond the Jabbok, and Numbers 21:26 speaks of Heshbon, well to the north of the Arnon, as having been Moabite before it was captured by Sihon. During the monarchy Moab certainly claimed this region as her own, and the Moabite Stone makes very evident that Mesha thought that the tableland of Medeba belonged to Moab and had been quite wrongly occupied by the Israelite king Omri.[3] It would seem, therefore, that these great canyons were essentially strategic boundaries rather than divi-

3. Pritchard, *ANET*, pp. 320–21.

66   **THE ARNON VALLEY**

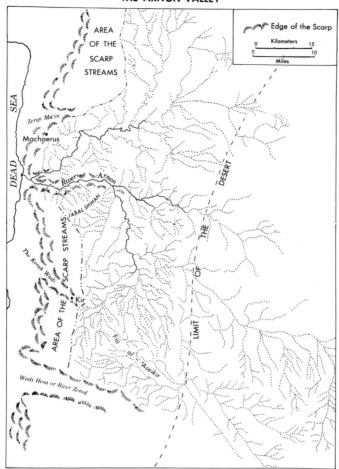

The Arnon Valley, illustrating how the scarp stream has cut back to capture the less powerful plateau streams.

sions between different ways of life. Victorious newcomers, such as the Amorites, who had driven a wedge between Ammon and Moab, and the Israelites, who dispossessed the Amorites, thought of them as natural defensive frontiers. So also did the Deuteronomic writers, for the use of these rivers as national or tribal divisions is very marked in the Book of Deuteronomy, but it must be remembered that this book was written when the northern kingdom of Israel was no more and by people who prob-

ably had little personal knowledge of the conditions east of the Jordan. We therefore have to recognize another, and much older, pattern transcending the physical divisions and tending continually to reassert itself. It cannot be too often insisted that traditional societies usually expand, even across the most imposing physical obstacles, to the limit of that area in which their own way of life is possible, and there their expansion normally stops. In the settled section of the eastern plateau there are four such

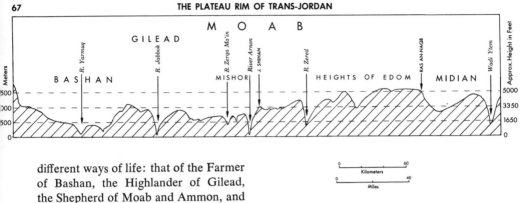

67   THE PLATEAU RIM OF TRANS-JORDAN

different ways of life: that of the Farmer of Bashan, the Highlander of Gilead, the Shepherd of Moab and Ammon, and the Trader of Edom. To these, farther to the east, we must add the Warrior of Mount Bashan (the Jabal Druze) and the Nomad of the desert steppes.

D.1. *The Plateau of Bashan, the Land of the Farmer*

Bashan, both the plateau and the mountain, lies for the most part beyond the limits defined for this study in Chapter I, but it cannot be left entirely out of consideration. Situated to the east of the Lake of Galilee and the Upper Jordan Valley, it is composed, very nearly everywhere, of dark, volcanic basalt, and all its heights are aligned from northwest to southeast. The most obvious of these NW–SE lines is that of the frowning mountains of Jabal Druze, extending northwestward into the region of the Leja and southeastward into Arabia, but parallel to this on the east is a lesser volcanic outflow, that of as-Safa, and also parallel to it on the western edge of the plateau lines of volcanic cones in what has come to be known today as the Golan Heights.

The plateau, which is the western section of Bashan, appears at first sight to be level, and the observer upon any height commands a panorama of wide, open plains, magnificently fertile. In fact, however, it slopes gently southward from about 2,800 feet (c. 850 m.) in the north to as low as 1,300 feet (400 m.) on the edge of the Yarmuq canyon and then rises again gradually to about 1,650 feet (500 m.). The northern limit is the rocky wasteland of al-Wa'arah some 15 miles (24 km.) southwest of Damascus, where the final outflow of the Leja basalt confronts the foot of Hermon. The southern limit is not the deep cleft of the Wadi Yarmuq, but the foothills of Gilead, some 5 miles (8 km.) south of the present Irbid-Mafraq road and corresponding fairly closely with the present IPC pipeline. The Wadi Yarmuq does, however, form one important division, for the plateau to the south of it is not basaltic, the edge of the continuous basalt being marked on a modern map by another of man's constructions, the railroad that runs north from Mafraq and then curves westward to descend the sinuous Yarmuq canyon to the Rift. We need, therefore, to distinguish three subregions, to which we may give names from the New Testament period: the *Gadarene Plateau* south of the Yarmuq, *Gaulanitis* overlooking the Galilee-Huleh section of the Rift Valley, and *Batanea* between this and the Jabal Druze.

The Gadarene Plateau south of the Yarmuq is shaped like a segment of a circle with the chord along the present

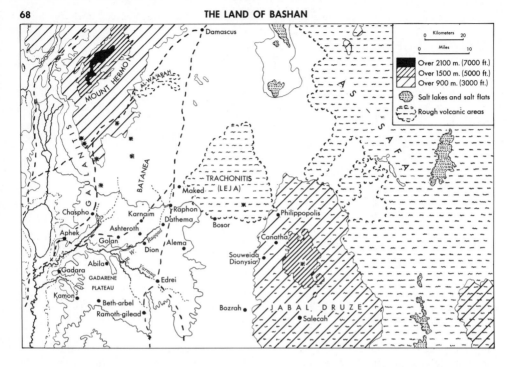

pipeline and the circumference formed by the railroad that follows the edge of the basalt. No less of a smooth plain than the region to the north, the rock here is mostly a soft chalky limestone of the Senonian-Eocene Type, and the soil is therefore less fertile, but more easily worked than the basalt to the north. In New Testament times all the Bashan Plateau was part of the Decapolis, and in this section Gadara stood to the west, on the edge of an outflow of basalt, at the modern Umm Qeis, and Abila toward the east at Tell Abil. From both these cities the inhabitants peered down into the Yarmuq Valley. In the Old Testament this was the region known as Havvoth-jair (Num. 32:41; Deut. 3:14; 1 Kings 4:13; 1 Chron. 2:23).[4] It was quite clearly a disputed

territory, claimed both by the Israelites from their strongholds in Gilead, who wished to make the Yarmuq Valley their boundary, and by the Syrians, who wished to push southward to the edge of Gilead, for "Geshur and Aram took . . . Havvoth-jair, Kenath and its villages, sixty towns" (1 Chron. 2:23). Havvoth-jair is described in Joshua 13:30 as being "in Bashan," which is the correct cultural description of it as part of the great plain of Bashan, but from the point of view of Manasseh it was held to be strategically part of Gilead. Ramoth-gilead, an outpost of the Israelites that they did not always manage to hold (1 Kings 4:13; 22:4ff.; 2 Kings 8:28; 9:1ff.; 2 Chron. 18:2ff.), was in this subregion, and presumably the name is an Israelite one.[5]

4. Translated as "villages of Jair" in 1 Kings 4:13 in *RSV* and "towns of Jair" in *KJV*.

5. Jair of Gilead is said to have been buried at Kamon (Judg. 10:5), the name of which is preserved at Qamm and

Gaulanitis was at one time the territory of the Geshurites, in the south, and the Maacathites, in the north, who were able to maintain a recognizably separate identity and at least some kind of semi-independence until the rise of the Israelite monarchy, or even later.[6] They were able to do so because of the *tulul,* those striking round volcanic cones which rise as much as 1,500 feet (450–500 m.) above the level plateau[7] and provide admirable strongholds for defense. Where the division between Geshur and Maacah was we do not know, but there is a certain difference between the south and the north of this subregion. The southern section is broader because of the alignment of the cones toward the southwest and is

6. B. Mazar, "Geshur and Maacah," *JBL,* LXXX (1961), 16–28. This is, as already stated, the region known today as the Golan Heights, but in view of the present political problem it is better to avoid this name in a book of this kind.

7. *Tulul* is the plural of *tell,* the word normally used for an archaeological mound, e.g., *Tell as-Sultan* or *Tulul adh-Dhahab.* It means any rounded hill, and throughout this volcanic region it is used for the volcanic cones. A very large number of the places in this part of Syria called tell so-and-so are volcanic hills. They are found all over the basalt plateau, but are concentrated in the west.

Qumeim, though the exact site is uncertain. These two villages lie about 7 miles (11 km.) west of Irbid (Beth-arbel, Hos. 10:14) on either side of the present road. Simons (*Geographical and Topographical Texts of the O.T.,* p. 9), speaks of the identification of Havvoth-jair with Bashan as incorrect, but this is because he is unaware of the double pattern of territorial divisions. Where Kenath was is far from certain. It is often identified with Qanawat in the Jabal Druze, but this seems much too far east. Simons (p. 134) suggests Kerak-Canatha between Dera'a and Souweida, which is possible. It is very likely, however, that it is the name of a clan territory.

carved by profound but narrow valleys cutting down southwestward, i.e., at right angles to the alignment of the volcanic cones, the most impressive being the Wadi al-Raqqad, which is continued by the lower Yarmuq. The northern section is narrower and much less dissected.

Batanea is almost certainly to be identified with the district of Argob in the Old Testament, traditionally containing sixty cities "fortified with high walls, gates and bars, besides very many unwalled villages" (Deut. 3:5; see 1 Kings 4:13), though it is wrong to extend this term, at least in its Old Testament sense, to the Leja, as some authorities do. Edrei, the city of the somewhat mysterious King Og (Num. 21:33; Deut. 1:4; 3:1, 10; Josh. 12:4, 13:12, 31), who seems to have ruled over Argob and Havvoth-jair, is the modern Dera'a, just at the junction of the basalt and the limestone. Here is the extraordinary underground city carved below the basalt in the soft limestone.

The cities of this plain certainly needed their high walls, their gates, and their bars, for they had little other protection on the open plateau and lay at the mercy of any invader. A strong government, such as that which Philip exercised in the days of Jesus, might maintain the peace, but whenever the authorities were shiftless or weak the robber bands of the Jabal Druze would descend upon them. Almost every mention of this region in the Old Testament is of some army coursing unopposed across it. So we are told that "Chedorlaomer and the kings who were with him came and subdued the Rephaim in Ashteroth-Karnaim" and marched through into Gilead (Gen. 14:5), and the Israelites long remembered how they had defeated King Og and that "there was not a city which we did not take from them" (Deut. 3:4; see also Num.

21:35: Josh. 9:10; Pss. 135:11; 136:
20). In the mid-ninth century we find
the Israelites fighting in defense of
Ramoth-gilead (1 Kings 22:3) and
also Aphek, where the Israelites "encamped before the Syrians like two
little flocks of goats" (1 Kings 20:27).
In 1 Maccabees 5:24-52 there is an
account of an expedition made by Judas
to rescue the Jews of Bashan and how
town after town fell before him.[8]

What unites these three subregions is
the common way of life. The winter
storms sweep almost unopposed across
the hills and basins of Lower Galilee to
water the rich volcanic soil which covers
so much of the plateau. Here the
primary crop is wheat, and the life is
an endless cycle of plowing and sowing,
threshing, winnowing, and gathering
into barns. In New Testament times it
was one of the great granaries of the
empire, and in the Old Testament also
its richness was proverbial. "Strong bulls
of Bashan" (Ps. 22:12) were needed
to till the heavy volcanic soil, and with
their help the level fields brought forth
harvests which were the envy of the
neighboring peoples. Where the ground
was too stony for cultivation, as well as
on the steep slopes of the *tulul,* the
animals found rich pasture, so that
Ezekiel could speak of "rams, of lambs,
and of goats, of bulls, all of them
fatlings of Bashan" (Ezek. 39:18), and
Amos earlier could liken the gross and
lazy noblewomen of Israel to "cows of

8. The twin cities of Ashteroth and
Karnaim were at Tell Ashterah and Sheikh
Sa'ad; Aphek was at Fiq, overlooking the
Lake of Galilee. Of the places mentioned
in 1 Maccabees Alema was at 'Alma,
southeast of the Sheikh Meskine; Chaspho
at Khisfin, northeast of Fiq; Bosor at Busr
al-Hariri; Bozrah (or Bosora) at Bosra
eski-Sham; Dathema at Tell Hamad, just
west of Sheikh Meskine; Raphon at ar-
Rafeh 5 miles (8 km.) to the northeast of
Dathema; and Maked at Tell Moqdad,
another 5 miles northeast.

Bashan . . . in the mountains of
Samaria" (Amos 4:1).

Except for the barrier of the Yarmuq
canyon and the precipitous valleys leading into it, there are few extended
obstacles to movement, and one may go
to fro across this plateau in almost any
direction. The roads southward from
Damascus, however, are determined by
the barrier of al-Wa'arah, which they
must circumvent. Therefore, one road
ran east of it almost due southward more
or less along the line of the present
road to Dera'a, avoiding both the forbidding Leja on the east and the dissected Yarmuq region to the west. It
was thus part of what has been called
the Pilgrim Road in Chapter VIII. The
other main road ran west of al-Wa'arah
along the foot of Mount Hermon, dividing later so as to enter Cis-jordan either
north or south of the Huleh marshes.
The road which crossed the Jordan south
of Lake Huleh by the Bridge of Jacob's
Daughters was the northern branch of
the Trunk Road, the southern branch
crossing south of the Lake of Galilee,
having descended the Wadi Yarmuq.

D.2. *The Mountain of Bashan, the Land
of the Warrior*

What Quennell has called "the tranquil outpourings of the Hauran,"[9] i.e.,
the older volcanic rocks, which flowed
out gently in thin horizontal sheets over
the Plateau of Bashan, were later succeeded by the more tempestuous activity
which produced the *tulul* of Gaulanitis
and the great mass of Jabal Druze, well
over 5,000 feet (1,500 m.) in the center and reaching its highest in Tell
Hauran (5,789 ft., 1,765 m.). This
great central mass is extended both
southeastward into Arabia and northwestward into the tormented lava region

9. *Op. cit.,* p. 47.

of the Leja, lower than the Jabal but so difficult that its very name means "Refuge." In the New Testament period it was known as Trachonitis and was part of the territory of Philip (Luke 3:1). The Romans, it is true, boldly built a road across it, as was their fashion, to ensure its obedience, but everyone else went round. Parallel to the Jabal Druze on the east is another excessively difficult region, as-Safa, but no part of this whole vast jumble of volcanic outpourings is in the least easy to penetrate. It is *par excellence* a region of refuge, to which the remnants oi a shattered army flee for safety (Ps. 68:22), and the home of a fiercely independent people, ever ready to ravage the skirting caravans and determined always to resist to the utmost the power of the government in Damascus.

The chief inhabited region is the Jabal itself, the "many-peaked mountain of Bashan" (Ps. 68:15), and especially, of course, the western slopes, which are plentifully watered in winter, both by torrential storms of rain and by the snow which every year falls on Zalmon (Ps. 68:14) and lies heavy until spring. Unfortunately, the brutal basalt renders the toil of the farmer tedious and difficult and has filled every tiny field with an almost incredible mass of stones. The mountain slopes must be coaxed to produce their mead of grain, though vines can be grown more easily, and sheep and goats are kept. The winters, however, are too cold for olives.

The lee slopes toward the east are more barren, but on the west, wherever there are no rocky fields, a thick tangle of *maquis* covers the ground. Doubtless there were more trees in the past, but even then they must have been stunted, for the hard rock gives no room for the roots of trees to develop. The scarcity of wood good enough for building is reflected in the ancient houses, where the somber basalt was used even for roofs, doors, and windows. The forests of Bashan were for the ancient Israelite as famous as those of Lebanon and Carmel, and he thought of them in the same terms. "Lebanon is confounded and withers away," said Isaiah; "Sharon is like a desert; and Bashan and Carmel shake off their leaves" (Isa. 33:9), and in Jeremiah 50:19 the promise is made that Israel shall "feed on Carmel and in Bashan." So also does Micah (7:14) say,

Shepherd thy people with thy staff,
the flock of thine inheritance,
who dwell alone in a forest
in the midst of a garden land;
let them feed in Bashan and Gilead
as in the days of old.

In both Nahum and Zechariah the destruction of a proud empire is pictured as the withering of Bashan and Lebanon (Nah. 1:4; Zech. 11:1–2).

XLVII. *Canatha.* Remains of the Roman temple at Qanawat, in the Jabal Druze, built out of the black volcanic basalt.

XLVIII. *Volcanoes at Shahba (Philippopolis).* Shahba stands where the Leja (Trachonitis) joins the main Jabal Druze. In the foreground may be seen a hard volcanic plug and in the distance softer cinder cones.

XLIX. *Herding Sheep near Salkhad (Salecah).* The rough, boulder-strewn nature of the basalt country is well shown here. Only with the greatest difficulty can tiny fields be coaxed to produce food.

Nevertheless, for the ancient Israelites the mountain of Bashan was something they had often heard of but had seen only from a distance, glimpsing the snow-clad summit in the crisp, clear air of winter. Dense and impenetrable the forest growth may well have been, but when Isaiah described the oaks of Bashan as "lofty and lifted up" like "all the cedars of Lebanon" (Isa. 2:13), he spoke as one who did not know them. So again did Ezekiel when he said of the ships of Tyre, "They made all your planks of fir trees from Senir; they took a cedar from Lebanon to make a mast for you. Of oaks of Bashan they made your oars; they made your deck of pines from the coasts of Cyprus, inlaid with ivory" (Ezek. 27:5–6). Only one town in the mountain of Bashan is ever mentioned in the Old Testament, Salecah, and this always as the most distant point of the habitable land toward the east (Deut. 3:10; Josh. 12:5; 13:11; 1 Chron. 5:11). It is to be identified with Salkhad, a very prominent landmark, perched upon the "plug" of an extinct volcano, and crowned today with the ruins of a medieval castle. It was the uttermost city to the east their eyes could perceive, but it should not be imagined that they normally went there. In the days of the Roman empire there were in the mountain such notable cities as Dionysia (Souweida), Philippopolis (Shahba), and Canatha (Qanawat), but for all that it remained beyond the purview of the New Testament writers.

D.3. *The Dome of Gilead, the Land of the Highlander*

As already explained (see page 12), this broad upwarp continues that of Judah, being divided from it by the rift valley of the Jordan. The western edge of the dome is therefore the plateau scarp. The eastern edge is a great curving line starting in the south near the mouth of the Zerqa Ma'in and then bending around east of Rabbah (the modern Amman) in the direction of the 'Ummayad ruin of Qasr Hammam as-Serakh. Within the boundaries formed by these two lines the land is everywhere mountainous, or at least hilly, in contrast to the level plateau both north and south of it, and is formed mainly of hard Cenomanian limestone. Throughout the main lines of relief run from southwest to northeast—that is to say, at right angles to those of Bashan—the only exception being the canyon of the Jabbok. This river rises at Amman, flows at first northeastward to Zerqa, and then curves around until it flows across the region due westward, cleaving the great dome into two parts.

The term "Gilead" is far from exact in the Old Testament and tends, indeed, to alter in meaning with the passage of time. It has been argued by some that the name originally applied to a relatively small section, possibly the area confined within the encircling arm of the Jabbok, partly on the grounds that the word *Jal'ad* in modern Arabic names is confined to this area.[10] However, in the Old Testament it normally applied to the land both north and south of the Jabbok canyon. The phrase "all the cities of the *mishor* (or tableland) and all Gilead and all Bashan" (Deut. 3:10) certainly distinguishes the highland region from the flat plateau on either side of it. Furthermore, in both Joshua and Deuteronomy we meet the expression "half of Gilead." In Joshua 12:2, 5, Sihon is said to have ruled "half of Gilead" south of the Jabbok and Og

10. The problems of the land of Gilead and its history are given very detailed examination by Magnus Ottossen in *Gilead: Tradition and History,* trans. by Jean Gray (Lund, Sweden, 1969).

69   **GILEAD AND AMMON**

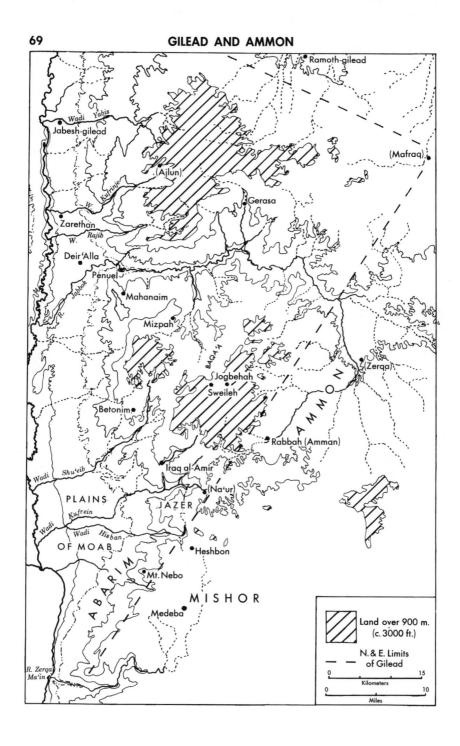

Ramoth-gilead

Wadi *Yabis*

Jabesh-gilead

(Mafraq)

(Ajlun)

Gerasa

Zarethan

W. *Rajib*

Deir 'Alla

Penuel

Mahanaim

Mizpah

BAQA'A

Jogbehah

Sweileh

AMMON

(Zerqa)

Betonim

Rabbah (Amman)

Wadi *Shu'eib*

Iraq al-Amir

PLAINS

(Na'ur)

JAZER

Kufrein

Wadi

Wadi *Hisban*

OF MOAB

Heshbon

Mt. Nebo

MISHOR

Medeba

R. Zerqa
Ma'in

	Land over 900 m. (c. 3000 ft.)
	N. & E. Limits of Gilead

0   15
Kilometers
0   10
Miles

to have ruled the other "half of Gilead" to the north. In Deuteronomy 3:12 and Joshua 13:31 the southern half of Gilead is said to have been alloted to Gad and the northern half to Manasseh.

The problem is where Gilead ended to the south and east. The eastern boundary did not coincide with the eastern edge of the hill country, because the Ammonites were thought of as living outside Gilead but continually threatening to penetrate into it (Judg. 11:4ff.; 1 Sam. 11:1ff.; Amos 1:3). That they normally remained obediently beyond the Jabbok eastward is clearly impossible, and they must have occupied the hills on both sides of Amman (Rabbah of the Ammonites), which was their chief city. Probably we ought to think of the true Gilead as ending at a line drawn from the town of Mafraq more or less directly southwestward through Na'ur to close to the mouth of the Zerqa Ma'in, leaving Amman a little to the east. The hills east of this line are normally lower than those to the west, though just southeast of Amman and Na'ur they rise to over 3,000 feet (900 m.), and they are everywhere broader, with less precipitous slopes. They were also less thickly wooded and their eastern slopes decidedly barren. The lack of a clearly marked distinction between these hills and the country of Gilead itself perhaps explains the continued tendency of the Ammonites to press up into the highlands.

What we have, then, is a triangle with its base on the present IPC pipeline and its apex in the south at the mouth of the Zerqa Ma'in. The southern extension of this triangle seems to have borne two names, the Abarim and Jazer. The Abarim (Num. 27:12; 33:47, 48; Deut. 32:49; Jer. 22:20) are the broad dissected slopes of the plateau edge, south of the latitude of Amman, carved into a tumble of hills and valleys by scarp streams, such as the Wadi Hisban. These hills are described as *harei ha-'abarim,* which all the English versions persist in translating as "the mountains of the Abarim," but this is misleading, for if we were standing on the plateau edge, at Mount Nebo, the Abarim would be beneath us. "Scarplands" would be very much better.

Jazer is the name of both a town and a district.[11] The town cannot be identified with any certainty,[12] but it would seem that the district is that broad, rather gentle, hill country, rising to over 3,000 feet (900 m.) in height, which lies between Amman and Na'ur, and evidently thought of as distinct from Gilead (Num. 32:3 and Josh. 13:25).

We are thus left with the territory north of a line drawn westward from Amman through Wadi Sir to the Wadi Shu'eib as being authentic Gilead. Raised high above the surrounding plateau, it receives excellent rainfall during the winter months and heavy dew in summer. Strong plentiful springs supply the villages tucked away among the limestone hills. Even today, when deforestation has been going on for century after century, the highest parts are still clothed with scrub oak, carob, and pine, and in early times the rich forests were almost as famous as those of Lebanon, the two often being mentioned together (Jer. 22:6; Zech 10:10). The medicinal balm was proverbial (Jer. 8:22; 46:11) and was exported to the Phoenicians at Tyre (Ezek. 27:17) and also to the

11. Numbers 21:32; 32:1, 3, 35; Joshua 12:25; 21:39; 2 Samuel 24:5; 1 Chronicles 6:81; 26:31.
12. It cannot be Kh. Jazzir, which is much too far west. I confess that in the *Atlas of the Biblical World* I accepted this identification, but I am convinced now that it is wrong. If, with the *RSV*, we accept the LXX version of Numbers 21:24, then Jazer must be in the Amman-Na'ur district.

Egyptians, for Joseph was sold to a traveling company of Ishmaelites, "coming down from Gilead, with their camels bearing gum, balm, and myrrh, on their way to carry it to Egypt" (Gen. 37:25). Wheat is grown, though there is little level land for extensive fields, save only north of Sweileh, where the Baqa'a provides something parallel to the basins of Galilee, but trees and shrubs are at home here. Olives grow well, especially on the western slopes, and vines are everywhere to be found, bringing forth grapes so superb that no others in the Palestinian realm may properly be compared with them.

L. *Gerasa: The Triumphal Arch.* This is the south gate of the city after it had been enlarged by the Emperor Hadrian. The carving at the base of the pilasters is an unusual feature.

LI. *Gerasa: A Colonnaded Street.* This is one of the side streets leading down to join the main street, which ran from the north gate to the forum, about a kilometer in length. Gerasa was one of the cities of the Decapolis, but though it has today the best preserved ruins it was not one of the larger cities.

The thickness of its forest cover probably meant that in Old Testament times it was not thickly inhabited, but since the three staples of wine, oil, and bread could be produced together here in the Israelite fashion, this was the only region east of the Jordan the Israelites ever made their own. The name "Gilead" came increasingly to mean for them "Israelite Trans-jordan," and so their forward fortress in Bashan was called Ramoth-gilead (1 Kings 4:13; 22:4ff.; 2 Kings 9:1ff., etc.) or Ramoth in Gilead (Deut. 4:43; Josh. 20:8, etc.). In 1 Maccabees 5:24ff., already referred to, even the plateau of Bashan is called "Gilead." As may be expected, it was also a region of refuge, especially when there was internal trouble in Cis-jordan itself. David fled to Gilead during the revolt of Absalom (2 Sam. 17: 21-22), as earlier the family of Saul had retreated here after his disastrous defeat on the mountains of Gilboa (2 Sam. 2:8). Mahanaim, which occurs in both stories, and the scene also of a vision of angels by Jacob (Gen. 32:2) and a city of refuge in Gad (Josh. 21:38), was evidently an important center, but where it was is far from certain.[13] Later, after the division of the kingdom, Jeroboam I fortified Penuel, where Jacob had wrestled with the angel (Gen. 32:30) and whose inhabitants had been punished by Gideon for failing to come to his help (Judg. 8:8–9, 17). The wording of 1 Kings 12:25 ("Then Jeroboam built Shechem . . . and dwelt there; and he went out from there and built Penuel") suggests that for a time he was forced to withdraw his capital east of the Jordan.

13. A wide variety of sites has been suggested, both north and south of the Jabbok. Tell Hajjaj, immediately south of Penuel and overlooking the Jabbok, has at present the most support, though Tell ar-Reheil farther up the Jabbok Valley is also a candidate.

Penuel must certainly be placed at Tulul adh-Dhahab, two impressive conical hills rising about 300 feet (nearly 100 m.) above the valley floor and enclosed in a meander of the Jabbok, not far above Tel Deir 'Alla, where the Jabbok enters the Jordan Rift. Again, in the tragic years at the end of the first century A.D. after the destruction of Jerusalem, many Palestinian refugees fled eastward to the Decapolis, which then included part of Gilead, and in 1948 the same sad trek occurred again.

Jogbehah (Num. 32:35; Judg. 8:11) may with some certainty be placed

LII. *Eastern Gilead.* Bringing wheat "on the backs of asses . . . and on the humps of camels," to sell in the markets of Amman. This picture shows also how the hillsides have been almost completely denuded of soil through the centuries after the protective woodland cover had been removed. These eastern slopes, being in the lee of the mountains, were always drier and more vulnerable than those on the west.

at al-Jubeihah about 1½ miles (2½ km.) east of Sweileh, and Betonim (Josh. 13:26) at Kh. Batneh northwest of as-Salt. About 6 miles (10 km.) northeast of as-Salt is Jal'ad, where most authorities today would place Mizpah, the important ancient sanctuary where Jacob and Laban set up the stone to mark the covenant between them (Gen. 31:49) and where the people of Gilead gathered at the time of the Ammonite attack to learn from the oracle who should be their leader (Judg. 10:17–18). Apart from these we have very little certainty and in consequence cannot discuss with any exactness the role of the different parts of Gilead. Northern Gilead is the higher of the two, reaching 4,090 feet (1,247 m.) in Jabal 'Amr ad-Daraj 2½ miles (4 km.) southeast of Ajlun, the highest point in southern Gilead being 3,654 feet (1,114 m.) just north of as-Salt. The Jabbok Valley, dividing the two halves, has cut down to the friable Nubian sandstone, which in this region of heavy rainfall is easily eroded. The valley, though narrow, is cultivated along its entire length and provides a relatively easy, though very meandering ascent onto the plateau. Gideon pursued the Midianites up this valley (Judg. 8:8), and in the nineteenth century Selah Merrill, who followed his footsteps, says that his muleteers often remarked, "What a fine road this is along the Zerka!"[14]

Just inside the Abarim region to the south is 'Iraq al-Amir, a unique palace in the steep-sided and fertile valley of the Wadi Sir. Built of gigantic limestone blocks in the Hellenistic period, it was the home of the Tobiad family, of whom an infamous earlier member had been that Tobiah who op-

posed Nehemiah.[15] The fertile region round about was densely settled in the Iron Age, and Paul Lapp has suggested that 'Iraq al-Amir is possibly the Levitical city of "Ramoth in Gilead" (Deut. 4:43; Josh. 20:8; 21:38; 1 Chron. 6:80).[16] That the Abarim were settled by the Israelites is good reason for including it as a southward extension of Gilead.

During the New Testament period the Abarim became the rather more extended territory of Perea, essentially the dissected scarplands as far south as the Arnon gorge, which formed part of the kingdom of Herod Antipas. Gilead itself was a southward extension of the region of the Decapolis, among whose inhabitants the fame of Jesus spread (Mark 5:20). These cities did not form a separate political division with a clearly marked frontier, but were rather a loose confederation of independent cities founded to protect the trade routes of Bashan and Gilead from the onslaughts of the Bedouin and the fierce inhabitants of the Jabal Druze and to provide a strong block of Hellenistic culture in an otherwise Semitic world. "The region of the Decapolis" where Jesus is said to have cured the deaf man who had an impediment in his speech and later to have fed the 4,000 (Mark 7:31–8:10) is the plateau region of

14. Selah Merrill, *East of the Jordan* (London: Richard Bentley & Son, 1881), p. 394.

15. Nehemiah 2:10, 19; 4:3, 7; 6:1ff.; 13:4ff. Tobiah is described as an Ammonite because the Abarim had been at this time taken over by Ammon, but he was almost certainly Jewish. His name, ha-'Ebed, the Servant, or Slave, meaning here an important official (cf. "minister"), is preserved in the present Arabic name for the palace, Qasr al-'Abd, the Castle of the Servant.

16. Paul Lapp, "Soundings at 'Araq el-Emir (Jordan)," *BASOR*, 165 (1962), 16–24. See also B. Mazar, "The Tobiads," *IEJ*, 7 (1957), 137–45, 229–38; and C. C. McCown, "The 'Araq el-Emir and the Tobiads," *BA*, XX (1957), 63–76.

Bashan east of the Lake of Galilee. We cannot now attempt to reconstruct any kind of journey for Jesus in this region, for that was not Mark's purpose, and it is absurd to argue, as some have done, that in imagining a journey from Tyre northward to Sidon and then around to the Decapolis Mark demonstrates his ignorance of Palestine. All this was pagan territory, and to look across the lake at Capernaum toward the lights on the other side was to be always conscious that over there were people who did not keep the feast. It is in this sense that Mark is envisaging all Syro-Phoenicia and the Decapolis. It is part of his argument that the deaf and stuttering Gentiles may be admitted to the Christian community because they now zealously proclaim the gospel and have indeed been fed in the wilderness, even as were the people of Israel.[17]

---

17. The cities of the Decapolis have been variously listed as ten, fourteen, and eighteen. The original ten, as given by Pliny, extend from Damascus in the north to Philadelphia (Amman) in the south, and from Scythopolis (Beisan, Beth-shan) in the west to Canatha (Qanawat) in the east. Within this area were Pella (Kh. Fahil) in the Ghor, Hippos and Gadara (Fiq and Umm Qeis) on the edge of the plateau, Dion (perhaps Tell al-'Ashari) and Raphana (ar-Rafeh) in the interior of Bashan, and Gerasa (Jerash) in the center of northern Gilead. Abila, which replaces Raphana in a second-century list, is Tell 'Abil. The finest ruins today are those of Jerash, followed by those of Umm Qeis. Amman has a magnificent theater and a few lesser remains, but nineteenth-century travelers, visiting the site when there was not so much as a village there, speak of the ruins as equaling those of Jerash.

CHAPTER **19**

Ammon, Moab, and Edom

Thus says the Lord:
"For three transgressions of Edom,
  and for four, I will not revoke the punishment;
because he pursued his brother with the sword,
  and cast off all pity. . . .
For three transgressions of the Ammonites,
  and for four, I will not revoke the punishment;
because they have ripped up women with child in Gilead,
  that they might enlarge their border. . . .
For three transgressions of Moab,
  and for four, I will not revoke the punishment;
because he burned to lime
  the bones of the king of Edom."

AMOS 1:11–2:1

D.4. *The Basin of Ammon*

This is a transitional zone, whose boundaries are difficult to define. Structurally it is a basin 20 miles long by 10 miles wide (32 by 16 km.), aligned from southwest to northeast. The last vestige of the Gilead Dome, it is enclosed on its desert side by an upfold which reveals once again the karstic Cenomanian limestone. The rounded hills within this hard and elevated rim are of the more easily worked Senonian-Eocene, and at their center is the broad valley of the Jabbok, with rich irrigable land along the river. The whole of this basin was Ammonite, with the capital at

Rabbah, i.e., Amman, "the city of waters" (2 Sam. 12:27), where the Jabbok rises in a powerful spring and the converging wadis have isolated a well-defended, flat-topped, dogleg hill. The Jabbok flows northeastward for about 12½ miles (20 km.) as far as Zerqa, but then encounters one of those NW–SE plateau depressions that continue the Bashan alignment and is deflected northwestward to enter a narrower section of its valley, carved out of the more resistant Cenomanian.

It was not only a small but an ill-defined area that the Ammonites could properly call their own, for on the north and west it merges imperceptibly into

Gilead, and on the south and east the hills descend but gradually to the level plateau. Hence they were forever seeking to enlarge their border or else withdrawing in time of weakness behind the defensive line of the Jabbok, and they survived only because of the great strength of their capital and the proximity of the desert steppe. Superbly defended by its steep slopes, the citadel hill at Rabbah was large enough to shelter a multitude of refugees in time of trouble, and the door to the east was always open. Thither a remnant could escape, trading space for time, and there remain to harass and trouble the conquerors, who found themselves with no strongly defensible line to protect them. Yet this same desert was also the enemy of the Ammonites, for while they remained in possession of the fertile fields along the Jabbok there were always other desert tribes ready to harass and trouble them. "Say to the Ammonites . . . : 'I am handing you over to the people of the east for a possession, and they shall set their encampments among you and make their dwellings in your midst; they shall eat your fruit and they shall drink your milk. I will make Rabbah a pasture for camels and the cities of the Ammonites a fold for flocks' " (Ezek. 25:3–5).[1]

Included within the Ammonite territory was the broad rolling high country of Jazer on either side of the present Amman-Na'ur road, Na'ur being prob-

ably the Abel-keramim of Judges 11:33. Martin Noth argues that it extended even farther to include the Baqa'a,[2] but this was an authentic part of Gilead, though doubtless coveted by the Ammonites, who probably seized it before they were driven out by Jephthah (Judg. 10:17ff.). Jazer is described quite rightly in Numbers 32:1 as excellent pastureland, almost certainly in this case for sheep.[3] Jazer itself, as we have seen, was probably one of the border towns on the edge of the plateau in the vicinity of Na'ur and Wadi Sir, the whole of this area being hotly disputed by Ammon, Moab, and the tribes of Reuben and Gad (Josh. 13:25). Unfortunately, we can no longer rely on the "megalithic" towers to assist us in drawing the boundaries of the Transjordanian kingdoms. The round *malfuf* towers in the neighborhood of Amman must apparently now be assigned to the Roman period, and it is possible that all the defensive border towers on the plateau are of a later date than was once thought.[4]

1. The best account of the Ammonites at present available in print is the article "Ammon" in the *Interpreter's Dictionary* by George M. Landes. This is essentially a summary of his Ph.D. thesis submitted to Johns Hopkins University, Baltimore, in 1956, to which the reader is referred for further details. See also his article, "The Material Civilization of the Ammonites," *BA*, XXIV (1961), 66–86, republished, though without maps, in Freedman and Campbell, ed., *The Biblical Archaeologist Reader*, 2 (Garden City, N.Y.: Doubleday, 1964).

2. Martin Noth, *The History of Israel* (New York: Harper and Row, 1960), p. 157.

3. There is once more a misunderstanding in the English translation here (see p. 87.) The word is again *miqneh*, meaning possessions reckoned in terms of animals, which in an agricultural society would be "cattle" in our sense of the word, i.e., cows and oxen, but the *miqneh* of the Patriarchs were sheep and goats, and the *miqneh* of the Midianites (Judg. 6:5) were camels.

4. Roger S. Boraas, "A Preliminary Sounding at Rujm el-Malfuf," to be published shortly in the Annual of the Department of Antiquities of Jordan. I am most grateful to Dr. Boraas for kindly letting me read this article before publication. Just as this book goes to press, however, there is information that some of the defensive Ammonite towers must be dated to the 6th or 7th century B.C. John H. Marks, *American Schools of Oriental Research Newsletter*, April, 1973, p. 2.

Pressed back apparently to Rabbah and the line of the Jabbok by Sihon, king of the Amorites, shortly before the Israelites encountered them (Num. 21:21–25), the Ammonites soon struggled to recover Jazer, which to them was *terra irredenta*. The account in Joshua 13 and 22 suggests that the tribal groups of Reuben and Gad, as well as some of the clans of Manasseh farther north, moved into Trans-jordan from the west, and this is supported by the presence of such names as Migdal-gad in Cis-jordan. They would therefore be pressing up onto the plateau with their flocks at the same time as the Ammonites were again pressing westward, for "to the land of the sons of Ammon you did not draw near, that is to all the banks of the river Jabbok and the cities of the hill country" (Deut. 2:37; cf. Num. 21:24; Josh. 13:25).[5] The extraordinary confusion in the accounts of Reuben and Gad in Numbers 32 and Joshua 13 indicates that neither tribe ever became properly established there.

The Ammonites allied themselves with anyone who would assist them to expand, with the king of Moab (Judg. 3:13) or with the Syrians (2 Sam. 10:6), and in times of Israel's weakness they pressed hard upon her, penetrating even to the Jordan (Judg. 10:9; 1 Sam. 11:1). The Ammonite king Nahash had been ready to befriend David when he seemed to be stirring up trouble for Saul, but when David himself became king, Hanun, the son of Nahash, opposed him (2 Sam. 10:2). This was a disastrous mistake, for David captured Rabbah in the infamous siege which cost Uriah the Hittite his life (2 Sam. 11:24), and the people were for a time reduced to abject servitude (2 Sam. 12:31), though David continued to support the royal house, with excellent results when he himself was forced to flee eastward (2 Sam. 17:27). Regaining their independence after Solomon's death, the Ammonites remained a perpetual nuisance to the kings of Israel and Judah. After the defeat of King Ahab at Ramoth-gilead they are said to have challenged Jehoshaphat of Judah, and probably again in the eighth century they had attacked Gilead (2 Chron. 20:1; Amos 1:13). Uzziah must have brought them to heel, but his son Jotham had once again to compel them to pay tribute, which they continued to do for at least three years (2 Chron. 27:5).

Inhabiting a climatically marginal area, where the rain becomes constantly less trustworthy toward the east, the Ammonites were a mixture of farmers and shepherds. All the hill farmers probably also had flocks of sheep and goats, and the eastern clans may well have been seminomadic, planting grain in the early winter and then returning in the spring to harvest it. It is true that they reaped considerable advantage from the position of Rabbah on the Pilgrim Road, for the excellent water supply made it an important staging post, but they were ever the weakest of the three plateau kingdoms and were oppressed both by the Moabites and by the rulers of Israel. They brooded continually on revenge, and when Jerusalem was overthrown they naturally rejoiced, causing Ezekiel to say angrily, "You have clapped your hands, and stamped your feet and rejoiced with all the malice within you" (Ezek. 25:6).

---

5. According to some authorities these names indicate rather that the Trans-jordan tribes tried to gain a foothold west of the Jordan. See, e.g., K. Elliger's article "Gad" in the *Interpreter's Dictionary*.

D.5. *The Tableland of Moab, the Land of the Shepherd*[6]

"Now Mesha king of Moab was a sheep breeder; and he had to deliver to the king of Israel a hundred thousand lambs and the wool of a hundred thousand rams. But when Ahab died, the king of Moab rebelled against the king of Israel" (2 Kings 3:4–5).[7] Such was the history of the Moabites. Both pastoral and proud, in the three relatively brief periods of Israel's strength they were reduced to vassalage, but more often they threw off her dominion and maintained a fierce independence behind the towering Dead Sea cliffs.

The territory they disputed between them was the wide open Mishor, the plateau around Medeba and Heshbon, stretching northward into Jazer and southward as far as the Arnon. Originally Reuben seems to have had the primacy here and in that critical time hymned by Deborah tarried "among the sheepfolds, to hear the piping for the flocks" (Judg. 5:16), but in the days of the monarchy it was known to both Israel and Moab as the land of Gad.[8] Reuben disappears from history, being mentioned only once again, when Hazael swept southward from Damascus to ravage the Mishor and drive Moab back beyond the Arnon, and in the

LIII. *The Mishor.* A Bedouin encampment on the level tableland of northern Moab, between Madeba and Umm al-'Amad (Bezer or Bozrah of the Old Testament).

expectations of Ezekiel both Reuben and Gad are to be allotted land *west* of the Jordan, for the eastern border of the country was to be "along the Jordan between Gilead and the land of Israel" (Ezek. 47:18; 48:6, 27). In the prophetic books Heshbon and the surrounding towns are always Moabite (Isa. 15:4; 16:8–9; Jer. 48:2ff.), though Jeremiah 49:3 classes Heshbon with Rabbah as Ammonite, for in the tragic final years of the kingdom Milcom, the Ammonite god, "dispossessed Gad" (Jer. 49:1).

Now that the Gilead Dome has been left behind, the geological strata are remarkably level, dipping slightly into a gentle basin north of the Arnon and rising equally gently to an upfold south of it. These broad undulations are aligned directly from west to east, as is also the forbidding gorge of the Arnon, but there is a remarkable change of direction in the south. In Gilead, north of the Mishor, the structural alignment had been from southwest to northeast, but in the southern part of Moab

6. See A. H. Van Zyl, *The Moabites* (Leiden: E. J. Brill, 1960).

7. One must protest against the attempt to make King Mesha and the prophet Amos, on the basis of linguistic parallels, into diviners. Words do not necessarily have the same meaning in related languages, and *noqed* in both 2 Kings 3:4 and Amos 1:1 is clearly related to the keeping of sheep (See Amos 7:14–15).

8. 1 Samuel 13:7; 2 Samuel 24:5; 2 Kings 10:33. See also "The Moabite Stone," Pritchard, *ANET*, pp. 320–21.

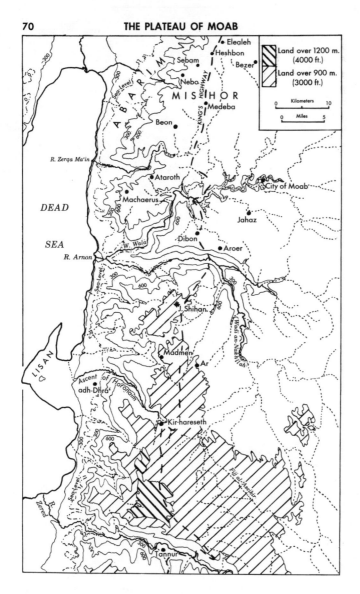

the faulting is all from northwest to southeast. Toward the south also the plateau rises steadily, and the red Nubian sandstone appears in the scarplands of the Rift. Basalt is once more present. North of the Arnon the outflows are confined to the scarp valleys, such as the Zerqa Ma'in, but south of the canyon the volcanic rock has poured out over a wide area from Jabal Shihan, preserving the hard edges of the canyon and preventing their erosion by the tributary wadis.

Upon the northern precipices of the Arnon stand Dibon and Aroer beside the King's Highway, which here must plunge suddenly down to the river nearly 2,300 feet (750 m.) below, crossing it just above the beginning of the narrow sandstone gorge. Three miles from Aroer is the southern rim, and this is the panorama envisaged by Jeremiah when he said, "Come down from your glory, and sit on the parched ground, O inhabitant of Dibon . . . stand by the highway and watch, O inhabitant of Aroer! Ask him who flees and her who escapes; say, 'What has happened?' Moab is put to shame, for it is broken; wail and cry! Tell it by the Arnon, that Moab is laid waste" (Jer. 48:18–20).[9]

Neither vines nor olives are greatly to be seen in Moab, and though the table-land is green with wheat and barley in the spring, the cultivable area grows steadily narrower southward. Everywhere, however, there are sheep, great flocks and converging lines of them, like the spokes of a limitless wheel, moving in clouds of golden dust to be given their water at the well. Black tents of the Bedouin cover the countryside, dwellings of people in all stages of that endless procession of settlement which has gone on throughout the centuries. Some are fully settled, save that they have not yet built houses of stone to replace the tents of hair, but this they will do in the next generation; others own fields to which they return for the seedtime and harvest, but move away in the meanwhile to find pasture for their flocks. There is great coming and going in Moab, for when the desert is safe even the true villager will take his sheep far out to the east during the rich season of spring, when clumps of huge dark irises burst out of the ground, and will return to the west only in the drought of summer.

The heartland of Moab lay between the Arnon and the Zered, and here was

9. RSV has "way," but *derech* here clearly means the King's Highway.

the capital city, Kir-hareseth, the present Kerak, an impressive stronghold at the head of a valley and one of the greatest of the fortresses along the King's Highway. From its walls, successors to those on which the king of Moab in desperation sacrificed his son (2 Kings 3:27), the ground drops away in a rush to the steep-sided wadi. At first open, with irrigated gardens in the soft Eocene limestone, it then cuts down to cleave a narrow gorge in the red sandstone northwestward to Bab adh-Dhra' and the Dead Sea. The road, which perforce must cling to the rim of the gorge, may perhaps be the "descent of Horonaim" (Jer. 48:5), but since we do not know where Horonaim was we cannot be sure.

It was from Kir-hareseth that Mesha sallied forth to recapture from the king of Israel his lost territory on the Mishor, for though he admits in the Moabite Stone inscription that "the men of Gad had always dwelt in the land of Ataroth and the king of Israel had built Ataroth

LIV. *Machaerus.* The characteristic sugar-loaf hill marks the site of one of Herod the Great's castles, this time on the east of the Rift, overlooking the Dead Sea. It was here, according to Josephus, that John the Baptist was beheaded. In the distance may be seen the plateau of Judah.

for them," he regarded the whole table-land as Moabite country, as for the most part it was.[10] He improved the road across the Arnon to facilitate his campaign and captured both Aroer and Dibon on its northern rim, making Dibon the headquarters for his further advance. He then drove northward along the King's Highway, striking out savagely both east and west of it, to capture the town of Madeba, which stands upon a slight eminence in the northern plain, but not the much stronger position of Heshbon, the cele-brated "City of Sihon" (Num. 21:25; 32:37; Isa. 15:4; 16:8, 9). From Madeba he was able to bring under his

10. See J. Liver, "The Wars of Mesha, King of Moab," *PEQ*, XCIX (1967), 14–17.

control both Nebo (Kh. al-Makhaiyat) to the northwest and Bezer (or Bozrah, Umm al-'Amad) on the road to Rabbah. It was probably after this invasion that Jehoram decided to seek the support of the king of Edom to attack Moab from the south (2 Kings 3:4ff.).

As with the plateau of Bashan north of Gilead, the level surface offers no obstacle to the invader, and once he has entered the Mishor, whether from the north or south, the whole of it usually falls into his hands, for the Wadi Wala, which enters the Arnon from the north, lacks the frowning cliffs which might check his advance. Only along the fretted plateau edge are there any ef-fective strongholds. "Ataroth, Dibon, Jazer, Nimrah, Heshbon, Elealeh, Sebam, Nebo, and Beon," listed in Num-

LV. *Kir-Hareseth.* Today the huge Crusaders' castle of Kerak crowns the hill on which once stood the capital of Moab, one of the series of strongly fortified positions which marked the course of the King's Highway.

bers 32:3 as the cities of Reuben and Gad, are all of them, as far as they can be identified, scarp towns.[11] Along this western scarp also Herod built the fortress of Machaerus (al-Mukawwar), only a couple of miles west of the earlier Israelite stronghold of Ataroth. In this castle, according to Josephus, John the Baptist was imprisoned and put to death.

Though the Mishor north of the Arnon was liberally endowed with towns and villages, to the south there are fewer. Constricted at first by the deep valley of the Wadi an-Nakhilah, one of the two main headwaters of the Arnon, they are then constrained by the increasing drought. We know, however, much less about the settlements of this region, for since it was never part of the Israelite territory it enters into their history only as an enemy or a vassal. That for the most part they were concentrated on either side of the King's Highway is certain, and they did not extend more than 7½ miles (12 km.) to the east of it, for here is the limit of permanent agriculture.

"Loftiness, pride, arrogance and haughtiness of heart" were the sins of which the Israelites accused the people of Moab (Jer. 48:29); cf. Isa. 16:6), and there was, indeed, a temptation for the Moabites to imagine that behind their bastions they were safe from conquest and foreign invasion. The prophets thundered denunciations against them, saying, "The hand of the Lord will rest on this mountain, and Moab shall be trodden down in his place . . . the Lord will lay low his pride together with the skill of his hands" (Isa. 25:10–11), and promised that because of his taunts

11. Ataroth is probably Kh. 'Attaruz; Dibon certainly Dhiban; Heshbon is Hisban; Elealeh, al-'Al; Sebam (Sibmah), probably Qurn al-Qibsh; Nebo, Kh. al-Makhaiyat; and Beon (properly Bethmeon, Beth-baal-meon, or Baal-meon) is Ma'in.

and boasts "Moab shall become like Sodom" (Zeph 2:9). But Psalm 60 shows that Moab had no monopoly of taunts and boasts, and in due course the pride of both Moab and Israel was humbled and each was forced to beg succor from the other. When Jerusalem was taken, the people fled to Moab and Edom (Jer. 40:11), and when Moab was attacked their refugees came "like fluttering birds, like scattered nestlings," to beseech the daughter of Zion: "Hide the outcasts, betray not the fugitive; let the outcasts of Moab sojourn among you" (Isa. 16:2–4).

D.6. *The Heights of Edom, the Land of the Trader*

Still farther south along the King's Highway the plateau is once again cleft by a mighty valley, striking back from the southern end of the Dead Sea. This is the valley of the Zered, probably the "Brook of the Willows" (Isa. 15:7), and for once a valley really was a frontier, dividing Moab from Edom to the south. We know very little about the relations of the two kingdoms, but since Amos tells us that the Moabites "burned to lime the bones of the king of Edom" (Amos 2:1) it seems clear that between them also raged that incessant internecine warfare which devoured the lives of all the Levantine states. Yet there is no suggestion that either side claimed the land across the canyon as its own, and the towns here quoted in the Old Testament remain quite steadily either Moabite or Edomite.

Already in the 12 miles or so (20 km.) south of Kir-hareseth the Moabite plateau has been climbing steadily until just south of Mazar it reaches 4,085 feet (1,285 m.), and indeed one point on the Zered rim, Jabal Dhabab, is as much as 4,280 feet (1,305 m.). South

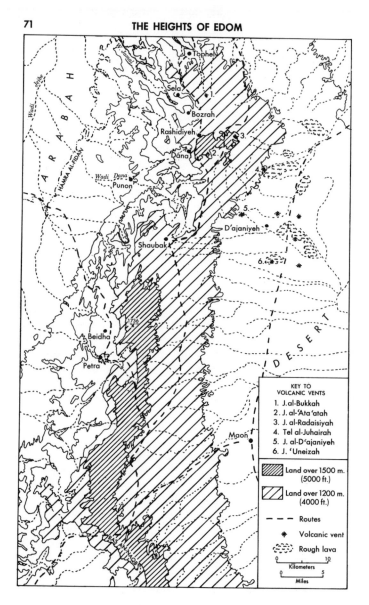

KEY TO
VOLCANIC VENTS
1. J.al-Bukkah
2. J. al-'Ata'atah
3. J. al-Radaisiyah
4. Tel al-Juhairah
5. J. al-D'ajaniyeh
6. J. 'Uneizah

Land over 1500 m.
(5000 ft.)

Land over 1200 m.
(4000 ft.)

— — — Routes

✳ Volcanic vent

Rough lava

Kilometers

Miles

of the canyon, however, the plateau has been pushed up even more sharply and takes the form almost of a ridge, over 5,000 feet (1,500 m.) for long distances, and dropping fairly steeply toward the more level desert country on the eastern side. It is possible that at some periods in ancient history the Zered marked the southern limit of settlement, for it seems now doubtful whether the kingdom of Edom existed as early as had previously been though, and it has been suggested that the eight "kings" of Genesis 36:31–39 were rather tribal chiefs.[12] Certainly the tableland of Moab is here at an end.

What may be called the "essential Edom," for it extended its power far beyond these limits, is a narrow ribbon of a country, more than 75 miles (120 km.) long but only a few miles wide, since there is room on this elevated ridge between the scarpland and the desert for no more than a single line of towns and villages. The scarplands themselves are much wider than in Moab, 12 to 13 miles across (about 20 km.), and for at least half of this distance toward the Rift the sandstone is exposed. The road, of course, keeps to the more level ridgeland, but from time to time it approaches the rim and the traveler peers dizzily down into a bizarre world of dark, gigantic cliffs and deep, terrifying gorges. Here is a region altogether apart, forbidding, and inaccessible, the home still of the leopard and such other animals as man in his ferocity has not yet succeeded in destroying.

The ridgeland of Edom is, in characteristic Trans-jordan fashion, divided into two unequal parts by the Punon (or Feinan) Embayment, which cuts back far enough into the scarp to interrupt the tenuous village zone. It is not merely a physical division but also a structural one. To the north was the region of Teman[13] and to the south southern Edom. In the smaller region of Teman great faults strike back southeastward from the Rift, such as that of the Wadi Tafileh and parallel to it to the south of the Wadi Jamal, and behind these NW–SE faults the highest lands are volcanic. There are some half-

dozen or more vents, all above 5,000 feet in height, such as Jabal al-Bukkah, Jabal al-'Ata'atah, Jabal ar-Radaisiyah, Tell al-Juhairah, Jabal ad-D'ajaniyah, and Jabal 'Uneizah, the last two being just to the east of the embayment itself. From this group of discontinuous basalt outflows the wadis drain off radially in every direction.

The Punon Embayment itself is fan-shaped, widening out eastward and narrowing toward the Rift. At its greatest it is some 12½ miles (20 km.) across and dominated on the southern rim by the isolated hill of Shaubak, crowned today by the Crusaders' castle of Montreal. Its main component is a remarkable fault valley, the Wadi Dana, cutting back absolutely straight northeastward toward the modern village of Rashidiyeh, itself an ancient Edomite site, on the plateau rim. To the south, however, another fault runs more directly eastward and minor NW–SE faults have widened the break in the plateau edge. At the foot of the Wadi Dana is Feinan, the ancient Punon (Num. 33:42-43), one of the most important of the copper mines centers along the eastern edge of the rift and certainly the place where Moses raised the serpent in the wilderness (Num. 21:4-9).

Southern Edom is longer and higher. From Shaubak in the north to Naqb Ishtar in the south is about 37½ miles (60 km.) as the crow flies, and the ridge exceeds 5,000 feet (1,500 m.) throughout, touching 5,704 feet (1,736 m.) at Rujm Tal'at al-Jum'ah in the north. Here the scarp faults all run parallel to the main direction of the Rift and the wadis generally follow the same direction. There are, indeed, two dissected platforms before the bottom of the Rift is reached. The first of these, the Petra-Beidha sandstone platform, is about 3,500 to 4,000 feet (1,100–

12. J. R. Bartlett, "The Rise and Fall of the Kingdom of Edom," *PEQ*, CIV (1972), 26–37.

13. It is now generally accepted that the word Teman refers to a region rather than a place. See Roland de Vaux, "Téman, Ville ou Région d'Édom?" *RB*, LXXVI (1969), 379–85.

2,000 m.) above sea level and 1,250 feet (1,000 m.) below the limestone heights of Jabal ash-Sharāh which dominate it on the east. The second is some 1,500 feet (500 m.) above the Rift Valley floor. Finally, southern Edom differs from Teman in that (a) along the edge of the Rift the underlying granite first begins to appear, climbing higher and higher as one proceeds south; (b) on the eastern side of the ridge the wadis run parallel to each other almost due eastward; (c) at the extreme southern end of the plateau edge, just before it turns southeastward, faulting has extended the Cenomanian and Eocene limestone westward in the region of Jabal at-Tur al-Abyad, bringing the Petra-Beidha platform to an end. Around this extension are frequent springs, and there is a marked increase in the number of Edomite settlements. Moreover, in this same region the faulting has made possible a route down to the oasis of Gharandal in the Wadi Arabah.

The winters in Edom are often icily cold, with howling, savage storms and snow that lies long upon the elevated ridge, but the summers are fresh and cool. So effectively do these heights catch the last fragments of the Mediterranean storms that even today there is a surprising amount of good scrub, and as late as World War I there was still so much wood here that the Turks built a branch of the Hejaz Railway out to Shobek to tap the supply. In ancient days it must have been a great deal more truly forest, and along the heights of Jabal Sharah oak, juniper, hawthorn, almond, and carob were all to be found,[14] so plentifully in fact that another name for Edom was Se'ir, i.e., "hairy" (e.g., Gen. 32:3; 36:8; Deut.

2:1; Josh. 24.4; Ezek. 25:8). These forests were strictly limited, both to the east and to the west, coming to an end with the more open sandstone westward and the rapid decline of the rainfall on the eastern lee slopes. Here, indeed, they passed quickly into desert, with only a narrow strip of steppeland between, and here were the forts which guarded the villages from the desert raiders. The outermost were Nabatean, Roman, or Byzantine, e.g., D'ajaniyeh, but others somewhat farther westward seem to belong to the Edomite period, though there is some argument concerning their date.[15]

A certain aura of mystery seems to have surrounded the country of Edom, and even today these heights have a decided quality of "otherness." In Old Testament times it must have been a strange and somewhat frightening region, where the villages, and fields, coaxed out· of the surrounding woodland, were exposed alike to the most violent tantrums of the Middle Eastern climate, the onslaught of the desert tribes, and the ever present menace of wild animals breathing close upon them from the desert, the forest, and the brutal sandstone crags. If the Edomites dwelt in clefts of the rocks (Obad. 3), carving their homes out of the friable sandstone, it was because this gave them security both from their enemies and from the weather. Their chief center seems to have been Teman, since all the Edomite sites mentioned in the Bible are in the north.[16] The chief

14. Hans Helbaek, "Pre-Pottery Neolithic Farming at Beidha: A Preliminary Report," *PEQ*, XCVIII (1966), 61–66.

15. Nelson Glueck, *The Other Side of the Jordan* (Cambridge, Mass.: The American Schools of Oriental Research, 1970), pp. 161–67.

16. Crystal-M. Bennett, "An Archaeological Survey of Biblical Edom," *Perspective*, 12 (Spring, 1971), 35–44; also "Des Fouilles à Umm el-Biyarah: Les Edomites à Petra," *Bible et Terre Sainte*, 84 (June, 1966), 7–16.

stronghold was Bozrah,[17] the modern Buseirah, on an isolated spur at the head of the Wadi Jamal and admirably placed not only to control the route which ran northwestward toward the end of the Dead Sea along the southern rim of this valley, but, even more important, to gain access by the road down the Wadi Dana to the vitally important copper mines at Punon (Feinan). Only 2½ miles (4 km.) to the northwest, on the northern rim of the Wadi al-Jamal, stand Sil', the biblical Sela which was captured by Amaziah (2 Kings 14:7; cf. Isa. 16:1) and perhaps also the "strong city" of Edom of Psalm 108:10. The traditional identification with the towering Umm al-Biyara at Petra must now be abandoned.

Strong though Bozrah and Sela undoubtedly were, agriculturally the richest city in Teman was certainly Tophel, the modern Tafileh (Deut. 1:1), wonderfully supplied with water from eight powerful springs and sufficiently protected, because it lies a little down the western scarp, for there to be extensive olive groves. It is, however, too easily accessible from the Zered by way of the long Wadi La'aban for it to have challenged Bozrah as the strategic center.

Perched upon their majestic heights, the Edomites could not hope to get their wealth by farming, nor maintain the huge Moabite herds of fat-tailed sheep, and were therefore taught by the stern land in which they lived to find their fortune in trade. Their riches came from the export of copper and from the lumbering caravans of the south, laden with the luxury products of southern Arabia, toiling wearily up from the hot deserts of the Wadi Hasma onto the heights of Edom, where the cultivated land stretched out a long arm into the wilderness to greet them. It was this trade that gave them their reputation for wisdom and strange knowledge, for it brought them into contact with a distant and legendary world that others knew only by hearsay.

The trade of these highlands was exceedingly ancient, and as early as 9,000 years ago the settlements on the Petra-Beidha platform obtained obsidian from Aksaray and Nigde in Turkey and probably also their pumice from the Anatolian plateau, for the local and north Arabian volcanoes do not produce it. These settlements lasted for some 500 years, from about 7000 to 6500 B.C., though experiments in agriculture had started much earlier and were connected with Jericho and other settlements of the same date in Anatolia and Mesopotamia.[18] There are signs also that trade with southern Arabia may have started as early as 6000 B.C.[19]

The Edomite greatness belongs to the seventh and sixth centuries B.C., and during this period they developed a rich and impressive culture. Some of the pottery discovered at Bozrah is "the most beautiful Iron Age pottery ever to be found in Jordan," rivaling even the delicate productions of the later Nabateans.[20] For the protection of their caravans they extended their authority

---

17. Genesis 36:33; Isaiah 34:6; 63:1; Jeremiah 49:13, 22; Amos 1:12. N.B. Bozrah in Moab in Jeremiah 48:24 is, of course, Umm al-'Amad south of Madeba.

18. Diana Kirkbride, "The Excavation of a Neolithic Village at Seyl Aqlat, Beidha, near Petra," *PEQ*, XCII (1960), 136–45; "Five Seasons at the Pre-Pottery Neolithic Village of Beidha in Jordan: A Summary," *PEQ*, XCVIII (1966), 8–72; "Beidha 1965: An Interim Report," *PEQ*, XCIX (1967), 5–13; "Beidha 1967: An Interim Report," *PEQ*, C. (1968), 90–96.

19. Diana Kirkbride. From a personal communication.

20. Crystal-M. Bennett, "Excavations at Buseirah, Southern Jordan, 1971: A Preliminary Report," *Levant*, V (1973), 1–11.

LVI. *The Heights of Edom*.   The tremendous scarp of the high Edomite plateau overlooking the Arabah. The cluster of houses in the center is Dana, at the head of the precipitous Wadi Dana, which is part of the Punon Embayment.

LVII. *Petra*.   These two temples, one above the other, are carved out of the pale yellowish Ram sandstone, which the visitor encounters before entering the narrow gorge of the *Siq*, leading into the heart of Petra.

far along the trade routes: across the Arabah into the Negeb, though probably intermittently; down to the Red Sea at Ezion-geber, where in the eighth century they seem to have wrecked the ships of Jehoshaphat (1 Kings 22:48), though some believe this was the result of a storm; and certainly well into Arabia, for Ezekiel speaks of the Edomites falling by the sword "from Teman even to Dedan" (Ezek. 25:13). Their readiness to take advantage of Judah's weakness in the sixth century earned them her lasting hatred (Ps. 137: 7; Isa. 34:5–17; Jer. 49:7–22; Ezek. 35; Mal. 1:2–4). The kingdom collapsed finally in the fifth century, though for what reason is not clear.

Some time in the third century B.C. the Nabateans began to move in from the desert, and by 100 B.C. they had ceased entirely to be a pastoral people. For the next two centuries, until their conquest by Trajan in A.D. 106, they controlled a wide trading empire, extending around Perea and the Decapolis as far north as Damascus and southward into Arabia to Madain Salah and probably beyond. Their caravans moved up and down the Wadi Sirhan, and they had harbors on the Mediterranean.[21] The fabulous city of Petra, with its huge classical façades carved out of the red or white sandstone, is today world-famous, but though Petra was the greatest of such cities, it was by no means the only one of its kind. Beidha, 4 miles farther north, and Madain Salah in Arabia are of the same style, and at Khirbet Tannur beside the Wadi Hesa a fine Nabatean temple has been excavated. The cliffs of Petra itself are honeycombed with caves, which served both as homes and as storehouses for

21. The most complete book on the Nabateans is Nelson Glueck, *Deities and Dolphins* (New York: Farrar, Straus and Giroux, 1965).

the merchants, as well as for tombs, but in the center a great semicircle of open ground was filled with buildings, though many of these seem to belong to the Roman period. The main approach in Nabatean days was from the west, by the road from the Arabah and from Gaza. After A.D. 106 the Romans built here a colonnaded street and a theater.

LVIII. *Petra: The "Urn Tomb."* **The facade of this great temple, carved out of the red Quweira sandstone shows how the wind-driven sand has eroded the foot of the columns. This constant undercutting close to the ground is the cause of the steep cliff formations which are so common in desert regions.**

The "triumphal arch," however, has now been shown to be the gateway to the temple known as Qasr Bint al-Fara'un.

The immense wealth which accrued to the Nabateans from their trade enabled them to cultivate economically areas which have never been cultivated before or since, using the most careful methods of irrigation and water conservation. They were extraordinarily skillful at this, but it is doubtful whether the produce of these fields would have justified the trouble taken over them if they had not been necessary for maintaining the complicated network of Nabatean trade routes.

The fantastic magnificence of Petra and the Nabatean kingdom enters hardly at all into the New Testament records, though the merchants of whom Jesus speaks must have been aware of it, for pearls of great price (Matt. 13: 45) from the Persian Gulf or Indian Ocean would doubtless have been part of their trade. Only twice does this kingdom stretch out a finger to touch the narrative directly, first when "wise men from the east" came to offer the infant Jesus gifts, "gold and frankincense and myrrh" (Matt. 2:1–12), and again when "the governor under King Aretas guarded the city of Damascus" in order to arrest Paul (2 Cor. 11:32), for the king of whom he speaks was that Aretas IV who resigned for forty-nine years (9 B.C.–A.D. 40) and was said to have "loved his people."[22]

---

22. *Ibid.*, p. 542.

CHAPTER 20

The Desert Wastes

Some wandered in desert wastes,
finding no way to a city to dwell in;
hungry and thirsty,
their soul fainted within them.
Then they cried to the Lord in their trouble,
and he delivered them from their distress.

PSALM 107:4–6

Enfolding the Palestinian region on the east and the south is "the great and terrible wilderness," the *midbar* which so alarmed the Israelites. It lay for the most part outside their direct experience and cannot therefore be examined in detail, but since it impinged so much upon their consciousness it must not be left without consideration. Part of it, the deep trench of the Arabah, has already been discussed, and the rest may be divided into four parts: the Plateau Desert of what today is eastern Jordan, the Wadi Sirhan, the Dissected Desert of southern Jordan, and the Wilderness of Zin, or Negeb. Except only in the far southeast, it is everywhere "tame desert," receiving occasional rain, sometimes no more than a shower or two and sometimes a real cloudburst coming very often in the

transitional seasons. In a dry year, however, the rain in the south and east may fail together.

E.1. *The Plateau Desert*

This is a large triangular region lying beyond the Hejaz Railroad. At the center is a Y-shaped upland section, seldom rising more than 500 feet (150 m.) above the general level of the plateau, but dividing the drainage into three distinct basins. The main backbone, so to speak, of these uplands is a long line of Eocene hills, continuously over 3,000 feet (900 m.), extending from southern Moab toward the southeastern corner of what is now the country of Jordan. About the middle, just northwest of the oasis of Bayir, these hills

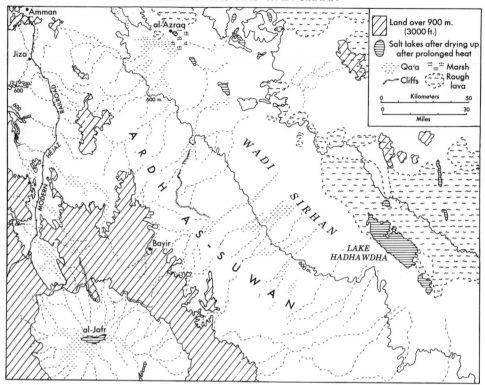

are joined by another, somewhat lower, line extending SSE from the direction of Amman. Between the two arms of the Y thus formed the wadis run off for the most part almost due northwest to join the scarp streams of the plateau edge. On the eastern side they run in almost parallel lines toward the Wadi Sirhan, and on the southwestern side the wadis, both from the central upland region and from the Edomite ridge-land, drain into the large oval basin of al-Jafr, where there are wide areas of salt flats and more than one intermittent salt lake.

Although the whole region is more or less level plateau, hardly at all interrupted by the central uplands, it must not be thought that movement is altogether easy. Before the invention of modern means of transport travel in the desert was everywhere limited by two things: where water was obtainable and where the camel could go. In the north wells are relatively frequent, but farther south the routes tend to converge on the two important sources of supply at Bayir and al-Jafr. The most difficult areas for camels were those which were either too rough or, in times of wet weather, too slippery, for a camel skids uncontrollably in the mud. Stretches of qa'a, or mud flat, such as occur extensively around al-Jafr and in many of the larger wadis, are perfectly possible, and indeed easy, in dry weather, for they are as flat as a billiard table, but even the slightest shower makes them treacherous and heavy rain renders them impassable for quite long periods, since the water pours down upon them through every surrounding wadi. Even slight hills could deflect the caravans because desert erosion creates typical butte or mesa formations with steep, almost clifflike sides that effectively deter the traveler. Though the central uplands are crossed by a large number of tracks, parts of them constitute more of an obstacle than would appear on the map.

Only one area, however, caused serious difficulty, and this was the Ardh as-Suwan, or flint desert, between the central uplands and the Wadi Sirhan. Here the ground is covered for miles and miles with innumerable sharp nodules of flint, every particle of sand having been blown or washed away. It is incredibly barren, with not a speck of green to be seen, and everywhere the unwinking flint throws back the light of the blazing sun. Not actually impassable, it was nevertheless distinctly to be avoided.

E.2. *The Wadi Sirhan*

This is not a wadi in the sense in which the word is normally understood, but a prolonged depression about 175 miles (280 km.) in length and some 50 or 60 miles wide (80–100 km.). The oasis of al-Azraq in the northwest is about 1,700 feet (525 m.) above sea level and the southeastern end of the depression about 1,400 feet (425 m.) Consequently there is a gradual descent toward the southeast, but the floor is far from even.

On the nearer side the Ardh as-Suwan slopes almost imperceptibly into the trough, and one arrives there almost without being aware of it, but on the farther side lies the formidable basalt barrier, a long line of mountains and plateaus, volcanic peaks, and great outflows of lava, rising to as much as 3,904 feet (1,190 m.). This lava belt is well

over 60 miles (100 km.) wide in places and stands about 750 feet (225 m.) above the depression, though of course the peaks are very much higher. It is true that opposite al-Azraq, where the barrier is lower and narrower, with occasional wide level areas, it can be crossed, though not easily, but in general the hardness and roughness of the rock and the great complexity of the terrain have combined to make this a region of quite singular difficulty, and the caravans usually made long detours to avoid it.

The Wadi Sirhan, therefore, lies between two regions in which desert travel is more than usually hazardous, and so all movement tends to be channeled along it, the more especially because in this low-lying depression there are fairly frequent wells, supplied by the wadis from the Ardh as-Suwan and from the rain which falls on the basalt heights.

LIX. *The Plateau Desert.* The boulder-strewn surface of the plateau desert in eastern Trans-Jordan.

There are also a number of salt marshes and intermittent lakes at the foot of the basalt, the largest of them being Bahairat Hadhawdha. The southeastern end of the basalt barrier is almost touched by a great shoulder of sand desert, the most northerly extension of the desolate Nefud of Arabia, which is almost as great an obstacle as the basalt itself. The sand and the basalt do not quite touch each other, however, and between them, leading into the Wadi Sirhan, are the oases of al-Jauf and Sakaka, through which all the major routes tend to be funneled.

The Wadi Sirhan trade route was much used by the Nabateans, who policed it and brought it under their control but did not apparently colonize it, for so far no clear-cut Nabatean pottery has been found there.[1] Bayir, however, farther west, has revealed considerable evidence of Nabatean occupation and must have been, then as now, an important center for controlling the desert. Apparently it was the difficulty of the Ardh as-Suwan which deterred further expansion and deflected all caravan movement around it to al-Azraq or al-Jauf at either end of the Wadi Sirhan. Since control of Bayir gave them access to these two important oases, the Nabateans would, therefore, have been able to command the Sirhan route.

The eastern desert does not enter very directly into biblical history, save as a threat to Israelite security. The Midianites, or Bedouin, had been a severe menace in the early period, and the victory of Gideon against them—when, apparently for the first time, the Israelites were exposed to camel raiders— was very long remembered (Judg. 6:1– 6; 7:1–25; Ps. 83:6; Isa. 9:4; 10:26). A passage in Numbers 31:1–12 recalls

1. Nelson Glueck, "Wadi Sirhan in Northern Arabia," *BASOR*, 96 (1944), 7– 17.

a struggle with the Bedouin during the Exodus, which of course is very probable, though the passage itself seems to be a late one and there is reason to wonder quite how historical it is. This part of the desert also provides the background for Isaiah 40, for what is there envisaged is a return across the Arabian plateau. The valleys which are below the general level are to be filled, and the rough, volcanic *harrah* is to be made a plain.

E.3. *The Dissected Plateau*

In the south of the present country of Jordan, 20 miles (32 km.) or so beyond the oasis town of Maon (Ma'an), the plateau breaks away along a NW–SE fault, stretching as far east as the Hejaz Railroad and then swinging round to a more northeasterly direction. Because of the steady elevation of the underlying plateau southward the protective limestone has been removed, and perhaps in the higher regions never existed. The friable sandstone beneath is exposed, and along its multitudinous cracks the desert storms have carved the plateau surface into a complex checkerboard of hills and gorges. The whole nature of the country changes. Instead of a wide open tableland there are narrow valleys and steep, gigantic cliff faces; instead of pale browns and russets there are dark reds and drifts of shining yellow sands; instead of freedom of movement there is constriction.

On the west is the high granite ridge of the mountains of Midian, joined to the Edomite highland by a shatter zone, where deep, sand-filled wadis have cut back across the mountains. The main mountain block is south of this, a towering gray massif, seamed with dark volcanic dikes and reaching at its highest

73   **THE DISSECTED PLATEAU**

point 5,222 feet (1,592 m.). East of this are sandy plains and passageways, shut in on every side by precipices and floored with drifting sand, *qa'a,* and wide alluvial fans. Out of this sea of sand rise hills and mountains, often 4,000 feet (1,200 m.) in height, startling masses of sandstone resting on a granite base. Though the plain and wadi bottoms often carry a reasonable cover of desert scrub, the hills are barren and easily eroded, the restless sand, forever driven by the wind against the foot of the cliffs, undercutting them and bringing down the cliff face in huge screes and drifts. At the foot of the northern scarp the Wadi Hasma stretches away southeastward and both to the east and south leads into even more constricted passages, many of which run directly from north to south and are spectacular almost beyond belief. The most famous is the broad Wadi

Ram, between Jabal Ram to the west and Jabal 'Ishrin to the east, two amazing bastions of red and yellow sandstone standing sheer out of the sandy floor. They are the highest points in the whole Palestinian realm, 5,753 and 5,750 feet respectively (1,754 and 1,753 m.), surpassing even the greatest summit in Edom. The springs at the foot of these mountains made this a sacred region from very early times, and here beside 'Ain Shellalah the Nabateans had a temple.[2]

Along these hot but splendid corridors the desert caravans slowly plodded in and out of Edom, dwarfed by the towering cliffs on either side, but protected by the Edomite merchants and even more stringently by the Nabateans, who built forts at frequent

2. Diana Kirkbride, "Le Temple Nabatéan de Ramm: Son Evolution Architecturale," *RB,* LXVII (1960), 65–92.

intervals along the more important roads. These were essentially three: southward along the eastern edge of the Midian Mountains and through the narrow Wadi Ytem at the southern end to Ezion-geber; southward again through Wadi Ram or by a more open passage farther along the Wadi Hasma to Madain Salah and Medina; or eastward to al-Jauf.

This eastward track, before it finally reached al-Jauf, had to skirt the even more fantastic region of Jabal Tubaiq in the southeastern corner of modern Jordan, a wide volcanic region which has amazed every visitor. Here one encounters "an abrupt escarpment, slashed and carved into a thousand intricate designs and rent by a mass of gullies. . . . The sandstone has been worn away while the lava has endured; coal-black cores of basalt stand sentinel over denuded sandstone slopes, where the refuse is piled in glorious ruin. Below and beyond the drift of ages silts up against the foothills like breakers surging on to a rock-bound coast. Beyond the Tubaiq lies the most grisly God-forsaken wilderness it has been my misfortune to behold."[3]

This is far indeed from the biblical story, but the Wadi Hasma is much closer. The author of Job knew of "the travelers of Sheba" who find the wells dried up and "turn aside from their course; they go up into the waste and perish," and in the prologue to the poem

3. Douglas Carruthers, "Reminiscences of Gertrude Bell," *RCAJ*, XLV (1958), 52–57.

LX. *The Dissected Desert.* A general view in the Wadi Ram region showing how the islands of rock, some small, some mountainous, rise out of the sea of sand.

the perils of desert herding are vividly described (Job 6:18–19; 1:13–19). By this route came the Queen of Sheba to confer with Solomon when she discovered that a new power had arisen to dominate the northern end of the trade route (1 Kings 10:1–5), and by the same road there came up from the wilderness "stacte, and onycha, and galbanum, sweet spices and frankincense" (Exod. 30:34) for use in the Temple, brought year by year "from Sheba . . . from a distant land" (Jer. 6:20; cf. Isa. 43:23–24). "Lift up your eyes round about, and see," said the Prophet to desolate Jerusalem,

A multitude of camels shall cover you,
    the young camels of Midian and Ephah;
    all those from Sheba shall come.
They shall bring gold and frankincense,
    and shall proclaim the praise of the Lord.
All the flocks of Kedar shall be gathered
    to you,
    the rams of Nebaioth shall minister
    to you;
they shall come up with acceptance on
    my altar,
    and I will glorify my glorious house.
                  [Isa. 60:4, 6–7]

E.4. *The Wilderness of Zin*

For convenience we may assume the northern boundary of this region to be a line drawn from Gaza through Beersheba to the southern end of the Dead Sea, and the southern and western boundary to be drawn from Elath westward along the Darb al-Hajj as far as Jabal al-Garfa and then due northward to the Mediterranean at Khan Yunis. The eastern boundary, of course, is the edge of the Wadi Arabah. It should be noticed, however, that strictly speaking the northwestern section is not really desert and that in the southwest the region as here defined extends well into the occupied territory of Sinai. It is

divided into two quite distinct parts by the backbone of uplands and highlands extending southwestward from the Dead Sea. Another dividing line runs along the northern foot of these highlands from the ancient Arad (Tell Arad) to Nessana (Nizzana or Auja al-Hafir). Thus we have to recognize from north to south four subregions: the Coastal Plains, the Western Slopes, the High Negeb, and the Paran Basin.

The Coastal Plains. This is gently rolling country, gradually sloping northwestward to the sea and drained by the "Brook Besor" (Wadi Ghazzeh or Nahal Besor; 1 Sam. 30:9, 10, 21), which is joined by the Beersheba Wadi. The southern part of the plain is largely covered with sand dunes, those around Khalasa (Horvat Haluja) being of great antiquity while the others are more recent, but the northern section between Beersheba and Khan Yunis is loess country and steppeland. Here in the north the landscape is dotted with fairly frequent wells and seems always to have been cultivated, and today is that region normally referred to in accounts of reclamation of the Negeb, settlements to the south being fewer and more experimental.[4] It might indeed be better to include it with the Philistine coast to the north than with the barbarous southern wilderness. In Old Testament times it was part of the territory of Simeon, later absorbed into Judah as the Negeb of Judah, and Sharuhen (Tell Fa'ra; Josh. 19:6) on the Brook Besor seems to have marked the frontier. Beyond toward the coast, or perhaps including the whole area, was the Negeb of the Cherethites (1 Sam. 30:14).

The Western Slopes. To the southwest of the previous region the land rises

4. See map in G. D. Blake, "Settlement in Israel's Negev Desert," *Geography*, 56 (1971), 135–37.

74   **THE WILDERNESS OF ZIN**

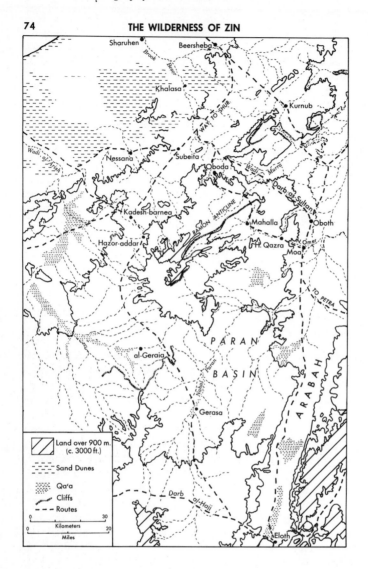

gently to the uplands in a countryside of broad wadis and wide, level spurs. Until recently the wadis were cultivated somewhat ineffectively, but regularly, by the Bedouin and in earlier days by the people of Judah, when the monarchy was strong enough to extend its control southward and, of course, most completely by the Nabateans. It is a relatively narrow zone, not more than 5 miles (8 km.) wide, of moderate para-steppeland, moistened with heavy dew from the sea and the occasional storms of the rainy season. Lying for the most part entirely between 1,000 and 2,000 feet (300–600 m.), these slopes receive about 6 inches (150 mm.) of rain a year, which is, however, very erratic, and considerable argument has developed in recent years both about the possibility of fluctuations in the rainfall pattern, which must surely have occurred, and also methods of ancient land use. Particular controversy has related to the purpose of the curious parallel heaps of stone known to the local Arab inhabitants as Teleilat al-'Anab, or "vine heaps." The majority of Israeli authorities believe that it can be demonstrated that they were intended to promote dew condensation or to direct the runoff, but this has been criticized as being too sophisticated and the result of wrongly applying modern methods to an ancient culture.[5]

However this may be, there is no doubt that this was the zone of Nabatean and Roman towns, which extended also into the edge of the plain. The most easterly were Kurnub and Oboda (Avdat or Abda), guarding the passages across the hills, and farther west were such cities as Nessana and Subeita.

5. There is very considerable literature, mostly in the form of articles, on this subject. By way of introduction see Reifenberg, *The Struggle Between the Desert and the Sown*; Michael Evenari and Dov Keller, "Ancient Masters of the Desert," *Scientific American*, 194 (April, 1956), 40–45; Y. Kedar, "Ancient Agriculture at Shivtah in the Negev," *IEJ*, 7 (1957), 179–89; "Water and Soil from the Desert," *Geog. Journal*, 123 (1957), 179–87; M. Evenari, Y. Aharoni, L. Shanan, and N. H. Tadmor, "The Ancient Desert Agriculture of the Negev: Early Beginnings," *IEJ*, 8 (1958), 231–68; "The Ancient Desert Agriculture of the Negev: V. An Israelite Settlement at Ramat Matred," *IEJ*, 10 (1960), 23–36, 97–111; Philip Mayerson, "Ancient Agricutural Remains in the Central Negeb: The Teleilat el-'Anab," *BASOR*, 153 (1959), 19–32; "The Agricultural Remains of the Central Negeb: Methodology and Dating Criteria," *BASOR*, 160 (1960), 27–37; Yehuda Kedar, "More About the Teleilat el-'Anab in the Negeb," *BASOR*, 176 (1964), 47–49; Philip Mayerson, "The Issue of the Teleilat el-'Anab," *BASOR*, 178 (1965), 69; "A Note on Demography and Land Use in the Ancient Negeb," *BASOR*, 185 (1967), 39–43.

Around them were smaller agricultural settlements, but it is doubtful whether the towns themselves developed in the first place as farming communities, for by any reckoning they stood upon the very edge of the cultivable zone. Rather they were started as posts intended to control the trade routes of a difficult and troubled region, and it was the huge volume of their trade which made agriculture economically possible. With this stimulus the farms did well and persisted for a prolonged period. The towns were dignified and comfortable, though they must have been expensive to build, for marble was imported in large quantities, and wood, which also

LXI. *Subeita.* The South Church at Subeita, one of the ancient cities of the Negeb. Built originally by the Nabateans, Subeita continued to be important in the early Christian period, but was already on the decline at the time of the Muslim conquest.

needed to be imported, was extensively used.

The High Negeb. The structure of this region has already been discussed in Chapter III, but here we need to notice the physical importance of the division made by the Biq'at Zin (Wadi Murra), which cleaves the hills so effectively that a wide scimitar of lowland cuts the hill country into two. Not only is this the major routeway of the Negeb, providing a relatively easy and low-lying passage for the Darb as-Sultan, but there is a marked difference between the country on either side of it. Both are characterized by the strange and striking *maksheshim,* but the hills to the north are very much lower, rising normally only slightly above 2,000 feet (600 m.) and touching no more than 2,348 feet (716 m.) at their highest point, which overlooks the lowland passage. To the south is the high oval-shaped Ramon (or Khurashe) Dome, which surpasses 3,000 feet (900 m.) over a wide area and reaches 3,395 feet (1,035 m.) in Har Ramon (Jabal Raman). Here there are no longer gentle slopes but steep precipices on every side, though tracks run outward in every direction along the steep wadis which cut down to the surrounding basins.

On the west, where the dome is widest, the ground drops steeply and even dangerously away into the wide basin of the Wadi al-'Arish, usually identified with the "River of Egypt" (Josh. 15:4), which was held to be the farthest border of Judah. That this was indeed the uttermost limit seems now to have been proved archaeologically.[6] At the foot of the northwestern promontory of the Ramon Dome are 'Ain al-Qudeirat and 'Ain Qudeis, both nestling

at the foot of steep cliffs.[7] 'Ain al-Qudeirat is the better supplied with water and is almost certainly the site of Kadesh-barnea, the center of the semi–nomadic wanderings of the Israelites in the Exodus period (Num. 13:26; 20:14, 22; 32:8; 34:4; Deut. 1:2; Josh. 15:3), and the site at a later date of a Judean fortress. Only 2 miles (3 km.) to the southeast is 'Ain Qudeis, where the springs are much less powerful and the water more scarce. It would probably be correct to identify this with Hazar-addar (Num. 34:5). The Kadesh-barnea region was unquestionably an important route center in ancient days, for not only did the excellence of the water supply attract the caravans, but the routes were here constricted between the cliffs which border the Ramon Dome and the mesa formations of Jabal Umm Hureiba farther to the northwest.

The Paran Basin. The whole southeastern side of the High Negeb is almost incredibly barren and sharply different from the gentler region to the northwest. Here the storms of the Pluvial period, cutting down to the low base level of the Arabah, have carved deep gorges in the hills and hewn out narrow corridors between high perpendicular cliffs. The wadis carry some desert scrub and can be used by the Bedouin for winter grazing, but they do not seem ever to have been cultivated.

South of the Biq'at Zin (Wadi Murra) and overshadowed on the northwest by the great cliffs and scarps of the Ramon Dome is the Paran Basin, an almost oblong depression stretching some 20 miles (32 km.) northeastward until it encounters the rift. It is a desolate world indeed, partly chalky and partly seamed

---

6. Nelson Glueck, "The Negev," *BA,* XXII (1959), 82–97.

7. See the description in Beno Rothenberg, *God's Wilderness: Discoveries in Sinai* (London: Thames and Hudson, 1961), pp. 33–56.

with long limestone ridges, but everywhere dry and forbidding. In many places the surface is as fragile as meringue and breaks away under the foot of the traveler, and elsewhere there are wide stretches of flinty desert, from which very speck of sand has been swept away by the scouring wind.

This region was everywhere difficult to cross, for the SW–NE cliffs and wadis run athwart the direction that most people wanted to go, and the drought of the Paran Basin tended to deflect all the routes northward, as far north indeed as the Darb as-Sultan. This was for the greater part of history the most important route across the hills, but not, surprisingly enough, in Nabatean and Roman days. Then the main road came from Gaza and Beersheba to Oboda and from there across the high country to enter the Maktesh Ramon at its northern end, leaving it by the gap at Qasr Mahalla and then directly to the Arabah across the mouth of the Paran Basin by way of the Nahal Omer (Wadi Siq) past Horvat Qazra and Moa. One route did cross the southern section of the Paran Basin by way of Gerasa (Kuntilla) northward toward the Wadi al-'Arish and Kadesh-barnea, and another skirted it on the south, closely hugging the foot of the mountains, westward across Sinai toward Suez. This is known as Darb al-Hajj (or Darb al-Hagg in Egyptian dialect), the Pilgrim Road, used up to the modern period by Egyptian Muslims on their way to Mecca.

A more northerly route across the Sinai peninsula from Ezion-geber went over the granite mountains bordering the Gulf of Aqabah, turned southwestward up the Wadi al-Heisi, and then made its way through the rugged mountains of southern Sinai until it passed the foot of Jabal Musa and down the

Wadi Feiran to the Gulf of Suez. Jabal Musa is, of course, the mountain traditionally associated with that Mount Sinai on which the Law was given to Moses (Exod. 19:11), though it must be admitted that the tradition is a very late one, and in the valley below it stands today the venerable monastery of St. Catherine. Recent study, however, has revealed the surprising fact that although this route was in use in the distant Chalcolithic period, about 3500 B.C., it was not used again until it became important for Nabatean trade.[8] Now, therefore, it seems impossible that this identification is correct. Unfortunately, if we are not to place Mount Sinai at Jabal Musa, we have no assurance where it was and are consequently at a loss for most of the other sites mentioned in this part of the Exodus wanderings. A number of possible sites for Sinai have been suggested, both in the broad peninsula itself and east of the Gulf of Aqabah in the district known as Madyan, but none of them has yet won general approval.

And so, upon a somewhat disturbing note of uncertainty, this study must be brought to a close. We have no reason at all, of course, to doubt the event, which is securely established in biblical history, but to realize that we cannot in fact say exactly where it happened is to be reminded of how much there is still to learn. Because of the researches of a multitude of people there is now a wealth of knowledge about the Bible at our disposal. "Others have labored and we have entered into their labor." Yet not every problem has been solved, and a book of this kind can never be more than an interim report.

8. Beno Rothenberg, "An Archaeological Survey of South Sinai: First Season 1967/ 1968, Prelminary Report," *PEQ*, CII (1970), 4–9.

Glossary of Geological Terms

[Words followed by an asterisk (*) are also explained in the Glossary]

Alluvium. Material usually fertile, brought down by a river. On the geological map the symbol for alluvium has been used to include also the loess* and the deposits of the Dead Sea when it was much larger than it is now. These last are salty and infertile.

Anticline. An upfolded region. See *Folding*.

Basalt. A black, volcanic rock. It is hard and therefore not easily eroded. In the region around the Lake of Galilee and in parts of Bashan and the northeastern Trans-jordan it forms the main building stone, but it is not easy to work. Basaltic soil is often very fertile, but the main basalt areas are usually fairly thinly inhabited, because the rock is very rough and hard and soil forms slowly.

Base level. See *Erosion*.

Basin. Structurally this term may be used for an area which has been depressed by either faulting* or folding.* An area may have a basin-shaped structure, but the land in the middle may actually be higher than the surrounding land if the rock of which the edges of the basin are composed is more easily eroded.

Cambrian. The first of the periods normally distinguished by geologists and the rocks belonging to that period. Rocks before this period are called *Archaean* or *Pre-Cambrian*. See *fig. 7*.

Cenomanian. The rock deposited after the Nubian sandstone and before the Senonian chalk. It is usually a hard limestone and sometimes forms steep cliffs and gorges.

Conformably, unconformably. If there has been no interruption in the process of deposition of sediments, one stratum* is said to lie *conformably* upon the one beneath it. If the sequence has been interrupted by a period of erosion, the later rock rests *unconformably* upon the earlier one.

Cretaceous. The period during which most of the Palestinian rocks were formed. It occurred just before the mountain-building storm* began.

Crystalline. Very old rocks have usually been changed in character ("metamorphosed") as a result of having been subjected to immense heat and pressure. Such rocks are very hard and resistant to erosion. The ancient platform of Arabia is composed of crystalline rocks.

Dikes. Long lines of volcanic rock which has been thrust up through cracks in the surrounding rock.

Dolomite. (adj. **dolomitic**). A hard limestone which tends to form massive cliffs.

Dome. Any dome-shaped land form, often a broad, short anticline,* as in Gilead.

Eocene. Literally, "the dawn of the recent" period. It is a term applied to the be-

253

ginning of the Quaternary. The Eocene rocks were laid down after the Senonian. In Palestine they are usually limestones.

Erosion. The cutting away of the rocks by the action of running water, water-borne particles, etc. The eroded material is carried away by rivers and wind and ocean currents. A river tends to erode down to its *base level*, the level at which it enters a lake or the sea. Thus the upper Jordan is eroding down to the level of Lake Huleh, the middle section to the level of the Lake of Galilee, and the final section to the level of the Dead Sea. If the level of the lake rises, erosion is stopped and deposition begins; if the level of the lake is lowered, the river will begin to erode more vigorously.

Fault, faulting. A crack in the layers of rock so that one side slips down and the other side is pushed up. Faults can have a "throw" of only a few inches or sometimes, as often in Palestine, of hundreds of feet. A great many of the steep scarps in Palestine are the result of faulting. This faulting has been caused by the great pressure which broke the Arabian platform during the mountain-building storm* (see also *rift valley*).

Folding. During periods of mountain building* the great pressure causes the less resistant rocks to become contorted. In Palestine this folding is relatively gentle, but in areas of high mountains it is often very severe.

Gondwanaland. A vast land mass which in Pre-Cambrian times lay south of the sea of Tethys.*

Granite. A hard, crystalline rock. The most important kind of rock in the great Arabian platform which underlies the Palestinian area, it is exposed only in the south of the Wadi Arabah.

"Ground swell." A name sometimes given to the gentle folding of the rocks in areas distant from the main mountain building.* In the Middle East the center of the mountain-building storm was in Turkey and Iran, and so the rocks in Palestine have been only gently folded.

Kurkar. Solidified, calcareous sand dunes forming ridges along the Cis-jordan coast.

Loess. A fertile, rather powdery soil which has been formed of material brought by winds from the desert. In Palestine it is found in the Gaza district.

Maktesh (pl. **makteshim**). A Hebrew word meaning "a mortar" used for the peculiar, cigar-shaped anticlines* in the Negeb, which have been broken open and scoured out by erosion* so that the center forms a deep, cliff-enclosed basin.

Marl. Normally a soil consisting of clay and carbonate of lime, which is a valuable fertilizer. However, in Palestine the *Lisan marls* are the salt-laden deposits of the Dead Sea, which are not fertile.

Monocline. A "single fold." Normally a fold, whether an upfold or downfold, has two sides. However, when a fault* occurs, the layers of rock may be pulled downward in a single fold of this type. The sides of the Jordan Valley are often marked by tremendous monoclines where the layers of rock have been pulled down toward the valley.

Mountain building. The periods of mountain building in geological history are divided by long periods of relative quiet during which new rocks are formed. Then there comes a period of slow, but tremendous, convulsion called an "orogeny" or "mountain-building storm." In the Middle East the main mountain building occurred after the Cretaceous* and produced the high mountains of Turkey and Iran.

Mousterian. The Mousterian deposits are part of the fairly recent rocks which make up the Coast Plain of Cis-jordan. They are bright red or orange sands which today form excellent orange groves, but in the past they were forested.

Nubian. A name given to the thick layers of sandstone found extensively in Transjordan and in one or two parts of southern Cis-jordan. They were laid down under desert conditions over a very long period.

Outcrop. An exposure of a layer of rock at the surface.

Pleistocene. The "most recent" period in geological reckoning. An important feature of the Pleistocene in Palestine is the thin thread of very low hills which line the coast and hinder the drainage.

Porphyry. A very hard, dark-red rock found in the southern Arabah. It forms a line of hills at the foot of the Punon Embayment.

Rift valley. A valley formed by the collapse of part of the earth's surface between two parallel series of faults.* The Jordan Valley and Wadi Arabah are part of an immense system of rift valleys extending through the Red Sea to Lake Nyasa in East Africa. The faulting on each side of the great rift valley in Palestine is very complicated. There are also smaller rift valleys, e.g., the Valley of Jezreel.

Senonian. The period between the Cenomanian* before it and the Eocene* after it. In Cis-jordan the Senonian deposits are usually a soft, infertile, easily eroded chalk, but over much of the Trans-jordan plateau they form a rather harder chert.

Stratum (pl. **strata**). A layer of rock. Rocks are laid down in level layers which may later be disturbed by *folding* or *faulting*.*

Tethys. A name given by geologists to the ancient sea which once lay in the Mediterranean-Turkey-Iran region.

Transgression. An extension of the sea over the land. This occurs when the level of the land has been lowered. Transgressions of the sea may be very extensive and endure for very prolonged periods. During a transgression marine deposits such as limestone and chalk are laid down.

Warping. A word used to describe the humping up of the rocks over a relatively wide area. It is really an immensely broad fold* but should not be confused with folding, which is more intense, though it may also cover wide areas.

Bibliography

I. ATLASES

Aharoni, Yohanan, and Avi-Yonah, Michael, *The Macmillan Bible Atlas*. New York: Macmillan Company, 1968.

Atlas of Israel. Jerusalem: Survey of Israel, Ministry of Labour; Amsterdam: Elsevier Publishing Company, 1970.

Baly, Denis, and Tushingham, A. D., *Atlas of the Biblical World*. New York: World Publishing Company, 1971.

Grollenberg, Luc H., *Atlas of the Bible*. New York: Thomas Nelson and Sons, 1957.

———, *Shorter Atlas of the Bible*. New York: Thomas Nelson and Sons, 1961.

Kraeling, Emil G., *Rand McNally Bible Atlas*. Chicago: Rand McNally, 1956.

May, Herbert G., ed., *Oxford Bible Atlas*. New York: Oxford University Press, 1962.

The Times Atlas of the World. Comprehensive ed. Boston: Houghton Mifflin Company, 1967.

Wright, George Ernest, and Filson, F. W., eds., *The Westminster Historical Atlas to the Bible*. Rev. ed. Philadelphia: Westminster Press, 1956.

II. MAPS

Archaeological Map of the Hashemite Kingdom of the Jordan. 1:250,000. 3 sheets. Amman: Department of Lands and Surveys of the Hashemite Kingdom of the Jordan, 1950.

Bordure Orientale de la Méditerranée: Carte Lithologique. 1:500,000. 2 sheets. Paris: Délégation General au Levant de la France Combattante, Service des Travaux Publics, 1942.

Carte Agricole du Liban. 1:200,000. Prepared by Boulos F. Boulos. Beirut: Imprimerie Catholique, 1963.

Carte Géologique du Liban. 1:200,000. Prepared by Louis Dubertret. Beirut: Ministère des Travaux Publics, République du Liban, 1955.

Carte Géologique du Moyen Orient. 1:2,000,000. Prepared by Louis Dubertret. Service Géographique des F.F.L., 1942.

Carte Géologique: Liban, Syria, et Bordure des Pays Voisins. 1:1,000,000. Prepared by Louis Dubertret. Paris: Museum Nationale de l'Histoire Naturelle, 1962.

Cart Pluviométrique du Liban. 1:200,000. Prepared by J. Rey, S.J., Observatoire de Ksara, Lebanon, 1954.

The Geological Map of Israel. 1:100,000. Prepared by L. Picard. 26 sheets. Jerusalem: Ministry of Development, Geological Survey, in publication.

Geological Map of Jordan (East of the Rift Valley). 1:250,000. 3 sheets. Prepared by A. Quennell. Amman: Government of the Hashemite Kingdom of the Jordan, 1959.

The Hashemite Kingdom of the Jordan. 1:100,000. 15 sheets. In Arabic. Amman: Department of Lands and Surveys of the Hashemite Kingdom of the Jordan, 1951.

The Hashemite Kingdom of the Jordan. 1:250,000. 4 sheets. Amman: Department of Lands and Surveys of the Hashemite Kingdom of the Jordan, 1949.

Israel. 1:100,000. In Hebrew. Jerusalem: Department of Surveys, Israel, 1962.

Israel. 1:250,000. 3 sheets. Jerusalem: Department of Surveys, Israel, 1971.

Jerusalem, Model of. 1:50. No publisher or date.

Jerusalem: The Old City. 1:2500. Prepared by F. J. Salmon, Commissioner of Lands and Surveys, Palestine, 1936, 1947. Republished Jerusalem: Survey of Israel, 1967.

Levant. 1:200,000. Paris: Institut Géographique Nationale, 1949.

Liban: Carte Touristique. 1:100,000. Beirut: Direction des Affaires Géographiques, 1965.

Old Testament Palestine. 1:500,000. Jerusalem: Department of Antiquities, Government of Palestine, no date.

Palestine. 1:100,000. 16 sheets. Jerusalem: Survey of Palestine, 1944.

Roman Palestine. 1:250,000. Jerusalem: Department of Antiquities, Government of Palestine, 1940.

Sinai. 1:250,000. 3 sheets. In Hebrew. Jerusalem: Department of Surveys, Israel, 1971.

Soil Map of Israel. 1:250,000. 2 sheets. Prepared by S. Ravikovitch. Jerusalem: Hebrew University and Survey of Israel, 1969.

The World. 1:500,000. Series 1404, Sheets 426, B,C; 427, A,D: 447, A,B,C,D; 446, A,D. London: War Office and Air Ministry, 1960.

III. GENERAL WORKS OF REFERENCE

Dictionary of the Bible, ed. by James Hastings. 5 vols. New York: Charles Scribner's Sons, 1902–4. Revised 1-vol. edition, ed. by Frederick C. Grant and H. H. Rowley. New York: Charles Scribner's Sons, 1963.

Encyclopedia Judaica. 16 vols. New York: Macmillan Company, 1971.

Encyclopedic Dictionary of the Bible, ed. and trans. by Louis F. Hartman. New York: McGraw-Hill, 1963.

The Interpreter's Dictionary of the Bible, ed. by George Arthur Buttrick. 4 vols. New York: Abingdon Press, 1962.

Manson, T. W., ed., *A Companion to the Bible.* Original ed., 1939. 2d rev. ed. Edinburgh: T & T Clark, 1963.

Miller, Madeleine S., and Lane, J., *Harper's Bible Dictionary.* New York: Harper & Row, 1973.

The New Bible Dictionary, ed. by J. D. Douglas. London: Inter-Varsity Fellowship, 1962.

North, Robert, *Stratigraphia Geobiblica: Biblical Near East Archaeology and Geography.* 3d ed. Rome: Biblico, 1970.

Pictorial Biblical Encyclopedia, ed. by Gaalyahu Cornfeld. New York: Macmillan Company, 1964.

Pritchard, James B., *Ancient Near Eastern Texts Relating to the Old Testament.* 2d ed. Princeton: Princeton University Press, 1955.

———, *The Ancient Near East in Pictures Relating to the Old Testament.* Princeton: Princeton University Press, 1954. N.B.: Selections from these two volumes are collected in Pritchard, ed., *The Ancient Near East: An Anthology of Texts and Pictures.* Princeton University Press, 1965.

———, *The Ancient Near East: Supplementary Texts and Pictures Relating to the Old Testament.* Princeton University Press, 1969.

Simons, J., *The Geographical and Topographical Texts of the Old Testament.* Leiden: E. J. Brill, 1959.

Thomas, D. Winton, ed., *Documents from Old Testament Times.* New York: Thomas Nelson and Sons, 1958.

IV. SLIDES

A very important set of 1,500 aerial photographs by Dr. Richard Cleave is in process of being published by Audio-View (Mideast) Ltd., Jerusalem, and will be an invaluable aid to geographical and archaeological study. Unfortunately, the first 375 slides reached me only a few days before the manuscript had to be given to the publishers, and consequently no use could be made of them in the preparation of this book.

BASIC BIBLIOGRAPHY FOR FURTHER READING

Since detailed reference has been made to books and articles in the footnotes, the titles listed here are of the more important books of general interest for further reading, and are normally confined to books in English.

General Geographical Studies

General Middle Eastern Geography

Birot, Pierre, and Dresch, Jean, *La Méditerranée et le Moyen-Orient*; Vol. 2: *La Méditerranée Orientale et le Moyen-Orient*. Paris: Presses Universitaires de France, 1955.

Brice, William C., *South-West Asia: A Systematic Regional Geography*. London: University of London Press, 1966.

Cressey, George B., *Crossroads: Land and Life in Southwest Asia*. Philadelphia: J. B. Lippincott Company, 1960.

Fisher, W. B., *The Middle East: A Physical, Social, and Regional Geography*. 6th ed. New York: E. P. Dutton and Co., 1971.

Grant, Michael, *The Ancient Mediterranean*. London: Weidenfeld and Nicholson, 1969.

General Geographical Studies of the Palestine Area.

Abel, F. M., *Géographie de la Palestine*. 2 vols. 1933–38. Reprint, Paris: Librarie Lecoffre, 1967.

Aharoni, Y., *The Land of the Bible: A Historical Geography*. Trans. by A. F. Rainy. Philadelphia: Westminster Press 1967.

Avi-Yonah, M., *The Holy Land from the Persians to the Arab Conquest: A Historical Geography*. Grand Rapids: Baker Book House, 1966.

Baly, Denis, *Geographical Companion to the Bible*. New York: McGraw-Hill Book Company, 1963.

Dalman, Gustav, *Sacred Sites and Ways*. New York: Society for Promotion of Christian Knowledge, 1934.

De Buit, M., *Géographie de la Terre Sainte*. 2 vols. Paris: Editions du Cerf, 1958.

Dubertret, L., *Aperçu de Géographie Physique sur le Liban, l'Anti-Liban et la Damascène*. 4 vols. Beirut: Imprimerie Catholique, 1945–48.

Karmon, Yehuda, *Israel: A Regional Geography*. New York: Wiley-Interscience, 1971.

Kopp, Clemens, *The Holy Places of the Gospels*. New York: Herder and Herder, 1963.

Orni, Efraim, and Efrat, Elisha, *Geography of Israel*. 3d rev. ed. New York: American Heritage Press, 1971.

Smith, George Adam, *The Historical Geography of the Holy Land*. 25th ed., 1931. Rev. ed. with introduction by H. H. Rowley. New York: Harper & Row, 1966.

Vaumas, Étienne de, *Le Liban: Étude de Géographie Physique*. 3 vols. Paris: Firman-Didot, 1954.

General Archaeological Studies

Albright, W. F., *Archaeology and the Religion of Israel*. New York: Doubleday & Company, 1969.

———, *The Archaeology of Palestine*. Rev. ed. New York: Penguin Books, 1960.

———, *From the Stone Age to Christianity*. New York: Doubleday and Company, 1967.

Anati, Emmanuel, *Palestine Before the Hebrews*. London: Jonathan Cape, Ltd., 1963.

The Biblical Archaeologist Reader, I, ed. by George Ernest Wright and David N. Freedman (1961); II, ed. by E. F. Campbell, Jr., and David N. Freedman (1964); III, ed. by E. F. Campbell, Jr., and David N. Freedman (1970). New York: Doubleday & Company.

Burrows, Millar, *What Mean These Stones?* First issued 1941. New York: Meridian Books, 1957.

The Cambridge Ancient History. 3d ed. Vol. I, pt. 2. *Early History of the Middle East.* Cambridge: University Press, 1971.

Frank, Harry Thomas, *Bible Archaeology and Faith.* Nashville: Abingdon Press, 1971.

Frank, Harry Thomas, and Reed, William L., eds. *Translating and Understanding the Old Testament.* Nashville: Abingdon Press, 1970.

Gray, John, *Archaeology and the Old Testament World.* New York: Thomas Nelson and Sons, Ltd., 1962. Reprinted by Harper & Row, 1962.

Kenyon, Kathleen, *Archaeology in the Holy Land.* New York: Frederick A. Praeger, 1960.

Noth, Martin, *The Old Testament World.* Trans. by Victor I. Gruhn. Philadelphia: Fortress Press, 1966.

Sanders, James A., *Near Eastern Archaeology in the Twentieth Century.* Garden City, New York: Doubleday & Company, 1970.

Thomas, D. Winton, ed., *Archaeology and Old Testament Study.* New York: Oxford University Press, 1967.

Williams, Walter G., *Archaeology in Biblical Research.* Nashville: Abingdon Press, 1955.

Wright, George Ernest, *Biblical Archaeology.* 2d ed. Philadelphia: Westminster Press, 1962.

Histories of Palestine

Abel, F.-M., *Histoire de la Palestine depuis la Conquête d'Alexandre jusqu'à l'invasion Arabe*; I, *De la Conquête d'Alexandre jusqu'uà la Guerre Juive.* Paris: J. Gabalda et Cie, 1952.

Ackroyd, P. R., *Israel under Babylon and Persia (The New Clarendon Bible).* London: Oxford University Press, 1970.

Alt, Albrecht, *Essays on Old Testament History and Religion.* Trans. by R. A. Wilson. Oxford: Basil Blackwell, 1966.

Anderson, G. W., *History and Religion of Israel* (The New Clarendon Bible). London: Oxford University Press, 1966.

Bright, John, *A History of Israel.* 2d ed. Philadelphia: Westminster Press, 1972.

Cambridge Ancient History. 3d ed. Vol. I, pt. 2; Vol. II, pt. 1. Cambridge: University Press, 1971–72.

Foerster, Werner, *From the Exile to Christ: Historical Introduction to Palestinian Judaism.* Trans. by Gordon E. Harris. Philadelphia: Fortress Press, 1964.

Heaton, E. W., *The Hebrew Kingdoms (The New Clarendon Bible).* London: Oxford University Press, 1968.

Josephus, Flavius, *The Works of Flavius Josephus.* Loeb Classical Library Edition. Trans. by H. St. J. Thackeray and Ralph Marcus. New York: G. P. Putman, 1926–65.

Kaufmann, Y., *The Religion of Israel, from Its Beginnings to the Babylonian Exile.* Abridged English trans. by Moshe Greenberg. Chicago: University of Chicago Press, 1960.

Maly, Eugene H., *The World of David and Solomon.* Englewood Cliffs, N.J.: Prentice-Hall, Inc., 1966.

McKenzie, John L., *The World of the Judges.* Englewood Cliffs, N.J.: Prentice-Hall 1966.

Myers, J. M., *The World of the Restoration.* Englewood Cliffs, N.J.: Prentice-Hall, 1968.

Noth, Martin, *The History of Israel.* 2d ed. Trans. by Stanley Godman. New York: Harper Brothers, 1960.

Oesterley, W. O. E., and Robinson, Theodore H., *A History of Israel.* 2 vols. Oxford: Clarendon Press, 1932.

Perowne Stewart, *The Later Herods.* Nashville: Abingdon Press, 1959.

———, *The Life and Times of Herod the Great.* London: Hodder & Stoughton, 1957.

Pfeiffer, Robert H., *History of New Testament Times, with an Introduction to the Apocrypha.* New York: Harper & Row, 1949.

Rowley, H. H., *From Joseph to Joshua.* London: Oxford University Press, 1950.

Russell, D. S., *The Jews from Alexander to Herod (The New Clarendon Bible).* London: Oxford University Press, 1967.

Some Useful Books on Special Subjects

GEOLOGY

Blake, G. S., *The Stratigraphy of Palestine and Its Building Stones.* Jerusalem: The Crown Agent for the Colonies, 1928.

Blake, G. S., and Goldschmidt, M. G., *Geology and Water Resources of Palestine.* Jerusalem: Government Printer, 1947.

Burdon, David J., *Handbook of the Geology of Jordan.* Amman: Government of the Hashemite Kingdom of Jordan, 1959.

Ionides, M. G., *Report on the Water Resources of Transjordan and Their Development.* London: Crown Agents for Overseas Governments and Administrations, 1939.

Kirkaldy, J. F., *General Principles of Geology.* 5th ed. London: Hutchinson & Co., Ltd., 1971.

Picard, L., *Structure and Evolution of Palestine.* Jerusalem: Geological Department of the Hebrew University, 1943.

Small, R. J., *The Study of Landforms.* Cambridge: University Press, 1970.

CLIMATE

Ashbel, D., *Bio-Climatic Atlas of Israel.* Jerusalem: Meteorological Department of the Hebrew University, 1950.

————, *Regional Climatology of Israel* (Hebrew). Jerusalem: Meteorological Department of the Hebrew University, 1951.

Barry, R. G., and Chorley, R. J., *Atmosphere, Weather and Climate.* London: Methuen & Company, Ltd., 1968.

Brooks, C. E. P., *Climate Through the Ages.* 2d. rev. ed. New York. Dover Publications, 1970.

————, *The Evolution of Climate.* London: Ernest Benn Limited, 1922.

Changes of Climate: Proceedings of the Rome Symposium Organized by UNESCO and the World Meterological Organization. Arid Zone Research. Paris: UNESCO, 1964.

Lamb, H. H., *The Changing Climate.* London: Methuen & Co., Ltd., 1968.

Raikes, Robert, *Water, Weather and Prehistory.* London: John Baker, 1967.

THE NATURAL HISTORY OF PALESTINE

Alon, Azaria, *The Natural History of the Land of the Bible.* Jerusalem: The Jerusalem Publishing House, 1969.

Bodenheimer, F. S., *Animal and Man in Bible Lands.* Leiden: E. F. Brill, 1960.

————, *Animal Life in Palestine.* Jerusalem: 1935.

Bunting, Brian T., *The Geography of Soil.* 2d ed. London: Hutchinson University Library, 1960.

Cansdale, G. S., *Animals of Bible Lands.* London: The Paternoster Press, 1970.

Crowfoot, J. W., and Baldensperger, Louise, *From Cedar to Hyssop.* London: Sheldon Press, 1932.

Moldenke, H. N. and A. L., *Plants of the Bible.* Waltham, Mass.: Chronica Botanica, 1952.

Newbigin, Marion I., *Plant and Animal Geography.* London: Hutchinson University Library, 1968.

Polunin, Oleg, and Huxley, Altheny, *Flowers of the Mediterranean.* London: Chatto and Windus, 1970.

Post, G. E., and Dinsmore, J. E., *Flora of Syria, Palestine and Sinai.* Beirut: Syrian Protestant College, 1932–33.

Reifenberg, A., *The Soils of Palestine.* 2d ed. London: Thomas Murby & Company, 1947.

————, *The Struggle Between the Desert and the Sown.* Jerusalem: Publishing Department of the Jewish Agency, 1955.

Zohari, M., *Plant Life of Palestine: Israel and Jordan.* New York: Ronald Press, 1962.

CIS-JORDAN

Glueck, Nelson, *The River Jordan.* New York: McGraw-Hill, 1968.

————, *Rivers in the Desert: A History of the Negev.* New York: Farrar, Straus and Cudahy, 1959.

Jeremias, Joachim, *Jerusalem in the Time of Jesus: An Investigation into Economic and Social Conditions during the New Testament Period.* Philadelphia: Fortress Press, 1969.

Kenyon, Kathleen, *Digging Up Jericho.* London: Ernest Benn Limited, 1957.

————, *Jerusalem: Excavating Three Thousand Years of History.* London: Thames and Hudson, 1967.

Parrot, André, *Samaria: The Capital of the Kingdom of Israel.* London: S.C.M. Press, Ltd., 1958.

Pearlman, Moshe, and Yannai, Yaacov, *Historical Sites in Israel.* London: W. H. Allen, 1964.

Pritchard, James B., *Gibeon, Where the Sun Stood Still: The Discovery of a Biblical City.* Princeton: University Press, 1962.

Rothenberg, Beno, *God's Wilderness: Discoveries in Sinai.* London: Thames and Hudson, 1961.

Simons, J., *Jerusalem in the Old Testament.* Leiden: E. J. Brill, 1952.

Wright, George Ernest, *Shechem: The Biography of a Biblical City.* New York: McGraw-Hill, 1965.

Yadin, Yeigael, *Masada: Herod's Fortress and the Zealots' Last Stand.* Trans. by Moshe Pearlman. New York: Random House, 1966.

TRANS-JORDAN

Glueck, Nelson, *Deities and Dolphins: The The Story of the Nabateans.* New York: Farrar, Straus and Giroux, 1965.

————, *The Other Side of the Jordan.* Cambridge, Mass.: American Schools of Oriental Research, 1970.

Harding, G. Lankester, *The Antiquities of Jordan.* Rev. ed. London: Lutterworth Press, 1967.

Ottoson, Magnus, *Gilead: Tradition and History.* Trans. by Jean Gray. Lund, Sweden: CWK Gleerup, 1969.

Van Zyl., A. H., *The Moabites.* Leiden: E. J. Brill, 1960.

"THE PEOPLE OF THE LAND"

Baramki, Dimitri, *Phoenicia and the Phoenicians.* Beirut: Khayats, 1961.

Bishop, Eric F. F., *Jesus of Palestine.* London: Lutterworth Press, 1955.

Bouquet, A. C., *Everyday Life in New Testament Times.* New York: Charles Scribner's Sons, 1954.

Brown, J. P., *The Lebanon and Phoenicia: Ancient Texts Illustrating Their Physical Geography and Native Industries.* Vol. 1: *The Physical Setting and the Forest.* Beirut: The American University of Beirut, 1969.

De Vaux, Roland, *Ancient Israel.* Vol. I: *Social Institutions*; Vol. II: *Religious Institutions.* New York: McGraw-Hill, 1961.

Dothan, T., *The Philistines and Their Material Culture.* Hebrew with English summary. Jerusalem, 1967.

Gray, John, *The Canaanites.* London: Thames and Hudson, 1964.

Harden, Donald, *The Phoenicians.* London: Thames and Hudson, 1962.

Heaton, Eric W., *Everyday Life in Old Testament Times.* New York: Charles Scribner's Sons, 1956.

Moscati, Sabatino, *The World of the Phoenicians.* London: Weidenfeld & Nicholson, 1968.

Index of Biblical References

OLD TESTAMENT

GENESIS

3:17–19	90
4:1–5	87
12:6	171
12:8	176
13:3	176
13:10–12	117
14:5	215
14:14	193
16:7	98
19:24, 28	25
19:25–29	117
19:29	204
25:29–34	84
27:28	45
27:28, 37	84
28:10–17	176
31:40	90
31:49	224
32:2	223
32:3	236
32:30	223
33:13	88
35:4	171
36:8	236
36:24	26
36:31–39	234
36:33	237n
37:17	149
37:25	222
37:33	107
43:11	87
46:32	87
46:34	89
49:10	177
49:15	151
49:17	193
49:20	123
49:22	164

EXODUS

3:8	84
10:9	89
12:29–30	52n
12:38	109
13:5	84
13:17	97, 131
13:21–22	25
14:11–22	109
15:3	75
15:22	103
16:3	109
19:11	251
19:18	25
20:4–5	109
23:14–16	84
23:15	85
29:22	88
30:34	247
33:3	84
34:18	85
34:18–24	85

LEVITICUS

20:24	84
23:9	85
23:39–43	85

NUMBERS

13:26	250
13:19–20	118
14:2	109
14:8	84
14:45	183
16:13–14	84
16:30–31	24
20:14–22	250

21:4–9	235
21:4–10	208
21:6	108
21:12	12
21:13	211
21:13, 18	103
21:20	117
21:21–25	228
21:24	221n, 228
21:25	232
21:26	211
21:32	221n
21:33	215
21:35	215–216
22:1	31, 202
23:14	117
27:12	117, 221
28:26	85
31:1–12	244
31:12	31
32	228
32:1	227
32:1, 3, 35	221n
32:3	221, 232–3
32:8	250
32:35	223
32:37	232
32:41	214
33:35	209
33:42–43	208, 235
33:43	206
33:47–48	117, 221
33:48	31
33:49	202
34:4	35, 250
34:5	250
34:7–9	11
34:8	98
34:11	98

DEUTERONOMY

1:1	237
1:2	250
1:4	215
1:7	140
1:7–8	115
1:19	102, 110
1:44	183
2:1	236
2:13	12
2:23	138
2:37	228
3:1, 10	215
3:4	215
3:5	215
3:9	193
3:10	219
3:12	221
3:14	214
3:16	211
3:27	3, 117
3:29	202
4:3	202
4:43	103, 223, 224
4:48	193
4:49	117
5:8	109
6:3	84
7:7	14
7:13	84
7:15	137
8:7	22
8:8	84, 87
8:9	21, 98
8:15	102, 108
11:9	84
11:10–12	69
11:14	51, 84
12:17	84
14:23	84
16:1–17	85
16:9	85
17:16	69
18:4	84
20:19–20	116
26:5	109
26:9	84
27:3	84
27:11–13	22, 171
28:51	84
28:60	137
32:10	103, 110
32:49	117, 221
33:15	174
33:19	151
33:22	193
33:24	123
33:28	45, 84

34:1	117
34:3	117

JOSHUA

2:1	202
3:1	202
3:16	167, 199
5:6	84
7:26	185
9:1	140
9:10	215–216
9:46–49	171
10:3ff.	139
10:10–15	134
10:11	50
10:12	22
10:38, 39	143
10:40	140
11:1	123, 162
11:2	26, 140
11:2, 16	140, 141
11:5	156
11:7–8	152
11:10	96, 196
11:17	98, 192
11:21	143
12:2, 5	219
12:4	215
12:5	219
12:7	98
12:8	140
12:13	143
12:18	133
12:20	123, 162
12:23	130
12:25	221n
13	228
13:3	138
13:5	98
13:9	31
13:11	219
13:12, 31	215
13:20	202
13:25	221, 227, 228
13:26	198, 224
13:30	214
13:31	221
15	181n
15:3	35, 250
15:4	250
15:11	138
15:13–19	93
15:15, 49	143
15:21	184
15:21–32	181
15:21, 33, 48, 61	181
15:31	143
15:33	140

15:34	142
15:36	134
15:39	142
15:41	134
15:42	142
15:43	142
15:44	142
16:4—17:13	165
16:7	201
16:8	128
16:9	117, 166
16:61	185
17:8	165
17:9	128
17:11	117, 121, 169
18:7	210
18:12	178
18:15, 23	175
18:21	201
19:1–9	181
19:5	143
19:6	247
19:12–13	162
19:14–27	125
19:15	162
19:18	162
19:24–31	121
19:26	121
19:28	121
19:35	198
19:36	125
19:40–48	135
19:42	134
20:7	117
20:8	223, 224
21:15	143
21:32	117
21:38	223, 224
21:39	221n
22	200, 228
24	169
24:4	236
24:26	171
24:32	171

JUDGES

1:9	140
1:11	143
1:11–15	93
1:16	184
1:27	98
1:31	127
1:31–32	123
1:35	134
1:36	35
3:3	98
3:13	228
4:2–13	123

JUDGES (*cont'd*)
4:5	*181*
4:6	*149*
4:16	*125*
5:6	*96*
5:16	*229*
5:17	*121, 123*
5:19	*151*
5:20, 4–5	*76*
5:20–21	*125*
5:21	*13*
6:1–6	*244*
6:3–4	*147*
6:5	*89, 227n*
6:35	*123*
6:38	*45*
7:1–25	*244*
7:12	*147*
7:23	*123*
8:4–17	*200*
8:7, 16	*105*
8:8	*224*
8:8–9, 17	*223*
8:11	*223*
9:4, 46	*171*
9:21	*161*
9:37	*3, 171*
9:50–57	*170*
10:5	*214n*
10:9	*228*
10:17ff.	*227*
10:17–18	*224*
11:4ff.	*221*
11:12–28	*211*
11:18	*12*
11:33	*227*
12:1–6	*200*
13:25	*141, 142*
14:1, 5	*141*
14:5	*107*
15:5	*86, 137*
18:7	*193*
18:27	*193*
18:30	*194*
20:1ff.	*181*
20:24–28	*175*
21:8ff.	*198*
21:8–12	*200*
21:19	*175*
22:10–34	*199*

1 SAMUEL
1:1	*174*
1:3	*175*
2:12	*181*
4:1	*133*
5—6	*137*
5:10	*139*

5:11	*175*
6:7–16	*100*
6:10–16	*141*
6:17	*138*
6:21	*106*
7:2	*142*
7:5ff.	*181*
7:14	*139*
7:16	*176*
7:17	*181*
8:2	*183*
9:12	*181*
10:1ff.	*179*
10:3	*181*
10:17	*181*
11:1	*228*
11:1ff.	*221*
11:1–11	*198*
11:8	*170*
11:12–15	*202n*
12:16–18	*75*
13:7	*229n*
13:19–20	*132*
14	*138*
14:1ff.	*179*
14:2	*87*
14:3	*175*
14:25–27	*84*
14:31	*22, 134*
15:34	*179*
17:1–54	*142*
17:28	*106*
17:34	*108*
17:52	*139*
22:1	*142*
22:2	*109*
22:6	*179*
22:11	*175*
23:1–5	*142*
23:3	*117*
23:15, 24	*103*
26:19	*87*
26:20	*184*
27:2	*139*
27:6	*143*
28:3–25	*149*
29:1	*133, 147*
30:1ff.	*143*
30:9, 10, 21	*247*
30:14	*138, 247*
30:26	*143*
31	*138*
31:8–13	*198*
31:12	*148*

2 SAMUEL
1:1	*143*
1:20	*139*

1:21	*45*
2:8	*223*
2:9	*123n*
2:12–17	*179*
2:24	*106*
2:29	*106*
3:26–27	*179*
5:11	*106*
5:17–25	*138*
5:25	*135*
6:2	*142*
8:1	*138*
9:4	*198*
10:2	*228*
10:6	*228*
11:16–17	*12*
11:24	*228*
12:27	*12, 226*
12:31	*228*
13:23	*174, 175*
15:18–22	*139*
15:23	*103*
17:21–22	*223*
17:27	*228*
18:2, 5	*139*
19:9	*138*
20:14	*193*
20:18	*193*
22	*76*
23:20	*50, 183*
24:5	*221n, 229n*
24:5–7	*121n*
24:18	*187*

1 KINGS
2:26–46	*139*
3:4	*181*
4:9	*134*
4:10	*128, 129, 172*
4:11	*98*
4:11, 16	*123*
4:13	*214n, 215, 223*
4:23	*108*
5	*106*
6:24–29	*90*
6:36	*209*
7:2	*105, 106*
7:45–46	*199*
7:46	*117*
8:65	*98*
9:10–14	*123*
9:11	*117*
9:15	*135, 150, 196*
9:17	*22, 134, 182*
9:18	*207*
9:26	*209*
9:27–28	*106*
10:1–5	*247*

1 KINGS (cont'd)
10:11   209
10:17, 21   105, 106
10:22   209
10:27   81, 106, 140, 141
10:28–29   89
11:26   174
11:26–40   169n
12:1ff.   169
12:21–34   182
12:25   223
12:26–33   176
12:28–29   89
12:29   194
13:24   108
14:1ff.   175
14:17   170
15:16–22   179
15:17   179
15:20   152, 192, 193
15:27   131, 169
15:33   170
16:8–23   170
16:15, 17   131
16:17   169
16:18   170
16:34   201
17:1   45, 70n
17:3   198
18:1   74
18:17–18   109
18:17–46   173
18:41   53
18:44–45   49
19:11   25
19:15   103
19:16   167
20:23   86
20:27   216
22:3   216
22:4ff.   214, 223
22:17   89
22:39   170
22:47   209
22:48   209, 239

2 KINGS
1:2   139
2:1, 11   64
2:4–6   201
2:16   108
3:4   229n
3:4ff.   232
3:4–5   229
3:4–27   63
3:25   116
3:27   231

5:12   11, 200
6:13   149
8:1–6   137
8:28   214
9:1ff.   169, 214, 223
9:27   98, 149, 150
10:11   148
10:29   194
10:33   229n
14:7   237
14:11   100, 141
14:22   209
14:23–24   142
14:25   11, 98, 191
15:14   170
15:29   117, 152, 192, 193
16:6   209
17:24–26   94
17:24–41   172
18:14   142
18:32   84
19:8, 35–37   137
22:1   142
22:8   85
23:8   177
23:21   85
23:22   85
23:29–30   150
23:33   98
25:4–5   185, 186
25:6, 21   98

1 CHRONICLES
2:23   214
5:11   219
5:16   128
6:58   143
6:76   117
6:80   224
6:81   221n
8:12   134
11:11–21   138
11:22   50, 183
13:5   106
13:6   142
14:16   135
16:37–42   181
20:4   135
21:29   181
26:31   221n
27:28   81, 140
27:29   128

2 CHRONICLES
1:15   106, 140, 141
2   106

4:17   117
8:17–18   106
9:16, 20   105, 106
9:27   140, 141
11:5–12   182
11:8   142
11:9   142
11:10   134
13:8–9   176
13:19   179
14:9–10   142
16:4   152
18:2ff.   214
20:1   228
20:1–30   206
20:16   100, 185
25:21   141
25:27   142
26:6   139
26:10   140
27:5   228
28:18   134, 140
30   85n
30:10   123
31:5   84
32:28   84
34:6   152
35:20–25   150

EZRA
2:33   134
10:9, 13   48

NEHEMIAH
2:10, 19   224n
4:3, 7   224n
5:11   84
6:1ff.   224n
6:2   134
7:37   134
10:39   84
11:35   131
13:4ff.   224n
13:5, 12   84

JOB
1:13–17   88
1:13–19   90, 246, 247
1:16, 19   64
6:15–20   50
6:18–19   246–247
12:24   101
21:18   46
24:4, 7   49
24:4–12   90
24:8   54
24:19   50

JOB (*cont'd*)
28:3–4   15
29:19   45
36:29   70
37:6–8   76
37:9   64
37:13   76
37:16–17   53
37:21   49
38:1   64
38:22–23   76
38:25–26   102
38:28–29   43
38:34   70
38:37–38   70
39:6   108
39:9–18   108
40:6   64

PSALMS

1:4   46
3:3, 10   76
4:7   84
18:7   25
19:9–13   76
18:16   84
22:12   216
23   89, 108
29:5   76
29:6   25
32:4   43
35:5   46
44:1–2, 9   76
48:7   52
50:3   76
60   233
65:5   4
65:5–8   198n
65:8   3
65:9–13   87
65:12–13   50
68:14   217
68:15   193, 217
68:22   217
72:16   87
74:1   89
74:12   3
74:12–17   86
78:19–20   111
78:40   103
78:47   71, 90
79:13   89
80:1   89
80:11   164
83:6   244
83:13   64
84:5   96
89:1–18   89

89:12   39
93:3–4   209
95   86
102:6–7   108
103:16   53
104   69
104:5–8   28
104:15   82
104:32   25
106:14   77, 103
107:4   6
107:4–6   241
107:7–8   91
107:40   101
108:10   237
128:2   87
128:3–4   87
132:6   106, 142
135:7   76
135:11   215–216
136:20   215–216
137:7   239
139:15   15
144:5   25
147:14   86
147:16–17   71

PROVERBS

1:27   64
10:5   86
10:25   64
14:4   89
22:13   108
22:17—24:22   70
25:14   49
28:3   76
30:29–30   108
31:13   86
31:21   71

ECCLESIASTES

5:9   101
12:5   87

SONG OF SOLOMON

1:5   88
2:1   128
2:8–9, 17   108
2:11   44, 80
2:15   85
3:6   104
4:3, 13   87
4:5   108
4:8   193
6:5   88
6:7, 11   87
7:3   108

8:2   87
8:14   108

ISAIAH

1:7–8   94
1:8   87
2:2–3   3
2:6   139
2:13   219
5:1–7   87, 183
7:2   190
7:15   84n
7:21–22   84n
7:23   116
7:23–25   106
7—8   84n
8:21–22   108
9:1   96, 117, 152
9:3   151
9:4   244
9:10   25, 81
9:12   141
9:18   106
10:9–10   188
10:17–18   106
10:23–24   188
10:26   244
11:14   141
15:4   229, 232
15:5   98
15:6   202
15:7   233
16:1   237
16:2–4   233
16:6   13, 29, 233
16:8–9   229, 232
17:13   64
18:4   45
20:1   134
21:1   64, 102
21:5   190
21:6   190
21:7   190
21:11–15   102
21:13   105
21:13–15   108
22:8   106
25:5   58
25:10–11   233
27:2   87
27:8   53
27:9   22
28:1   144, 151
28:2   50, 71
28:15   190
28:18   7
28:22   144
28:27   87

ISAIAH (*cont'd*)
29:1   185
29:17   106
30:6   71, 97, 108, 110
30:10–11   190
31:4   107
32:15   106
33:7–8   96
33:9   128, 217
34:5–17   239
34:6   237n
34:13–14   102
35:2   120, 128
36:17   84
37:12–13   188
37:24   105
40   244
40:6–8   53
40:11   89
40:24   64
41:16   64
43:19, 20   103
43:14, 23   105
43:23–24   247
57:20   6
60:4, 6–7   247
63:1   237n
62:10   96
65:10   128

JEREMIAH

1:11–12   87
2:2   110
2:21   87
2:23   88
4:6   190
4:11   52
4:20   90
5:24   51
6:20   247
7:12   176
8:22   221
11:5   84
11:13   179
11:16   87
12:5   200
13:1–11   179
13:17   89
14:2–6   90
14:3   76
14:4   49
14:13   190
17:26   140
21:14   106
22:6   221
22:20   117, 221
23:1   89
23:19   64

24:2   87
25:20   139
25:32   64
25:36   89
30:23   64
31:10   89
31:21   96
32:22   84
32:44   140
33:13   140
34:7   142
36:22   58
39:5–6   98
40:7–12   181
40:11   233
41:4   172
46:11   221
46:18   39
47:1–12   186
47:4   138
48:2ff.   229
48:5   98, 231
48:18–20   231
48:24   237n
48:29   233
49:1   229
49:3   229
49:7, 16   13
49:7–22   239
49:13, 22   237n
49:19   108, 200
50:17   108
50:19   89, 217
50:44   200
52:9, 10, 26, 27   98

LAMENTATIONS

1:4   64, 96
2:12   84

EZEKIEL

1:4   64
3:17   190
13:13–14   71
17:10   53
19:10–14   87
20:6, 15   84
20:46   105
25:3–5   227
25:6   228
25:8   236
25:13   239
25:16   138
27:5–6   219
27:8, 11   98
27:17   221
27:26   52

28:2–3   13
31:2ff.   106
33:7   190
34:1–31   89
34:25   101, 106
35   239
39:18   216
47:15–17   11
47:18   229
48:6, 27   229

DANIEL

1:8   84

HOSEA

1:5   148
2:5, 8, 22   84
2:12   106
2:14–15   110
2:22   87
3:4   110
6:3   51
6:4   46
8:9   108
9:10   87, 110, 202
10:1   87
12:1   53
13:3   46
13:5–8   89
13:7–8   107
13:15   53
14:5   45

JOEL

1:2—2:10   90
1:10   84
1:12   87
1:20   103
2:17–19   84
2:22   103
2:23   51

AMOS

1:1   25, 229n
1:3   221
1:8   139
1:11—2:1   226
1:12   237n
1:13   228
2:1   233
3:15   170
4   74
4:1   216
4:7   49, 51, 72
4:10   137
5:5   183

AMOS (*cont'd*)
5:11   90
5:19   107
5:25   110
6:2   10, 139
6:4   170
6:13   198
7:1   90
7:4   106
7:13   176
7:14   87, 89, 141
7:14–15   229n
8:14   194
9:7   138

OBADIAH

3   236
19   140

JONAH

4:8   53

MICAH

1:10   139
1:11   143

1:15   142
4:1–2   3
4:4   87
5:7   45
6:5   202
6:15   90
7:1   87
7:14   217

NAHUM

1:4   217
3:12   87

HABAKKUK

1:8   89
2:1   190
3:3, 10   76
3:7   64

ZEPHANIAH

1:11   187
2:4   139
2:5   138
2:9   233
3:3   107

HAGGAI

1:6, 9   90
1:10   45
1:11   84
2:17   71, 90
2:19   87

ZECHARIAH

3:10   87
7:7   140
8:12   45
9:5   139
9:17   84
10:3   89
10:10   221
11:1–2   217
11:2   105
11:3   108, 200
13:7   89
14:5   25

MALACHI

1:2–4   239

THE APOCRYPHA

1 ESDRAS

5:54–55   106

2 ESDRAS

3:19   76

WISDOM OF SOLOMON

10:7   25

ECCLESIASTICUS

12:5   87
39:26   84

1 MACCABEES

3:13–24   134
3:28—4:25   134
3:40   134n
4:15   143

5:2   160
5:3   35
5:24–52   216, 223
5:40   12
5:66   143
10:89   139
13:22   50

2 MACCABEES

12:35, 38   143

NEW TESTAMENT

MATTHEW

2:1–12   240
3:4   84
3:7   110
3:12   46
4:1   102
4:1–11   111
4:23   152
4:25   198
6:13   111

7:10   110
7:27   48
8:20   110
9:36   89
10:6   89
10:16   110
11:21   196
12:11   89
13:45   163, 240
15:24   89

15:33   111
16:3   49
21:28–31   86
21:33–41   87
23:23   87
23:24   89n
23:33   110
24:20   58
25:14   163
25:32   89

MATTHEW (*cont'd*)
27:51   25

MARK

1:6   84
1:12   111
1:12–13   102, 111
4:2–20   87
4:26–29   87
4:28   85
5:1–20   198
5:20   198, 224
6:34   89
6:35–36, 39   111
7:31   198
7:31–37   198
7:31—8:10   224
8:1–10   111
8:29   194
8:31   195
10:25   89n
14:27   89
15:38   25

LUKE

2:8   106
3:1   217
3:7   110
3:17   46
4:1–13   102, 111
4:5   185
4:29   145
7:5   197
7:11   163
7:11–17   149
9:51–56   172
9:58   110
10:19   110

10:29–37   186
11:11–12   110
12:24   87
12:32   89
12:55   53
13:32   110
15:3–7   89
15:13   163
19:28   186
19:41   190
24:13   134n

JOHN

1:28   202
1:44   197
2:1   163
4:4   172
4:5   170
4:12   171
4:20   171
6:35   111
7:37   86
10:1–18   89
10:12   110
11:54   175
12:24   87
15:1   87
18:18   58
19:13   187

ACTS

8:1–25   172
8:4   171
15:3   172
21:27–36   187
23:31   133
27:4   44
27:9   44

1 CORINTHIANS

11:26   197
15:20–33   85
15:36–38   87

2 CORINTHIANS

11:32   240

GALATIANS

1:17   102

2 TIMOTHY

14:17   110

HEBREWS

11:33   110
11:37–38   102

JAMES

1:11   53

1 PETER

2:25   89
5:8   110

JUDE

12   49

REVELATION

4:7   110
5:5   110
9:8, 17   110
10:3   110
13:2   110
16:15   151

Index of Names and Subjects

NOTE: *Figures in italics refer to maps and diagrams. Place names beginning with the Arabic article "al-" or its equivalent are listed under the first letter of the name, e.g., al-Azraq, ar-Rafeh, ash-Shaghur. Names beginning with Jabal, Har, Khirbet, Nahal and Wadi are listed as Tubaiq, Jabal and Fahil, Kh. etc., but names beginning with 'Ain, Horvat, Tel (Hebrew) or Tell (Arabic) are listed under the first word, e.g., 'Ain Qudeis, Horvat Qazra.*

Abana   11, 14
Abarim   117, 221, 224, *41, 69, 70*
'Abbad, Kh.   142
Abda   21, 99, 249
Abdon   124, 155, *44*
'Abdullah, Wadi   149, 151
Abel-beth-maacah   98, 193, *62*
Abel-keramim   227
Abel-meholah   167, *58, 63*
Abel-shittim   202, *64*
Abijah, King   179
Abila   214, 225, *68*
'Abillin   *44*
'Abillin, Wadi   124, *44, 55*
Abimelech   170, 171
Abner   106, 179, 181
Abraham   116, 193, 200
Absalom   223
Abu Mukheila   *73*
Abu-Nar, Wadi   149, 168
Acchabare   157, *54*
Acco   40, 50, 98, 99, 100, 124, 152, 153, 157, 161, *11, 16, 39, 40, 44, 50, 53*
Acco, Bay of   8, 40, 124, 144, 146
Acco-Beth-shan   Corridor   144ff., 152, 157, 164
Achan   185
Achor, valley of   185
Achshaph   123, *44*
Achzib   124, *44*
Acre   124, *11*
Adam   167, 199, *58, 63*
'Adathir, Jabal   155n
Adir, Har   155n
Adithaim   134
Adoraim   177, 182, *61*
Adullam   142, 143, 182, *49, 61*
Adummim   178, 185, 186, *60, 61*
Aelia Capitolina   187, 188

Affuleh   55
Africa   23
Agriculture   11, 12, 22, 79, 82, 89, 93, 156, 157, 168, 183, 184, 196, 202, 206, 216, 217, 228, 233, 237, 240, 247, 248, 249
Ahab, King   97, 109, 170, 194, 196, 209, 228, 229
Aharoni, Yohanan   87n, 93n, 94n, 100n, 123n, 135n, 138n, 139, 142n, 150n, 181n, 183n, 184n, 249n
Ahaz, King   134
Ahaziah, King   149, 150, 209
Ai   *60*
Aiath   188, *60*
Aijalon   36, 99, 134, 142, *47*
Aijalon, valley of   22, 50, 134, 141, 166, 174, 182, 190, *16, 40*
'Ain   *65*
'Ain al-'Arus   207
'Ain ad-Dafiyah   24
'Ain Feshka   203, *64*
'Ain Gharandal   209, *65*
'Ain Ghudyan   209, *65*
'Ain Harod   145
'Ain Hosb   206
'Ain Khanazir   206, *65*
'Ain al-Qattar   *73*
'Ain al-Qudeirat   250
'Ain Qudeis   250
'Ain Shellalah   245
'Ain at-Taiyebah   208
'Ain Tamar   207, *65*
'Ain Weiba   206
Ajlun   72, 91, 199, 224, *69*
Akbara   155, 157
Aksaray   237
al-'Al   233n
Alalakh   *39*

271

Albian limestone   174
Albian series   19
Alema   216, *68*
Aleppo   96, *39*
Aleppo pine   80, 82
Aleppo-Euphrates Depression   8, *3*
Alexander   170, 185
Alexandrium   199, *58, 63*
Allenby, General   151
Allonim hills   162
Alluvial fans   27, 206, 208, 245
Alluvial Plain   196
Alluvial soils   78, 79, 168
Alluvium   26, 34, 39, 78, 79, 81, 124, 130,
    134, 141, 146, 162, 168
'Alma   155, 216, *54*
Almond   87, 236
Alon, Azariah   82n
Alt, Albrecht   94n
Amad, Wadi   22
'Amal, Jabal   155, 156, *54*
Amalekites   143, 147, 183
Amarna letters   94, 142, 198
Amathus   198
Amaziah, King   100, 141, 142, 237
Amiran, Ruth   138n, 184n, 187n
Amman   29, 31, 61, 72, 103, 219, 221,
    225n, 227, 242, *11, 12, 69, 72*
Ammon   185, 212, 213, 226ff., *42, 69*
Ammon, basin of   226ff., *69*
Ammonites   198, 211, 221, 224, 228
'Ammud, Nahal   41, 155
Amorites   211, 212, 228
Amos   110
'Amr ad-Daraj, Jabal   224
Anah   26
Ananiah   *60*
Anathoth   179, 188, *60*
Anati, Emmanuel   206
Anatolia   5, 9, 16
Anatolian mountains   17
Anderson, Bernhard H.   171n
Andrew   197
Anti-Lebanon mountains   7, 11, 29, 192
Antiochus III   127
Antiochus VII   127
Antipatris   133, 174, *47*
Antonia fortress   187
Aphek (i) i.e., Ras al-'Ain   13, 97, 98,
    130, 133, 134, *40, 47*
Aphek (ii), in Asher   124, *44*
Aphek (iii), in Trans-jordan   216, *68*
Apollonia   130
Aqabah   209, *13*
Aqabah Basin   26
Aqabah, Gulf of   13, 24, 251
Ar   *70*
'Ara, wadi   150
'Arab, River   198, *63*
Arabah Rift   12, 35, 101, 191
Arabah, Wadi   13, 19, 27, 30, 34, 35, 42,
    61, 62, 72, 73, 98, 99, 117, 120, 128,
    206–209, 236, 239, 241, 247, 251, *13,
    14, 41, 71, 74*
Arabia   17, 18, 19, 23, 25, 97, 105, 213,
    237, 239, 244

Arabia, desert of   80, 102
Arabo-Nubid mountains   17
Arad, biblical   36n, 100, 184, 185, 247,
    40, 61
Arad, modern town of   36
al-'Araj   197
Ararat, Mount   5
Araunah   187
Arbela   160, *56, 63*
Archelais   200, *64*
Arculf, Bishop   3
Ardh al-Hima   160, 162, *56*
Ardh as-Suwan   104, 243, 244, *72*
Aretas IV, King   240
Argob   117, 215
al-'Arish, Wadi   250, 251, *74*
Aristobulus   157
Ark, the   100, 137, 141, 142, 175, 176,
    181
Armageddon   151
Armenian mountain knot   5
Arnon, Canyon and River   12, 14, 24, 29,
    31, 103, 205, 211, 229, 230, 231, 232,
    233, *5, 12, 64, 66, 67, 70*
Aroer (i) in the Negeb   *61*
Aroer (ii) in Trans-jordan   230, 231, 232,
    70
Arpad   188
Arraba   172
Arsuf   130, *46*
Arubboth   172
Aruma   165, *58, 59*
Arvad   98, *39*
Asa, King   142, 179
Ascent of Blood   185
Ascent of Gur   98, 149
Ascent of Horonaim   *see* Horonaim
Ascent of the Scorpions   35, 206
Ashbel, D.   44n
Ashdod   28, 97, 133, 137, 138, *40, 48*
Ashdod-yam   138
Asher, coasts of   121ff.
Asher, regional name   117, 123, 144, *16,
    41, 44, 45, 55*
Asher, tribe of   *42*
Ashkelon   28, 36, 42, 97, 137, 138, *40,
    48*
Ashkelon trough   28
Ashnah   142, *49*
Ashteroth   216, *68*
al-'Ashu'shir   206, *65*
Asira ash-Shamaliyah   168
'Askar   170
Ass, asses   89, 108
Assyria   7, 9, 144, 188, 192
Assyrians   127, 142, 170, 172, 176, 188,
    196
al-'Ata'atah, Jabal   235, *71*
Ataroth(i) in Ephraim   *58*
Ataroth (ii) in Trans-jordan   231, 232,
    233, *70*
al-Athelah, Kh.   202n
Athlit   126, *45*
'Attaruz, Kh.   233n
Auja al-Hafir   62
Auja at-Tahta   201

Autumn transitional season   43
Avdat   99, 249
Avigad, N.   130n, 184n, 187n
Avi-Yonah, Michael   94n, 147n, 187n
Ayyalon, Nahal   131, 134
Azekah   142, 182, *49*, *61*
al-Azraq   30, 31, 91, 243, 244, *12*, *72*
'Azziyeh, village of   155
'Azziyeh, Wadi   155

Baalath   *47*
Baalbek   11, 14, 98, 191
Baal-Berith   171
Baalgad   98, 192, *62*
Baal-hazor   174, *59*
Baal-meon   233n
Baal-peor   202
Baasha, King   169, 179
Bab adh-Dhra'   205, 231, *64*
Babylon   9, 196
Babylonians   127, 142, 150, 170, 186
Badlands   78, 199, 204, 206
Baghdad   70
Bahairat Hadhawdha   *see*   Hadhawdha
    Lake
Balkha   *73*
Balm   221, 222
Balsam   206
Baly, Denis   87n, 169n
Bananas   59
Banias   193
Banyasi, River   193, *62*
Baqa'a (i), in Gilead   31, 82, 222, 227,
    12, 69
Baqa'a (ii) in Lebanon   11, 14, 192
Bar Kochba   157, 185
Barada, Wadi   14
Bar-Adon, P.   184n, 204n
Barak   125, 149
Bar'am   153, 157, *53*, *54*
Bareighit, River   192, *62*
Barley   81, 82, 84, 85, 86, 115, 137, 210,
    231
Bartlett, J. R.   235n
Basalt   8, 13, 24, 25, 26, 31, 34, 40, 91, 96,
    98, 104, 105, 155, 160, 161, 195, 196,
    213, 214, 215, 217, 230, 243, 244, 246
Basaltic soil   79, 213
Bashan   94, 117, 124, 197, 213, 223, *11,
    41*
Bashan, mountain of   156, 213, 216–219
Bashan, plateau of   24, 31, 79, 213ff.,
    216, 223, 224–225, *67*
Batanea   213, 215–216, *68*
Batneh, Kh.   224
Bayir   63, 242, 244, *72*
Bears   11, 107, 108
Bedouin   64, 71, 75, 88, 104, 147, 184,
    224, 231, 244, 248
Bedouin raids   97, 101, 244
Beehive houses   9, 10
Beer   160
Beeroth   *60*
Beersheba   6, 26, 35, 61, 62, 72, 73, 74,
    78, 91, 93, 98, 177, 181, 183, 209, 247,
    251, *14, 39, 40, 42, 61, 74*

Beersheba Basin   181
Beersheba depression   35, 80, 183
Beersheba Gap   24
Beersheba Wadi   247
Beersheba-Zered Depression   8, 29, *3*
Beidha   20, 74, 239, *71*
Beirut   30, 98, *40*
Beisan   225n
Beit Dajan   166, *58*
Beit Lid   167, *58*
Beit Natif   142
Beit Nesib, Kh.   142
Bell, Gertrude   70, 146
Belvoir, castle of   160, *56*
Benaiah   50, 183
Benhadad, King   179, 192
Benhesed   128
Benjamin, Saddle of   36, 94, 99, 138, 176,
    177, *16*
Benjamin, tribe of   87, 178, 182, 201, *42*
Bennett, Crystal-M   236n, 237n
Benoit, P.   187n
Beon   232, 233n, *70*
Besor, Brook   247, *74*
Besor, Nahal   247, 183
Beten   *44*
Bethany beyond Jordan   202
Beth-arbel   215, *68*
Beth-baal-meon   233n
Beth-dagon   134, *47, 48*
Bethel   89, 94, 106, 133, 134, 169, 170,
    171, 174, 175, 176, 178, 179, 180, *40,
    58, 59*
Beth-emek   124, *44*
Beth-ezel   143, *49*
Beth Guvrin   142
Beth-haccerem   *60*
Beth-haggan   149
Beth-horon, Ascent of   22, 99
Beth-horon, Lower   134, 166, 178, 182,
    58, 60, 61
Beth-horon, Upper   134, 174, *60*
Beth-jeshimon   99
Beth Kerem Basin   *see*   Biq'at Beth
    Kerem
Bethlehem   20, 36, 98, 103, 106, 182, 183,
    61
Beth-meon   233n
Bethpeor   202, *64*
Bethsaida   197, *63*
Beth-shan   12, 39, 42, 46, 59, 79, 91, 97,
    98, 99, 138, 145, 147, 148, 164, 225n,
    39, 40, 50, 58, 63
Beth-she'arim   157, 162, *55*
Beth-shemesh   100, 141, 142, 166, *40,
    49, 61*
Beth-zur   182, *61*
Betonim   224, *69*
Bezek   170, *58*
Bezer   103, 232, *70*
Bihn, H. G.   127n
Bilad al-Hawa   160
Bint Jebail   153, 157, *53, 54*
Biq'at Beth Kerem   153, 161
Biq'at Beth Netofa (Sahl al-Battauf)   40,
    161

Biq'at Zin   35, 99, 206, 250, *14, 40*
Bir Asluj   62
Bir ad-Dahr, Jabal   192, *62*
Bir Madhkur   208
Bira, Wadi   160, *56*
Biran, A.   193n, 194n
Bitumen   205, 206
Black Sea   4
Blad al-makhzan   101
Blad as-Sibā'   101
Blake, G. D.   247n
Blake, G. S.   20n
Booths, living in   85
Boraas, Roger S.   227n
Bosor   216, *68*
Bosora   216
Bosra eski-Sham   216
Bozez   179
Bozkath   142, *49*
Bozrah (i), in Bashan   216n, *68*
Bozrah (ii), in Edom   91, 99, 237, *40, 65, 71*
Bozrah (iii), in Moab   232, 237n
Bridge of Jacob's daughters   96, 195, 216, *62*
Brigands   96, 160, 186, 215
Bronze Age   26, 130, 139, 171, 199
Bronze Age, early   116, 130, 184, 205
Bronze Age, middle   68, 93
Brook Besor   *see* Besor
Brook of the Willows   233
Brooks, C. E. P.   65n, 66n
Broom   80
Brown forest soils   79
al-Bukkah, Jabal   235, *71*
Bulbs   80
Bull, Robert J.   171n
al-Buqei'a (i) in Galilee   155, *54*
al-Buqei'a (ii) in Judah   185
al-Buqei'a (iii) in Manasseh   167, 168, 170, *58*
Burdon, D. J.   21, 23n, 24n, 26n, 27n, 30n
Buruqin   174, *59*
Buseirah   237
Busr al-Hariri   216
al-Buteiha   196
Byblos   98, 127, *39*

Cabul   123, *44, 55*
Caesarea   42, 127, *45, 46, 51*
Caesarea Philippi   194, 195
Callirhoe   202, 205, *64*
Calno   188
Cambrian limestone   18, 20
Cambrian period   17, 18, 20
Cambrian Sea   17
Camel   88, 210, 242, 244
Camel thorn   80, 206
Campbell, Edward F., Jr.   171n
Campus Asochis   40, 161
Cana of Galilee   86, 163, *55, 56*
Canatha   219, 225n, *68*
Canterbury   179
Canyons   12, 24, 31, 32, 199, 211ff.
Capernaum   197, 225, *63*

Cappadocia   89
Caradon, Lord   71
Caravans   11, 104, 245
Carchemish   188
Carmel (in Judah)   184, *61*
Carmel, Mount   12, 13, 22, 24, 29, 38, 39, 58, 72, 81, 97, 98, 99, 117, 120, 123, 124, 125, 128, 141, 144, 149ff., 217, *11, 16, 41, 53*
Carmel range   22, 106, 160, 167, 172ff.
Carmel Upwarp   38, 40, *17*
Carnac   179
Carob   80, 82, 221, 236
Carruthers, Douglas   246n
Caspian Sea   4
Causeway   96, 146, 150
"Cave of the Treasure"   203
Caves   141, 162, 184
Cedar   10, 76, 106, 219
Cenomanian epoch   19, 22, 38, 40, 164
Cenomanian highlands   22, 36, 167, 168
Cenomanian limestone   19, 31, 34, 36, 38, 79, 142, 149, 154, 161, 164, 172, 174, 181, 203, 219, 226, 236
Cenomanian, upper   172, 174
Cenomanian-Turonian   21, 167
Central Highlands (Palestine)   28, 57
Central Rift Valley   7, 9, 10, 14, 29, 191ff.
Central Upwarped Region   34
Central Valley of Lebanon   11, 13
Cereals   78
Chalcolithic period   67, 93, 105, 184, 251
Chalk (*see also* under Senonian)   16, 21, 22, 98, 136, 141, 142, 149, 150, 162, 166, 167, 168, 184, 208, 250
Chartres   179
Chaspho   216, *68*
Cherith   198
Chesulloth   162, *55, 56*
Chorazin   196, 197, *63*
Cilicia   9, 89
Cis-jordan   5, 9, 11, 12, 16, 17, 19, 23, 30, 80, 86, 88, 91
Cis-jordan, hills of   55ff., 72
Cis-jordan, structure of   34ff.
Citadel of Jerusalem   187
Cities of the Plain   205
Citrus   26, 78, 81, 128
City of Moab   *70*
City of Salt   185, *61*
Claudius Ptolemaus   66
Cleopatra   206
Cliffs   42, 128, 136
Climatic change   64–68, 93
"Climatic optimum"   65, 66, 67
Clouds   49
Coast Plain   7, 12, 13, 23–24, 26, 29, 34, 36, 42, 54ff., 87, 143, 149, 157, 172, 190
Coast Road   98
Cold   50, 58, 72, 73, 80, 86, 90, 183, 236
Colomb, B.   82n, 157n
Copper   21, 98, 104, 207, 209, 235, 237
Corbo, Père V. C.   197n
Covenant Code   85
Craftsmen, Valley of   131–136, *47*

Creation, the 86
Cretaceous period 18, 19, 21, 34
Crete 138
Crocodile River 121, 127, 128, *45, 46*
Cross, F. M. 185
Crown, Alan D. 67
Crusaders 31, 133, 151, 157, 160, 235
Crystalline rocks 17
Cultivation *see* Agriculture
Cyclones 47, 48, 51, 64, 66, 216
Cypress 10, 106
Cyprus 9, 44, 48, 138, 219

Daberath 162, *55, 56*
Dahi, Jabal 161
D'ajaniyeh 236, *71*
ad-D'ajaniyeh 235, *71*
Dallita 155
Dalton 155, *54*
Damascus 9, 11, 14, 96, 97, 98, 103, 163,
  188, 200, 213, 216, 217, 239, 240, *39,
  40, 68*
Dan, city of 59, 89, 183, 191, 193, 202,
  42, 62
Dan, tribe of 135, 193, *42*
Dana 33, *13, 71*
Dana, Wadi 34, 235, 237, *71*
Danielus, Eva 128n
Darb al-Hagg *see* Darb al-Hajj, ii
Darb al-Hajj (i) *see* Pilgrim Road
Darb al-Hajj (ii), in Sinai 247, 251, *74*
Darb-al-Hawarnah 100
Darb as-Sultan 35, 99, 250, 251, *74*
Dates 87
Dathema 216, *68*
David, King 106, 107–108, 138, 139,
  142, 143, 147, 181, 184, 185, 223, 228
Dead Sea 7, 8, 11, 13, 14, 19, 24, 26,
  27, 29, 35, 36, 42, 59, 61, 78, 98, 100,
  103, 117, 181, 184, 185, 202–206, 211,
  247, *5, 12, 13, 41, 61, 64, 65*
Debir (i), near Hebron 93, 139, 143,
  185, *48, 49*
Debir (ii), near Jerusalem 198, *60*
Deborah 181
Decapolis, the 148, 185, 198, 214, 223,
  224–225, 239
Deciduous plants 80
Dedan 239
Deir 'Alla 71, 138, *63, 69*
Deir Istiya 166, *57*
Deir az-Zor 8
Deiraban 166
Delougaz, P. 138n
Dera'a 30, 216
Descent of Horonaim *see* Horonaim
Desert 31, 50, 51, 61–64, 77, 82, 91,
  101ff., 138, 206, 211, 227, 235, 236,
  241ff.
Desert animals 108ff.
Desert, Dissected 241, 244–247, *73*
Desert, Plateau 241–243, *72*
Desert Fathers 102, 184
Desertic soils 77–78
Dever, William G. 135n
Dew 44ff., 221, 248, 249

Dhabab, Jabal 233
adh-Dhahariyah 57, 181–182, *61*
Dhiban 233n
adh-Dhra' 29, *70*
Dibon 230, 231, 232, 233n, *12, 40, 70*
Dimona ridge 35, *14*
Dimona upfold 184, *61*
Dion 68
Dionysia 219, *68*
Docus 201, *64*
Donkeys 88
Dor 98, 121, 123, 126, 127, 141, 150,
  40, 45, 51
Dor, Heights of 26
Dothan 98, 149, 168, 170, *51, 58*
Dothan, basin or plain of 39, 170, 172,
  17
Doubbeh, Wadi, or basin of 155, 156,
  157, *16*
Doum palms 82
Downfaulted basins 24, 30, 39, 40, 124,
  134, 145, 153, 166, 168
Drought 72, 73, 74–75, 76, 80, 137, 233,
  251
ad-Druze, Jabal 24, 50, 80, 94, 156, 193,
  213, 215, 216ff., 224, *12, 68*
Dumah 102
Duncan, Alistair 25n
Dune sands 26, 35, 36, 42, 79, 81, 102,
  124, 130, 138, 247
Dura 177
Dust storms 64
ad-Duwaiyima 142

Eagle 173
Earth movements 22
Earthquakes 24, 76, 157, 199, 209
East African lakes 23
Eastern plateau 7, 11, 12, 14, 29, 50
Ebal, Mount 12, 22, 38, 164, 168, 171,
  59
Ebenezer 133, *47*
Ecbatana 8
Edom 8, 9, 12, 13, 21, 61, 71, 91, 93,
  94, 104, 117, 185, 207, 209, 213, 232,
  233–240, 245, *41*
Edom, Exaltation of 9, 12
Edom, heights of 12, *13, 14, 67*
Edom, plateau of 12, 33, 34, 72, 82,
  233ff.
Edrei 97, 215, *68*
Efrat, Elisha 18n, 52n, 59n, 154n
Eglon 139, *48*
Egypt 11, 69, 70, 89, 109, 137, 138, 147,
  150, 206
Egypt, River of 250
Egyptians 133, 173, 209, 222
Eilabun 153, 157, *53*
Eitan, A. 187n
Ekron 138, *48*
Elath 17, 35, 104, 191, 202, 209, 247, *14*
Elah, valley of 142, *48, 49*
Elealeh 232, 233n, *70*
Elijah 45, 74, 108, 109, 173, 198
Elisha 63, 109, 137, 149, 167
Elliger, K. 228n

Eloth   209, *40, 65, 74*
Emek Peq'in   155
Emmaus   134, *47*
En Bokek   202
En Gev   198
Endor   149, *50, 56*
En-gannim   144, 146, 149, 171, *58*
Engedi   36, 98, 100, 183, 184, 185, 202, 203, *64*
En-shemesh   *60*
Entrance of Hamath   98
Eocene chalks   21, 34, 79, 155, 162, 164, 172, 226
Eocene limestones   21, 34, 36, 38, 79, 81, 124, 155, 160, 164, 214, 231, 236, 241
Eocene period   19, 22, 39, 40, 135, 161, 167, 168
Eocene Sea   20, 34
Ephraim, Dome of   164, 173–176, *11, 16*
Ephraim, region of   38, 39, 87, 94, 117, 118, 133, 173–176
Ephraim, town of   175
Ephraim, tribe of   12, 141, 164–166, 201, *42, 60*
Ephraim upwarp   38, 177, *16*
Ephron   174, 175, 178, *59, 60*
Eremos   102, 111
Erg, or sand desert   102, 244
Erosion   17, 18, 21, 24, 35, 36, 52, 76, 77, 78, 115, 116, 128, 136, 141, 178, 206, 211, 224, 230, 250
Esdraelon corridor (*see also* Acco-Beth-shan corridor)   40
Esdraelon, Plain of   3, 12, 13, 30, 39, 55, 75, 79, 81, 87, 94, 98, 144ff., 162, 169, 172, *16, 53, 55*
Eshtaol   141, *49*
Etam   182, 183, *61*
Etesian winds   44
Ethbaal   70
Euphrates, river (i) in Mesopotamia   8, 9
Euphrates, river (ii) in Benjamin   179
Euro-Siberian vegetation   82
Evenari, M.   64n, 249n
Evergreens   80
Execration Texts   133
Exodus, the   86, 90, 103, 105, 109, 111, 117, 244, 250
Ezion-geber   209, 239, 246, 251, *65, 73*

Fahil, Kh.   198, 225n
Fahn, A.   65n
Fajjas   160
Falama   167, *58*
Famine   90, 137, 198
Fari'a, Wadi   14, 29, 30, 38, 167, 168, 170, 179, 199, *11, 16, 58, 63*
Farmers   10, 11, 22, 71, 90, 91, 93, 117, 163, 228
Fasayil, Kh.   200
Fault, faulting (*see also* downfaulted basins)   22, 24, 28, 29, 30, 31, 33, 34, 39, 40, 42, 124, 132, 134, 135, 149, 154,155, 160, 161, 166, 168, 172, 177, 208, 230, 235, 236

Fault scarp   145, 166, 202
Fault systems   11
Feast of Booths   86
Feast of Weeks   85
Feasts   84–86, 96, 118, 175, 199
Feinan   21, 33, 207, 235, 237, *13*
Feiran, Wadi   104–105, 251
Ferocious Land, the   101, 104, 106, 184
Fertile Crescent   5, 6, 16
Festivals   *see* Feasts
Fig Sycamore   *see* Sycamore
Fig trees   81, 84, 87
Fijj al-'Aseikir   29, 32, *13, 66, 70*
Fiq   216, 225n
Fir   219
First fruits   85
Fish   197
Fish ponds   81
Fisher, W. B.   19n
Fitzgerald, G. M.   188n
Flash floods   34
Flint   31, 243
Flint-strewn desert   243
Floods   48, 70, 72, 73, 76, 79, 125, 130, 133,134, 137, 147, 199, 205, 208, 209
Folding   17, 19, 22, 23, 29, 31, 34, 184
Forests   78, 81, 82, 94, 105, 116, 127, 128, 156, 162, 172, 173, 174, 178, 193, 217, 219, 221, 223, 236
Former rains   *see* Rain
Fortresses   91, 116, 135, 151, 184, 185, 187, 196, 204, 207, 209, 223, 231, 245, 250
Forty Oaks   173
Foxes   110
Franken, H. J.   199n
Frankincense   240, 247
Freund, R.   22n
Frost   15, 49, 55, 70, 71, 86
Fureidis, Jabal   156

Gabbatha   187
Gad   211, 221, 223, 227, 228, 229, 231, *42*
Gadara   198, 214, 225n, *63, 68*
Gadarene plateau   213–214, *68*
Galil   117, *41*
Galilee   19, 21, 22, 24, 29, 73, 100, 117, 123, 124, 130, 152ff., 179, *53*
Galilee, hills of   81
Galilee, Lake, or Sea of   8, 13, 14, 26, 27, 30, 34, 39, 40, 59, 97, 98, 155, 160, 196ff., 216, 225, *5, 16, 53, 63*
Galilee, Lower   8, 12, 24, 29, 40, 57, 73, 93, 94, 124, 153, 157–163, 166, *55, 56*
Galilee, Upper   12, 29, 30, 40, 57, 72, 81, 93, 124, 152, 154–157, 160, 161, *54*
Galilee-Beth-shan Basin   42, 79, 196–198
Galilee-Bashan Depression   8, 30, *3*
Gallim   188, *60*
al-Garfa, Jabal   247
Garigue   81
Gath   138, 139, 142, *48, 49*
Gath-padalla   168, 172, *46*
Gath-rimon   *47*
Gaulanitis   213, 215, 216, *68*

Gav ha-Arava   206
Gaza   6, 12, 28, 42, 44, 55, 61, 78, 91, 97, 99, 137, 138, 239, 247, 251, *39, 40, 48*
Gazara   143
Gazelle   108
Geba   177, 179, 188, *60*
Gebim   188
Gennesaret   160, 161, 196, *63*
Gentiles   111, 197, 198, 225
al-Geraia   *74*
Gerasa (i), in Gilead   85, 198, 225n, *69*
Gerasa (ii), in Sinai   251, *74*
Gergesa   198, *63*
Gerizim, Mount   3, 12, 22, 164, 168, 171, *59*
Geshur   215
Geshurites   215
Gezer   135, 143, 174, *47, 48*
Ghab, marshes of the   10
Ghar, Wadi   183
Gharandal   236
Gharra, Kh.   183
Ghazza, Kh.   184, 185, *61*
Ghazzeh, Wadi   247
Gheish, Wadi   32
Ghor   91, 144, 198, 199ff.
Ghouta   11
Gibbethon   131, 133, 135, 169, *47, 48*
Gibeah of Saul   98, 175, 179, 188, *60*
Gibeon   106, 134, 179, 181, *60*
Gideon   45, 105, 123, 147, 223, 224, 244
Gilboa, Y.   40
Gilboa, Mount   24, 39, 99, 145, 147, 168, 223, *16*
Gilead   19, 29, 72, 73, 86, 93, 94, 117, 148, 169, 198, 199, 211, 213, 214, 217, 219–225, 227, 228, 229, *11, 41, 67*
Gilead, Dome of   7, 12, 19, 30, 31, 38, 82, 219–225, 226, 229, *11, 12*
Gilead upwarp   *16*
Gilgal (i), in the Ghor   99, 202
Gilgal (ii), in Sharon   130, *46*
Ginnosar   155, 160
Ginzburg, C.   65n
Gischala   157, *54*
Giv'at Ha-More   161
Glaciers   65, 66
Glueck, Nelson   93, 99n, 116n, 209, 236n, 239n, 244n, 250n
Goats   88, 108, 184, 210, 217, 228
Golan   103, *68*
Golan Heights   213, 215
Gold   209, 240, 247
Golgotha   187
Goliath   142
Gomorrah   25, 204, 205
Gondwanaland   16, 17, *6*
Gophna   174, *59*
Gorges   36, 38
Gorgias   134
Grain   81, 86, 87, 134, 162, 163, 183, 197, 217, 228
Grain & wine & oil   82–84, 87, 210
Grain Sabt   26
Granite   17, 20, 30, 34, 208, 236, 245

Grapes   86, 163, 183, 211, 222
Grassland   10, 94
Gravel   27, 34
Grigg, David   75n
Ground swell   17
Gulf Stream   67
Gur, ascent of   *see* Ascent of Gur

Ha'ari, Har   155n
Hadar   128
Hadera   42, 130
Hadera, Nahal   128
Hadhawdha, Lake   244, *72*
Hadhira, Jabal   35
Hadhira, wadi   35
Hadid   *47*
Hadrian, Emperor   187, 188
Hafira, wadi   31, *12*
Haidar, Jabal   155n
Haifa   12, 24, 44, 55, 57, 62
Hail   50, 63, 71, 73, 74, 75, 76, 90
Halazun Basin   161
Halazun, Wadi   124, 161, *44, 55*
Haleisa, Jabal   155, *54*
Hamada   78
Hamadan   8
Hammam, Wadi   160, *56*
Hamath   10, 96, 188, *39*
Hamath, Pastures of   9
Hammath   198, *63*
Hammath Gader   *63*
al-Hammeh   26, 198
Hammond, Philip C.   206n
Hamra al-Fidan   207, *71*
Hannathon   100, 125, 152, *40, 53, 55*
Harab, Jabal   105
Haraba al-Abyad   *73*
Haram ash-Sharif   187
Haramiyeh, Wadi   175, *59*
Harbors   127, 130
Harel, M.   185n
Harod, River   14, *63*
Harosheth of the Gentiles   99, 123, 125, 144, 145, *50, 51*
Harrah   244
Harun, Jabal   155, *54*
Harvest   49, 50, 216
Hasbani, River   192, *62*
Hasbaya   192
Hasma, Wadi   31, 34, 97, 104, 208, 209, 237, 245, 246, *13, 65, 73*
Hathira, Jabal   35
Hathira, Wadi   19, 35
Hatira ridge   35, *14*
Hattin, Horns of   96, 160, *56*
Hauran, the   156, 163
Havvoth-Jair   214, 215
Hawthorn   82, 236
Hazael, King   229
Hazar-addar   250
Hazera ridge   35, *14*
Hazor   96, 98, 149, 152, 195, *39, 40, 62*
Hazor, Nahal   195
Hazor-addar   *74*
Hazzur, Jabal   160, 161, *55*
Heat   46, 80, 90, 184

Hebron   12, 36, 57, 73, 91, 93, 94, 98,
    100, 103, 139, 177, 181, 182, 183, 185,
    42, 61
al-Heisi, Wadi   251
Hejaz railway   29, 31, 50, 82, 91, 211,
    213, 214, 236, 241, 244, *13*
Helbaek, Hans   236n
Helez   *48*
Helez-Negba anticline   137
Helkath   *44*
Hellenistic period   94, 157, 170, 224
Hepher   130, *46*
Hermon, Mount   14, 30, 31, 96, 156, 191,
    192, 195, 196, 213, 216, *11, 62, 68*
Herod Antipas   224
Herod the Great   130, 160, 170, 172, 185,
    187, 194, 202, 204, 232n
Herodium   156
Hesa, Wadi   239, *66*
Heshbon   99, 211, 229, 232, 233n, *40,
    69, 70*
Hezekiah, King   123, 142
High pressure system   47, 48, 66
Highway   96, 175
Hillazon Basin   161
Hillel, Har   155n
Hinnom   186
Hippos   198, 225n, *63*
Hiram   123
Hisban   233n
Hisban, Wadi   202, 221, *64, 69*
Holy Sepulcher, Church of   187, 188
Homs   9, *39*
Homs, Lake of   8
Homs-Palmyra Corridor   8, 9, 11, *3*
Honey   84
Horbah   101
Hormah   183, *61*
Horns of Hattin   *see* Hattin
Horonaim   231
Horonaim, Ascent, or Descent of   98,
    205, 231, *40, 64, 70*
Horses   89, 211
Horvat Haluja   247
Horvat Qazra   251
Hosea   110
Hot springs   26, 160, 167, 198, 202
House of the Forest of Lebanon   106
Huleh Basin   8, 26, 30, 42, 59, 73, 79,
    82, 191ff., 195
Huleh, Lake of   13, 26, 96, 192, 195, 216,
    62
Hureish, Jabal   168, *58*
Hyksos   196
Hymn to the Aton   69–70
Hyrcania   185
Hyrcànus, John   171, 172

Ibleam   39, 98, 99, 149, 150, 170, *40,
    50, 51, 58*
Ibziq, Kh.   170
Ice   67, 76
Ice Age   67
Idna   142
Idumeans   35
Ijon, plain of   98, 192, *62*

Ikhnaton, Pharaoh   69, 169
Immanuel   84n
Imwas   134
Incense (*see also* Frankincense)   209
Incense trade route   102, 104
Inn of the Good Samaritan   178, 185, 186
Instruction of Amen-em-ope   70
Ionides, M.G.   20n
IPC pipeline   213, 214, 221
Iphtah   142, 177, *49*
Iphtah-el, River   125, 161, *44, 55*
Iran   5, 16
Irano-Turanian vegetation   80, 82
'Iraq al-Amir   224, *69*
Irbid   31, 215
Iris   81, 231
Iron   116
Iron Age   130, 183
Irrigation   70, 75, 196, 198, 200, 240
Irrigation society   11
Isaiah   84
Ishmaelites   222
'Ishrin, Jabal   245
Iskanderun, River   128, 130, *46*
Israel, kingdom of   11, 12, 14, 116, 135,
    179, 193
Israel, modern state of   143, 151, 191
Israelite, Israelites   93, 117, 118, 120,
    121, 127, 128, 131, 133, 137, 141, 152,
    178, 183, 211, 212, 214, 223, 228, 244
Issachar   151, 162, 169, *42*
Isserlin, B.S.J.   94n, 105n
Ivory   170, 209, 219

Jabal, Jibal   156, 181, 217
Jabbok, River   12, 14, 21, 30, 31, 199,
    211, 219, 221, 223, 224, 226, 227, 228,
    5, *11, 12, 63, 67, 69*
Jabesh-gilead   148, 170, 198, *63, 69*
Jabneel   100, 138n, 157, *47, 48*
Jacob   107, 171, 176, 223
Jacob's well   170
Jaffa   55, 133
al-Jafr   242, *13, 72*
Jair of Gilead   214
Jal'ad   224
Jaljuya   130
al-Jamal, Wadi   237
Jamnia   157
Jamnith   *54*
Janoah   165, 166, *58*
Jarmaq, Jabal   41, 152, 155n, 157, 160,
    54
Jarmuth   139, *49*
al-Jau'aliyat, Jabal   31, *11*
al-Jauf   244, 246
Jazer, district of   221, 227, 228, 229, *69*
Jazer, town of   221, 232
Jazzir, Kh.   221n
Jdeideh   191
Jehoash, King   141
Jehoram, King   232
Jehoshaphat, King   209, 228, 239
Jehu, King   148, 149, 150, 169, 170
Jeibe, Wadi   208, *65, 71*
Jenin   39

Jepthah   211, 227
Jerash (*see also* Gerasa)   198, 225
Jeremiah   110, 171, 176, 179
Jericho   26, 36, 46, 50, 54, 58, 59, 72,
   99, 116, 174, 178, 179, 185, 186, 201,
   206, 237, *16, 40, 60, 61, 64*
Jeroboam I   89, 174, 175, 176, 194, 223
Jeroboam II, King   170
Jerusalem   3, 4, 22, 36, 50, 54, 55, 57, 60,
   62, 72, 73, 74, 75, 93, 94, 98, 100,
   103, 106, 134, 141, 142, 143, 170, 171,
   178, 179, 182, 185–190, *16, 39, 40, 42,
   60, 61*
Jerusalem, Western Hill of   94, 187
Jeshanah   179, *59*
Jeshimon   101, 103
Jeshimon, region of   36, 54, 80, 81, 103,
   117, 181, 182, 183, 184–185, 203, *41,
   61*
Jesus   102, 111, 115, 149, 162, 172, 184,
   186, 187, 190, 194, 196, 197, 224, 225,
   240
Jet stream   47
Jezreel Corridor   39, *11*
Jezreel, town of   148, *50, 58*
Jezreel, Valley of   8, 29, 30, 39, 40, 72,
   87, 97, 99, 144ff., 147, 160, 168, 169,
   16, 41
Jinsafut   167, *57, 58, 59*
Jirafi, Wadi   208
Jish   157
Jisr ad-Damiyeh   167
Jisr al-Ghajar   192, *62*
Jisr al-Harithiyeh   125
Jiza   *72*
Joab   179, 181
Jogbehah   223, *69*
John the Baptist   46, 185, 233
John of Gischala   157
Johnson, Aubrey R.   86n
Jokneam   39, 99, 144, 149, 150, *50, 51,
   52*
Jonathan   22, 134, 138, 147, 179
Jonathan Maccabeus   139
Joppa   12, 26, 98, 134, *48*
Jordan, modern state of   172, 191, 241
Jordan, rift valley   7, 29, 30, 39, 190,
   223, *11, 16*
Jordan, River   ᑈ, 13, 14, 27, 82, 99, 117,
   160, 167, 191ff., 211, *5, 53, 58, 63, 64*
Jordan valley   12, 26, 28, 59, 162, 191ff.
Jordan "Waist"   30, 198
Jordan-Dead Sea Lake   24, 26
Jordan-Huleh Rift   30
Joseph   149, 171, 222
Joseph of Arimathea   174
Josephus   58, 157, 160, 161, 162, 187,
   233
Joshua   22, 133, 134, 139, 142, 152, 156,
   192, 196, 198
Josiah, King   150
Jotapata   161, *55*
Jotham, King   228
al-Jubeihah   224
Judah   14, 19, 22, 34, 36, 73, 94, 116,
   117, 118, 141, 143, 172, 219, 248, 250

Judah, highlands of   7
Judah, hill country of   12, 21, 36, 81, 94,
   181ff., *61*
Judah, kingdom of   12, 35, 177ff., 179, *61*
Judah, tribe of   12, 36, 139, *42, 60, 61*
Judah, wilderness of (*see also* Jeshimon)
   20, 36
Judah-Gilead Dome   29, 30
Judas Maccabeus   35, 134, 143, 216
Judean moat   22, 36, 142, 166, 177, 181,
   182, *49*
Judean upwarp   36, 177
Judges, period of the   93, 169
Jungle   82
Juniper   236
Jurassic period   19, 20, 21
Juttah   177, 182

al-Kabir, Jabal   38, 167
al-Kabir, Jabal (upwarp)   *17*
al-Kabir, Nahr   8
al-Kabir, Wadi   131, 134, 135, *47, 48*
al-Kabri   124, *44*
Kabzeel   183, *61*
Kadesh   98, *39*
Kadesh-barnea   250, 251, *40, 74*
Kafr 'Abbush   167, *58*
Kafr Jammal   167, *58*
Kafr Kanna   163n
Kafr Qaddum   167, *58*
Kafr Qasim   71
Kafr Yasif   124, *44*
Kafr Zibad   167
Kammana, Jabal   160, 161, *55*
Kammon, Har   161
Kamon   214, *68*
Kanah, River   128, *57*
Kaplan, J.   138n
Karen Karmel   173
Karmon, Yehuda   19n, 26, 40n, 50n, 98n,
   128n, 134n, 141n, 146n, 154n, 167n,
   168n, 195n
Karnaim   97, 216, *40, 68*
Katarina, Jabal   104
Katsnelson, J.   50n, 71n
Kedar, Yehuda   82n, 157n, 249n
Kedesh Naphtali   103
Keilah   142, *49*
Keller, Dov   249n
Kelso, James L.   176n
Kena'an, Har   155
Kenath   215
Kenites   184, 209
Kenyon, Kathleen M.   26n, 116n, 188,
   201–202
Kerak   29, 31, 32, 231
Kerak Rift   32
Kerak trough   *12*
Kerak, Wadi   14, 29, 98, 205, *66*
Kerak-Canatha   215
Kermanshah   8
Keziv, Nahal   124, 155
Kfar Tavor   153, 157, *53*
Khalasa   247, *74*
al-Khalidi, Kh.   *73*
Khallat Batrakh, Kh.   182

Khamsin   52
Khan Yunis   247
Khisfin   216
Khurashe Dome   250
Khurashe Upwarp   34
al-Khureij, Jabal   19, 30, 206, *65*
Kidron, River   186
Kiev   179
Kikkar   117, 199–202, *41*
Kina'an, Jabal   41, 57, 155, *54*
King Solomon's mines   104, 209
Kinglake, A. W.   97n, 184
King's Highway   97, 230, 231, 231n, 232, 233, 235, *70*
Kir-hareseth   31, 91, 116, 205, 231, 233, *12, 13, 39, 40, 66, 70*
Kiriath-jearim   106, 141, 177, 178, *60*
Kirkbride, Diana   11n, 74n, 93n, 237n, 245n
Kishon Gate   39
Kishon, River   13, 125, 144, 146, *5, 44, 55*
al-Kithara, Kh.   *73*
Kraabel, A. Thomas   157n
Krown, Leo   75
Kufrein, Wadi   14, 202, *64, 69*
Kufrinje, Wadi   14, 199, *63, 69*
Kuntilla   251
Kurkar   26, 36, 42, 124, 126, 127, 128, 130, 134, 138
Kurnub   249, *74*
Kurnub sandstones   21, 31
Kurnub Upwarp   34, 35
Kurnub-Hosb region   24
al-Kursi   198
Kuweikat   124, *44*

La'aban, Wadi   237
Laba'yu   169
Lachish   100, 137, 139, 142, 182, *49, 61*
Lacus Asphaltitis   206
Ladder of Tyre   123, 124, *44*
Laish   193, 194
Laishah   188, *60*
Lamb, H. H.   65n, 66n
Lance, H. Darrel   135n
Land and sea breezes   46, 59
Land of Obedience   101, 103
Landes, George M.   227n
Lapp, Paul W.   151n, 205n, 224
Latter rains   *see* Rain
Laurel   80
Lebanese Rift   192
Lebanon, modern country of   128, 153, 155, 156, 157, 173, 191, 192
Lebanon, Mount   7, 10, 106, 156, 217
Lebanon mountains   7, 8, 14, 28, 29, *11*
Lebanon, valley of   98, 105, 191
Lebo-hamath   98
Lebonah   175, *59*
Legio Maximinopolis   150
Leimun, Wadi   41, 155, 157, 160, *54, 55*
Leja   213, 215, 216, 217, *68*
Lejjun   150
Leopard   11, 104, 107, 173, 235
Levant   6, 14

Levant bridge   6, *39*
Levant Coast   5, 6
Libnah   137, 139, 142, *48, 49*
Liddani, River   193, *62*
Lifta   178
Limestone   16, 18, 19, 21, 26, 31, 136, 141, 162, 164, 168, 173, 183, 192, 208, 214, 215, 221, 224, 244, 251
Lions   107, 108, 110, 193
Lisan marls   26, 27, 78, 79, 82
Lisan Peninsula   29, 204, *64, 70*
Lisan Sea   26, 27
Litani river   14, 98, 154, 155
"Little Ice Age"   66
Liver, J.   232n
Locusts   90
Lod   29, 42, 133, 134, *47, 48*
Lo-debar   198, *63*
Loess   26, 42, 78, 247
Lubban   38, 175
Lumber   82, 199
Lydda (*see also* Lod)   *21, 23*

Maacah   215
Maachites   215
Ma'ale ha-Aqrabbim   35
Ma'ale Tamar   35
Ma'an   19, 62, 72, 74, 99, 244, *13*
Maccabees   142, 143, 152, 204
Machaerus   233, *66, 70*
Madain Salah   239, 246
Madeba   73, 81, 103, 104, 232
Madeba Map   206
Madmen   *70*
Madmennah   188
Madyan   105, 251
al-Mafjir, Kh.   202n
Mafraq   213, 221, *69*
Magdala   96, 160, 197, *40, 56, 63*
Mahalla   *74*
Mahanaim   223, *69*
Mahaneh-dan   141
al-Mahjara, Jabal   166
Ma'in, Kh.   177
Majdal   160
Majdal Yaba   133, 174
Maked   216, *68*
al-Makhaiyat, Kh.   232, 233n
Makmish   130
Maktesh, Makteshim   34, 187, 250
Maktesh ha-Gadol   19, 22, 35
Maktesh ha-Qatan   35
Maktesh Ramon   19, 34, 251
Malamat, A.   196
Malawi, Wadi   198
Malfuf towers   227
al-Malih, Wadi   167
Malik, Wadi   125, 161
Manasseh   38, 39, 118, 172, 214, 221
Manasseh, basin of   12, 40, 41, 164, 174, *11*
Manasseh, tribe of   12, 164ff., 166, 228, *42*
Manasseh upfold   *16*
Manei'yeh, Jabal   209
Manei'yeh, Wadi   104

al-Manjir   *73*
Maon (i) in Judah   177, 184, *61*
Maon (ii) in Trans-jordan   97, 99, 103, 184, 244, *40, 65, 71*
al-Maqteh, Kh.   207
Maquis   80, 81, 105, 155, 156, 173, 217
Mar Jirius   184
Mar Saba   184
Marda   174, *59*
Mareshah   142, 143, 182, *48, 49, 61*
Margalit, Hanna   147n
Mari   8, 96, 196
Marisa   142, 143
Marj'ayoun, city of   191, *62*
Marj'Ayoun, plain of   30, 42, 191, 192, *62*
Marj Sannur   39
Marks, John H.   227n
Marl   199
Maroun ar-Ras   154, *54*
al-Marsad, Wadi   *73*
Marshes   10, 78, 79, 81, 82, 97, 98, 121, 124, 125, 127, 128, 130, 135, 137, 146, 147, 150, 192, 195
Masada   36, 185, 204, *61, 64*
Mayerson, Philip   249n
Mazar   61, 233
Mazar, B.   215, 224n
Mazeva, Har   206
McCaw, G. T.   204n
McCown, Chester C.   58n, 224n
McDowell, Margaret Dean   71n
Mecca   97, 179, 251
Medeba (*see also* Madeba)   211, 229, 232, *12, 69, 70*
Medina   246
Medinet Habu   138
Mediterranean Sea   4, 16
Mediterranean soils   79ff.
Mediterranean vegetation   80, 81, 82
Meek, Theophile J.   117n
Meeroth   157
Megiddo   39, 96, 97, 99, 146, 149–150, 151, 169, 173, 196, *39, 40, 42, 50, 51, 52, 58*
Megiddo Basin, or downfold   38, *16, 17*
Megiddo hills   40
Megiddo, pass of   95, 97, 149, 173
Merchants (*see also* Trade)   11, 104, 151, 163, 179, 209, 239, 240, 245
Merom   *53, 54*
Merom, waters of   155
Meron   153, 157
Meron, block, or massif   41, *11*
Meron, Har   41, 152, 155n, 157, *16*
Merrill, Selah   224
Mesha, king of Moab   211, 229, 231–232
Mesillah, Mesilloth   96
Mesopotamia   6, 11, 69, 70, 71
Metullah   192, *62*
Meyers, Eric M.   157n
Michmash   22, 134, 179, 188, *60*
Midbar   101ff., 115, 128, 167, 184, 241
Midian, mountains of   17, 20, 30, 104, 208, 244, 246, *13, 14, 65, 67*
Midianites   88, 123, 147, 224, 244

Mifjir, Wadi   128, 168, 46
Migdal   160
Migdal-gad   228
Migron   188, *60*
Milik, J. T.   185n
Milk   84
Miocene period   24, 141
Miocene-Pliocene   22
Miqneh   87, 227
Mishash, Kh.   *61*
Mishash, Wadi   *61*
Mishmar-ha-Emek   151
Mishor (*see also* Tableland)   12, 103, 117, 219, 229ff., *41, 67, 69, 70*
Mist   45
Mizpah (i) in Benjamin   98, 179, 181, *60*
Mizpah (ii) in Trans-jordan   224, *69*
Mmst   181
Moa   251, *74*
Moab   8, 12, 13, 73, 91, 93, 103, 116, 185, 211, 212, 213, 227, 228, 229–233, 241, *42*
Moab lily (*see also* Iris)   81
Moab, plains of   30, 202, *69*
Moab, tableland of (*see also* Mishor)   67
Moabite Stone   211, 229n, 231
Mojjib, Wadi (*see also* Arnon River)   12
Monarchy   94, 130
Monarchy, Israelite   185
Monarchy, United   *see* United Monarchy
Monocline, monoclinal fold   29, 30, 31, 181
Monsoons   44
Montfort, castle of   124
Montreal (*see also* Shaubak)   235
Moreh, Hill or Mount of   24, 39, 149, 161, 163, *56*
Moreh, plateau of   8, 40, 145, 160
Moreshath-gath   182, *61*
Moses   11, 89, 208, 235, 251
Mosul   71, 156
Mountain building   16, 19
Mountain of Lebanon   10
Mountain ranges   16
Mountfort, Guy   110n
Mousterian red sands   26, 42, 78, 81, 128, 129, 134, 135
Mozambique   23
Mu'awwat, Wadi   185
Mudeisisat, Jabal   31, *12*
Mughar   160, *56*
al-Muhraqa   173
al-Mukawwar   233
Mules   89
al-Muqanna, Kh.   139
Murra, Wadi   35, 99, 206, 250, *14, 40, 65, 74*
Musa, Jabal   104, 105, 251
Musa, Wadi   208
Mycenae   138
Myrrh   222, 240
Myrtle   80

Naaman   200
Na'aman, Wadi   124, *44*

Nabateans   12, 68, 93, 104, 105, 185, 206, 208, 239, 244, 245, 248, 251
Nabi Musa   185
Nablus   29, 38, 73, 93, 100, 164, 172, *16*
Nafud   102, 244
Nahalol   *44*
Nahash, King   228
an-Nahas, Kh.   207
Nain   149, 163, *50, 56*
an-Nakhilah, Wadi   233
Napthali, tribe of   125, 149, 152, *42*
Napoleon   151
Naqb Ishtar   235
Nari   141, 162
Nathanya   128, *46*
Natural regions   *see* Regions
Na'ur   61, 221, 227, *69*
Naveh, J.   139n
Nazareth   40, 55, 57, 145, 160, 161, 162, 163, *16, 50, 55, 56*
Nazareth scarp (*see also* Qafsa, Jabal)   *11*
Neapolis   172, *58*
Neballat   *47*
Nebo   232, 233n, *70*
Nebo, Mount   221, *69*
Necho, Pharaoh   150
Negba   *48*
Negeb   12, 21, 34, 61, 62, 67, 72, 73, 74, 78, 80, 93, 94, 102, 117, 143, 183, 184, 239, *41, 61, 74*
Negeb, coastal plains of   247
Negeb, High   247, 250
Negeb of the Cherethites   247
Negeb of Judah   181, 182, 247
Negeb, structure of   34, *14*
Negeb uplands   7, 12, 30, 206
Negeb, western slopes of   247–250
Negeb, Wilderness of   9, 12, 42, 71, 103, 105
Negev, A.   104n
Nehemiah   170, 224
Neolithic period   11
Nephtoah   178, *60*
Nessana   104, 247, 249, *74*
New Year festival   86
Nezib   142, *49*
Nigde   237
Nile Valley   6
Nimrah   232
Nimrin, waters of   202, 210, *64*
Nir, Dov   42n, 127n, 136n
Nizzana   247
Nob   175, 188
Nomads   104
Northern Kingdom   131, 151, 169
Northern Realm   9
Noth, Martin   87n, 89n, 100n, 117n, 227
Nubian sandstone   18, 20–21, 203, 208, 224, 230, 231, 235, 236, 239, 244, 245, 246
Nusairi, Jabal   156
Nuseiriyeh Mountains   7, 8, 9, 14

Oak   81, 82, 130, 162, 173, 219, 221, 236
Oak, evergreen   82

Oak, Mediterranean   80
Oak, Tabor   80
Oases   11, 81, 91, 204, 205, 236, 244
Oboda   99, 104, 249, 251, *40, 74*
Oboth   98, 207, *40, 65, 74*
Obsidian   237
Og, King   215, 219–221
Oleanders   210
Oligocene epoch   20, 22
Olive oil   84
Olives   81, 82, 84, 86, 87, 116, 125, 137, 162, 167, 168, 173, 174, 183, 210, 211, 217, 222, 231, 237
Olives, Mount of   178, 188, 190, *60*
Omer, Nahal   251, *74*
Omphalos   3
Omri, King   169, 170, 211
Ono   134, *47, 48*
Ophrah   175, *58*
Orni, Ephraim   18n, 52n, 59n, 154n
Orontes, River   10, 14
Ostrich   108
Ottossen, Magnus   219n
Overgrazing   115
Owl   108
Ox, oxen   89, 108, 216

Palestine   5, 14, 93, 109
Palestine bridge   7
Palestine, natural regions   *see* Regions
Palestinian Realm   9, 11
Palmyra   8, *39*
Paneas   193, 194, *62*
Papyrus   79, 82, 195
Paran Basin   103, 247, 250–251, *14, 74*
Paran, Mount   76
Paran, Nahal   *14, 65, 74*
Paran, plateau of   34
Paran, Wadi   34, 208
Parod   153, 157, *53*
Parod-Eilabun-Kafr Tavor road   153, 157
Passover   85, 89, 123, 171
Pastoralism   71, 87ff., 93
Patriarchs, the   68, 93
Paul, Saint   102, 187, 240
Pear, wild   82
Peat   79
Pella   198, 225n, *63*
Penuel   223, *63, 69*
Perea   185, 224, 239
Persia   8
Persian Gulf   4
Persian period   94, 130, 139, 171
Persians   127, 170
Peter, Saint   194, 197
Petra   20, 30, 74, 97, 185, 208, 237, 239, *40, 65, 71*
Petra-Beidha platform   235, 236, 237
Pharpar, River   11
Phasaelis   200, *63*
Philadelphia   225n
Philip, the Apostle   197
Philip, the Tetrarch   194, 215, 217
Philippopolis   219, *68*
Philistia, Philistine plain   36, 81, 131ff., 247, *48*

Philistines   12, 22, 36, 86, 93, 106, 140, 141, 142, 143, 147, 150, 175, 176, 179, 181, *42*
Phoenicia   10, 11, 12, 13, 70, 106, 170, 193, *42*
Phoenicia, Mountain of   9
Phoenician coast   127, 162
Phoenicians   173, 221
Picard, Leo   17n, 19n, 22n, 24n, 34, 40
Pilate, Pontius   187
Pilgrim Road   97, 104, 216, 228, *40*
Pines   81, 219, 221
Pisgah   11, 117, *41*
Pistachia   80, 87
Plagues   137
Plantain   82
Plants of Palestine   80–82, *37*
Pleistocene epoch   24, 26
Pliny   225n
Pliocene epoch   24, 26
Pluvial period   13, 26, 27, 34, 126, 250
Pomegranates   84, 87
Porphyry   17, 34, 207
Potash   205
Precipitation, Mount of   145
Prepottery Neolithic   116, 201
Pride   13, 29, 233
Pride of Jordan   200
Pritchard, James   96n, 98n, 127n, 134n, 150n, 199n, 211n, 229n
Prophet   110, 190, 233
Ptolemais   124, 162, *44*
Pulses   84, 86
Pumice   237
Punon   21, 98, 99, 207, 208, 235, 237, *13, 40, 65, 71*
Punon Embayment   99, 207, 235

Qa'a   208, 242, 245
Qafsa, Jabal   145, 161, *56*
Qamm   214
Qana, Kh.   163, 167
Qana, Wadi   128, 130, 165, 166, 167, 174
Qanawat   215, 219, 225
Qarn, Wadi   124, 155, *44*
Qaruni, River   *62*
Qasr al-'Abd   224n
Qasr al-Hallabat   31
Qasr Hammam as-Serakh   219
Qasr Mahalla   251, *74*
Qattara   199, 204
Qazra, Har   *74*
Qedummin, Har   161
Qilt, Wadi   178, 179, *60*
Qubeibah, Wadi   142, *48, 49*
Quennell, A. M.   20, 23, 27n, *9*
Qumeim   215
Qumran community   102, 109, 203
Qumran, Kh.   185, *64*
Qurn al-Qibsh   233n
Quruntul, Jabal   156, 184, *61*
Quweira   *73*
Quweira sandstone   20, 21

Rabbah, Rabboth Ammon   29, 31, 97, 219, 221, 226, 227, 228, *39, 40, 69*

ar-Radaisiyah, Jabal   235, *71*
Rafah   42, 55
ar-Rafeh   216n, 225n
Rain, rainfall   6, 12, 14, 15, 21, 36, 48, 49, 50, 51, 54, 55, 57, 60, 61, 62, 67, 70, 71ff., 93, 123, 125, 137, 155, 167, 172, 173, 174, 183, 196, 198, 202, 206, 211, 217, 221, 224, 228, 241, 243, 248, *24–31*
Rain, former   49, 51, 73, 74, 75
Rain, latter   50, 51
Rain shadow   59, 61, 203
Rainfall factor   78ff., *36*
Rainy season   43, 47ff., 77, 80, 85, 248
Rajib, River   199, *63, 69*
Rakhma, Jabal   35
Ram   *73*
Ram al-'Atiq   *73*
Ram, Jabal   20, 245, *13*
Ram sandstone   20
Ram, Wadi   18, 20, 63, 97, 104, 245, 246, *73*
Ramah (i) in Benjamin   98, 177, 179, 181, 188 , *60*
Ramah (ii) in Galilee   125
Ramallah   29, 36, 38, 179, *16*
Raman, Jabal   250
Raman, Wadi   19, 34
Ramathaim-zophim   174
Ramath-mizpeh   224
Rameses II, Pharaoh   98
Rameses III, Pharaoh   138
Ramleh   55, 132, *47*
Ramon anticline   206, *74*
Ramon dome   250
Ramon, Har   34, 250, *14*
Ramon Upwarp   34, 35, 82, *14*
Ramoth-gilead   97, 99, 103, 169, 214, 216, 223, 228, *40, 68, 69*
Ramp valley   23, *8*
Raphana   225n
Raphon   216, *68*
al-Raqqad, Wadi   215, *68*
Ras al-'Ain   71, 130
Ras an-Naqb   33, 34, 104, *13, 67, 71*
Ras an-Naqura   42, 123, 124, 154, 155, *44*
Rasridiyeh   235, *71*
ar-Ratama, Jabal   *73*
Red Sand   *see* Mousterian Red Sand
Red Sea   4, 13, 19, 23, 97, 191, 239, *65*
Refugees   108, 139, 184, 198, 223, 227, 233
Regions, natural   118–119, *41, 43*
Regions of refuge   162, 217, 223
Rehoboam, King   134, 142, 182
Reifenberg, A.   77, 249n
Renan, Ernest   102
Rendzina soils   79
Reuben, tribe of   103, 211, 227, 228, 229, *42*
Riblah   98
Richard I, King   143
Rift   30, 31
Rift Valley   7, 11, 16, 17, 23, 24, 26, 28, 30, 31, 34, 38, 39, 41, 44, 72, 78, 81,

Rift Valley (*cont'd*)
82, 103, 120, 146, 155, 160, 167, 191, 219, *8*
Rift Valley Road   98
Ritual Decalogue   85
River of Egypt   *see* Egypt, River of
Rivers   124, 126, 137, 155, 203, 211, *5*
Roads   22, 95–100, 124–125, 129, 130, 134, 136, 137, 142, 156, 162, 170, 171, 172, 174, 178, 182, 185, 199, 203, 206, 216, 224, 239, 244, 246, 250, 251, *40*
Rock rose   80
Roman period   124, 130, 150, 157, 185, 198
Romans   204, 206, 210, 217, 239, 251
Rome   185, 197
Rosh ha-'Ayin   13, 71
Rosh ha-Niqra   42
Ross, James F.   171n
Rothenberg, Beno   105n, 209n, 250n, 251n
Rujm Tal'at al-Jum'ah   235
Rumman, Wadi   *73*

as-Safa   213, 217, *68*
Safad   152, 155, 156, 157
Saffuriyeh   162
Sagebush   80, 206
Sahara   80, 81, 102
Saharo-Sindian vegetation   80, 81
Sahl al-Battauf   24, 100, 125, 161, 162, 163, *53, 55, 56*
Sahl Kafr Istuna   175, *59*
Sahl Makhna   170, 175, *59*
Sahm al-Jaulan   103
St. Catherine's Monastery   251
St. David's   179
Sakaka   244
Saladin   160
Salecah   219, *68*
Saliha   155
Salim   166, 167, *58*
Salkhad   219
Salmon, T. J.   204n
as-Salt   31, 60, 61, 72, 91, 224, *12*
Salt   78, 202, 204, 205
Salt flats   206, 242
Salt marshes   31, 244
Saltbush   82
Samaria, basin of   19, 164, 166
Samaria, city of   22, 100, 149, 170, 171, 172, 188, *42, 58*
Samaria, district of   29, 81, 149, 172
Samaritans   171, 172
Samson   107, 141, 142
as-Samt, Wadi   139, 142, 177
Samuel   174, 175, 176, 179, 181, 183
Samuniyeh, Kh.   162
Sanballat   134, 170
Sanctuaries   193, 199, 203, 245
Sand   18, 42, 135, 136, 137, 208, 244, 245, 247
Sandstone (*see also* Nubian sandstone)   16, 18, 19, 27, 30, 34, 78, 205, 208, 245, 246
Sandstorm   64

Sanhedrin   157, 162
Santiago di Compostella   179
Sanur Basin   168, 170, *58*
Sara, Wadi   132
Sarepta   98
Sarida, Wadi   133, 174
Saul, King   22, 133, 134, 143, 147, 149, 150, 170, 184, 198, 223
Savanna   81
Scorpions   110
Scrub   11, 141, 156, 167, 172, 184, 236, 245
Scythopolis   147, 225
Sdom   26, 35, 59, *14*
Sdom, Har   26, 204, *64*
Sea breeze (*see also* land and sea breezes)   46, 54, 59, 60
Sea Peoples   127, 137
Sebam   232, 233n, *70*
Sebaste   170, 171, 172
Sebastiyeh   57
Sebhka   35, 206, *65*
Sede Boqer   35, *14*
Se'ir   12, 236
Sela   237, *71*
Seleucids   142
Seneh   179
Senir   193
Sennacherib, King   137
Senonian chalk   21, 31, 34, 36, 38, 79, 142, 156, 164, 166, 169, 170, 172, 174, 181, 214, 226, *17*
Senonian epoch   19, 22, 23, 167, 168
Sepph   157, *54*
Sepphoris   160, 162, 163, *50, 55*
Seron   134
Serpent, snake   107, 108, 110
Shaalbim   134
Shaduf   70
Shafa 'Amr   124, 162, *44, 55*
ash-Shaghur basin   29, 40, 153, 155, 161, *53, 55*
ash-Shagur fault   30, 40, 124, 125, 152, 155, *11, 16, 54, 55*
Shahba   219
ash-Shaikh, Jabal   156
Sha'ir, Wadi   174, *59*
Shanan, L.   64n, 249n
ash-Sharah, Jabal   236
Sharav (*see also* sirocco)   52
Sharon, plain of   12, 26, 42, 78, 81, 91, 94, 97, 98, 100, 117, 120, 127–130, 131, 149, 164, 217, *16, 41, 46*
Sharuhen   247, *74*
Shatter zone   30, 208, 244
Shaubak   33, 61, 235, 236, *13, 65, 71*
Shearing movement   23
Sheba   97, 193
Sheba, Queen of   209, 247
Shechem   22, 94, 98, 100, 103, 130, 131, 166, 167, 169, 170, 171, 172, 175, *39, 40, 42, 58, 59*
Sheep   70, 71, 87, 88, 137, 210, 217, 227, 228, 231
Shefar'am   157, 162

Sheikh Abu Zarad   165
Sheikh Banit, Kh.   157
Sheikh Madhkur, Kh.   142
Sheikh Meskine   216
Sheikh Sa'ad   216
Sheikh Salman, Jabal   168
Sheluhat Zeva'im   160, 161, *56*
Shenek, Wadi   183
Shephelah   22, 36, 81, 106, 117, 120, 134, 135n, 137, 139, 140–143, 177, 181, 182, *41, 61*
Shephelah, Galilean   162, *55*
Shepheleh, Israelite   141, 149, 173
Shepherd   10, 71, 87, 88, 89, 90, 104, 106, 107, 108, 228
Shezor, Har   155
Shihan, Jabal   24, 31, 230, *66, 67, 70*
Shihan, volcano of   *see* Shihan, Jabal
Shihor-libnath   121
Shiloh   98, 174, 175, 179, *40, 58, 59*
Shimei   139
Shimron   162, *55*
Ships of Tarshish   *see* Tarshish
Shishak, Pharaoh   150
Shittim   202
Shu'eib, Wadi (*see also* Sha'eb)   14, 202, 221, *69*
Shulhat Zeva'im   *see* Sheluhat Zeva'im
Shunat Nimrin   202
Shunem   147
Shur, Midbar of   103
Shur, Way of   98, *40, 74*
Shuweika   168
Shuweikat ar-Ras, Kh.   128
Sibmah   233n
Sidon   8, 30, 98, 121, 127, 225, *11, 39, 40*
Sidon-Wadi Sirhan depression, or trough   30, *11, 12*
Sihon   211, 219, 228, 232
Sil'   237
Siloam, Pool of   86
Simeon, territory of   181, 182, 247, *42*
Simonias   162
Simons, J.   215n
Sin, Midbar of   103
Sinai   62, 68, 102, 103, 247, 251
Sinai, Isthmus of   4
Sinai, Mount   25, 251
Sinai mountains   34
Sind, desert of   80
Sinjar, Jabal   156
Siq, Wadi   251
Sir, Wadi   221, 224, 227
Sirhan, Wadi   8, 30, 31, 91, 239, 241, 242, 243–244, *40, 72*
Sirion   193
Sirocco   51, 52–53, 61, 64, 72, 80
Sisera   76, 123, 124, 144, 149
Smith, George Adam   140, 141n, 150n, 151n, 168n, 190, 201
Snakes   *see* Serpents
Snow, Snowfall   48, 50, 55, 60, 66, 70, 71, 72, 74, 75, 76, 160, 191, 193, 217, 219, 236
Socoh (i), in Sharon   100, 128, 130, 131, 168, 171, 181, *40, 46, 51, 58*

Socoh (ii), in Judah   142, *49, 61*
Sodom   25, 204, 205
Soeurs de Zion   187
Soil   77ff., 117
Solomon, King   22, 89, 97, 123, 134, 135, 150, 169, 181, 182, 187, 188, 196, 207, 209, 228, 247
Solomon's Quarries   22, 209
Song of Deborah   123
Sorek, Valley of   132, 135, 138, 139, 141, 178, *47, 48, 49, 60*
Southland, realm of   9, 12, 13, 29
Souweida   219, *68*
Spices   87, 209, 247
Spina christi   80, 82, 206
Spring (transitional season)   43, 51, 228
Springs   10, 93, 94, 95, 98, 116, 124, 150, 173, 191, 193, 198, 203, 206, 209, 221, 226, 245
Spring line   11, 91, 94, 167, 199
Stager, Lawrence E.   140n
Steppe, steppeland   10, 61, 67, 71, 77, 78, 81, 82, 88, 90, 103, 137, 175, 227, 236, 247
Stock, night-scented   81
Strange, James M.   157n
Styrax   80
Subeita   249, *74*
Succoth   105, 199
Sudanian vegetation   80
Sulam   147
Summer   43, 44–46, 236
Summer drought   13, 22, 77, 231
Surar, Wadi   132
Suwanet ath-Thaniyeh   202n
Suweilit, Wadi   *48, 49*
Suweinit, Wadi   179, *60*
Sweileh   31, 222, *12, 69*
Sycamore, i.e., Fig Sycamore   89, 106, 141, 173
Sychar   170, *58, 59*
Synagogues   157, 197
Syria   9, 25, 193, *42*
Syrians   143, 196, 214, 228
Syro-Phoenicia   225
Syro-Phoenician Realm   9, 10, 11

Taanach   99, 149, 172, *50, 51, 58*
Tableland (*see also* Mishor)   9, 103, 104, 210, 211, 229ff., 235
Tabor, Mount   3, 39, 40, 148, 153, 160, 161, 195, *11, 53, 56*
Tadmor   *39*
Tadmor, N. H.   64n, 249n
Tafileh   237, *13*
Tafileh, Wadi   33, 235
at-Taiyebeh   175, 178
Taiyebeh, Wadi (i) in Gilead   198, *63*
Taiyebeh, Wadi (ii) in Edom   *65*
Talluza   168, *58*
Talmon, Shemaryahu   103
Tamar   207, *65*
Tamarisk   80, 82, 200
Tammun, Jabal   167, *58*
Tannur, Kh.   239, *70*
Tappuah   142, 165, 166, 174, *49, 57, 58, 59*

Tarqumiyeh   142
Tarshiha   155, 157, *54*
Tarshish, Ships of   209
Tavor, Nahal   160
Tekoa   89, 182, *61*
Tel 'Adashim   144, 146, 150
Tel Aviv   13, 55
Tel Bornat   139, 142
Tel Qasile   130, 138
Tel Zeror   130
Teleilat al-'Anab   249
Tell Abil   193, 214, 225
Tell al-Afshar   130
Tell al-'Amr   123, 125
Tell al-Aqra'   *45*
Tell Arad   247
Tell al-'Ashari   225n
Tell Ashterah   216
Tell 'Asur   174
Tell Balatah   170
Tell Beit Mirsim   116
Tell Deir 'Alla   199, 202n, 223
Tell Dibbine   191
Tell Durur   130, *46*
Tell ad-Duweir   116, 142
Tell Fa'ra   247
Tell al-Fukhkhar   124
Tell Hajjaj   223n
Tell Hamad   216
Tell al-Hammam   202
Tell Hauran   216
Tell al-Hesi   139
Tell al-Hila   167
Tell Hum   197
Tell al-Juhairah   235, *71*
Tell al-Kheleifeh   209
Tell al-Khuweilfeh   143
Tell Maqlub   198n
Tell al-Milh   183
Tell Moqdad   216
Tell an-Najila   139, *48*
Tell an-Nasbeh   179
Tell Qades   103
Tell al-Qadi   193
Tell Ramith   103
Tell ar-Ras   171
Tell ar-Reheil   223n
Tell as-Sa'eidiyeh   199
Tell as-Safi   139
Tell Sandahanna   142
Tell ash-Sharia'   139
Tell Sheikh al-'Areini   139, *48*
Tell Zakaria   142
Tema   102
Teman   13, 76, 235, 237, 239
Temperature   54, 59, *21, 25, 28–30, 32–34*
Temperature range   55, 59, 61, 64, *23, 28–30, 32–34*
Temple, general   187, 199
Temple, Jerusalem   22, 176, 181, 184, 209, 247
Temple Area   25
Temptation, Monastery of   189
Temptation, Mount of   156, 178, 201, *60*
Terebinth   80, 82

Terra rossa   21, 79, 167, 172, 174
Terraces, terracing   10, 94, 116, 183
Tethys, Sea of   16, 17, *6*
ath-Thamad   62
Thebez   167, 170, *58*
Thekel   127
Thesiger, Wilfred   102n
Thomson, W. M.   146, 156, 157
Thunder, thunderstorms   49, 50, 51, 63, 64, 67, 72, 73, 202, 206
Thutmose III, Pharaoh   94, 133, 149, 150
Tiberias   46, 50, 59, 157, 160, 162, 198, *56, 63*
Tiberias-Beth-shan basin   26
Tibnine   153, 154, 155, 157, *53, 54*
Tiglath-pileser III, King   192
Timber   10, 106
Timnah   139, 141, *47, 48, 49*
Tir'an, Har   161
Tirzah   22, 98, 167, 169, 170, *40, 58*
Tobiad family   224
Tobiah   224
Tohu   101
Toombs, Lawrence E.   171n
Tophel   91, 237, *65, 71*
Tower of Aphek   174
Towns and villages   125, 167, 168, 174, 183, 198
Trachonitis   217, *68*
Trade (*see also* Merchants)   13, 104, 127, 138, 151, 209, 224, 237, 244, 249
Trajan, Emperor   239
Transfiguration, Mount of   195
Transitional seasons   51–53
Trans-jordan   5, 9, 12, 16, 17, 19, 23, 29, 30, 60ff., 62, 72, 73, 78, 80, 82, 91, 185, 223, *12, 13, 33, 38, 65–73*
Trans-jordan plateau   20, 26, 71, 73, 80, 88, 208
Trans-jordan, Plateau edge   *67*
Trans-jordan, structure of   31ff.
Trans-jordan, Tableland of   *see* Mishor, Trans-jordan Plateau
Trees (*see also* Forests)   78, 116, 137, 156, 217
Triassic period   20
Tribes, Israelite   *42*
Tripoli   8
Tristram, Canon   147n, 151n
Trunk Road   96–97, 98, 100, 130, 131, 133, 134, 137, 138, 144, 147, 149, 156, 157, 160, 168, 169, 171, 190, 195, 197, 216, *56*
Trypho   50
Tsiyyah   101
Tubaiq, Jabal   18, 21, 31, 246
Tubas   167
Tulkarm   100, *58*
Tulul   215, 216
Tulul adh-Dhahab   223
Tunisia   75
at-Tur   188
at-Tur al-Abyad, Jabal   236
Tur'an, Jabal   160, 161, *55, 56*
Tur'an basin   161, 162, *55*
Turkey   23

Turonian   164, 167
Tushingham, A. D.   169n, 187n
Tyre   13, 98, 123, 154, 157, 221, 225,
    16, 39, 40
Tyropoeon Valley   186, 187

Ugarit   10, 138, *39*
Ugarit, Promontory of   9
Umm al-'Amad   103, 232
Umm al-Biyara   237
Umm ad-Dabar   198
Umm al-Fahm   38, 106, 149, 157, 167,
    168, 172, 173, *11*
Umm al-Fahm Upwarp   38, 40, 164, *16,
    17*
Umm Hureiba, Jabal   250
Umm Qeis   198, 214, 225n
Umm al-Quseir   *73*
Umm Sahm, Jabal   20
Umm Sahm Sandstone   20
'Ummayad empire   11
'Uneizah, Jabal   235, *71*
United Monarchy   98, 127, 134, 138, 142,
    147
Unleavened Bread, Feast of   85
Upwarps (*see also* Warping)   12, 164,
    168
Urartu   5
Uriah the Hittite   12, 228
al-'Urma, Kh.   165
Usdum, Jabal   204
Usha   157
Ussishkin, David   204n
Uzu   98
Uzziah, King   25, 139, 182, 209, 228

Valley of Craftsmen   *see* Craftsmen
Valley of the Robbers (Ephraim)   *see*
    Haramiyeh, Wadi
Valley of the Robbers (Galilee)   22, 160,
    175
Van Zyl, A. H.   229n
de Vaux, Roland   85n, 86, 173, 235n
Vegetables   81, 87
Veryard, R. G.   66n
Vespasian, Emperor   157
Via Dolorosa   187
Via Maris   96
Villagers   108
Villages (*see also* Towns and Villages)
    91, 93, 116, 134, 137, 147, 162, 167,
    173, 178, 179, 203, 235, 236
Vines   58, 82, 84, 85, 86, 87, 162, 168,
    183, 210, 217, 222, 231
Vintage festival   85
Vita-Finzi, C.   66n
Volcanic cones   215
Volcanic dikes   18, 207, 244
Volcanic eruptions   25, 26, 160
Volcanic gases   26
Volcanic outcrop   146, 150, 173, 213
Volcanic regions   24, 213ff., 244, 246
Volcano   25, 31, 216, 219, 237
Vulture   108

al-Wa'arah   213, 216, *68*
Wachs, Naomi   65n
Wadis (*see also* Rivers)   13, 211, *5*
Wala, Wadi   211, 232, *70*
Waqqas, River   195, *62*
Warping   17, 22, 34
Washburn, Roger   79n
Waterfalls   192, 202, 205
Water, underground supply   150, 196,
    199
Water-parting   36, 148, 174, 175
Water-parting Road   98, 182, 183, 185
Waters of Nimrin   210
Waters of Merom   155
Way of the land of the Philistines   97
Way to Shur   98
Weippert, Manfred   94n, 123n
Weiser, Artur   86
Wells   91, 95, 116, 231, 242, 243, 247
Wen Amon   127
Western Highlands   7, 12, 14, 29, 50, 98,
    126
Wheat   10, 81, 82, 84, 85, 86, 87, 115,
    137, 162, 168, 183, 210, 211, 216, 222,
    231
Whirlwinds   64
Wild beasts   115
Wilderness   9, 11, 12, 101ff.
Willis, B.   23n
Wine   223
Winnowing   46, 60, 64, 187, 216
Winter   47–51
Winter storms   12, 236
Winton, Thomas D.   108n
Wisdom   13, 237
Wolves   11, 107, 110
Woodland (*see also* Forests)   12
Wright, George Ernest   138n, 171n
Wright, G. R. H.   171n

Ya'ar   105ff., 115, 128, 150, 172, 176
Ya'bad   172
Yabis, Wadi   198, *63, 69*
Ya'bud   149
Yadin, Yigael   96n, 150n, 181n, 196n
Yalu   134
Yanun, Kh.   165
Yarkon, River   13, 97, 128, 130, 131,
    132, 133, 134, 138, *47*
Yarmuq, River   8, 12, 14, 26, 31, 94, 97,
    103, 160, 198, 211, 213, 214, 215, 216,
    5, 11, 12, 63, 67, 68
Yatta   177, 181, *61*
Yavneel   56
Yavneel, Har   160, *56*
Yavneel, valley of   160
Yir'on   155, *54*
Yirun   153, *53, 54*
Yogurt   84, 88
Yotvata   209
Ytem, Wadi   97, 246, *67, 73*
Ytem al-'Umran, Wadi   *73*

Zababida   *58*
Zababida Basin   168, 170

Zagros mountains   6
Zalmaveth   108
Zalmon   217
Zanoah   142, *49*
Zara   202
Zarethan   199, *63, 69*
Zebulun, tribe and territory of   125, 149, 151, 152, 162, *42*
Zedekiah, King   186
Zeimar, Wadi   100, 128, 130, 167, 168
Zeita   166, *57, 58*
Zeita, Wadi   139, 142, *49*
Zenifim, Nahal or Wadi   34, *14*
Zered, River   8, 12, 14, 18, 29, 32, 35, 63, 204, 211, 231, 233, 234, *5, 66, 67, 70*
Zeredah   174, *59*
Zerqa   12, 61, 219, 226, *69*
Zerqa, Wadi   19

Zerqa Ma'in, Wadi   14, 18, 26, 27, 31, 202, 205, 211, 219, 221, 230, *12, 64, 66, 67, 69, 70*
Ziklag   143
Zimri   170
Zin, Wilderness of   103, 104, 241, 247–251, *74*
Ziph   103, 181, 182, 184, *61*
Zippori, Nahal   161
Ziqlab, River   198, *63*
Zir'in   147
Ziz, Ascent of   100, 185, *40*
Zohar, Nahal   185
Zon, R.   116n
Zone of Greater Complexity   29–30
Zone of Relative Simplicity   29, 35
Zone of Reversed Tendencies   29, 30–31
Zor   27, 82, 105, 200
Zorah   141, 182, *47, 49, 61*

74 75 76 77 10 9 8 7 6 5 4 3 2 1

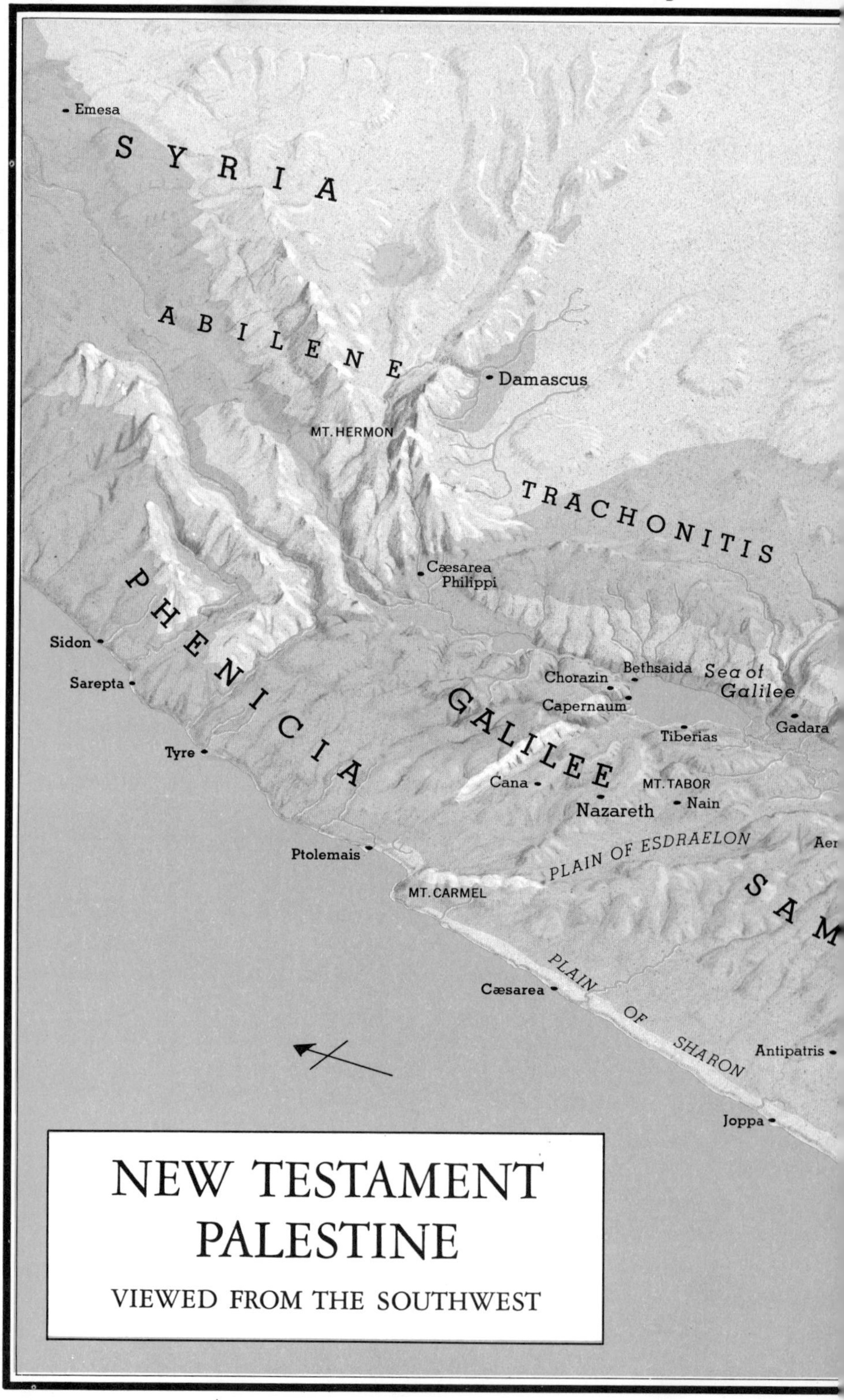

NEW TESTAMENT
PALESTINE

VIEWED FROM THE SOUTHWEST